Xenophon

The Shorter Writings

A volume in the series
AGORA EDITIONS

General Editor
Thomas L. Pangle

Founding Editor
Allan Bloom

A full list of titles in the series is available at
cornellpress.cornell.edu.

Xenophon
The Shorter Writings

Edited by

GREGORY A. MCBRAYER

CORNELL UNIVERSITY PRESS

ITHACA AND LONDON

First published 2018 by Cornell University Press

Printed in the United States of America

Library of Congress Cataloging-in-Publication Data

Names: Xenophon, author. | McBrayer, Gregory A. (Gregory Alan), 1978– editor.
Title: The shorter writings / Xenophon ; edited by Gregory A. McBrayer.
Description: Ithaca : Cornell University Press, 2018. | Series: Agora editions |
    Includes bibliographical references and index.
Identifiers: LCCN 2017039249 (print) | LCCN 2017043060 (ebook) |
    ISBN 9781501718519 (pdf) | ISBN 9781501718526 (epub/mobi) |
    ISBN 9781501718496 (cloth : alk. paper) | ISBN 9781501718502
    (pbk. : alk. paper)
Subjects: LCSH: Xenophon—Translations into English.
Classification: LCC PA4495.A4 (ebook) | LCC PA4495.A4 M37 2018 (print) |
    DDC 883/.01—dc23
LC record available at   https://lccn.loc.gov/2017039249

Contents

Xenophon
The Shorter Writings

Editor's Introduction

GREGORY A. MCBRAYER

In the last half century or so, there has been resurgence in the study of Xenophon, across a variety of disciplines and methodological approaches.[1] We hope to encourage or contribute to this resurgence by offering new, literal translations of Xenophon's eight shorter writings along with interpretive essays on each work: *Hiero, or The Skilled Tyrant; Agesilaus; Regime of the Lacedaemonians; Regime of the Athenians; Ways and Means, or On Revenues; The Skilled Cavalry Commander; On Horsemanship;* and *The One Skilled at Hunting with Dogs.*

Other collections of Xenophon's works are available, but each has its shortcomings. Many are very old, most provide inadequate translations, and none of the alternatives contains interpretive essays along the lines of what we provide. Where introductory remarks are found, they are usually brief, and where they are longer, they focus more on historical context than textual analysis. Additionally, only two contain all of the works included here in a single volume: Rev. J. S. Watson's *Xenophon's Minor Works*[2] and E. C. Marchant's edition in the Loeb series.[3]

Of all previous translations, that done by Watson is probably the best. Watson's volume includes all of Xenophon's shorter works, as well as three of his shorter Socratic works. It is the most accurate previous translation, though even it is not without flaws (Watson anachronistically translates *polis* as "state," for example). Also, his introductory remarks are exceedingly brief. But above all, Watson's translation is no longer available in print, it being over 150 years old.

H. G. Dakyns published his first volume of Xenophon's works in 1890, and while he went on to translate Xenophon's entire corpus, his translations of Xenophon's shorter writings were published across various volumes.[4] Moreover, his introductory remarks are typically brief, and his translations are far from literal. Although he aims to remain true "to the sense and spirit of the original," he occasionally feels compelled to embellish Xenophon's words. For example, consider Dakyns's translation of the following passage from *The One Skilled at Hunting with Dogs*:

> Naturally, those from whose souls and bodies the sweat of toil has washed all base and wanton thoughts, who have implanted in them a passion for manly virtue—these, I say, are the true noble souls. Not theirs will it be to allow their city or its sacred soil to suffer wrong. (12.9)

The terms "naturally," "manly," "noble," "souls," and "sacred" are not found in the text.[5]

E. C. Marchant, the editor and translator of the Loeb text, holds Xenophon in low regard: he calls him a pedantic and tedious writer, and holds that Xenophon's mind produces elementary thoughts. Finding Xenophon's repetition tiresome, he accordingly alters the terms.[6] G. W. Bowersock followed Marchant's lead in his later addition to the series, going so far as to say that he "found it impossible always to render these [key] terms in the same way."[7]

Robin Waterfield's edition contains many of the works included in this volume, but it omits Xenophon's treatises on the regimes of Lacedaemonia and Athens, works that must inform any understanding of Xenophon's political thought.[8] Moreover, despite having translated numerous works of Xenophon, Waterfield does not accord him the respect that he deserves as a thinker of the highest rank. While Waterfield claims to be more sympathetic to Xenophon than many other scholars—as he may well be—he still sees Xenophon "very much as a product of his times. He did not have the largeness of spirit, or whatever it takes to transcend one's time and even to change them."[9] Waterfield's view that Xenophon is a conventional thinker leads him to doubt "whether Xenophon can be shown to be a penetrating or even consistent philosophical theorist."[10]

Waterfield's judgment of Xenophon as a thinker encourages a certain carelessness in translation. Waterfield translates key terms — such as *aretē* (virtue) and *sophia* (wisdom) — inaccurately and inconsistently. In the *Hiero*, he translates *aretē* as "quality" (2.2), "good points" (6.15), "good" (7.9), and "excellence" (11.5, 11.8). In the *Agesilaus*, he translates the term as "virtue" the first three times it occurs, and then changes it to "bravery" (6.2) before returning to "virtue" (10.2, 11.9), and, finally, decides on "courage" (11.16). Thus one cannot follow Xenophon's use of the term *aretē* in either work, let alone across works. Again in the *Hiero*, Waterfield alternates between translating *sophia* as "learned" (1.1) and "clever" (5.1), and in *On Hunting* — the title of which he inaccurately translates — he translates *sophia* differently each time it occurs: "clever" (6.17), "intelligence" (12.16), and "knowledge" (13.7). At the beginning of his translation of this work, Waterfield leaves out a key philosophical term, *physis* or "nature" (1.3). Of course, the Greek sometimes has a range of meaning different from any one English word, and occasionally one may be compelled to translate a Greek term with more than one English equivalent. In such cases, however, the translator should indicate deviations and explain the complexities of the terms. Waterfield's translations offer no such guidance to the reader.

J. M. Moore provides translations only of Xenophon's *Regime of the Lacedaemonians* and *Regime of the Athenians*.[11] While Moore's edition has its virtues, it is not without its problems. Attributing the *Regime of the Athenians* either to the "Old Oligarch," as most do, or to someone else "manifestly prejudiced," as Moore does (21), alienates someone interested in Xenophon's political thought and discourages anyone from undertaking a sustained inquiry into the treatise. Moore's introductions, outlines of the main topics, and commentaries are quite useful, but he often falls short in his aim to be faithful to the Greek text. For example, Moore translates *polis* as "state," thus importing the foreign distinction between state and civil society characteristic of modern liberalism. Moore usually translates what is perhaps the single most important word in these two treatises, *politeia*, as "constitution." The best English term for *politeia* is "regime," since *politeia* refers to a broader phenomenon than a constitution: the *politeia* is comprehensive, the ruling order inasmuch as it profoundly shapes the character of its citizens and their way of life. Moore leaves *politeia* untranslated in his title of the *Regime of the Lacedaemonians*, a decision that would perhaps be unobjectionable if consistently followed. Unfortunately, in the body of that work, he translates the term as "constitution." Moreover, this variation obscures the very obvious comparison between Xenophon's *Regime of the Athenians* and his *Regime of the Lacedaemonians*.

Perhaps most troubling is Moore's decision, in the *Regime of the Lacedaemonians*, to change the order of the text as it has come down to us, since the order as it occurs in the manuscripts does not fit with his interpretation of the text. Taking for granted Xenophon's pro-Spartan allegiance or bias, Moore deems chapter 14 an intrusion into the text, saying, "It is impossible to conceive that this chapter was originally designed to stand between XIII and XV as the manuscripts transmit it." Moore unjustifiably inserts his interpretation of the text into the translation, hampering the ability of new readers to form their own judgment about the text.[12] Moore's choices unduly influence readers' interpretation of Xenophon's texts, and reinforce the prejudice that Xenophon is simply an oligarchic Laconophile with very little to offer of philosophical import.

The eight scholars who have contributed the translations in this volume have striven to remain faithful to the spirit guiding the other translations of Xenophon in the Agora series. This means that the translations aim at being as literal as is compatible with English usage. We have tried to remain consistent in rendering key Greek terms with the same English equivalent, indicating in notes the most important departures from such consistency. Notes to the translations also clarify Xenophon's historical and literary references, identify relevant allusions to his other writings, explain the complex meaning of important Greek terms, and highlight important difficulties or ambiguities in the Greek texts. All of this is with a view to helping students and general readers alike understand these works.

Accompanying the annotated translations are interpretive essays that have been commissioned for this volume. The essays seek, if in different ways, to show that these works are masterful achievements that raise important moral, political, and philosophical questions. The authors treat Xenophon as a distinguished student of Socrates and a serious thinker of the first rank, whose writings deserve careful and sustained study. Accordingly, we appreciate that Xenophon is a graceful, subtle writer who sometimes raises fundamental questions in seemingly innocuous ways—the problem of justice, for example, in a children's dispute over tunics.[13] The interpretive essays aim to elucidate the subject matter where it may be ambiguous and to uncover larger themes or fundamental questions that Xenophon may have been content to leave beneath the surface. The essays also situate the works within Xenophon's corpus and draw out the ways in which these works inform one another.

Five of these shorter writings of Xenophon are unmistakably devoted to political matters. The *Agesilaus* is a eulogy of a Spartan king, and the *Hiero, or the Skilled Tyrant* recounts a searching dialogue between a poet and a tyrant. *The Regime of the Lacedaemonians* presents itself as a laudatory examination of what turns out to be an oligarchic regime of a certain type, while *The Regime of the Athenians* offers an unflattering picture of a democratic regime. *Ways and Means, or On Revenues* offers suggestions for how to improve the political economy of Athens' troubled democracy. The other three works included here treat skills that are appropriate for gentlemen, but they do touch on matters of political importance, especially in regard to war. *The Skilled Cavalry Commander*, for example, tackles the question of leadership, or how to rule, a topic of clear political import (1.1). Moreover, political order of the day depended on a class of knights available for military service. Horsemanship, the subject of the treatise *On Horsemanship (Peri Hippikēs)*, was for the sake of cavalry service. And Xenophon's *The One Skilled at Hunting with Dogs (Kunēgeticus)* opens with an extended apology meant to highlight hunting's moral, martial, and political utility: many of Greece's most renowned heroes were educated in hunting with dogs, and that education seems to have been key to their military and political success. Indeed, Xenophon elsewhere says, "It is not easy to find anything missing from hunting that is present in war."[14]

With the exception of the *Hiero* and perhaps the *Regime of the Lacedaemonians*, the writings here collected are still relatively unexplored in the scholarly literature. In some cases, this is because the subject matter, such as the skill of hunting with dogs, commanding a cavalry, and horsemanship, no longer appears to be relevant. But the titles of Xenophon's writings may not always indicate their subject matter clearly or unambiguously. In the case of a writer as skilled as Xenophon, whose great apparent simplicity of style is married to profundity of thought, readers cannot be so sure that *The One Skilled at Hunting with Dogs*, for example, is simply a treatise about hunting. In addition to the many things it has to teach about hunting, it also undeniably has *something* to do with sophistry, since that is the subject of its final chapter, and sophistry is still a topic of interest to scholars of ancient thought. Moreover, Xenophon often mentions hunting in relation to philosophy,[15] and the interpretation of *The One Skilled at Hunting with Dogs* offered here does much to clarify this connection. Similarly, horsemanship, the topic of *On Horsemanship*, figures prominently in the *Anabasis of Cyrus* and the *Education of Cyrus*, as well as in Xenophon's Socratic writings. As Amy L. Bonnette points out, Xenophon's only complete description of Socrates' course of education in the *Memorabilia* is initiated in a bridle shop.[16] A different problem attends the *Regime of the Athenians*: Xenophon is not thought to be its author. The treatise was preserved in antiquity as having been written by Xenophon, but, in the twentieth century, scholars came to doubt the work's authenticity largely on the basis of its style and supposed date of composition. In fact, the treatise is now all but universally attributed in the English-speaking world to the so-called Old Oligarch, a term coined by Alfred Zimmern to denote that the treatise was written by an otherwise unknown author with clear antidemocratic prejudices. The essay in this volume on the *Regime of the Athenians* accordingly takes up the question of the work's authorship and aims to show that the grounds adduced in support of the denial of Xenophon's authorship are not demonstrably settled and are in fact questionable. While the authorship of the *Regime of the Athenians* cannot be established beyond doubt, the interpretation offered in this volume is open to the possibility, at least, that it came from Xenophon's hand. As a result, it pursues possible lines of inquiry and interpretation that have been closed off to other interpreters who did not take this possibility seriously. Whoever its author, the treatise gives us one of the few sustained treatments of Athenian democracy written by someone who had firsthand experience of it.

Each of Xenophon's works included in this volume is worthy of study in its own right, and the translations and essays offered here are meant to encourage sustained study of these difficult and sometimes strange texts. We hope that by bringing together Xenophon's shorter political writings, we will also help all those interested in Xenophon understand better the core of his thought, political as well as philosophical.

CHAPTER 1

Hiero, or The Skilled Tyrant

Translated by David K. O'Connor

_～ Chapter 1 _～

(1) Simonides the poet once visited Hiero the tyrant.[1] When both had some leisure, Simonides said, "Would you be willing, Hiero, to tell me about something it is likely you know better than I?"

"And what sort of thing could it be," said Hiero, "that I could know better than you, who are so wise a man?"[2]

(2) "I know you used to be a private person and are now a tyrant; since you have experienced both, you are likely to know better than I how the tyrannical life and the private life are distinguished in the enjoyments and pains of human beings."[3]

(3) "Well," said Hiero, "why don't you, since for now at least you are still a private person, remind me of what goes on in the private life? That way I think I would best be able to make clear to you what distinguishes each from the other."

(4) Simonides gave this reply: "I believe, Hiero, that I have noticed private persons being pleased and bothered by things seen through the eyes, by things heard through the ears, by smells through the nose, by foods and drinks through the mouth—and as for sex,[4] we all know through what. (5) As for things cold and hot and hard and soft and light and heavy, I believe it is with the whole body that we judge of being pleased or pained by them. By things good and bad, we are sometimes pleased and pained through the soul by itself, I believe, and sometimes through both the soul[5] and the body in com-

mon. (6) That we are pleased by sleep, I have perceived, I believe; but of how and through what and when," he said, "I believe I am somehow more ignorant. And perhaps it isn't surprising if experiences while we're awake provide us with clearer perceptions than experiences in sleep."

(7) To these things Hiero answered: "I for my part," he said, "would not be able to mention anything the tyrant might perceive other than the things you have just related. So at least up to this point, I do not know if in anything the tyrannical life is distinguished from the private life."

(8) And Simonides spoke: "But in this," he said, "it is distinguished: it enjoys many more things through each of these, and has many fewer of the painful things."

And Hiero said, "That is not how these things stand, Simonides, but know well that tyrants have much less enjoyment than private persons who live within measure, and have many more and much greater pains."

(9) "What you are saying is incredible," said Simonides. "For if things were that way, how could many desire to be tyrants, with this applying even to those believed to be men of great capacity? How could everyone be emulous[6] of tyrants?"

(10) "Because, by Zeus," said Hiero, "they are considering the issue without experience of both activities. But I will try to teach you that the things I am saying are true, starting from sight—for I believe I remember you too starting to speak from there. (11) First, when I reflect on the spectacles contemplated through sight, I find the tyrants get less.[7] There are different spectacles worth contemplating in different places, and private persons can travel to each of them, and to whichever cities they want, for the sake of spectacles, and also to the common festivals,[8] where the spectacles human beings believe are most worth contemplating are gathered together. (12) But the tyrants have little to do with contemplating. For it is not safe for them to go where they will not be stronger than those who will be present, nor are their possessions at home so secure that they can turn them over to others to go on a trip. For it is to be feared that they might both be deprived of the rule and become powerless to take revenge on those who perpetrate the injustice. (13) Now perhaps you will say, 'But things of this sort come to them while they remain at home.'

But, by Zeus, Simonides, only a few of the many, and these are at such a price to the tyrants that the exhibitioners, whatever they present, expect to leave the tyrant after getting much more in a short time than they obtain in their entire life from the rest of human beings."

(14) And Simonides said, "But if you[9] get less of spectacles, surely through hearing you get more, since of the most pleasant thing to hear, praise, you are never in short supply. For all in attendance on you praise whatever you say and whatever you do. And the harshest thing to hear, blame, you do not hear; for no one is willing to accuse a tyrant before his eyes."

(15) "And how do you think," Hiero said, "those who say nothing bad can be enjoyed when one knows clearly that these silent persons are all thinking of nothing but bad things for the tyrant? And how do you believe those who praise can be enjoyed when they are under the suspicion of feigning their praises for the sake of flattery?"

(16) And Simonides said, "This indeed, by Zeus, I for my part certainly concede to you, Hiero: that the praises of those who are most free are the most pleasant. But look, you still could not persuade any human being of this: that, regarding the things through which we human beings are nourished, you do not have much more enjoyment."

(17) "I do know, Simonides," he said, "that most people judge us to drink and eat more pleasantly than private persons, because they believe they would also themselves dine more pleasantly on the food served to us than that served to them. For it is what exceeds the habitual things that provides pleasures. (18) Thus all human beings anticipate with pleasure the feasts, except tyrants; since their tables are always abundantly provisioned, there is no special addition to them for feasts. So in the first place, they get less than private persons of this enjoyment of expectation. (19) And furthermore," he said, "I know well—and you too have experienced—that to the extent one is served luxuries beyond what would be sufficient, by so much does satiety more quickly take over the feasting. So also in the duration of pleasure, one served many things gets less than those who have a measured regimen."

(20) "But, by Zeus," said Simonides, "for so long as the soul is eager, so long do those nourished by expensive provisions have much more pleasure than those served inexpensive ones."

(21) "Well, Simonides," said Hiero, "do you think that he who is especially pleased by something has the most erotic interest[10] in the activity concerning it?"

"Surely," he said.

"Well, do you see tyrants going to their own provisions with any more pleasure than private persons to theirs?"

"No, by Zeus," he said, "not at all, but rather with less interest, as many believe."

(22) "And then," said Hiero, "have you noticed these many contrivances that are set before tyrants, acid and bitter and astringent and things akin to these?"

"Surely," said Simonides, "and I very much believe these to be against nature for human beings."

(23) "Then do you think," said Hiero, "these foods are anything but the objects of desire of a soul made soft and weak? For I at least know well that those who eat with pleasure—and you surely know it too—have no need for these additional sophistications."[11]

(24) "And surely," said Simonides, "these expensive scents with which you are anointed are enjoyed more by those nearby, I think, than by you yourselves, just as offensive scents are not perceived by the one who has eaten, but rather by those nearby."

(25) "And it is this way," said Hiero, "with foods: he who always has all sorts takes none of them with longing, while it is he who is in short supply of something who with satisfaction gets his fill, when it happens to appear before him."

(26) "Perhaps it turns out," said Simonides, "that only the enjoyments of sex produce the desires in you to be tyrants. For in this, it is open to you to have intercourse with[12] whatever you see that is most beautiful."[13]

(27) "Now, indeed," said Hiero, "you have spoken of a matter in which, know clearly, we get less than private persons. First, in the case of marriage, surely one with those superior in wealth and power is believed to be finest, and to provide an honor to the groom that comes with pleasure. Second is one with those who are similar; while a marriage with those who are inferior is held to be very dishonorable and worthless. (28) Now the tyrant, unless he marries a foreigner, of necessity must marry with those inferior. Thus what satisfies does not easily come to him. In addition, the attentions of

the proudest[14] women are much the most enjoyable, while the attentions of slaves are not at all satisfying when they are given, and produce terrible anger and pains if they are at all lacking. (29) As for sex with boys,[15] the tyrant gets still less of enjoyments [compared to private persons] than with child-producing sex. For we all surely know that sex accompanied by erotic longing provides a very distinguished enjoyment. (30) But erotic longing[16] is not at all willing to arise in the tyrant, since erotic longing aims at the pleasures provided not by persons at one's disposal, but by those who are objects of one's hopes. Just as one who has no experience of thirst cannot enjoy drinking, so he who has no experience of erotic longing has no experience of the greatest pleasures of sex."

(31) So said Hiero. But Simonides laughed. "What are you saying, Hiero?" he said. "Do you deny that erotic longing for boys naturally springs up in a tyrant? What about," he said, "your erotic love for Dailochus, who is called most beautiful?"

(32) "Because, by Zeus," he said, "Simonides, it is not what seems at my disposal that I most desire to get from him, but rather what it is inappropriate for a tyrant to attempt by superior power. (33) For indeed, I have an erotic interest in Dailochus, for exactly those things nature perhaps forces human beings to ask from the beautiful. But these things that I have an erotic longing to get I very strongly desire to get with friendship[17] and from someone who is willing; to take them by force from him I desire less, I believe, than to do something bad to myself. (34) For with enemies, I hold the pleasantest of all things is to take from them when they are unwilling; but with boys, I think the most pleasant favors come when they want to give them. (35) For example, from one who returns love, pleasant are the exchanged gazes, pleasant the questionings, pleasant the replies; and most pleasant and sexually arousing the fights and quarrels. (36) But to enjoy unwilling boys is more like robbery, I believe," he said, "than sex. Though at least robbery provides some pleasures in the profit and the harming of an enemy. But to get pleasure from someone whom one erotically longs for when that person is being hurt, and to be hated when one loves, or to be bothersome when one touches: how could this not be a distressing and pathetic experience? (37) And indeed for the private person there is direct proof, whenever the object of his erotic longing renders some service, that

the erotic object gratifies him out of love, since he knows that there is no necessity for the service; but the tyrant can never trust that he is loved. For we know those who render service out of fear liken themselves as much as they can to the services of those who love. Indeed, the plots against tyrants arise from none more than those who make a pretense of loving them most."

∾ Chapter 2 ∾

(1) To these things Simonides said, "Well, I for my part believe all these things you are talking about to be very small. For many," he said, "who are believed to be men I at least see willingly getting less of foods and drinks and delicacies—and sex too, keeping themselves away from it. (2) But it is in the following that you are very much distinguished from private persons: you make great plans, and accomplish them swiftly; you have many luxuries, and possess horses distinguished in virtue, weapons distinguished in beauty, outstanding ornament for women, the most magnificent houses, and these furnished with things of great value; further you possess a multitude of knowledgeable servants, the best, and you are most capable of harming enemies and benefiting friends."

(3) To these things Hiero said, "That the multitude of human beings, Simonides, is deceived by tyranny does not surprise me. For the mob, I believe, guesses merely by what it sees that some are happy and others wretched. (4) Tyranny spreads out for all to see and contemplate a wide display of those possessions believed of much value; but as for the difficulties tyranny possesses, they are hidden away in the souls of tyrants—which is just where being happy and being unhappy lie for human beings. (5) Now, that this escapes the multitude does not, as I said, surprise me. But that you[18] too are ignorant of these things, you who are believed to contemplate most affairs more finely, using your judgment rather than your eyes, this I believe is surprising. (6) But from experience I know clearly, Simonides, and tell you, that tyrants share least in the greatest goods and possess most of the greatest bad things. (7) For example, if peace is believed to be a great good for human beings, it is least shared by tyrants. And

if war is a great bad thing, tyrants have the greatest share of this. (8) For example, it is possible for private persons, unless their city is fighting a common war, to travel wherever they wish without fear that someone will kill them; but all tyrants travel everywhere as if through hostile territory. At least they think it necessary to go about armed themselves, and to be always surrounded by other armed guards. (9) Next, private persons, even if they should go on campaign somewhere in hostile territory, at least when they return home think themselves safe. But tyrants, when they return to their own city, then know they are among the most enemies in war. (10) And if stronger outsiders campaign against a city, the weaker side believe they are in danger as long as they are outside the walls, but at least when they come inside the fortress they all hold they are established safely. But the tyrant is not out of danger even when he comes inside his house. Indeed, it is there that he thinks he must be most on guard. (11) Next, for private men, rest from war comes through treaties and peace, while for tyrants peace never comes with those over whom they tyrannize, nor can the tyrant ever dare to trust treaties.

(12) "There are wars that cities fight, and wars tyrants fight against those whom they use force against. Now with regard to these wars, all the difficulties the war of a city has, the tyrant also has: (13) for both must be armed and stand guard and run risks, and if they suffer something bad by being defeated, they will each be pained by this. (14) So up to this point the wars are equal; but the pleasures that the wars of cities against other cities have, these tyrants no longer have. (15) For when cities prove stronger in battle than their opponents, it is not easy to describe how great the pleasure is they take in having turned their enemies in war, and how great in pursuing them, and how great in killing them, and how they exult over the accomplishment, how they cover themselves with shining glory, how they enjoy the city, holding that they have made it greater! (16) Each one pretends to have shared in the planning and to have killed the most, and it is difficult to find a place they are not telling lies, claiming to have killed more than all who really died. So beautiful a thing do they believe it is to win a great victory. (17) But when a tyrant has suspicions and, perceiving that some people are in fact plotting against him, kills them, he knows he is not making the whole city greater, and he knows he will be ruling fewer people; and he cannot

be openly pleased nor boast of his deed. Rather he minimizes what has happened as much as he can, and defensively claims even as he acts that he has done nothing unjust. Thus not even he believes he has been done anything beautiful. (18) And when those he feared are dead, he is no more confident because of this, but is even more on his guard than before.

"And so the tyrant is always engaged in a war of the sort that I have shown."

∾ CHAPTER 3 ∾

(1) "Now with regard to friendship, contemplate how tyrants share in it. First we should consider whether friendship is a great good for human beings. (2) Surely when someone is loved by others, those who love him see him with pleasure, and with pleasure do well by him, and also long for him when he is gone and welcome him with great pleasure when he comes back again, and share his pleasure when he has good things, and come to his aid if they should see him take a false step. (3) Nor has it escaped the notice of cities that friendship is the greatest good and most pleasant to human beings. At least many of cities hold that adulterers alone can be killed legally, clearly because they hold them to be destroyers of the friendship of women for their men. (4) Nevertheless, when a woman has been forced to have sex by some misfortune, their men do not honor them any less on this account, if of course the friendly love of the women remains untainted. (5) I judge being loved to be so great a good that I hold goods really come automatically to one who is loved, from both gods and human beings. (6) And it is of just this sort of possession that tyrants get less than everyone. But if you want to know that what I am saying is true, Simonides, consider it this way. (7) Surely the most secure friendships are believed to be of parents for children, children for parents, brothers for brothers, women for their men, and companions for companions. (8) Now if you are willing to consider it closely, you will find private persons are most loved by these persons, while many tyrants have killed their own children, many have been destroyed by their children, many brothers who were partners

in tyranny have become each other's murderers; and many tyrants have even been ruined by their own women, or even by the very companions believed to be their best friends. (9) How then can one think that such persons can be loved by anyone else, so hated are they by those who should be prompted by nature especially to love them, and compelled by law?"

~ CHAPTER 4 ~

(1) "Furthermore, how can he who has least share in trust not get less of a great good? What sort of intercourse is pleasant without trust for one another, what sort of association of man and woman is sweet without trust, what attendant is pleasant who is not trusted? (2) Yet in this, trust in relation to others, a tyrant shares the least— when he even approaches his food and drink without trusting, and before the offering to the gods, they first order their servants to taste of them, out of distrust lest even in this situation they might eat or drink something bad. (3) Further, their fatherlands are most valuable to other human beings. For citizens guard one another, without pay, from the slaves, and guard against evildoers so that none of the citizens will die a violent death. (4) They have gone so far in guarding that many have made a law that not even the associate of a murderer is guiltless. Thus because of their fatherlands, each of the citizens lives in safety. (5) But for tyrants, things are again reversed. For instead of avenging them, cities greatly honor one who kills the tyrant;[19] indeed, instead of excluding them from the temples, as they do the murderers of private persons—instead of this, cities even set up in the temples statues of those who have done it.

(6) "And if you think that because the tyrant has more possessions than private persons he also gets more enjoyment from them—it is not that way, Simonides. Rather, just as with athletes, for whom it is not enjoyable to prove stronger than private persons, yet it hurts them to prove weaker than their competitors, so with the tyrant: it is not when he clearly has more than private persons that he gets enjoyment, yet when he has less than other tyrants, he is pained by it. For he thinks them his competitors for wealth. (7) Nor does what

he desires come more easily to the tyrant than to the private person. For the private person desires a house or field or domestic slave; the tyrant desires cities or much territory or harbors or strong citadels, which are much more difficult and dangerous to take over than the objects of private desire. (8) You will even see that though few private persons are poor, many tyrants are. For it is not by number that what is many and what is few are judged, but with a view to use. Thus what exceeds the sufficient is many, while what falls short of the sufficient is few. (9) And for the tyrant, very much is less sufficient for necessary expenses than for the private person. For it is possible for private persons to cut down their expenses for daily affairs whenever they wish, but for tyrants it is not possible. For their greatest expenses, and the most necessary, are for the guards of their life;[20] to cut down on these is believed to be ruinous. (10) And again, who will pity as poor those able to have with justice whatever they need? But as for those forced by need to live by contriving something bad and base, how could one justly not call them wretched and poor? (11) Well now, tyrants are most forced to steal unjustly from temples and human beings because of always needing more money for necessary expenses. For just as if at war, they are forced always to maintain an army, or perish."

~ CHAPTER 5 ~

(1) "I will tell you, Simonides, of another difficult suffering of tyrants. They recognize no less than private persons the well-ordered and wise and just. But instead of admiring them, they fear them: the manly, lest they dare something for the sake of freedom; the wise, lest they contrive something; the just, lest the multitude desire to be governed by them. (2) When out of fear they use stealth to get rid of such people, who else is left for them to use but those who are unjust and lacking self-control and slavish? The unjust are trustworthy because they fear, just as tyrants do, that the cities may sometime become free and gain control over them; those lacking self-control are trustworthy for the sake of the existing lack of restraint; and the slavish are trustworthy because they do not even deem themselves

worthy of freedom. And so I believe this also is a difficult suffering, to hold that some are good men, but be forced to use others.

(3) "Further, the tyrant too must be a lover of the city. For without the city he can neither preserve himself nor be happy. But tyranny forces tyrants to run down even their own fatherlands. For they are not glad to be supplied with citizens who are valiant and well armed; instead they are more pleased to make foreigners more formidable than the citizens, and these they use as personal guards.[21] (4) And when there is a good growing season and an abundance of good things, not even then does the tyrant share the enjoyment. For when [the citizens] are needier, [tyrants] think them more submissive to the tyrants' treatment."

∾ CHAPTER 6 ∾

(1) "But I wish, Simonides, to make clear to you," he said, "all the enjoyments I had when I was a private person that I perceive I am now deprived of since becoming tyrant. (2) For I used to have intercourse with those of my age, taking pleasure in them and they in me, and had intercourse with myself when I desired quiet, and I passed the time at drinking parties, often almost forgetting every difficulty there might be in human life, often almost immersing my soul in songs and revels and dances, and indeed often to the point where I and the others desired only to go to bed. (3) But now I am deprived of people taking pleasure in me, since I have slaves instead of friends for companions, and am also deprived of taking pleasure myself in associating with these people, since I see in them no good-will for me. Drunkenness and sleep I guard against like a snare. (4) To fear a mob, but to fear isolation too; to fear being unguarded, but to fear the very guards themselves; and to want not to have un-armed persons around oneself, yet not to contemplate with plea-sure their being armed: how could this not be a troubling problem? (5) Further, to trust foreigners more than citizens, and barbarians more than Greeks; to desire to have the free as slaves, and be forced to make slaves free: do you not believe that all of these things are the marks of a soul terrified by fears? (6) Indeed, the fear is not only itself

painful when it is present in souls, but becomes the mutilator of all the pleasures present with it.

(7) "And if you are experienced in the affairs of war, Simonides, and have ever been drawn up near the enemy's phalanx, recollect what sort of food you had at that time, and what sort of sleep. (8) For just the sort of pains you had then are had by tyrants, and even more formidable ones. For tyrants hold that they see enemies not only facing them, but on every side."

(9) On hearing these things, Simonides interrupted and said, "I believe you have spoken exceedingly well on some things. For war is a fearful thing. Nevertheless, Hiero, we at least, when we were on campaign, set up forward guards in order to get our share of food and sleep in confidence."

(10) And Hiero said, "Yes, by Zeus, Simonides; for the laws are forward guards of the guards, so that they fear for themselves, but also on your behalf. But tyrants get guards for a wage, just like field hands. (11) And surely there is nothing the guards need to be able to do so much as to be trustworthy. But it is more difficult to find one trustworthy person than very many workers for whatever work you want, especially when the guards are in attendance for the sake of money, and it is possible for them to get much more in a little time by killing the tyrant than they will get from the tyrant during a long time of guarding.

(12) "As for you being emulous of us on the grounds that we are able best to do well by our friends, and that we defeat our enemies more than anyone else, this is also not the case. (13) How could you hold you are doing well to friends when he who gets the most from you is pleased to get out of your sight as fast as he can? For no one who gets something he wants from a tyrant holds it to be his own until he is out of the tyrant's control. (14) And how could you claim tyrants are most able to defeat enemies, when they know well that their enemies are all whom they tyrannize over, yet they cannot execute or imprison all of them—for then who would be left to rule over? Though they know these persons are enemies, nevertheless they are forced to use them even as they are on guard against them. (15) And know this well too, Simonides: any of the citizens they fear, tyrants find it difficult to see alive, but also difficult to kill. It is just as with a horse that, though good, makes one afraid it will do something deadly, so that it would be difficult to kill it, because of its

virtue, yet difficult to use it while it is alive, since one must beware lest in dangers it work some deadly damage. (16) And similarly all other possessions that while difficult are also useful give pain to those who possess them, but also to those who do away with them."

~ CHAPTER 7 ~

(1) When Simonides had heard these things from him, he said, "It is likely, Hiero, that honor is a great thing, in the pursuit of which human beings undertake every labor and undergo every risk. (2) And you, as is likely, though tyranny has such problems as you mention, nevertheless eagerly bear them for its sake, so that you will be honored and everyone will serve your every command without excuses, and all will gaze at you, rise from their seats, and make way on the road; and all in attendance will always give you gifts of honor in word and deed. For those who are ruled do things of this sort for tyrants, and for anyone else whom they happen to honor at any time. (3) And I believe, Hiero, that a man is distinguished from the other animals by this: he pursues honor. All animals alike seem to take pleasure in foods and drinks and sleep and sex; but the love of honor does not spring up by nature in the irrational animals, nor in all human beings. But those in whom erotic longing for honor and praise naturally springs up are in fact the most distinguished from cattle, and hold themselves to be men, and no longer merely human beings. (4) Thus I believe you reasonably endure all these things that you bear in tyranny, since indeed you are distinguished in honor from other human beings. For no human pleasure is believed to be nearer the divine than the enjoyment concerned with honors."

(5) To these things Hiero said, "But, Simonides, the honors of tyrants, I believe, are just as I have demonstrated to you their sexual relations are. (6) For we do not believe the services of those who do not return love are gratifying, nor do forced sexual relations appear pleasant; and similarly, services from those who are afraid are not honors. (7) How could we claim that people who are forced to rise from their seats rise in order to honor those who do injustice? Or that those who make way on the road for stronger people make way in order to honor those who do injustice? (8) And the many surely give

gifts to those they hate, especially when they are most afraid that they may suffer something bad from them. So I think these are reasonably held to be acts of slavishness; but honors, I believe, come from those the opposite of these. (9) For when human beings think some man is a capable benefactor, and hold that they enjoy good things from him, then with praises they have him on their lips, and contemplate him as each person's own special good, and willingly make way for him in the road, and rise from their seats out of love, without fear, and crown him because of his public virtue and benefaction, and want to give him gifts: these persons, I believe, truly honor that man when they render these services, and he who is deemed worthy of them is really honored. (10) And for my part, I deem him blessed[22] who is so honored. For I perceive that he is not plotted against, but inspires concern that nothing happen to him, and without fear, without being envied, without danger, with happiness, he passes his life. But know well, Simonides, that the tyrant passes both night and day as if judged worthy of death for injustice by all human beings."

(11) When he had heard all these things through, Simonides said, "Then why is it, Hiero, if being a tyrant is this bad and you recognize the fact, that such a bad thing is not gotten rid of by you, nor does anyone else ever willingly give up tyranny who once obtains it?"

(12) "For a reason," he said, "Simonides, that makes tyranny most wretched: it is not possible to get rid of it. For how could a tyrant ever have the capacity to pay back the money to all from whom he has stolen, or suffer a return in imprisonment for all he imprisoned; and how for all he killed could he hand over enough souls to die in return? (13) Indeed, Simonides, if it profits anyone to hang himself, know," he said, "that I find it profits the tyrant most. For him alone it profits neither to keep nor to put aside the bad things."

∾ CHAPTER 8 ∾

(1) And Simonides interrupted by saying, "That at the moment, Hiero, you are dispirited with tyranny does not surprise me, since you hold it to be an impediment to your desire to be loved by human beings. But I can, I believe, teach you how ruling does not at all

prevent being loved, but even gets more than living privately. (2) In considering if this is so, let us not yet consider if because of his greater power the ruler also has the power to give more gratification, but even if the private person and the tyrant do similar things, reflect on which obtains more gratitude from the same things. I will begin for you with the pettiest examples. (3) First, the ruler and the private person see someone and greet him in a friendly manner. In this case, which greeting do you hold would be more enjoyable to the one who receives it? Or this case: if both praise the same person; which praise do you believe contributes more to enjoyment? Let each honor [someone] at a sacrifice; the honor from which, do you believe, gets the greater gratitude? (4) Both offer the same services to someone who is sick; is it not clear that the services of the most powerful people also produce the greatest gratitude? Or the two give equal gifts; is it not also clear in this case that half of what the most powerful offer can give more gratification than the whole gift of the private person? (5) I believe even from the gods there is some honor and favor that accompany the man who is a ruler. Not that it makes a man more beautiful; but we do contemplate with more pleasure the same person when he rules than when he lives privately, and are more glorified by conversing with those of high honor than with those who are from a [station] equal to ours. (6) And as for boys, with regard to whom you especially blamed tyranny, they are least bothered by old age, and take least account of ugliness, in a ruler with whom they happen to associate. For the very fact of being honored is an added ornament, so that what is bothersome is made inconspicuous, while what is beautiful shines out more brilliantly. (7) So when you get more gratitude from the same services, how is it not in fact fitting, since after all you can do much more to benefit [people], and can give many more gifts, that you would also be much more loved than private persons?"

(8) And Hiero immediately interrupted: "Because, by Zeus," he said, "Simonides, we must also busy ourselves much more than private persons with the things through which human beings become hated. (9) Money must be exacted if we are going to be able to afford what is required, and someone must be compelled to guard what needs to be guarded; the unjust must be punished, and those who want to act with hubris hindered; and when the critical moment

comes for a speedy expedition by land or sea, there must be no tolerating the laggards. (10) Further, the man who is a tyrant needs mercenaries, and there is no heavier burden on the citizens than this. For they hold that these are supported by tyrants not for the sake of equality in honors, but for the sake of getting more."

~ CHAPTER 9 ~

(1) To these things Simonides again replied: "But I am not saying all these things do not need to be taken care of, Hiero. Still, I believe that taking care of some things leads very much to enmity, while taking care of others is productive of gratitude. (2) For to teach what is best, and to praise and honor someone who accomplishes it most beautifully, this caring gives rise to gratitude; but to criticize someone who does something poorly, and to force and punish and correct, necessarily give rise instead to hatred. (3) So I assert that a man who rules must assign others to correct the person who needs to be forced, while he must himself give out prizes. What happens now gives witness that this is a beautiful approach. (4) When we wish to have choruses compete for us, the ruler offers the prizes, but the order to assemble the choruses is given to chorus directors, and to others is given the order to teach [the choruses] and to apply force to those who are doing something poorly. So in these matters what is gratifying comes straight from the ruler, and things of the opposite type through others. (5) And what then prevents other political affairs from being handled this way? For all cities are divided up, some into tribes, some into divisions, some into regiments, and rulers are set up over each part. (6) Now, if one offered prizes to these just as to choruses, for good armament and military order and horsemanship, and valor in war and justice in contracts, it is likely that all of these too would be practiced eagerly, through competition for victory. (7) And yes, by Zeus, they would rush, indeed, more quickly to where they ought to be, pursuing honor, and more quickly contribute money when there was the critical time for it. And even that most useful thing of all, least accustomed to be practiced for the sake of love of victory, namely, farming, would show much increase if one

offered prizes by fields or villages to those who most finely worked the land; and from those citizens who turned with vigor to this would come many good things. (8) For the revenues would increase, and moderation would very much follow on the lack of leisure. And acts of wrongdoing too naturally arise less among those busy with work. (9) And if commerce is of any benefit to a city, the honoring of whomever does this best would also attract many people engaged in commerce. And if it becomes manifest that one who discovers a painless source of revenue for the city will be honored, this subject of investigation will not be left unworked, either. (10) In summary, if in everything it is manifest that one who introduces something good will not be unhonored, it will set many to applying themselves to this work of investigating something good. And when what is beneficial is the concern of many, necessarily much will be both discovered and achieved. (11) But if you fear, Hiero, that awarding prizes to many will incur many expenses, reflect that no commodities are less expensive than those that humans purchase with prizes. You see in competitions in horsemanship, athletics, and the choruses how small prizes draw out of human beings great expenses and many labors and much care."

∿ CHAPTER 10 ∿

(1) And Hiero said, "Yes, in all of this, Simonides, I believe you have spoken beautifully. But with regard to mercenaries, can you say anything about how to avoid being hated because of them? Or do you say that by obtaining friendship, a ruler will not need personal guards?"

(2) "Oh yes, by Zeus," said Simonides, "he surely will need them. For I know that just as it happens among horses, so it happens among some human beings, that to the extent they have an abundance of what they need, they become that much more hubristic. (3) Such persons are made more moderate by their fear of the personal guards. On the other hand, I believe there is no one through whom you could provide the gentlemen[23] with as many benefits as you can provide through the mercenaries. (4) Now, no doubt you

support them to guard yourself; but it is also the case that many masters have been killed by their slaves. So if the first command to the mercenaries was to aid everyone if they perceived some such thing [was going to happen], as if they were the personal guards of all the citizens—for, as we all know, wrongdoers are sure to arise in cities—if they would be ordered to guard the citizens too, then the latter would know that in this they are benefited by the mercenaries. (5) In addition, the mercenaries would also be likely to be especially able to provide confidence and safety to workers and cattle in the country, both those belonging to you and those throughout the land. And surely they would be capable of providing leisure for the citizens to take care of their private [affairs] by guarding critical positions. (6) In addition, who would be more prepared to perceive beforehand or to prevent secret and sudden invasions by enemies in wars than those who are always armed and in military order? Furthermore, what is more beneficial to the citizens on a military campaign than mercenaries? For these are likely the most prepared to lead in labors and dangers and guarding. (7) And is it not necessary for the bordering cities to desire peace very much, because these are always armed? For those in military order are most able to protect the things of friends and to destroy the things of enemies. (8) And when the citizens recognize that these mercenaries are not doing anything bad to anyone who does no injustice, and that they hinder those who wish to be wrongdoers, and aid those done injustice, and look out for and face dangers for the citizens, how will it not be necessary that the expense of them be most pleasant? At any rate, they support guards even privately for things less important than these."

⁓ CHAPTER 11 ⁓

(1) "You should not, Hiero, hesitate to spend from your private possessions for the common good. And I for my part believe that what a man who is a tyrant expends on the city contributes more to what is required than what he expends for his private [affairs]. (2) Let us consider them one by one. First, do you think a house decorated at extraordinary expense provides you more of an ornament

than the whole city fitted out with walls and temples and colonnades and markets and harbors? (3) And do you appear more formidable to enemies in war by being yourself ornamented with extremely striking arms, or by the whole city being well armed by you? (4) And do you believe there will be more revenues if you have only your private [possessions] at work, or if you contrive to have the [possessions] of all the citizens at work? (5) And with regard to what is held to be the most beautiful and magnificent undertaking of all, namely, raising horses for the chariot races, which do you believe would be more of an ornament: if you yourself sponsor the most teams among the Greeks and send them to the common festivals, or if from your city there are the most horse breeders and the most competitors? Do you believe it is more beautiful to be victorious in the virtue of a chariot team or in the happiness of the city that you lead? (6) For I claim it is inappropriate for a man who is a tyrant to attempt to compete against private persons.[24] If you are victorious, you are not admired, but envied, since you draw on many households for your expenses; but if you are defeated, you would be more ridiculous than anyone. (7) I claim instead that for you, Hiero, the contest is with the other leaders of cities, and if you make the city you lead the most happy, [you will][25] be victorious in the most beautiful and magnificent contest among human beings. (8) First, you would surely have achieved being loved by those you rule, which is just what you happen to desire. Next, there would be no one who does not herald forth your victory, but all human beings would sing hymns to your virtue. (9) Not only would you attract the gaze of private persons, but you would also be esteemed by many cities, and be admired not only privately, but publicly by everyone. (10) And because you would be safe, you could, if you wished, travel somewhere to contemplate [the spectacles], or do this while remaining here. For there would always be a festival gathered around you of those who wish to display something, whether wise or beautiful or good, and of those who desire to serve you. (11) Everyone in attendance would be your ally, everyone absent would desire to see you. Thus you would not only be loved by human beings, but even attract their erotic longing; and the beauties you would not court, but would need to put up with being courted by them; you would not fear that you might suffer something, but would produce this fear in others; (12) you would have people who voluntarily obey you, and contemplate people who willingly look out for you; if any danger should arise, not only would you see allies to fight with you, but eager protectors to fight for you. Deemed worthy of many gifts, you would not be without some good-tempered person to share them with; and everyone would share your gratification at good things, and fight for your [own private affairs] as much as for their own private ones. (13) And so you would have treasures in all the wealth of your friends. (14) So be bold, Hiero, enrich your friends, for you will enrich yourself; make the city greater, for you will attach power to yourself; obtain allies for it; hold the fatherland your household, the citizens your companions, your friends your own offspring, your children just as your own soul; and try to win victory over all of these in benefaction. (15) For if you master your friends by benefaction, your enemies would be unable to stand against you. And if you do all these things, know well that you would possess the finest and most blessed of all the possessions of human beings; for you would be happy without being envied."

An Introduction to the Hiero

David Levy

As the complexity of its title suggests, Xenophon's *Hiero, or the Skilled Tyrant* focuses on two questions: whether tyrannical life is preferable to private life, and how a tyrant should rule. The course of the dialogue, in which Simonides offers his account of how a tyrant should rule in response to Hiero's criticisms of the tyrannical life, suggests that the latter question is subordinate to the former. The question of how a tyrant should rule is ostensibly taken up to show Hiero how, by ruling differently, he would find tyrannical life more choiceworthy. Insofar as the implementation of Simonides' proposals would remove Hiero's dissatisfactions with tyranny, that advice shows how the tyrant can have a good life. It appears that a full evaluation of tyrannical life requires consideration of that life at its best, when the tyrant rules most effectively. Indeed, Simonides seems to show not merely how to improve tyrannical life, but that it is through well-run tyranny—through the intelligent use of absolute power to promote the happiness of one's city—that a man can obtain the love of his citizens and the admiration of all human beings; this beneficent ruler, it seems, will reach the peak of virtue and human happiness (11.7–15).

The *Hiero* thus seems to defend the superiority of tyrannical life. That it defends only the life of the beneficent tyrant may lessen the reader's sense that the dialogue teaches injustice, but it remains the case that Simonides praises very highly the life of a man who may have acquired power in the most unscrupulous manner and whose way of life requires that he deprive his subjects of freedom. Still, unsettling as the dialogue's praise of tyrannical life may be, we must consider that Xenophon's desire to discover the truly best way of life required him to take seriously the possibility that tyrannical life is superior to private life, and that we too must be willing to consider this possibility if we seek to make a rational decision about how to live. We must also note that the dialogue's praise of tyranny does not by itself suffice to establish Xenophon's view on the subject. For Xenophon presents Hiero and Simonides in a situation in which neither can be expected to be completely honest, and both characters indicate as much. We therefore cannot take at face value the claims of either character or accept without scrutiny what the conversation seems to imply about each character's preferences. Accordingly, before we attempt in this essay to grasp what the *Hiero* teaches about the relative ranks of the tyrannical and private lives, we must first consider how the motives each character has for hiding his own beliefs affect the course of the conversation. Only then can we discern what Hiero truly finds dissatisfying about his own life, determine how well Simonides' advice addresses these dissatisfactions, and thereby uncover what the *Hiero* teaches about the choiceworthiness of the tyrannical life.[26]

Very early in the conversation, we see the first sign that what Simonides says about tyranny may not be entirely honest. In the course of praising the tyrannical life, he observes that everyone praises everything a tyrant says and does and that no one is willing to criticize a tyrant to his face (1.14). Simonides' praise of tyranny can then be expected to be exaggerated for this reason, but the course of the conversation shows that Simonides has an additional reason to be less than perfectly candid. He evidently tries to persuade Hiero to make some changes in the way he rules, and Simonides therefore has an incentive to exaggerate his praise of the tyranny that is ruled in accordance with his advice. Furthermore, in order for Hiero to be receptive to advice, he must first be somewhat aware of the defects of tyrannical life as he currently lives it. And since it would be offensive and hence dangerous for Simonides to inform Hiero about the defectiveness of tyrannical life, Simonides has an incentive to speak in such a fashion as to bring it about that Hiero condemns tyranny.

Hiero, for his part, claims that tyrants generally cannot trust others (1.15, 4.2), which implies that they cannot be expected to be entirely frank in any conversation, and he indicates that he has an additional reason to be wary of Simonides. For Hiero regards Simonides as a wise man (1.1; cf. 2.5), and Hiero observes that tyrants are particularly frightened of wise men (5.1). According to Hiero, tyrants fear that the wise will "contrive something," and although he does not explain what kind of thing tyrants fear the wise will contrive, the context of his remark allows us to make a suggestion.[27] Here, Hiero also reports that tyrants fear both brave and just men; tyrants fear that the brave may "dare something for the sake of freedom" and that the just might be desired by the multitude to rule (5.1). Hiero thus distinguishes the wise from both the brave and the just while distinguishing what exactly he fears from the brave from what exactly he fears from the just. It is reasonable to conclude that Hiero also distinguishes what exactly he fears from the wise from what he fears from either the brave or the just: he does not particularly fear that the wise will dare something for the sake of freedom or that the wise will be desired by the multitude to rule. But Hiero's whole remark concerns the threat these three classes of men pose to his rule. What does Hiero fear that the wise will contrive?

The distinction Hiero makes between what he fears from the brave and what he fears from the just implies that the just and the brave have different aims: the tyrant is not said to fear that the just, as opposed to the brave, will seek freedom. Hiero does not suggest that the just would actively seek to threaten his rule; the just are a threat because others would desire them to rule. This accords with Hiero's earlier indication that those who would deprive him of his rule would be unjust (1.12). On the other hand, the wise are said to contrive something, which implies that they, like the brave, would actively seek to undermine his rule. But the distinction between the wise and the brave suggests that the wise do not aim at freedom when they seek to undermine a tyrant's rule. If Hiero does not fear that the wise desire to form a free regime, but does fear that they plot against his rule, it is reasonable to conclude that he fears the wise will contrive to take tyrannical rule for themselves. Hiero had earlier professed surprise at the possibility that a wise man such as Simonides would be jealous of tyrants (2.5), but Hiero's willingness to attempt to persuade Simonides of the badness of tyrannical life shows that Hiero is not sure that wise men do not wish to be tyrants

(1.10; 2.6). Furthermore, since Hiero acknowledges that the desire for tyranny is very widespread (1.9–10; 2.3–5), and since his distinction between the wise and the just means that he does not know the wise to be restrained by justice, it is quite understandable that Hiero would suspect the wise of using their wisdom to obtain tyrannical power. When we add that Hiero also regards Simonides as a manly man or a "real man" (1.1),[28] that Simonides praises tyranny highly and gives the impression that real men tend to seek tyrannical power (1.8–9; 2.1–2; 7.3–4), that Hiero regards Simonides as being emulous of tyrants (6.12), and that Hiero once even refers to Simonides as being "still" a private man (rather than a tyrant) (1.3), it seems we must regard Hiero as having some fear that Simonides aspires to be a tyrant. Since Simonides is a stranger in Hiero's city (1.1), and since strangers are not likely to be especially dangerous to tyrants (5.3; 6.5), we may conclude that Hiero's fear of Simonides is not overwhelmingly great. Perhaps Hiero has no more than a vague suspicion of Simonides, but even this would be an incentive for Hiero to exaggerate his criticisms of tyranny in order to counteract Simonides' apparent jealousy of tyrants.[29]

Hiero's desire to criticize tyranny, which Simonides' initial praises of tyranny only encourage, serves Simonides' purpose of preparing Hiero to listen to his advice. Regardless of whether Hiero's criticisms of tyranny are genuine, by making them he gives Simonides a pretext for offering advice. Furthermore, in the course of criticizing tyranny as harshly as possible, Hiero is likely to recall and mention his genuine grievances, which would help to make him receptive to Simonides' advice. The conversation can thus reach the result that Simonides intends in spite of the limited honesty of its two participants. Let us now see more precisely how Simonides leads Hiero to listen to his advice.

The portion of the conversation that prepares Hiero to listen to Simonides' advice is divided into three sections by three distinct statements Simonides makes about the superiority of the tyrannical life; each statement provokes Hiero's criticisms of the tyrannical life, and each of the latter two statements comes with a denial of the importance of the preceding criticisms (1.8–9; 2.1–2; 7.1–4). Simonides first praises tyranny for its ability to provide more pleasures and fewer pains of all kinds than private life provides, which leads everyone to be emulous of tyrants (1.8–9). However, Hiero is able to show with relative ease that tyrants do not necessarily have an advantage over private men in their ability to obtain many kinds of pleasure (1.14, 16, 21, 24, 26), and it is hard to believe that, at the outset of the conversation, Simonides could have been unaware of the kinds of objections that Hiero raises to his initial praise of tyranny.[30] Furthermore, once Hiero has shown the defectiveness of tyrannical life with respect to many kinds of pleasures, Simonides observes that real men, who are the kind of men he implies have tyrannical ambition, regard many of these pleasures as insignificant (2.1–2; cf. 1.9; 7.1–4). Now, Simonides will continue to use the preferences of real men as his standard for determining the worth of various pleasures and pains (cf. 7.1–4), while never indicating that he regards any other standard as superior to that of the real man, and it makes sense for him to use this standard. For Hiero appears to have a rather low regard for virtue,[31] so he could not be expected to be impressed by a comparison of private and tyrannical life in terms of the virtues or excellences available to each. But Hiero also does not regard all pleasures as equally choiceworthy (cf. 2.6), and since real men can be plausibly characterized as having tyrannical ambitions, their preferences could be expected to appeal to Hiero. Accordingly, Hiero does not object to Simonides' use of the real man's preferences as a standard. But Simonides could not have been unaware at the outset of the conversation that many of the pleasures for which he initially praises tyranny are insignificant in the eyes of real men. We must therefore regard Simonides' initial praise of tyranny as intentionally misleading. However, precisely by not initially adopting the real man's point of view, Simonides' first praise of tyranny would seem to characterize him as someone who is unlikely to pursue tyrannical rule for himself.[32] Simonides thus initially presents himself as being relatively harmless, and we may suggest that by so doing he makes it easier for Hiero to trust him and enter the conversation (cf. 4.1), enticed by the prospect of easily refuting a man he regards as wise.

Simonides offers his second major statement about tyranny once Hiero is invested in the argument and has shown the relative defectiveness of the tyrannical life in terms of its ability to provide many kinds of pleasures. Now, having indicated the insignificance of many pleasures in the eyes of the real man (2.1), Simonides praises tyranny for the various kinds of power and wealth in which tyrants surpass private men (2.2), and he mentions specific examples of tyrannical wealth, such as virtuous horses, beautiful weapons, and magnificent houses, with which Hiero himself is concerned, as Simonides' advice in chapter 11 implies (11.2–5). In chapter 11, Simonides presents the concern with these very kinds of wealth as signs of errors on the part of a tyrant, and thus his praise of these kinds of wealth here cannot be entirely serious, but this praise serves perfectly to arouse Hiero's suspicion that Simonides is emulous of tyrants and seeks the very things that inspire real men to become tyrants (cf. 6.12).

Hiero responds precisely as our observation of his fear of the wise would lead us to expect. He immediately increases his criticisms of tyranny. In chapter 1, Hiero had claimed that tyrants "have much less enjoyment than private persons who live within measure, and have many more and much greater pains" (1.8); now, he does not limit himself to comparing tyrannical life only to moderate private life, and he claims that tyrants "share least in the greatest goods and possess most of the greatest bad things" (2.6). In order to support this claim, Hiero makes a number of questionable criticisms of tyranny. Since Hiero cannot straightforwardly deny that tyranny affords him the kinds of wealth and power that Simonides had praised (cf. 2.4; 4.6), he tries to show that the enjoyment of these kinds of power and wealth is rendered negligible by the evils that attend tyranny. His account of these evils appears to be exaggerated. Perhaps most strikingly, Hiero had admitted previously to finding acts of violence toward enemies "the pleasantest of all things" (1.34), and he admits now that citizens may take great pleasure in their wars with other cities (2.15–16). But he overlooks the pleasure that tyrants, who, after all, lead their cities in war (8.9), will take in these wars (cf. 2.16), and denies that tyrants can enjoy the war they constantly wage against their subjects (2.14–18). Hiero conceals the pleasure he takes in acts of violence, a kind of pleasure that would be especially available to a tyrant. As Hiero's criticisms of tyranny receive virtually no response from Simonides (cf. 6.9), he increases their vehemence, emphasizing the way tyranny cuts him off from friendship (3.1–9; 6.2–3), leaves him in danger of being killed (2.9, 11; 3.8; 4.1–5, 9; 6.3–8, 10, 14–16), and he expresses great dissatisfaction with the injustices he must commit (2.17; 4.10–11; 5.1–2).

Simonides finally addresses Hiero's complaints with his third major statement on the tyrannical life. Simonides grants that Hiero has mentioned a number of shortcomings of tyranny, but denies that these are decisive. Simonides takes up again the concerns of real men and gives the impression of believing that such men are superior human beings who willingly accept the toil and danger of tyranny for the sake of the honor that tyranny provides, since "no human pleasure is believed to be nearer to the divine than the enjoyment concerned with honors" (7.1–4). Simonides' praise of tyranny now, coming as it does with the acknowledgment of the difficulties Hiero had mentioned, and without any apparent concern for the moral defects of tyranny, seems strongly to suggest that Simonides could have tyrannical ambitions. Hiero thus resumes criticizing tyranny, denying that it can provide true honor, and putting together more clearly than ever his fear of being killed and his sense of his own injustices: "The tyrant passes both night and day as if judged worthy of death for injustice by all human beings" (7.5–10). We note that Hiero's fear of being executed is somewhat exaggerated: he had earlier admitted that tyrants could trust some human beings, if only the unjust, incontinent, the slavish, and foreigners (5.2; 6.5).

In response, Simonides merely asks why neither Hiero nor any other tyrant has ever given up his tyranny (7.11). The question puts Hiero in a corner: despite his claims against it, Hiero holds onto his rule. Hiero can only deny that it is possible to surrender his tyranny. Hiero, however, had earlier observed that his rule could be taken from him if he were away traveling, and he made no mention of his being put to death after his rule was taken (1.12). Moreover, Hiero's earlier admission that tyrants trust both foreigners and the unjust suggests that, at the court of another tyrant, a former tyrant could hope to find a relatively safe place to live, reducing the envy and blame directed at himself (5.2–3; 6.5). Hiero cannot credibly claim that it is impossible for a tyrant to give up his tyranny and escape with his life. Therefore, Hiero denies that it is possible to give up tyranny because it is impossible for the tyrant to atone for all his crimes (7.12). It could seem that a moral concern prevents Hiero from giving up his tyranny, but by remaining a tyrant he will continue to commit injustices rather than atone for any of his past crimes. Just as Hiero exaggerates his fear of being executed, he exaggerates his concern about his own injustice. Thus, in the first chapter, prior to Simonides' indication that he might be jealous of tyrants especially for their power and wealth, Hiero presented the tyrant as a victim of injustice rather than a perpetrator of it, and in chapter 8, once Simonides has gained Hiero's trust, Hiero portrays the tyrant as an enforcer of justice (cf. 1.12 and 8.9 with 5.1–2 and 7.10). Hiero's concern with his guilt cannot be the true reason he refuses to give up his tyranny. Despite his claims to the contrary, Hiero does not dislike the tyrannical life sufficiently to want to give it up. Therefore, when Hiero concludes his lament with the claim that it does not profit a tyrant to go on living (7.13), we cannot take this as his genuine assessment of his life.

Simonides, of course, does not respond to Hiero's complete condemnation of the tyrannical life by calling it an exaggeration, but Simonides does not appear to regard it as altogether sincere. He will advise Hiero to change how he rules, but Simonides does not suggest that, given how little Hiero says he has to lose, he should be willing to take great risks in making these changes. If anything, Simonides attempts to conceal the riskiness of his proposals, as we shall see below. Nor does Simonides respond to Hiero's complete condemnation of tyranny in such a manner as to aggravate further Hiero's fear of the wise. A man with as little attachment to his life as Hiero claims to have could easily be encouraged to attempt something risky that would make it easier for someone else to take his power, but Simonides responds by comforting Hiero, showing him that tyranny need not be so bad (8.1ff.). Therefore, in his remaining remarks, Hiero speaks far more moderately about tyranny and agrees with many of Simonides' praises of it (8.8–10; 10.1).

Our analysis of the argument therefore shows that Simonides has provoked Hiero's harshest but not his most honest criticisms of tyranny. Still, as mentioned above, we do not conclude from this observation that Hiero's criticisms of tyranny are entirely false. Simonides' attempt to advise Hiero makes sense only if he regards Hiero as somewhat dissatisfied with his current way of ruling, and we can interpret and evaluate Simonides' advice only if the conversation shows us the sources of Hiero's discontent. Fortunately,

Hiero's and Simonides' subsequent remarks confirm that Hiero has expressed some genuine dissatisfactions with his life (8.1, 6, 8; 9.1; 10.1; 11.8). We must now consider what these dissatisfactions with tyranny are, but we cannot focus on Hiero's discontent alone. The interpretation of Simonides' advice also requires that we determine which aspects of tyranny Hiero finds attractive, that is, what in fact motivates him to live as a tyrant. For this task, those of Hiero's statements that, contrary to his intention to criticize tyranny, imply that he finds something about tyranny desirable provide crucial clues.

So what are Hiero's true concerns? Despite the weakness of his concern for justice and his apparent willingness to harm his subjects, Hiero has several concerns that incline him to be kind to others. Most remarkable is Hiero's desire to be loved.[33] According to Simonides, it is because Hiero desires to be loved and regards tyranny as an impediment to his being loved that he is disappointed by tyranny (8.1). Early in the conversation, Simonides refers to Hiero's love for the boy Dailochus (1.31), which shows that Simonides had observed something of Hiero's concern with love prior to the conversation, but the conversation itself gives further evidence of Hiero's desire to be loved. In the first chapter, in response to Simonides' suggestion that tyranny provides greater sexual satisfaction than private life provides, Hiero objects very strongly: this is "a matter in which, [Simonides should] know clearly, [tyrants] surely get less than private persons" (1.27).[34] Hiero then speaks at greater length about his sexual dissatisfactions, which center above all on his doubt that his love for Dailochus is reciprocated, than about any other subject in chapter 1 (1.27–38). Later, Hiero has such confidence in the strength of this discussion of love that he refers to it as a demonstration (7.5). And Hiero does not wish to be loved only by those to whom he is sexually attracted: though Simonides had not mentioned the subject,[35] Hiero praises friendship more highly than any other subject, and he does not limit his praise to sexual friendships (3.1, 3, 5; cf. 1.34; 2.7; 4.1, 3). Then, in his response to Simonides' claim that tyrants receive greater honors than do private men, Hiero argues that honor is analogous to sexual favors: each is desirable only when it is given willingly (7.5–6). And in his subsequent description of a man who is truly honored, whom he would count "blessed," Hiero makes clear that the honors he most desires must come with affection from those who bestow them, and gives voice to his wish to be loved by his fellow citizens in general (7.9–10). Furthermore, although Hiero's comments about love draw attention primarily to his wish to be loved rather than his love for others, Hiero also loves others. Thus he admits that he loves Dailochus (1.33); he characterizes the time he and his companions spent together prior to his becoming a tyrant in terms of the mutual pleasure they felt with one another and the desire they felt for one another, which are mutual pleasures and desires he now claims to miss (6.2–3); he describes the loving honors he desires as responses to benefits given, which, among other things, could confirm that the one honored is a benefactor (7.9–10). Now it would appear to belong together with the concern Hiero feels for his fellow citizens—his desires for honor and love from them and his care for their well-being—to feel an attachment to his own city or a patriotic spirit, and Hiero shows traces of just such an attachment. This appears most conspicuously in his claim that a tyrant can neither preserve himself nor be happy without his city (5.3), a claim he makes in spite of the fact that his earlier discussion of the fatherland suggested only that it is needed for safety (4.3–4).[36] Because Hiero finds that his tyrannical rule sets his fellow citizens against him and requires him to weaken his city, his attachments to his city and its citizens are major reasons for his discontent with tyranny, but these attachments also give him a need for his city and are thus major reasons for his unwillingness to consider giving up his tyranny and abandoning his city.

We must note, however, the relative weakness of Hiero's attachment to his city and fellow citizens. Simonides, perhaps finding support in the way Hiero had emphasized his sexual dissatisfaction in particular (1.27), claims that it is Hiero's desire to be loved by boys, not by his fellow citizens in general, that is most responsible for his dissatisfaction with tyranny, and Hiero does not deny this claim (8.6).[37] Hiero's desire to be loved by his fellow citizens in general is weaker than his desire to be loved by his sexual favorites, and his love for his fellow citizens is similarly weak: Simonides exhorts Hiero to regard his fellow citizens as his comrades (11.14), which suggests that Simonides regards Hiero as capable of feeling this kind of affection for his citizens, but also implies that Hiero has hitherto failed to feel sufficient affection for them. The relative weakness of Hiero's concern for his fellow citizens is not the only source of tension between Hiero and them. In his criticism of the wealth available to tyrants, Hiero makes clear that he is very concerned to be wealthy: he is satisfied not by surpassing other private men but only by surpassing tyrants in wealth (4.6), and Hiero's description of honors, unlike Simonides' preceding description of them, includes gifts as signs of honor (cf. 7.2 with 7.7–9). Thus, Simonides has to advise Hiero to be concerned not with his own private wealth but with that of his city (11.1–6). Hiero also enjoys very much the exercise of his power, and enjoys, in particular, exercising it in cruel ways. As we noted above, he regards acts of violence toward enemies not as mere necessities but as "the pleasantest of all things" (1.34; cf. 2.14–16), and the objection he thinks to raise against the killing or imprisoning of his whole city is that he would be without people to rule if he gave in to this temptation (6.14). Simonides, accordingly, must also advise Hiero to see his city's power as his own and to direct his competitiveness toward other rulers (11.3, 6–7, 13). Thus, although Hiero's interest in ruling is motivated in part by concern for those he rules, he also enjoys his own private wealth and exerting power over his subjects.[38] These concerns of Hiero run counter to his kinder inclinations, set him against his subjects, and set them, in turn, against him. Accordingly, Hiero must also always be concerned for the safety of his life.

Since Hiero's concerns are complicated in this manner, we can safely conclude that though he is not so dissatisfied by tyranny as to consider giving it up, he also does not find the tyrannical life as he currently lives it altogether fulfilling. It is clear that all the desires we have mentioned, with the possible exception of his concern for his own safety, contribute to Hiero's attraction to rule, but in satisfying those of his desires that set him against his city, he frustrates those desires that incline him to serve it. How, then, does Simonides address Hiero's dissatisfaction with the tyrannical life?

Because Hiero's disappointment with tyranny stems above all from his belief that it prevents his being loved, Simonides prefaces his advice about how to rule with the encouraging observation that acts of kindness from rulers receive more love in return than do equal or greater acts of kindness from private men, for ruling "makes a real man nobler," and we enjoy the sight of a man ruling more than the sight of that same man as a private person (8.1–5). Hiero tacitly grants that this true, as far as it goes, but notes "immediately" that tyrants must also do many more hateful things than private men have to do (8.8).

Simonides' comforting statements have provoked Hiero to focus on a characteristic weakness of tyrannical government. He first mentions five hateful things that tyrants must do, all of which could be easily justified as being for the city's good: tyrants must exact money to pay for necessities, compel men to guard what needs guarding, punish the unjust, restrain the insolent, and prevent idleness on necessary expeditions (8.9). These acts, of course, are not simply pleasant for the citizens, but even if they must be opposed by some of the citizens, why would they not be endorsed by the majority as being in their own interest? An earlier exchange suggests that these acts would be popularly endorsed in a city with a nontyrannical regime. There, in response to Simonides' claim that during military campaigns the guards that were posted mitigated the fear he felt, Hiero observed that those guards were obedient out of fear of the laws, but that tyrants have to pay their guards, and these guards cannot be trusted (6.9–11; cf. 4.3–4). Hiero thus implied that tyrannical government is characterized by the absence of law and that where there are laws, citizens more willingly perform their unpleasant tasks.[39] Tyranny, even the beneficent tyranny that Simonides proposes, is distinguished by the absoluteness of the ruler over any laws that could restrain him, and this lawlessness of his rule—which means the citizens have no ultimate share in ruling (cf. 7.2; 11.14)—leads to less acceptance on their part of the necessary but unpleasant acts their ruler must require of them. In his earlier statement, Hiero also noted that, in the absence of law-bound guards, tyrants must rely on mercenaries (6.10; cf. 4.3–4 with 4.9); accordingly now, in chapter 8, he adds to the five hateful things he must do that the mercenaries he needs are the heaviest burden of all: the mercenaries are both a large expense for which the citizens must pay and the means of ensuring inequality in honor between the citizens and the tyrant (8.10).

Simonides concedes that these concerns of Hiero require attention (9.1), but he shows Hiero that there is a way of taking care of them that minimizes the hatred they incur: Hiero must delegate to others the unpleasant yet necessary acts of coercion, while taking for himself the gratifying task of awarding the citizens many prizes for good behavior (9.3). Prizes should be offered for military virtues, justice in contracts, farming, and commerce; in general, no one who introduces something good should go without honor (9.6–10). The citizens would then participate more enthusiastically in military matters and in paying money when necessary (9.7); those farming would be busy and therefore less troublesome (9.8); the city's economy would improve (9.8–9). And these prizes would be a bargain for Hiero, because men will exert themselves a great deal for relatively small prizes (9.11); the appeal of the prizes surpasses their cost to Hiero. Simonides thus shows Hiero how, by offering prizes to encourage useful activity among the citizens, he can both decrease animosity toward himself and increase the citizens' willingness to do what the city requires, all at little expense to himself.

But Simonides has not addressed Hiero's concern about his mercenaries. Accordingly, while Hiero grants the soundness of Simonides' advice, he asks now about how to avoid the hatred provoked by his mercenaries. Perhaps the prospect of having armed and trained citizens has led him to humor the possibility that he could dispense with mercenaries altogether, but he remains sure that his current use of them produces hostility (10.1; cf. 5.3). Simonides emphatically denies that Hiero can do without mercenaries to guard himself, and thereby implies that Hiero cannot become so well-loved as to expect his citizens adequately to defend him (10.2, 4). Simonides can only suggest that Hiero employ the mercenaries also for the defense of the citizens from criminals and foreign enemies (10.3–6). Having elaborated this suggestion, Simonides asks Hiero a number of questions concerning the usefulness of the mercenaries for the citizens, leading up to the question of whether the public-spirited use of the mercenaries will not lead the citizens to find paying for them "most pleasant" (10.8). Hiero does not answer. It is true that Simonides' questions here appear rhetorical, and he follows each of them with a comment that indicates the answer he seeks, thus lessening the need for a reply from Hiero. But we can safely say that unlike Simonides' previous advice, this advice about the mercenaries does not sufficiently impress Hiero to provoke his praise of it. It is not difficult to see why Hiero would be less impressed by this advice: even if the mercenaries do benefit the citizens, the mercenaries also preserve the inequality between the tyrant and his citizens, which the citizens resent (8.10); it would therefore not be surprising if the citizens were not happy to pay for the mercenaries, to say nothing of their finding this expense "most pleasant" to pay.

In the absence of a response from Hiero, Simonides exhorts him to be willing to spend his private possessions for the "common good" (11.1). By responding to Hiero's silence with this new consideration, Simonides appears to concede that Hiero cannot obtain the love or even the freedom from hatred he desires unless he is willing to give himself more fully to his city and fellow citizens (cf. 10.1). But, as is suggested by Simonides' mention of the "common good," in giving to his city, Hiero also would be giving to himself: "Be bold, Hiero, in enriching your friends, for you will enrich yourself. Make the city greater, for you will attach power to yourself" (11.14). By giving to the city, Hiero will gain finer adornments, strength against enemies, greater revenues, and, indeed, the love of his subjects and the praise of all human beings (11.2–5, 8). Simonides then concludes his advice by telling Hiero to "hold the fatherland your household, the citizens your companions, your friends your own offspring, your children just as your own soul; and try to surpass all of these in benefaction" (11.14). If Hiero can do this, Simonides promises he will receive the "finest and most blessed" possession: happiness without being envied (11.15). Hiero, however, remains silent.

Simonides has managed to dominate the conversation; he has put himself in a position to advise a tyrant to change his ways. Much of Simonides' advice has won Hiero's approval (10.1), and Simonides has shown himself to be thoughtful about many aspects of human life. Simonides certainly appears wiser than Hiero. We may thus be inclined to think Xenophon regards Simonides' advice as wholly satisfactory, but nothing would have been easier for Xenophon than to follow Simonides' advice with Hiero's high praise of it. Hiero's failure to respond to both Simonides' advice about the mercenaries and his exhortations to spend for the common good therefore raises a question about how satisfactory the advice is and whether Hiero will attempt to follow it. If we examine Simonides' concluding advice more closely and compare it to what we have seen about Hiero's concerns, we can see why Hiero is not so satisfied by the advice that he praises it.

Simonides advises Hiero to give to the city from his private wealth for the sake of the common good, but as this advice implies, Hiero has not yet managed to regard expenditures for the city as being equally expenditures for himself. What is more, Simonides' advice casts doubt on how fully Hiero can be expected to regard his expenditures this way. For Simonides also tells Hiero to seek to surpass his friends and fellow citizens in the benefactions he offers them, which implies that Hiero, in benefiting these others, would distinguish his good from theirs and would not believe that he enables them equally to benefit him. Simonides accordingly advises Hiero to regard others with more friendly affection: Hiero should regard his fellow citizens as companions and his friends as his own offspring (11.14). If Hiero could do this, he would be inclined to distinguish less sharply between his own good and that of others (cf. 3.2), and hence would feel less acutely the difficulty of following Simonides' advice. But we have seen that Hiero's affection for his fellow citizens has its limits, and Hiero's character and situation will not make it easy for him to overcome these limits. For Hiero is set against his citizens by his desire to rule over them. Hiero would not be held in equal honor with them—indeed, he would treat even his friends as his children—and it is doubtful that the citizens will cease to regard the mercenaries that preserve Hiero's rule as an onerous burden (8.10; 11.14). Hiero's subjects, therefore, would feel some animosity toward him, and although Hiero could expect to become more lovable by following Simonides' advice, that mercenaries would continue to be necessary shows the limits of the love that the citizens can be expected to feel for him. It is then understandable that Hiero would struggle to regard his subjects as his comrades (cf. 4.1). We have also seen that Hiero is concerned with his own safety, and following Simonides' advice would surely be risky. Hiero would arm and train his citizens for war, but he cannot trust them sufficiently to rely on them as a bodyguard. The implementation of Simonides' advice might gradually lessen the danger the armed citizens pose to Hiero, but the transition period would be especially risky. What is more, even after the transition is complete, Simonides admits that precisely the good conditions provided by Hiero's rule would lead some people to become more insolent, and these insolent men may well be heavily armed and thoroughly trained (10.2; cf. 5.4). Hiero's love for his fellows and his desire to be loved by them would have to be greater than we have seen them to be for him to follow all of Simonides' advice. Thus Hiero has very great reasons not to be totally satisfied with the tyrannical life even when that life is lived in accordance with Simonides' suggestions. And this is not even to mention the perhaps mild annoyance a man who enjoys ruling might feel at having to honor and follow the advice of whoever "introduces something good" (9.10), or the irritation at having to delegate punishments to others that would be felt by a man who finds violence toward enemies most pleasant (1.34).

The reforms Simonides proposes therefore come with significant drawbacks, and it is fitting that we are left with doubt that Hiero will implement them. Perhaps Simonides will succeed in persuading Hiero to adopt only the easiest and safest of the reforms. However, precisely because Simonides' advice is not perfectly satisfying, it serves a crucial function for the dialogue's evaluation of tyrannical life: Simonides' advice brings to light the essential tension in Hiero's life. Hiero cannot be satisfied by the tyrannical life as he currently lives it, but he also cannot be satisfied by Simonides' reforms; Hiero's desire to be loved and his care for his city are opposed by his concern for himself and his own things.[40] Furthermore, although tyrants will surely differ from one another in terms of the relative strengths of their different desires, it is reasonable to expect that the tension in Hiero's life will manifest itself somehow also in the lives of other tyrants. A man who takes power in what is widely regarded as an illegitimate manner must be willing to incur the hatred of many citizens, and his desire to be loved by his fellow citizens in general must therefore be somewhat limited. But Hiero's observation that a tyrant must take considerable pains to protect the city and punish the unjust shows that one cannot rule without attempting—at great risk to oneself—to secure some very important goods for many of one's subjects (8.9), and a man who is willing to make this attempt can be expected to suffer to some extent if he is not loved in return.[41] In this case, Simonides' inability to offer Hiero a wholly satisfactory way of life is an indication of the defectiveness of the tyrannical life in general.

Still, merely by indicating that the tyrannical life is defective, Simonides does not show that it is inferior to private life. It remains possible that, defective as it is, tyranny is preferable to living as a private man. Hiero is acutely aware of the intensity of the desire for tyranny among at least many human beings (1.10; 2.3, 5; 3.8–9), and Simonides goes so far as to claim that all are emulous of tyrants (1.9). If Simonides' claim is true, then all who are free of the dissatisfactions characteristic of living as a tyrant are plagued by the pain of not being a tyrant. Furthermore, Hiero's reluctance seriously to consider leaving the tyrannical life for the private appears to prove that, at least in his view, the tyrannical life, defective as it is, is preferable. But is this the view of Simonides, who appears to be the much more competent character in the dialogue? Since Simonides has reasons to conceal his own view throughout the dialogue, it could seem impossible to determine what that view really is. However, if we scrutinize his claims about tyranny more closely, we can see that he retracts or qualifies his praises of tyranny quite carefully, in many cases when it could have served his purpose to praise tyranny more highly, and that he thereby points to the possibility of a private life that is preferable to the tyrannical life.

Simonides implies that universal emulation of tyrants is a consequence of the fact that tyrants receive more of all kinds of pleasures and fewer pains than do private men (1.8–9), but he then concedes more or less explicitly throughout chapter 1 that tyrants do not have an advantage over private men in regard to many kinds of pleasures (1.14, 16, 24, 26). Simonides thereby opens up the possibility that those who understand the defectiveness of tyranny with regard to some kinds of pleasures might not wish to be tyrants. In chapter 2, when Simonides denies that real men are seriously concerned with many kinds of pleasures (2.1), he goes on to praise the various kinds of wealth and power that tyranny provides, but he does not say that real men necessarily desire such wealth and power (2.2; cf. 2.3–5). Simonides thus leaves open the possibility that real men, or at least some real men, are unconcerned with tyrannical wealth and power. When Simonides returns to the topic of real men, he indicates that their characteristic desire is for honor (7.3), the pleasure of which he praises more highly than any other (7.4). His primary purpose here is to explain that tyrants endure the difficulties Hiero has mentioned for the sake of honor as well as to praise tyrannical life for the honor it provides, and this makes all the more striking Simonides' additional observation that others can receive the same kinds of honors as tyrants receive (7.2). Simonides does go on, it seems, to claim that tyrants are honored above other human beings, but, in fact, what he says is ambiguous: what he actually says could mean merely that tyrants are honored "differently" (*diapherontos*) from other human beings (7.4).[42] In chapter 8, Simonides allows that ruling makes a real man appear finer and that the same man is beheld with more pleasure when ruling than when leading a private life (8.5). Simonides appears to go out of the way to avoid comparing the ruler to someone who never rules; he certainly does not say, although it would have been most appropriate in the context, that a ruler can receive more honor than can someone who never rules. Simonides thus leaves open the possibility that private life can provide superior honors to those available to a ruler. In his concluding praise of beneficent tyranny, when Simonides has a strong incentive to praise such tyranny as highly as possible, he claims that, by ruling as he suggests, Hiero would win "the finest and most magnificent contest among human beings" (11.7). Simonides does not say that this is the best contest or that real men necessarily compete in this contest. Finally, in the dialogue's concluding sentence, when Simonides could be expected to exaggerate his praise of beneficent tyranny as much as possible, he tells Hiero that by following his advice he will obtain "the finest and most blessed possession" available to human beings: being happy without being envied (11.15). Even if we overlook the likelihood that Simonides' claim that a successful tyrant could avoid being envied is ironic,[43] we still must note that Simonides does not say that the tyrant will live the best life. He says merely that the tyrant will obtain a "possession," and does not even say it is the best possession. As for why Simonides would call being happy a possession, he has not said what he means by the happiness of an individual, but his earlier references to the happiness of the city suggest he means happy in the sense of possessing great power and wealth (11.5, 7).[44] We have already seen that Simonides does not insist that real men are concerned with the possession of tyrannical power and wealth. Simonides therefore appears to have constructed his praises of tyranny carefully in order to leave open the possibility that there is a private life that is preferable to the tyrannical.

We could seem, however, to have overlooked Simonides' unambiguous argument that rulers can receive more love than can private men (8.1ff.). That Simonides praises nothing more highly than honor and that he distinguishes the real man by his desire for honor seems to indicate that the choice between the private and tyrannical lives depends on who receives more honor. And if rulers have the advantage in terms of being loved, while being loved, as Hiero suggests, is essential to the most choiceworthy honors (7.5–9), then it would seem that Simonides must prefer the life of a tyrant who is well loved to the life of a private man. But it is Hiero, and not Simonides, who insists that the honors he seeks be accompanied by love; Simonides gives no indication that he is concerned with being loved. Thus, when Hiero brings up the topic of friendship, he feels the need to attempt to show Simonides that it is a great good (3.1ff.); Simonides never expresses agreement (cf. 7.1–2). Simonides implies that honor need not be accompanied by love with his claim that the beneficent tyrant will be loved by his subjects but honored by all human beings (11.8): the class of those who honor the tyrant is larger than the class that loves him. Simonides indicates his preference regarding honor by his emphatic statement that "the praises of those who are most free are the most pleasant" (1.16), whereas Hiero makes clear that he is especially concerned with honors from those who believe they have been benefited by him, who not only honor him but love him and care for his well-being (7.9–10; cf. 11.8).[45] Simonides does not explain whom he means by "those who are most free," but it is obvious that many who have been benefited by a tyrant will not be the freest human beings. What is more, Simonides indicates his preference for praise from the freest in response to Hiero's criticism of the praise available to tyrants, which includes his observation that praise of tyrants must be suspected of being mere flattery (1.15). Even Hiero wishes to be praised truthfully. But the truth of praise that derives from benefits given and affection for the benefactor must be doubted, for those who love their benefactor may well conflate the pleasure they take in his company as well as his goodness for themselves with his goodness simply. Simonides' indication of his preference for praise from the freest together with his failure to profess any desire to be loved then suggests that he seeks praise from those who are free in the sense that their ability to evaluate him is not constrained by ulterior motives, such as love. Therefore, in granting that rulers can receive more love than private men receive, Simonides does not indicate that rulers will receive more of the honor with which he is concerned.

We must acknowledge that it is doubtful whether Simonides truly regards honor as the greatest pleasure and prefers private life solely or primarily because of the honors it provides. Not only does his interest in advising Hiero give Simonides a reason to present himself as more desirous of honor than he really is, but he also praises honor only in a qualified way: he says that honor "seems" to be a great thing (7.1), and that no pleasure "is *believed* to be nearer the divine than the enjoyment concerned with honors" (7.4, my emphasis). Simonides thus leaves open the possibility that he is equally or more concerned with pleasures other than honor. But his statements about praise and honor, when contrasted with Hiero's on honor and love, nevertheless serve to distinguish Simonides' concerns from Hiero's. When compared, the two characters' statements call attention to the fact that Hiero's preference for the life of a ruler depends in part on his desire for love and such honors as are accompanied by love, while suggesting that private men such as Simonides can be free of this need for love and honors. The honors of greatest concern to Hiero combine an expression of admiration for one's excellence with an expression of loving affection; Simonides presents himself as concerned only with the former aspect of honor. Because of his manifest thoughtfulness about many aspects of human life, as well as his reputation for wisdom (1.1), Simonides appears to be a man who places great importance on being wise, and it makes sense that such a man would also be concerned with praise from the freest human beings. The expressions of admiration that come from those who are not bound by ulterior motives to praise him could reasonably be hoped to provide him with a pleasant awareness of his goodness. That is, such praise could offer a pleasant contribution to his self-knowledge.

As for why Simonides would not indicate that, apart from seeking such praise, he also shares Hiero's desire to be loved, some of Hiero's remarks about the pleasures of spending time with friends allow us to make a suggestion. When Hiero discusses the pleasures that he claims to miss since becoming a tyrant, he focuses primarily on the mutually pleasant time he spent with his companions, and his account culminates in the observation that spending time with others at banquets permitted him almost to forget "every difficulty there might be in human life" as he immersed himself in revelry with them (6.2). While Hiero's claim that he now lacks such pleasures may be exaggerated, his statement indicates that a significant aspect of his enjoyment of friendship is the pleasant forgetting it permits.[46] Furthermore, although this pleasant forgetting is available to private men, Simonides' depiction of the life of the beneficent tyrant helps to show how being loved could offer rulers further opportunities for similar enjoyments. For this tyrant would live amid a constant "festival," listening to songs of his virtue, surrounded by those who would display their wise, beautiful, or good things to him, and by those merely longing to serve him, while those who are beautiful attempt to seduce him (11.8, 10–11; cf. 8.6). He would thus have ample opportunities to immerse himself in activities with others.[47] But insofar as a man strives to be wise, as Simonides appears to do, he must be unwilling to forget even the gravest difficulties in human life.

We therefore conclude that the *Hiero* is not ultimately a defense of the tyrannical life. By presenting Hiero's complaints and Simonides' advice, Xenophon indicates the essentially defective character of the tyrannical life. Through Simonides' remarks about honor and his unconcern with the advantages he indicates ruling offers, Xenophon suggests that there is a private life that is superior to the tyrannical: the life of the man concerned with wisdom and honor, who is free of Hiero's need to rule with all its attendant toils and risks. We should conclude, however, by noting some of the questions that this interpretation has not answered. In the first place, a question remains about Xenophon's view of tyranny as a political regime. To what extent or in what ways is a free and lawful community superior to Simonides' beneficent tyranny, in which excellences of many kinds are promoted and the ruler is free to implement any beneficial reforms? The investigation of this question would necessarily take up those indications in the *Hiero* and Xenophon's other works of his view of law, and it would therefore shed light on another question that our interpretation of the *Hiero* has left unanswered. By presenting Simonides as being free of concern with the advantages he indicates ruling offers, the *Hiero* could seem to suggest the superiority of private life to any life characterized by political ambition. But Simonides'

comments about the advantages of rulers are meant to appeal to
Hiero, and as Simonides' failure even to mention the term "law" suggests, he does not necessarily address the specific attractions ruling
may have for the nontyrannical political man whose political ambition is limited by or compatible with his willing obedience to the
law. Our study therefore raises questions about Xenophon's view
of the relative ranks of private and nontyrannical political life. To
what extent can a political man be law-abiding in his heart and thus
free of the desire for tyranny? Insofar as he can do this, what goods
and evils follow from his doing so, and how does his life compare
to that of a private man such as Simonides? Finally, in attempting
to answer these questions, we cannot take for granted the adequacy
of the standard in light of which the *Hiero* suggests the superiority
of the private to the tyrannical life: the rank in the eyes of the real
man of the pleasures and pains each life offers. This standard may
be most appropriate to a conversation with a tyrant, and it certainly
suffices to bring to light Hiero's dissatisfaction with his own life. But
it remains unclear whether the real man is adequately defined in the
Hiero, and above all, whether Xenophon could have regarded the
pleasures and pains of this man as his ultimate standard in judging
between private and political life.

CHAPTER 2
Agesilaus

TRANSLATED BY ROBERT C. BARTLETT

∽ CHAPTER 1 ∽

(1) I know that it is not easy to write a praise worthy of both the virtue and reputation of Agesilaus, but nonetheless it must be attempted. For it would not be a fine state of affairs if, because a man was perfectly good, he should not, for that very reason, attain even lesser praises [than those he deserves].

(2) Concerning his good birth, then, what greater and nobler thing might someone have to say than that still, even now, his lineage going back to Heracles[1] is remembered, in the recounting of his ancestors, and these no private persons but kings descended from kings? (3) But not even in this respect, at any rate, might someone be able to blame them—on the grounds that, though they rule as kings, they do so over some chance city. Instead, just as their familial line is held in very high regard in their fatherland, so their city is very much honored in Greece. As a result, they do not occupy the first place among second-raters but exercise leadership among leaders. (4) In this respect, at least, both the fatherland and his familial line are deserving of shared praise: the city never attempted to put down their rule because it begrudged them their preeminent honor, and the kings never longed for things greater than those specified when they first acceded to the kingship. For that very reason, while no other rule is manifest as having lasted without interruption—neither

democracy nor oligarchy nor tyranny nor kingship—this kingship alone endures uninterrupted.

(5) That even before he came to rule, Agesilaus was held to be worthy of the kingship, there are the following indications. For Agis met his end while ruling as king,[2] and a contentious struggle for the rule ensued between Leotychides, on the grounds that he was son of Agis, and Agesilaus, on the grounds that he was son of Archidamus; and the city, judging Agesilaus to be more unimpeachable in point of both familial line and virtue, established him as king.[3] And when one is judged, by those who are best, to be worthy of the noblest reward in the strongest[4] city, what sorts of additional evidence are still needed of his virtue, at least prior to his ruling?

(6) All such things as he accomplished in the kingship I will now relate, for from the deeds I believe his ways will, in the finest manner, be quite clear. Now Agesilaus was still young[5] when he attained the kingship, and he had just come to rule when it was announced that the King of the Persians was gathering a great armed force, both naval and infantry, for the purpose of attacking the Greeks. (7) While the Lacedaemonians and the allies were deliberating about these things, Agesilaus promised that, if they gave him thirty Spartiates, three[6] thousand *neodamodeis*, and a contingent of allies numbering six thousand, he would cross over to Asia and attempt to establish peace or, if the barbarian wished to wage war, he would deprive him of any leisure to march against the Greeks. (8) Many were immediately much delighted by the very fact that he desired this—since the Persian had previously crossed over to attack Greece, [Agesilaus] would cross over to attack him in return; and by his choosing to proceed against [the Persian] rather than waiting to be attacked by him; and by his wish to wage war at [the Persian's] expense rather than at that of the Greeks. But judged to be finest of all was the fact that at stake in the contest was, not Greece, but Asia.

(9) Now once he obtained an armed force and sailed off, how might one set forth more clearly the way that he exercised his generalship than by relating the actions he undertook? (10) This, then, was the first action in Asia: Tissaphernes[7] swore an oath to Agesilaus, to the effect that if he should observe a truce until the arrival of the messengers whom he had sent to the King, he would bring it about for him that the Greek cities in Asia be left autonomous. Agesilaus for

his part swore that he would observe the truce without guile, speci-
fying a three-month period for the action indicated. (11) Now Tissaphernes immediately betrayed the oaths he had sworn, for instead of
acting for peace he sent for a great armed force from the King to add
to the one he possessed already. And although Agesilaus perceived
these things, nonetheless he abided by the truce. (12) To me this
seems to be the first noble thing he accomplished, for by showing
Tissaphernes to be a breaker of oaths, he made him untrustworthy
in the eyes of everyone; and by showing himself, by contrast, to be
someone who abides by his oaths, in the first place, and, second, one
who does not betray his compacts, he encouraged everyone—both
Greeks and barbarians—to enter into compacts with him, should he
ever wish to do so.

(13) Now when Tissaphernes, on account of his haughtiness at the
thought of the army then marching to the coast, declared war on
Agesilaus, unless Agesilaus should withdraw from Asia, the rest of
the allies and the Lacedaemonians present made manifest their great
consternation, for they believed Agesilaus's present power to be less
than that available to the King. But Agesilaus, with a brightly beaming face, ordered the envoys to report back to Tissaphernes that he
was very grateful to him because, by betraying his oaths, he had acquired the gods as enemies but made them allies of the Greeks. (14)
Immediately after this he announced to the soldiers that they should
prepare themselves as if for a campaign. To those cities it was necessary to visit in his march to Caria, he sent word to prepare a marketplace. And he wrote to the Ionians, Aeolians, and Hellespontines
to send to him at Ephesus those who would campaign together with
him. (15) Now Tissaphernes believed that his own home in Caria
was Agesilaus's real target, both because Agesilaus did not have a
cavalry (Caria was impracticable for cavalry) and because he held
Agesilaus to be angry with him on account of the deception; and so
he conveyed the whole infantry in that direction while the cavalry
he brought around to the plain near the Meander River, in the belief
that, with his contingent of horses, he was capable of dealing a blow
to the Greeks before they could reach the areas where it is difficult
for horses to maneuver. (16) But Agesilaus, rather than proceeding
immediately to Caria, turned and headed for Phrygia instead.[8] Collecting and leading on the powers that met him along the way, he

began to put down the cities and, because he set upon them unexpectedly, took a great many goods.[9]

(17) This too, then, was held to be an accomplishment characteristic of a skilled general, for once war was declared and deception subsequently became both pious and just, he showed Tissaphernes to
be a child when it came to deception, whereas he seemed then prudently to enrich his friends as well. (18) For since so many goods had
been taken, everything was being sold for next to nothing, and he
sent word to his friends to buy, saying that he would then go down
to the sea, bringing with him his army in formation. He ordered the
auctioneers to write down how much they sold something for and
to release the goods [to his friends]. As a result, though his friends
spent no money in advance and did no harm to the public treasury,
they all obtained a great many goods. (19) Further, whenever deserters, as is only likely, went to the king in their wish to point out to him
where there were goods to be found, he saw to it that such goods
were seized by his friends so that they might be both wealthy and
held in higher repute. On account of these things, he immediately
made many lovers of his friendship.

(20) But recognizing that a land that had been plundered and
made desolate could not long maintain an army, whereas one that
is inhabited and cultivated would supply unending sustenance, he
saw to it that his opponents were not only subdued by violence, but
also brought over by gentleness. (21) He announced many times to
the soldiers not to take vengeance on those seized, as on those who
are unjust, but rather to guard them, on the grounds that they are
human beings; and many times, whenever he moved camp, if he
perceived little children of merchants left behind, whom many tried
to sell because they believed it impossible to bring them along and
rear them, he saw to these too and had them conveyed somewhere
together. (22) As for those prisoners, in turn, who were captured in
battle on account of their old age, he gave orders for them to be cared
for, so that they would be destroyed by neither dogs nor wolves. As
a result, not only those who learned of these things, but even the
very people seized by him became well disposed toward him. As for
the cities he brought over to himself, he relieved them of all those
services slaves perform for their masters and ordered them instead
to do all those things freemen are persuaded to do for their rulers;

and through his philanthropy[10] he brought under his control the fortifications not taken by assault.

(23) Since, however, he was unable to campaign in the plains even in Phrygia, on account of Pharnabazus's[11] cavalry, it seemed to him that a cavalry force had to be provisioned, so that he would not have to wage war while taking flight. He therefore enlisted the wealthiest people from all the cities in the region to raise horses. (24) He also proclaimed that whoever might supply a horse, arms, and a man who could pass muster would be exempt from going on campaign, and he thus made each eager to do these things, just as one would eagerly seek out somebody to die in one's stead. He also appointed cities from which the horsemen were to be supplied, in the belief that it was of course from the cities that rear horses that those who are especially confident in their horsemanship would come. This too, then, he was held to do in admirable fashion, because he thus outfitted his cavalry that was from the outset both mighty and ready for action.

(25) At the first appearance of spring, he brought together at Ephesus the whole of his armed force. In his wish to train it, he proposed prizes both for the cavalry squadrons, whichever one should be strongest at riding, and for the companies of hoplites, whichever one might be best in bodily conditioning. He proposed prizes for the targeteers and archers as well, whichever of them came to sight as strongest in the deeds appropriate to them. As a result of this, it was possible to see the gymnasia full of men exercising and the racecourse full of cavalrymen riding, and the javelin throwers and the archers pursuing their targets. (26) In fact he made the whole city in which he resided a sight worth seeing. For the marketplace was full of all manner of arms and horses for sale, and the coppersmiths and the carpenters, as well as blacksmiths and cobblers and painters— all were supplying implements of war. As a result, you might have believed that the city really was a workshop for war. (27) And someone upon seeing it would have been heartened, in the first place by Agesilaus, then also by the other soldiers wearing wreaths as they came from the gymnasia and dedicating their wreaths to Artemis.[12] For wherever men revere gods, train for warfare, and practice obedience, how is it not to be expected that all things there are full of good hope?

(28) And because he believed that feeling contempt for enemies too would foster a certain strength for fighting, he announced to the heralds that the barbarians seized by raiders would be put up for sale naked. When, then, the soldiers saw that they were pale, on account of their never stripping down, as well as fat and unexercised on account of always being in carriages, they believed that the war would be no different than if it had to be waged against women. He announced this too to the soldiers—that he would quickly lead them by the shortest route to the strongest parts of the territory, so they might prepare themselves for him then and there, in body and judgment, as do men about to engage in a contest.

(29) Yet Tissaphernes believed that [Agesilaus] was saying these things because he wished to deceive him once again, and that he now really was going to invade Caria. Just as before, then, [Tissaphernes] had the infantry cross over into Caria and stationed the cavalry in the plain of the Meander. Agesilaus, however, did not play false, but instead, just as he announced, he moved immediately into the region around Sardis, and, making his way for three days through land barren of enemies, he furnished the army with much in the way of provisions. But on the fourth day the enemies' cavalry arrived. (30) To the person in command of the baggage train, the leader [of the Persian cavalry] said to cross the Pactolus River and there make camp; [the cavalry] themselves, upon catching sight of the Greeks' camp followers who were dispersed for purposes of plunder, killed many of them. Perceiving this, Agesilaus ordered the cavalry to go to their aid. The Persians, in turn, when they saw this aid, banded together and arranged themselves in battle formation with their full complement of cavalry. (31) At this, Agesilaus, recognizing that the enemies' infantry was not yet present and that he himself lacked nothing in point of preparations, regarded it as an opportune moment to join battle, if he could. After offering sacrifice, then, he immediately led the phalanx against the cavalry arrayed opposite him, and he ordered those of the hoplites of the ten-year class[13] to run to close quarters with them,[14] and he told the targeteers to lead the way on the double. He also sent word to the cavalry to attack, while he and the whole army followed. (32) Those who were good among the Persians received the cavalry; but when all that was terrible fell upon them at once, they gave way, and some of them were immediately

cut down in the river, others began to flee. The Greeks who followed seized even their army camp; and the targeteers, as is to be expected, began to turn to plunder. Now Agesilaus made his camp in a circle that encompassed all things, those of friends as well as of enemies;[15] (33) but when he heard that the enemies were in confusion because they were blaming one another for what had happened, he immediately led on toward Sardis. And there he burned and sacked the areas around the town and simultaneously made clear by proclamation that those requesting liberty should come to him as to an ally. But if some claim Asia as their own, then they should come against its liberators, who will decide the matter by means of arms. (34) When no one came out in opposition, however, he henceforth campaigned fearlessly, seeing the Greeks who had previously been compelled to prostrate themselves now being honored by those by whom they had been continually treated with hubris; and as for those who deemed themselves worthy of reaping even the honors due the gods, these he rendered unable even to look the Greeks in the face. And while making the land of friends inviolate, he reaped such harvest from that of enemies that, over the course of two years, he dedicated more than one hundred talents as a tithe to the god in Delphi.[16]

(35) The King of the Persians,[17] however, believing Tissaphernes to be the cause of his own affairs going so badly, sent down Tithraustes and had Tissaphernes' head cut off.[18] After this, the affairs of the barbarian were still more dispirited, whereas those of Agesilaus were stronger by far. Ambassadors from all the nations came seeking friendship, and many even revolted in his favor, in their longing for liberty, with the result that Agesilaus was leader, no longer of Greeks only, but also of many barbarians. (36) And indeed he deserved to be exceedingly admired, he who, though he ruled over very many cities on the mainland and ruled over islands too—for the city delivered into his hands the naval force as well[19]—and though he grew in both renown and power, he to whom it was possible to make use of many good things in whatever way he liked, and—what is the greatest thing beyond these—while intending and expecting to dissolve the empire that had previously campaigned against Greece, nonetheless he was overpowered by none of these things. Instead, when the order came from those in office back home to aid

the fatherland, he obeyed the city in a manner no different than if he happened to be standing alone in the office of the ephorate before the Five: he made it very clear that he would accept neither the whole earth in place of the fatherland nor his newly acquired friends in place of ones of long standing, nor shameful and risk-free profits rather than the just and noble things accompanied by risks.[20]

(37) For so long, then, as he remained in office, how could the following deed not show him to be a king deserving of praise, namely, that he who, in coming upon all the cities in the grip of civil strife because their regimes had been changed when the Athenian empire came to an end, cities to which he had sailed with the intention of ruling them, brought it about that, without recourse to exile or executions, the cities were governed harmoniously and continued to be happy for so long as he was present? (38) For that very reason, the Greeks in Asia were pained when he left, on the grounds that he was not just a ruler but also a father and comrade. And in the end they made clear that the friendship they supplied was not counterfeit; at any rate, they were willing to join him in aiding Lacedaemon, even though they knew that they would have to battle against those who were not inferior to themselves.

This, then, was the end of his actions in Asia.

∼ CHAPTER 2 ∼

(1) Upon crossing the Hellespont, he proceeded through the same nations as had the Persian with his very great armament;[21] and the path on which the barbarian had spent one year, Agesilaus covered in less than one month, for he was eager not to come too late for the fatherland.[22] (2) When he had passed through Macedonia and arrived at Thessaly, Larisaeans, Crannonians, Scotousaeans, and Pharsalians, who were allies of the Boeotians—in fact all the Thessalians except those who happened to be in exile at the time—kept doing him harm as they followed along. For a while he led the army in a hollow square, having half the cavalry in the front, the other half in the rear; but when the Thessalians prevented his progress by setting upon those in the back, he sent along to the rear that part of

the army that was in the van and those with him himself.[23] (3) When they were arrayed against one another [in battle formation], the Thessalians, believing it not to be a noble [or propitious] circumstance to conduct a cavalry fight against hoplites, turned and withdrew at a walking pace; and the others followed them, very foolishly.[24] Agesilaus, recognizing the errors each side was making, sent those with him — very stout cavalrymen — with orders to announce to the others to pursue at full strength, and to do so themselves as well, and to grant the enemy no further opportunity to wheel round. When the Thessalians saw, contrary to their expectation, the forces charging them, some of them did not even turn to wheel round, others were seized in the very attempt to do so, their horses standing athwart [the enemy]. (4) Polycharmus, however, the Pharsalian cavalry commander, did wheel round and, in the course of fighting together with the men around him, died. When this happened, a headlong flight ensued; as a result some of them died, others were taken alive; and they did not come to a halt until they reached Mount Narthacium.

(5) And at that time Agesilaus erected a trophy between Pras and Narthacium, and there he remained, very much pleased by the deed because, with a cavalry he himself had contrived, he had been victorious over those who pride themselves on their horsemanship. On the next day he crossed the Achaean mountains in Phthia and proceeded along the entire path that now remained, through friendly territory, until he reached the borders of Boeotia.[25] (6) Here, upon discovering arrayed in opposed battle formation the Thebans, Athenians,[26] Corinthians, Aenianians, Euboeans, and both Locrians,[27] he did not at all delay but drew up in battle formation in plain sight, having one and a half *morae*[28] of Lacedaemonians and, of the local allies, only the Phoceans and Orchomenians, together with the army he himself had led.[29] (7) I am not going to say this, that though his forces were both much smaller and much worse, he nonetheless joined in fight; for should I say these things, I think Agesilaus would come to sight as senseless, and I myself as a fool, if I were to praise someone who takes risks haphazardly when the greatest things are at stake. Instead, I admire rather more these things about him: that he provided for himself an army not inferior in number to that of the enemies, and he so equipped them that all appeared to be bronze, all crimson. (8) He also saw to it that the soldiers would be capable

of enduring the labors involved, and he filled their souls with resolve, such that they would be competent against any they might
have to fight. Further, he instilled in those with him, in each of them,
the ambition to outdo one another in appearing best. He instilled in
all of them the hopes, at any rate, that many good things would be
theirs, if they should become good men, because he believed that it is
on the basis of such things that human beings most zealously battle
enemies.

(9) And indeed he was not proved false. I will relate the battle as
well; for it was unlike any other in our time. They came together in
the plain of Coronea, Agesilaus with his men coming from the Cephi-
sus [River], the Thebans with their men from Mount Helicon. They
saw that the phalanxes on both sides were very equally matched,
and the cavalry too on each side were very nearly equal. Agesilaus
held the right wing of those on his side, Orchomenians were on his
extreme left; and the Thebans, in turn, were on the right, the Argives held the left. (10) Upon their coming together, a great silence
arose from both; but when they were a stade's distance from one
another, the Thebans gave the battle cry and charged at a run. When
there was still a distance of three plethra between them, [the merce-
naries] from Agesilaus's phalanx, under the command of Herippi-
das, charged in their turn (11) (these were among the men who had
marched together with Agesilaus from home and some troops who
had served with Cyrus[30]) as well as Ionians, Aeolians, and the Hellespontines who bordered them. All of these were among those who
ran forward together, and when they crossed spears, they routed
those opposite them. Indeed, the Argives did not receive Agesilaus's
men, but instead fled to Mount Helicon. And at this, certain of the
foreigners were already preparing to place a victory wreath on Agesilaus—when someone announced to him that the Thebans, having
cut through the Orchomenians, were in among the baggage carriers.
He immediately extended his phalanx and led it against them. The
Thebans, in turn, seeing that their allies had fled to Mount Helicon
and wishing to force their way through to their own men, began a
mighty charge. (12) Here it is possible to say indisputably that Agesilaus was courageous, and yet[31] he did not choose for himself the
safest things: for although it was possible for him to let pass the men
charging and then to pursue and defeat their rear, he did not do

this but came to blows with the Thebans head-on. Shield clashing against shield, they were being thrust backward, they battled, they killed, they died. And there was no war cry, but neither was there silence; there was instead a certain sound such as anger as well as battle might supply. In the end, some of the Thebans forced their way through to Mount Helicon, but many died while withdrawing.

(13) When victory was with Agesilaus, he himself was conveyed, wounded, to the army's main body, and some of the cavalry came up and said to him that eighty of the enemy, with their arms, were at the temple, and they asked what they ought to do. Now although he had many wounds everywhere and from every sort of weapon, nonetheless he was not forgetful of the divine, but he ordered [his men] to allow [the Thebans] to depart wherever they might wish, and he forbade the committing of any injustice against them, and he commanded his cavalry to accompany them until they were in safety. (14) Now that the battle was over, it was possible to observe the earth made damp with blood, there where they fell upon one another, corpses of friend and enemy lying with one another, shields smashed to pieces, spears broken, daggers stripped of their sheaths, some on the ground, some in bodies, others still in men's hands. (15) At that point, then—for it was already late in the day—having dragged together the corpses of the enemies within their camp, they had their evening meal and slept. At dawn, he ordered Gylis the polemarch to put the army in battle formation, to set up a trophy, to have all wear a wreath in honor of the god, and to have all the aulos players play. (16) And they were doing these things— when the Thebans sent a herald, asking for a truce to bury their dead. And so it was in this way that the truce came about, and Agesilaus withdrew for home, choosing, instead of his being the greatest in Asia, to rule in a lawful manner and to be ruled in a lawful manner, at home.[32]

(17) After this, when he realized that the Argives were reaping the fruits of things at home, and had got hold of Corinth, and were taking pleasure in the war, he campaigned against them.[33] Having laid waste to the whole of their land, he immediately crossed from there through the narrow passes to Corinth and seized the walls that extend to Lechaeum.[34] And having thus opened up the gates of the Peloponnesus and then withdrawn toward home at the time of the Hyacinthian Festival,[35] he aided in completing the paean to the god,

taking the place assigned him by the chorus master. (18) After this, when he perceived that the Corinthians were keeping all their flocks in Peiraeum[36] and sowing and harvesting the whole of Peiraeum, and because he held it to be a very great thing that the Boeotians were setting forth with ease from Creusis[37] so as to support the Corinthians, he campaigned against Peiraeum. Seeing that it was being guarded by many, he moved his camp after the morning meal toward the city center [of Corinth itself], making it seem as though the city were on the point of being delivered up [by some fifth columnists inside]. (19) And once he noted that support had come in haste, under cover of night, from Peiraeum into the city, he pivoted at break of day and seized Peiraeum, finding it emptied of its guards; and he took, in addition to its contents, also the walls that had been built there.[38] Once he had done these things, he withdrew toward home.

(20) After these things, the Achaeans, eager for alliance and asking [the Spartans] to campaign together with them in Acarnania [. . .];[39] and when the Acarnanians set upon them in the narrow passes, he with his light infantry[40] captured the heights above their heads and engaged in battle; and, after killing many of them, he erected a trophy; and he did not let up until he made the Acarnanians,[41] Aetolians, and Argives[42] friends with the Achaeans, and allies with himself. (21) When the enemies[43] sent an embassy, in their desire for peace, Agesilaus spoke against the peace[44] until he compelled the cities of the Corinthians and Thebans to permit to return home those who had been exiled on account of [their having sided with] the Lacedaemonians. And later on, in turn, he restored those of the Phliasians who were exiled on account of the Lacedaemonians, he himself having campaigned against Phliasia.[45]

And if someone may reproach these things for some other reason, at least it is manifest that they were done through friendship for comrades. (22) For when his opponents were killing the partisans of the Lacedaemonians in Thebes, he came in turn to their aid and campaigned against Thebes.[46] On discovering everything surrounded by a trench and a palisade, he crossed over the heights of Cynoscephalae[47] and ravaged the territory up to the town, offering to meet the Thebans in battle on both the plain and the hills, should they wish it. He also campaigned again, the following year, against Thebes; and, after crossing the trenches and palisades at Scolus, ravaged the rest of Boeotia.[48]

(23) So as regards matters up to this point, both he himself and the city together enjoyed good fortune; but as for all such blunders as happened after this, no one would say that they were done when Agesilaus was leader. For when the misfortune at Leuctra[49] had occurred and his adversaries, together with the Mantineans, were killing his friends in Tegea and his guest-friends, and all the Boeotians, Arcadians, and Elians were already in league, he campaigned with the force of the Lacedaemonians[50] only, although many believed that it would be a long time before the Lacedaemonians would even venture forth from their own land. But only once he had ravaged the land of those who killed his friends, did he then withdraw toward home.[51]

(24) After this, all the Arcadians, Argives, Elians, and Boeotians campaigned against Lacedaemon, together with the Phocians, both Locrians, the Thessalians, Aenianians, Acarnanians, and Euboeans.[52] In addition to these, the slaves and many of the cities of *perioikoi* were in revolt,[53] and despite the fact that at least as many of the Spartiates themselves died in the battle at Leuctra as survived it, nonetheless he kept vigilant guard over the city—and this, although the city is unwalled. He did so by not leading out the army to where the enemies would have the upper hand in everything, but instead by vigorously taking up positions for battle where the citizens would have the upper hand, for he believed that, by going out onto level ground, he would be surrounded on all sides, whereas by staying put in the narrows and the heights, he would prevail in everything. (25) When the army indeed withdrew, how could someone deny that he handled himself judiciously? For given that by now old age prevented him from campaigning, both on foot and on horseback, when he saw the city in need of money, if it was going to gain anyone as an ally, he applied himself to providing this. He also contrived a way to do all such things as he was able to do while remaining at home, and he did not shrink from pursuing whatever the opportune moment allowed; neither was he ashamed to be sent out as an envoy rather than a general, if he should thus bring about some benefit for the city.

(26) Nonetheless, even as an envoy he accomplished the deeds of a great general: for when Autophradates was besieging Ariobarzanes,

an ally [of Sparta], at Assos, he withdrew and fled, for fear of Agesilaus.[54] And Cotys, in turn, while besieging Sestos when it still
belonged to Ariobarzanes, broke up and brought an end to his siege.
As a result, it was not unreasonable that a trophy over his enemies
was erected for him, stemming from his being an envoy as well.
Indeed Mausolus,[55] besieging both of these places by sea with one
hundred ships, sailed away toward home, not because he was afraid,
but because he had been persuaded to do so. (27) Here too,[56] then, he
accomplished things worthy of wonder. For those who believed they
were well treated by him as well as those who fled before him—both
gave him money. Tachos[57] and Mausolus—the latter also contribut-
ing money to Lacedaemon, on account of a prior guest-friendship
with Agesilaus—sent him off toward home and gave him a magnificent escort.

(28) After this, when he was about eighty years old, he came to
understand that the king of the Egyptians desired war with Persia and had a large infantry, a large cavalry, and much money; he
was delighted to hear that [the king] had sent for him, promising
him, in fact, the leadership of these [forces]. (29) For [Agesilaus] believed that, with one and the same sally, he would return a favor
to the Egyptian for the benefactions he had done Lacedaemon, he
would set free again the Greeks in Asia, and he would impose a just
penalty on the Persian both for previous matters and because now,
while claiming to be an ally, he demanded that Messene be let go.[58]
(30) When, however, he who had sent for him did not give the leadership over to him, Agesilaus thought over what he ought to do, on
the grounds that he had suffered the greatest deception. After this,
to begin with, those Egyptians who were campaigning separately[59]
revolted from the king, and then all the others abandoned him. And
he himself, in his fear, withdrew in hasty flight to Sidon in Phoenicia,
while the Egyptians who were engaged in civil strife chose two kings.
(31) Here Agesilaus realized that, if he should assist neither one, neither would pay wages to the Greeks and neither would supply a
marketplace, and that whichever of the two might gain the upper
hand would be hostile but that if he assisted one of the two, this
one would in all likelihood be a friend because he had been treated
well. And so, having decided which of the two seemed to be more
a friend to the Greeks, he campaigned together with him, defeated

the enemy of the Greeks in battle, and helped establish the other [as king].[60] And having made him a friend to Lacedaemon and received in this way a great deal of money, he sailed for home, although it was the middle of winter, he being in a hurry so that the city would not be idle in attacking its enemies in the coming summer.

∼ CHAPTER 3 ∼

(1) And as many deeds of his as were accomplished with the greatest number of witnesses have been stated. For such things need no additional proofs: it is sufficient just to call them to mind and they are immediately trusted. But now I will attempt to make clear the virtue in his soul, the virtue through which he did these things and loved all that is noble and shunned all that is shameful. (2) For Agesilaus so revered the divine things that even his enemies held his oaths and his treaties to be more trustworthy than their friendship among themselves [since they sometimes][61] shrank from proceeding to meet at the same place, but they entrusted themselves to Agesilaus. And so that no one distrust this, I want even to name the most conspicuous of them. (3) Spithridates the Persian knew that Pharnabazus was bringing about a marriage with the King's daughter but that Pharnabazus wanted to take Spithridates' daughter without benefit of marriage; and so, regarding this as an act of hubris, he entrusted himself, his wife, his children, and his power to Agesilaus. (4) Cotys, ruler of the Paphlagonians, did not submit to the King, though the King sent a pledge of friendship, for fear that he might be seized or be compelled to pay a great deal of money or even be killed [by the King]. But because he trusted in the treaties of Agesilaus, he entered the latter's army encampment and, concluding an alliance with him, chose to campaign together with Agesilaus, having two thousand horses and four thousand targeteers.[62] (5) And Pharnabazus too came to Agesilaus to parley and struck an agreement that if he himself should not be installed as general over the whole army, he would revolt from the King. "If, however, I do become general," he said, "I will wage war against you, Agesilaus, to the greatest extent I can." And in saying these things, he trusted that he would suffer nothing

in violation of the treaty.[63] So great and noble a possession is it, both for all others and especially for a man who is a general, to be and to be known to be pious and trustworthy. This, then, about pious reverence.[64]

∼ CHAPTER 4 ∼

(1) As for his justice in regard to money [or goods], what sorts of evidence might one have that could be greater than the following? For no one ever lodged a legal complaint of being deprived [of money] by Agesilaus, but many agreed that they were treated well by him in many respects. And how would he, who derived pleasure from giving of his own things for the advantage of human beings, be willing to take what belonged to others, at the price of a bad reputation? For if he should desire money, it would be much less trouble to guard his own things than to take what did not belong to him. (2) And how indeed would he who is unwilling to withhold favors [or gratitude], where no legal action is possible against the person who fails to give them, be willing to deprive others of what the law in fact prohibits depriving them? But Agesilaus judged to be unjust not only the withholding of favors but also the failure to give them, for one capable of doing so, in greater measure [than any received]. (3) As for stealing what belongs to the city, in what way might anyone plausibly accuse him of this, he who gave over to the fatherland even the reaping of the gratitude [or favors] that were owed him? And whenever he might wish to benefit with money either a city or friends, he was able to profit them by taking from others — is this too not great evidence of his continence as regards money? (4) For if he had sold his favors or performed benefactions for pay, no one would have held that they owed him anything. But as for those who have been treated to benefactions as a free gift, it is they who always serve their benefactor with pleasure, both because they were treated well and because they were trusted in advance to be worthy of guarding the favor [or gratitude] thus deposited. (5) But whoever prefers having less, accompanied by well-born nobility, to having more, accompanied by injustice — how could such a person not shun mak-

ing shameful profits to the greatest degree? At any rate, although he was judged by the city to own the goods of Agis in their entirety, he gave half of those goods over to his relatives on his mother's side, because he saw that they were impoverished. That all these things are true, the city of the Lacedaemonians is a witness. (6) And when Tithraustes offered him a great many gifts, if only he should withdraw from the land, Agesilaus answered: "Tithraustes, it is believed among us that it is nobler for the ruler that his army become rich rather than that he become so, and that he try to take spoils of war from the enemy rather than gifts."

∽ CHAPTER 5 ∽

(1) Moreover, when it comes to pleasures that master many human beings, by what sorts of pleasure does anyone know of Agesilaus's having been defeated—he who supposed that one must abstain similarly from drunkenness as from gluttony, and similarly from food beyond what is fitting as from error?[65] Although he received a double portion at the public meals, this was not so that he might make use of both himself; instead, he distributed them and left neither portion for himself, believing that this double portion had been granted to the king, not for the sake of satiety, but so that he might be able with this to honor whomever he might wish. (2) He did not deal with sleep as with a master but rather as with something ruled by the actions [he had to undertake], and if he failed to have the lowliest bed among his associates, the shame he felt was not unclear. For he believed it fitting for a ruler to be preeminent over private persons, not in point of softness, but in endurance. (3) In the following things, however, he felt no shame in having a greater share: of the sun in summer, of the cold in winter. And indeed, if it ever happened that the army endured hardships, he voluntarily labored beyond the others, believing that all such things were an encouragement to the soldiers. To sum up, Agesilaus delighted in toiling but put up with no easygoingness whatever.

(4) As for his continence concerning sexual matters, is it not worthwhile to call it to mind, if for no other reason than for the

wonder of it? For anyone would say that it is only human to abstain from the things one does not desire; but, when he was in
love with [the boy] Megabates, the son[66] of Spithridates, as the
most intense nature loves what is most beautiful, then—since it is
a customary practice among the Persians to kiss those whom they
honor—when Megabates attempted to kiss Agesilaus, he fought
mightily against being kissed—is not *this* instance of moderation
even overly crazy[67]? (5) And when Megabates henceforth did not
attempt to kiss him again, in his belief that it was as if he had been
dishonored, Agesilaus had a word (*logos*) conveyed by one of his
comrades to persuade Megabates to honor him again. And when
the comrade asked whether [Agesilaus] would kiss him, should
Megabates be persuaded, Agesilaus then said, after having remained silent: "No, by the Twins,[68] not even if I should immediately become exceedingly beautiful and strong and swift among
human beings! I swear by all the gods that I much prefer to fight
the same battle again than that all I see turn to gold for me."

(6) And as for what some people suppose about these things, I am
not ignorant of it. Yet I know, I think, that many more are able to gain
mastery over their enemies than over things of this sort. Should only
a few know these matters, then many could distrust them; but we all
know that the most prominent human beings least of all escape notice in whatever they do, and nobody ever reported seeing Agesilaus
do anything of this sort, and neither would anyone be held to speak
in a trustworthy way if he made such conjectures. (7) For when away
from home, [Agesilaus] did not lodge in any home but was always
either in a temple, where it is of course impossible to do such things,
or out in the open, thus making the eyes of everyone witnesses of
his moderation. And if I am lying about these things, when Greece
knows contrary things about him, then I offer no praise at all but
blame myself.

~ CHAPTER 6 ~

(1) Of his courage, at any rate, it seems to me that he supplied
proofs that are not immanifest, by always undertaking to wage war

against the strongest enemies both of his city and of Greece and, in the contests against them, stationing himself in the fore. (2) Where the enemies were willing to engage with him in battle, he did not attain victory by turning them through fear, but rather raised a trophy after having overpowered them in an equally matched battle, thus leaving behind deathless memorials of his own virtue, and personally carrying off clear signs of having fought with spiritedness. As a result, his soul could be tested[69] by those who had not merely heard of him, but seen him. (3) Indeed, it is just to believe that the trophies of Agesilaus were not all those that he actually raised but rather all such campaigns as he waged. For he overpowered his enemies no less when they were unwilling to do battle with him, in a manner less dangerous to and with greater advantage for both the city and the allies. And in contests too, they who are victorious over those who put up no fight win the wreath no less than when victorious over those who do.

(4) As for his wisdom, moreover, which of his actions do not display it—he who, in dealing with his fatherland such that he was most obedient,[70] and in his eagerness in dealing with comrades, acquired friends who never made excuses? He certainly had available to himself soldiers who were at once obedient and disposed as friends toward him. And yet how could a phalanx become stronger than by its being in good battle order, through its ready obedience, and by its being present in a trustworthy way, through its friendship for its ruler? (5) He had enemies who, though they were unable to reproach him, were compelled to hate him. For he always contrived a way for his allies to have the advantage over them, using deceit wherever the opportunity might arise, beating them to the punch wherever speed should be needed, being stealthy wherever that should be advantageous, practicing toward enemies the contraries of all the things he did toward friends. (6) For he made use of the night as he did the day, and the day the night, it often being unclear where he was or where he was going or what he might do. As a result, he rendered even strongholds unsafe for enemies; some strongholds he bypassed, some he crossed over, some he took by thievery. (7) Indeed, whenever he was marching with the knowledge that it was possible for the enemy to engage in battle should it wish to do so, he led on the army in such a battle formation as would make it possible for it

to be of most aid to him, and in as calm a manner as the most moderate virgin would proceed, believing that in this sort of thing resides
what is free of tumult, least given to confusion, without commotion,
least subject to error, and most difficult to attack. (8) At any rate, in
doing such things he was terrible in the eyes of enemies, whereas he
instilled confidence and strength in friends. As a result, he continued
to be free of the contempt of enemies, unpunished by fellow citizens,
unreproached by friends, and much beloved and much praised by
all human beings.

∼ CHAPTER 7 ∼

(1) That he was a lover of his city would be a large matter to write
of instance by instance. For I suppose that none of the actions taken
by him did not tend in this direction. But, to speak briefly, we all of
us know that Agesilaus, wherever he supposed he would in some
way benefit the fatherland, did not cease toiling or stand aside from
risks; neither did he spare money or body, or claim as an excuse his
old age. Rather he believed that this deed belonged to a good king:
doing as many good things for the ruled as possible. (2) And among
the greatest benefits he performed for the fatherland I place also this
one: while possessing the greatest power in the city he was especially
manifest in serving the laws. For who would wish to be disobedient
when he sees the king being obedient? And who, because he believes
he has too little, would attempt some revolution, when he knows
that the king endures even submission in a lawful manner? (3) He
behaved even toward those at odds with him in the city as a father to
children. For he reproached them for their errors but honored them
if they should do something noble, and he stood by them if some
misfortune should befall them, believing that no citizen is an enemy
but being willing to praise all because he believed it a profit if all
are preserved, putting it down as a loss if even one of little worth
should perish. But if they should remain quiet, within the confines
of the laws, he clearly calculated that the fatherland would always be
happy, and that it would be mighty when the Greeks make a practice of moderation.

(4) If, again, it is noble for one who is a Greek to be a lover of Greece, who knows of another general who was either unwilling to take a city, whenever he supposed that doing so would be to destroy it, or who believed that victory in a war against Greeks was a misfortune? (5) And when news came to him that, in the battle at Corinth, eight Lacedaemonians but about ten thousand others had died, he it was who was manifestly not pleased but in fact said: "Alas, Greece, when those who have now died were, while alive, capable of gaining a victory in battle over all the barbarians!" (6) And when the Corinthian exiles said that the city would be handed over to them, and showed him the devices by means of which they had every hope of taking the walls, he was unwilling to launch an assault, saying that one should not enslave Greek cities but make them moderate.[71] "And if," he said, "we obliterate those among us who have erred, we must see that we not be without those needed to prevail over the barbarians."

(7) If, again, it is noble also to hate what is Persian, both because of him who long ago campaigned with the intention of enslaving Greece and because of him[72] who now allies with whichever side he supposes will inflict the greater harm [on Greece], and who now gives gifts [or bribes] to those who he supposes will, once they receive them, do the greatest harm to the Greeks, and who aids in attaining such a peace as he believes will most make us wage war among ourselves—these things everyone sees. And who else, apart from Agesilaus, ever was concerned either that some nation revolt from the Persian,[73] or that one that had revolted not perish or, in general, that the King, being plagued by evils, would be unable to cause trouble for the Greeks? And even when the fatherland was at war with the Greeks, he nonetheless did not neglect the common good of Greece, but set sail intending to do the barbarian whatever harm he could.

∼ CHAPTER 8 ∼

(1) But it is worthwhile not to be silent about his graciousness[74] as well. At any rate, when honor was conferred on him and power was

at his disposal and, in addition to these, a kingship, one that was not plotted against but greeted fondly, no one could have seen arrogance in him but, even without looking for it, one would have grasped instead his love of affection and inclination to care for friends. (2) Moreover, with very great pleasure he partook of playful speeches, but with his friends he treated seriously everything that ought to be so treated. And on account of his hopefulness and good spirits and always being cheerful, he drew many people to him, not only for the sake of accomplishing something, but also for the sake of just spending the day pleasantly. And while being least of all the sort to engage in big talk, he nonetheless listened without vexation to those who praise themselves because he believed that they did themselves no harm but rather professed to be good men. (3) But one must also not leave out the loftiness of sentiment he made use of when it was appropriate to do so. For once when a letter came to him from the King, brought to him by the Persian who was with Callea the Lacedaemonian,[75] a letter pertaining to a guest-friendship and friendship with him, he did not accept it. Instead, he said to the person carrying it to report to the King that letters should in no way be sent to him privately, but if the King were manifestly a friend to Lacedaemon and well disposed toward Greece, then he himself would be a friend to him to the utmost of his ability. "If, however," he said, "he is caught hatching plots against them, let him not suppose that he will have me as a friend, not even if I accept a great many letters from him."

(4) I, then, praise this too about Agesilaus, that he looked down on a guest-friendship with the King, in comparison to his being pleasing to the Greeks. And I admire this as well: he believed that, of the two of them, it was not he who had more money and ruled over greater numbers who ought to feel greater pride, but rather he who was himself better and exercised leadership over better [people]. (5) And I praise also this instance of his forethought: believing it to be good for Greece that the greatest possible number of satraps revolt from the King, he was not overcome either by gifts or by the King's strength so as to be willing to accept a guest-friendship with him; instead, he guarded against becoming untrustworthy in the eyes of those who wished to revolt. (6) Who indeed would not admire this about him? For the Persian, believing that, if he had the greatest amount of money, he would make everything subordinate to himself, for this

reason attempted to collect for himself all the gold there is among human beings, all the silver, and all that is most valuable. But [Agesilaus] outfitted his house in just the opposite way, such that he had no additional need of any of these things. (7) And if somebody distrusts these things, let him see the sort of house that satisfied [Agesilaus], and let him observe its gates. For someone might conjecture that these gates are still those ones that Aristodemus, the descendant of Heracles, got hold of and set up, when he returned from exile.[76] And let him undertake to observe the provisions within, and reflect on how [Agesilaus] entertained during the sacrifices; and let him hear how he[77] used to go down to Amyclae in a public carriage made of wicker.[78] (8) Accordingly, then, he adjusted his expenditures to his income in such a way that he was not at all compelled, for the sake of money, to commit injustice. Now, it seems a noble thing to possess walls unassailable by enemies; yet I for my part judge it to be much nobler to render one's own soul unassailable by money and by pleasures and by fear.

∼ CHAPTER 9 ∼

(1) I will say, moreover, how also the manner he adopted differed from the boastfulness of the Persian. For, in the first place, the latter affected a solemn air by being rarely seen, whereas Agesilaus exulted in always being plainly visible, believing that while being unseen is fitting for shameful action, the light supplies adornment to a life given over to what is noble. (2) Second, the one affected a solemn air by being difficult of access, whereas the other delighted in being readily accessible to everyone; the one prided himself on accomplishing things slowly, the other was most delighted whenever he might send off those who very quickly attained whatever it was they needed. (3) Moreover, it is worthwhile to grasp also how much more easily and readily Agesilaus attained his comforts: for the Persian has people seeking the whole world over for what he might drink with pleasure, and ten thousand people artfully contriving what he might eat with pleasure; and no one could even say in how many ways they concern themselves so that he might fall asleep.

But Agesilaus, on account of his being a lover of toil, drank with pleasure anything that was ready to hand, and he ate with pleasure anything he chanced on; and as for his falling asleep contentedly, any place was sufficient for him. (4) And he not only took delight in doing these things, but he also exulted in reflecting on the fact that he himself dwelled in the midst of good cheer, whereas he saw that the barbarian, if he was going to live free of pain, had to have gathered together for him, from the ends of the earth, things that would delight him. (5) And he himself was of good cheer also in these respects: he knew that he was capable of dealing painlessly with the way the gods had arranged things, whereas he saw the other fellow fleeing the heat and fleeing the cold, on account of the weakness of his soul, thus imitating a life, not of good men, but of the weakest beasts. (6) How indeed is this not something noble and indicative of lofty sentiments, that he adorned his own house with the deeds and possessions of a man, rearing many hunting dogs and war horses, but persuaded Cynisca, his sister, to raise chariot horses and thus showed that, when she won a victory, this animal is an indication, not of manly goodness, but of wealth? (7) And how indeed does this not clearly bear on the well-born character of the judgment he made, namely, that if he won a victory over private persons in a chariot race, he would thus become renowned to no greater degree, but that if he should hold the city above all to be a friend, if he should come to possess the greatest number of and the best friends the whole world over , and if he should be victorious in benefiting the fatherland and comrades while exacting vengeance on adversaries, then he would thus be the victor in the noblest and most magnificent contests and become most renowned both while alive and after having met his end?

∾ CHAPTER 10 ∾

(1) I therefore praise Agesilaus for these sorts of things. For these are not comparable to the following: if someone should happen across a treasure, he would become wealthier but not at all more skilled in household management; and if someone should overcome

his enemies because an illness befalls them, he would be luckier but not at all more skilled as a general. But he who is first in endurance when the moment is right for toil, in stoutness wherever a contest calls for courage, and in judgment wherever a deed requires counsel—he it is, in my opinion, at any rate, who would be justly held to be a perfectly good man. (2) And if the carpenter's rule and measure are a noble invention for human beings to produce good works, then in my opinion the virtue of Agesilaus is a noble model for those wishing to make a practice of manly goodness. For who by imitating someone pious could become impious, or someone just, unjust, or someone moderate, hubristic, or someone continent, incontinent? For indeed Agesilaus boasted, not because he was king over others, but because he ruled himself, and not because he led the citizens against enemies, but because he led them to every virtue.

(3) But let no one believe that this account is a lamentation for the sake of praising him now that he has met his end, but much rather an encomium. For, in the first place, the very same things he used to hear while alive are being said about him now as well. And, second, what belongs less to a lamentation than a life of renown and a death in due season? And what would be more deserving of encomiums than victories of the greatest nobility and deeds of the greatest worth? (4) And he would justly be deemed blessed whoever, passionately desiring immediately from boyhood to be famous, attained this beyond all those of his day. And being naturally a lover of honor to the greatest degree, he lived his life undefeated, once he became king. And once arrived at the outer limit of a human lifespan, he met his end free of blame, as regards both those whom he led and those against whom he waged war.

∾ CHAPTER 11 ∾

(1) I wish, in summary fashion, to go back over his virtue, so that the praise may be more easily remembered. Agesilaus revered even the temples of his enemies, believing that one ought to make allies of the gods no less in enemy territory than in that of a friend. And to suppliants of the gods he did no violence, not even to those who

were hostile, believing it irrational to call those who steal from temples "temple robbers" but to regard those who drag suppliants from temples as piously reverential. (2) Indeed, he never ceased descanting on the fact that he supposed the gods to be pleased no less by pious deeds than by pure temples. Moreover, whenever he might enjoy good fortune, he did not look down on human beings but was instead grateful to gods. He offered greater sacrifices when emboldened than prayers when in doubt; and he was accustomed to appearing cheerful when afraid but gentle when enjoying good fortune. (3) He especially welcomed as friends, not the most powerful, but those most eager. He hated it, not if someone who was suffering something bad defended himself, but if someone who had enjoyed some benefaction should appear ungrateful. He delighted in seeing impoverished those who had made shameful gains and in enriching those who were just, in his wish to make justice more profitable than injustice. (4) He made a practice of associating with people of every sort, but he had dealings [only] with the good. Whenever he heard some people either blaming or praising others, he supposed that he would learn no less about the ways of those speaking than about those of whom they spoke. He did not blame those deceived by friends, but he heaped blame entire on those deceived by enemies; and he judged it to be wise to deceive those who were distrustful but impious to do so with the trusting. (5) He also delighted in being praised by those who were also willing to blame whatever was unacceptable to them, and he was irked by none of those who spoke freely, but he guarded against those who hid their thoughts as against those lying in ambush. Slanderers he hated more than thieves, believing it a greater penalty to be deprived of friends than of money. (6) And the errors of private persons he bore gently, whereas those of rulers he regarded as great, judging the former to bring about few ills, but the latter, many. He believed, not easygoingness, but nobility and goodness[79] to be appropriate to the kingship. (7) And he shunned having erected any likeness of his body, though many wished to bestow this gift on him, whereas he never ceased laboring to make memorials of his soul, believing the former to be the work of sculptors, the latter of him himself, the former belonging to the wealthy, the latter to the good. (8) Indeed, as regards money, he made use of it not only in a just but also in a liberal manner, believing it sufficient for a just person to leave be the things of others, whereas a liberal person must benefit others from his own resources. He also always feared the divine,[80] believing that those who live nobly are not yet happy, whereas those who have met their end accompanied by fame are blessed. (9) He judged it to be a greater misfortune to neglect good things knowingly than in ignorance. He desired no reputation for which he did not perform the labors peculiar to it. But together with few [other] human beings, he seemed to me to believe virtue to be a matter not of endurance, but of enjoyment. At any rate, he took greater pleasure in being praised than in acquiring money. Moreover, courage he displayed more with good counsel than with risks, and he practiced wisdom in deed rather than in speeches. (10) While very gentle with friends, he was very frightening to enemies; and while he endured labors especially, he nonetheless yielded with great pleasure to comrades, although he desired noble deeds more than beautiful bodies. And because he knew how to be moderate while faring well, he was able to be of good confidence amid terrible things. (11) He also put into practice his graciousness not by means of jokes but in his manner, and when he was disdainful,[81] he was such, not with hubris but with judgment; at any rate, while looking down on the over-proud, he was humbler than those who observed due measure. For in fact he prided himself on the paltriness of what accompanied his body, on the one hand, and on the adornment that accompanied his army, on the other; and on the fact that while he himself needed the fewest things possible, he benefited his friends as much as possible.

(12) In addition to these things, he wielded a very heavy hand as an antagonist but a very light one once he had prevailed; to enemies, he was very difficult to deceive, to friends, very easy to persuade. And while he always placed in safety what belongs to friends, he took as his task always to damage what belongs to enemies. (13) His relatives used to call him a devoted family man; those who dealt with him, never one to rely on excuses; those who rendered him some service, one who remembered; those done injustice, an ally; and indeed those running risks with him, a savior next in rank to gods. (14) In my opinion, at least, he alone among human beings showed forth this: that while the force of the body grows old, the strength of the soul of good men is unaging. He, at any rate, did not

give up striving for great and noble [reputation, for so long][82] as his body was able to bear the strength of his soul. (15) To what sort of youthful age, then, did his old age not come to sight as superior? For who in the bloom of youth is as frightening to his enemies as Agesilaus was at the extreme of old age? And at whose removal were enemies more pleased than were those of Agesilaus, although he was elderly when he met his end? And who supplied such confidence to allies as did Agesilaus, although he was by then "at the mouth of life"[83]? And what young person did his friends miss more than [those of Agesilaus missed] Agesilaus, who died in old age? (16) So perfectly advantageous for the fatherland did the man continue to be that, even once he had met his end and was led down to his eternal home, he was still magnificently advantageous to the city, having acquired memorials of his own virtue the world over and attaining a kingly burial in the fatherland.

An Introduction to the Agesilaus

ROBERT C. BARTLETT

The purpose of the *Agesilaus* is clear. Xenophon wishes to write an "encomium" (10.3) of the Spartan king because he regards him as a "perfectly good man" (1.1; 10.1).[84] As such, Agesilaus is deserving of praise, even if it is "not easy" to do justice to anyone of such high quality. Xenophon clearly feels an obligation to pay tribute, within the limits of his abilities, to Agesilaus: the perfection of a man is hardly a fine reason to prefer silence to such (insufficient) praise as one is capable of giving. The avowed inadequacy of Xenophon's encomium is especially striking once one sees the extraordinary qualities it succeeds in attributing to Agesilaus. He was, for example, a man unimpeachable in point of ancestry and virtue according to the leading city of Greece; an outstanding general, combining jaw-dropping physical courage with cagey prudence; generous to friends, harsh toward enemies, but noble in victory; devoted in all things to the good of Sparta and always obedient to her laws, whatever the cost to himself, and capable of leading his fellow citizens to "every virtue" (10.2 end). Yet he was concerned for the well-being of all of Greece too, and he exhibited an attractive "philanthropy" or love of human beings (1.22). Accordingly, Agesilaus was "much beloved and much praised by all human beings" (6.8).

There are only two individuals in Xenophon's writings who might be thought to rival Agesilaus in stature, Cyrus the Great and Socrates. But in neither case—not even in that of Socrates—does Xenophon ever say that he was a "perfectly good man." The reason for this must be that Agesilaus alone combines the greatest virtues in action—pious reverence, courage, endurance, and moderation among them—with "judgment" (10.1; 11.11) and indeed "wisdom" (6.4; 11.9, 4). One might say then that Agesilaus combines the best of Socrates with the best of Cyrus, contemplation and action, and so is a peak beyond those admittedly high peaks. Xenophon singles out Cyrus for praise, we remember, because he solved the problem of the instability of regimes—and yet, as the end of the *Education of Cyrus* makes plain, that accomplishment was fleeting: it was the kingship of Sparta, not the empire of Cyrus, that "alone" solved that problem in fact (1.4 end). And Agesilaus himself did much to foster that stability, given that he was one of the longest-serving kings on record (consider 11.14–15). Even Xenophon the dutiful student of Socrates could never say of his teacher, whose premature end was marked by undeserved disgrace, what he can and does say of Agesilaus: "So perfectly advantageous for the fatherland did the man continue to be that, even once he had met his end and was led down to his eternal home, he was still magnificently advantageous to the city, having acquired memorials of his own virtue the world over and attaining a kingly burial in the fatherland" (11.16). Agesilaus deserves to be remembered, then, as a "perfectly good man," the only such man known to Xenophon. In reading the *Agesilaus*, we come to understand what Xenophon regards as the peak of goodness or excellence, and the writing thus forms an important part of Xenophon's answer to *the* question of the best way of life for a human being.

This reading of the *Agesilaus* is open to at least two objections. According to the first, the preceding may characterize accurately enough Xenophon's intention, but it is blithely unaware of the inadequacy of the portrait Xenophon gives us. For Xenophon was a friend of Agesilaus and much indebted to him, especially once Xenophon was exiled from Athens and hence dependent on his Spartan patron. As a result, he is simply unable to see, or at least unwilling to state, *any* of the man's defects: he is unwilling or unable to do what Plutarch, for example, did in spades.[85] The *Agesilaus* is the "concentrated essence of Xenophon's morbid veneration for his model Spartan warrior."[86] Even if readers ignore Xenophon's unfortunate "laconizing" tendency and his unpalatable oligarchic sentiments, even if as a result they allow that the *Agesilaus* is a fond tribute of one friend to another, they must admit that it is neither sound history nor objective biography. The most that one can say, paraphrasing Xenophon himself, is that while "someone may reproach these things for some other reason, at least it is manifest that they were done through friendship for his comrade" (see 2.21 end). At all events, any sensible reading of the *Agesilaus* must take into account Xenophon's limitations as a writer and even as a human being.

The second objection maintains that not only our initial statement but also the first objection to it are naïve: both are "blithely unaware" of Xenophon's irony. This suggestion of the decisive importance of Xenophon's irony must be traced back to Leo Strauss's essay of 1939, "The Spirit of Sparta or the Taste of Xenophon."[87] For in that article Strauss first and "most notoriously"[88] dissented from the universal view that the *Constitution of the Lacedaemonians* is laudatory of Sparta and of all "laconizing": read with the proper care, Strauss argues, that work demonstrates Xenophon's mastery of irony and indeed satire. According to this approach, then, Xenophon, far from being oblivious of the failings of Sparta, was keenly aware of them and indicated them in his understated, playful manner. Strauss also suggests in that early essay that the *Agesilaus* is "the work of his [Xenophon's] which is in every respect nearest akin to the *Constitution of the Lacedemonians*."[89] Almost thirty years later, Strauss offered this assessment: "I would not hesitate to say that Agesilaus was not a man after Xenophon's heart. How could a man with Xenophon's lack of pomposity and even gravity have unqualifiedly liked a man as absurd, as pompous, as theatrical as the Agesilaus of Xenophon's description (as distinguished from his explicit judgments)?"[90] The proof of this is evidently available once one reflects on the facts that "large parts of the *Hellenica* are 'repeated' in the *Agesilaus*," and that in "a good author, who as such is not prolix, a repetition is never a mere repetition and very rarely a literal repetition; in a good author a repetition always teaches us something we could not have learned from the first statement."[91] It falls to the reader of the *Agesilaus*, then, to compare the *Hellenica* with the more or less verbatim "repetitions" in the *Agesilaus*, especially in its first two chapters. By thus bringing together the relevant sections of the history with those of the encomium, one begins to observe Xenophon's judgment as reflected in his literary choices: in what he chose to omit from the encomium but include in the history, for example, or to add to the encomium but leave out of the history.[92]

The following remarks will offer a reading of the *Agesilaus* in part to test the suggestion, which we believe to be sound, that Xenophon is a writer of supreme irony. And if the second objection does prove sound, it will do away with the first. Whatever one may ultimately think of this procedure of reading the *Agesilaus* in the light of the *Hellenica*, it is not unpleasant in itself. For it affords readers a glimpse into Xenophon's workshop, and, by bringing Xenophon the encomiast together with Xenophon the historian, or by putting two and two together, readers even become a party to Xenophon's enterprise and help bring it to completion.

∾ Overview and the Opening of the Work ∾

The organization of the *Agesilaus* is relatively straightforward. A brief preface establishes both the purpose of the writing—to offer a praise worthy of the "virtue and reputation" of Agesilaus—and the difficulty inherent in such an undertaking (1.1–5). Xenophon then turns to discuss Agesilaus's deeds because it is these that will make "quite clear" the man's characteristic ways or character (*tropoi*: 1.6 beg.). These deeds prove to be the ones that can claim the most witnesses or are altogether public (3.1 beg.) and concern partly Agesilaus's actions in Asia Minor against the Persian King (1.6–38), partly those in Europe or Greece pertaining to both friends and enemies (2.1–31). This account of Agesilaus's deeds takes up slightly more than half of the whole work. Xenophon then turns to discuss "the virtue in [Agesilaus's] soul" that prompted him to love all that is noble and shun all that is shameful (3.1–8.3). The most important of these virtues are pious reverence (3.2–5); justice (4.1–6); mastery over pleasures, or continence (5.1–7); courage (6.1–3); wisdom (6.4–8); patriotism or love of his fatherland (7.1–3), together with love of Greece (7.4–6) and hatred of Persia (7.7); graciousness (*eucharis*: 8.1–2); and loftiness of sentiment or judgment (*megalognōmosynē*: 8.3). After this, Xenophon praises Agesilaus and states the various grounds of his admiration of him, above all his manifest superiority to the Persian

King (8.4–10.4). The elucidation of Xenophon's own praise and admiration compels him to take up once again both Agesilaus's "character" or "manner" (*tropos*: 9.1 beg. and context) and his "virtue" (10.2 and context). Finally, Xenophon concludes his encomium by summarizing Agesilaus's virtue in a single chapter so that the praise of the man may be more easily remembered (11.1–16). The central of the five main sections of the *Agesilaus* is thus devoted to an account of the virtue of the man's soul, which is immediately surrounded by a longer account of his deeds, on the one hand, and by Xenophon's shorter statement of praise and admiration, on the other.

The title of the work reminds of that of the *Hiero*, for only these two titles in Xenophon's corpus consist of a proper name.[93] Both works concern Greek rulers. But whereas the *Hiero* is a dialogue between a wise man and a Greek tyrant of a time before Xenophon's own, the *Agesilaus* is Xenophon's account, stated emphatically in the first person singular (compare, e.g., *Education of Cyrus* 1.1.1), of a legitimate Greek king—not a "tyrant"—who was Xenophon's contemporary and acquaintance. If Xenophon is present also in his four Socratic writings, for example, and in them addresses the reader directly by stating at the outset (and elsewhere) an opinion of his, or something that he has often wondered about, the *Agesilaus* is the only work of Xenophon that begins with a strong statement of something he claims to know: "I know . . ." (*oida*).

Now *what* Xenophon claims to know is striking: "I know that it is not easy to write a praise worthy of both the virtue and reputation of Agesilaus." Xenophon goes on clearly to imply that the difficulty stems from the fact that Agesilaus was a "perfectly good man." The logic of this is somewhat obscure. Is the difficulty that no writer, not even Xenophon, can do justice to the facts, that these are too great to be encompassed by the encomiast's art? Or is the difficulty connected with Pericles' complaint, stated in his funeral oration, that it is impossible to praise a fallen soldier in a satisfactory way: for those who knew the man in question, no praise is sufficient, while for those who did not know him, all such praise will seem excessive (Thucydides 1.35.2)? This division of opinion would seem inapplicable in the case of Agesilaus, however, given that he was (to repeat) "much beloved and much praised by *all* human beings." But then again, Xenophon is compelled to admit that at least the enemies of

Agesilaus "hated" him and were pleased when he died (compare 6.8 end with 6.5; 11.15). We remain puzzled by Xenophon's contention. Still, Xenophon says only that it is "not easy" to offer a worthy praise: he does not say that it is impossible. And we learn late in the work that others evidently found no difficulty whatever in praising Agesilaus—as a family man, as one who shunned excuses, as one mindful of services done him, as a helpmate to victims of injustice, and as a savior, to those running risks, next in rank only to the gods (11.13). But none of these, it is true, went so far as to call him a "perfectly good man."

The burden of the remainder of the introduction is to show that, even before he acceded to the kingship, Agesilaus was deserving of it. Under this heading, Xenophon considers first Agesilaus's "good birth" or family lineage: he was a descendant of kings born of kings themselves descended from Heracles, as memory tells us. This may remind one of the opening of the *Education of Cyrus*, where Xenophon begins by sketching the family line of Cyrus, which can also be traced to a son of Zeus (*Education of Cyrus* 1.2.1). But to this consideration Xenophon adds an account of the man's "nature" and "education": Xenophon never speaks of either the nature or the education of Agesilaus. These latter are important in understanding Cyrus because he ascended to a peak that (to put it mildly) was not his by simple inheritance—he became the king of all Asia while his father the "king" of Persia was still living. Agesilaus's rule as king, by contrast, was wholly determined by his familial line. This goes together with the fact Xenophon here stresses, namely, that Spartan kingship and it alone enjoyed great stability and hence longevity (1.4).

But this is not quite true. For Xenophon is compelled to indicate immediately that Agesilaus's claim to the throne was highly controversial. In fact a "contentious struggle" (*erisantōn*) for the kingship broke out upon the death of King Agis (1.5). As we learn in greater detail in the *Hellenica*, Leotychides, son of Agis, had the much more obvious claim to inherit as the only son of the just-deceased king, and it was assumed that he would succeed his father. Yet Agesilaus alleged that Leotychides' father had denied paternity of the boy. In this way Xenophon alludes to the unhappy fact that the familial line of the Spartan kings was murky indeed, and it was so for a reason he makes clear enough in the *Constitution* (1.6–9): the Spartan women

in general and the queens in particular were not models of propri-
ety (consider also Aristotle, *Politics* 1269b22–23 and context). Just ask
Alcibiades, who was rumored to be Leotychides' father (Plutarch,
Alcibiades 23.7). One can only wish that the Spartan women had imi-
tated the Spartan men, or Agesilaus, as they or he entered battle "in
as calm a manner as the most moderate virgin would proceed" (6.7).
The obscurity of Leotychides' lineage casts a shadow on questions
not only of immediate but also of ultimate ancestry: Heracles indeed.[94] What then of Agesilaus's claim? In the encomium, Xenophon
mentions only that it rested on his being (a) son of King Archidamus. This is true but inexhaustive. Agesilaus was in fact the younger
son of Archidamus from the latter's second wife, Agis the elder son
from the first. Accordingly, Agesilaus's claim to the throne was very
weak, and in the *Hellenica*, Xenophon confines himself to mentioning
only that Agesilaus was the (half-)brother of Agis (compare *Hellenica*
3.3.1 end with 1.5; consider also 4.5 and *Hellenica* 5.3.9 [the bastard
sons of the Spartiates]).

Xenophon also indicates in the *Hellenica*, and not of course in the
encomium, that the alleged bastardy of Leotychides did not yet
clear the path to Agesilaus's accession. This required the intervention of the greatest naval commander of Sparta, Agesilaus's lover,
Lysander. Given the obscurity attending such human affairs, the
question came down to the judgment of the gods. One oraclemon-
ger or seer supported Leotychides' claim on the grounds that an
oracle of Apollo had warned Sparta against the "lame kingship":
we learn only in the *Hellenica* that Agesilaus, in addition to being
quite small, was also born with a gimp leg.[95] (It may have been
something other than becoming modesty, then, that led Agesilaus
to prohibit having any statue of his body erected: 11.7.) Lysander,
naturally relying on no seer, countered that that phrase referred
to anyone occupying the kingship who was not descended from
Heracles. "Having heard such sorts of things from both sides, the
city chose Agesilaus as king" (*Hellenica* 3.3.4). Piety, led or guided
by doubts about the queen's virtue, prompted the city not to see
the plain facts and so to prefer Agesilaus, already in his midforties by the time he became king (but "still young"! [1.6]). "And
when one is judged, by those who are best, to be worthy of the
noblest reward in the most excellent city, what sorts of additional

evidence are still needed of his virtue, at least prior to his ruling?" (1.5 end).

∾ THE DEEDS OF AGESILAUS: ASIA MINOR ∾

"All such things as he accomplished in the kingship I will now relate, for from the deeds I believe his ways will, in the finest manner, be quite clear" (1.6). The reader of the encomium learns first that, "just" after (*arti*) Agesilaus came to rule as king, word came that the King of Persia was marshaling a great armed force so as to attack the Greeks. In response, Agesilaus promised to thwart that attack by bringing the fight to the Persians in Asia, provided he receive the number and kind of men he requested (1.6–7). Xenophon compresses events here by leaving out the following facts. When Agesilaus had been in office not yet a full year, the prophet announced, after the King had performed one of the assigned sacrifices on behalf of the city, that the gods were revealing a most terrible plot. A subsequent interpretation of a second sacrifice confirmed this dire warning. Only once sacrifices to the averting ("apotropaic") and saving gods were performed did they finally receive good omens. Yet those good omens seemed premature. At any rate, within five days Cinadon launched his revolutionary plot against the Spartan elite in the name of greater equality (consider 7.2 end), a plot that included the participation of a certain prophet (*Hellenica* 3.3.11). In this way Xenophon permits us to glimpse the surprising fragility of the Spartan oligarchy, with its ever-shrinking number of citizens enjoying full rights ("Spartiates") and hence ever-increasing proportion of Helot slaves, *perioikoi*, and other subordinates, all of them more or less hostile to the regime but vital to its survival (consider 2.24). And only now, once we see both this fragility, with its mundane cause, and Agesilaus's reliance on prophets, do we learn of the threat from Persia. Sparta, the great victor in the Peloponnesian War, which succeeded in humbling imperial Athens, is threatened from within and without. One need not be a prophet to know that Sparta's reign as "the most excellent" (or merely "strongest") city of Greece (1.5) will likely be short-lived. It is one of the purposes of the *Hellenica* to confirm this "prophecy."

Xenophon also declines to mention in the *Agesilaus* that it was Lysander who weighed the merits of a royal incursion into Persian territory—he remembered in particular the impressive return of the army that had marched upcountry with Cyrus—and that it was Lysander who "persuaded" Agesilaus to venture to Asia, the first Spartan king to do so (*Hellenica* 3.4.2). Here we note more generally that the elevation of the name "Agesilaus" requires that the names of the greatest men of the day—Lysander, Dercylides,[96] Epaminondas, Pelopidas, Alcibiades—never appear in the encomium. Similarly, the *Agesilaus* makes it easy to miss the fact that the Spartan kingship was not a powerful monarchy but rather a duarchy of fairly limited powers, at home certainly, but to some extent even abroad (consider *Hellenica* 2.4.36; 3.4.2, 8, 20). The longevity of the Spartan kingship was due partly to the fact that it really was no kingship at all but a religious-military office subordinate to the commands of a tight oligarchy: the real power, the political power, lay rather with the five ephors (consider 1.36 and, e.g., Aristotle, *Politics* 1270b13–16).

As for Agesilaus's deeds in Asia Minor, the *Hellenica* and *Agesilaus* agree about this beginning point: when Tissaphernes the Persian satrap immediately violated a truce struck with Agesilaus upon the latter's arrival—Tissaphernes sent for massive reinforcements from the Great King, not for permission to make peace as he claimed—Agesilaus perceived this "deception" (1.15) but nonetheless abided by the treaty, which he had sworn an oath to uphold (see 1.10–11; *Hellenica* 3.4.6 and context). Here the two accounts diverge. While the reader of the encomium hears Xenophon's praise of Agesilaus's fealty—"the first noble thing he accomplished"—Xenophon makes plain in the history that Agesilaus did precisely nothing in the face of this treachery—he acted "as though (*hōs*) there was peace and he was at leisure" (*Hellenica* 3.4.7 beg.)—and that it was *Lysander* who commanded such respect in the region that "Agesilaus came to sight as a private person, Lysander as king" (3.4.8). This led to a break between the men, and Agesilaus complied with Lysander's request to be sent away, north to the Hellespont, thus voluntarily depriving himself of the commander's expertise. But nature will out: in short order Lysander effected the rebellion of Spithridates, a man in the

Great King's service, and delivered him, together with his possessions, his family, and two hundred cavalry, to Agesilaus. When Xenophon later tells this story in the encomium, he omits all mention
of Lysander, of course (see 3.3), and adduces it as evidence of Agesilaus's great trustworthiness, even in the eyes of the Persians, stemming from his piety. One begins to wonder whether Agesilaus was
not so trustworthy because he was a little too trusting (consider also
2.30: Agesilaus suffered "the greatest deception" at the hands of the
Egyptian; compare 11.12).

Agesilaus, it is true, proceeds to deceive Tissaphernes twice about
his military intentions. He does so once by heading north from Ephesus (to Phrygia) instead of south, as expected, to the satrap's home in
Caria, and once by heading north from Ephesus (to Sardis) instead of
south, as expected, to the satrap's home in Caria. In the interval between these two excursions, as we learn in the encomium (1.17–22),
Agesilaus collected a great deal of booty from unsuspecting towns,
with which he dealt quite gently (1.20–22), and with which booty he
greatly enriched his friends and so made many lovers of his friendship (1.17–19). Here we may note Agesilaus's interest in, and expertise in acquiring, money (e.g., 2.25–31: "envoy" is a euphemism
for "mercenary"); one can avoid the bad reputation for taking what
belongs to others if one gives what one takes to friends or the city,
thereby practicing liberality of a kind (compare 4.1 with 4.3 end; 11.8
[on liberality]); if Agesilaus "took greater pleasure in being praised
than in acquiring money," he surely took very great pleasure in being
praised for acquiring money (11.9). While Xenophon is conveying
to the reader of the encomium these pleasing facts, we learn from
the *Hellenica* that Agesilaus suffered his first defeat, at Dascyleum,
and that, after the liver of a sacrificial victim proved to be missing a
lobe, he began to retreat to the sea (*Hellenica* 3.4.13–15). This defeat
brought home to him his need for a cavalry, and he now set about
to establish one (1.23–24; *Hellenica* 3.4.15). This he did quickly and
efficiently. The ensuing battle around Sardis (and, in the *Agesilaus*,
also *in* Sardis: 1.33–34) brought defeat to Tissaphernes and sometime
thereafter his execution at the hands of his Persian replacement, Tithraustes (1.35).

In this way Agesilaus can claim (a) victory in Asia. Xenophon declines to tell the reader of the encomium that Agesilaus was partly

responsible also for a naval disaster. When the Spartan authorities took the unprecedented step of giving Agesilaus command over both the army and the navy, he chose to appoint as naval commander his inexperienced brother-in-law, Peisander (*Hellenica* 3.4.29; 1.36), who in turn brought the Spartan navy to defeat at Cnidus, which ended any Spartan pretensions to naval power. What is more, Agesilaus proceeded not only to lie to his troops about this defeat, in order not to deflate their spirits, but also to sacrifice as if for a victory and have the sacrificial meats distributed. Agesilaus evidently agreed with Xenophon's view that "once war was declared . . . deception subsequently became both pious and just"—even deception that makes use of the gods (1.17). And this means in turn that Agesilaus did not consistently follow his own dictum that it is "impious" to deceive those who trust you (11.4 end).

But to return to Agesilaus's victory over Tissaphernes, one must wonder what it accomplished. It prompted the Great King to replace Tissaphernes with Tithraustes, which made no appreciable difference to the Greek cause. What is more, or worse, it prompted the King to have money funneled to Sparta's enemies in Greece to stir up trouble there and so to force her to turn her attention away from the Persian mission. And what precisely was that mission? For even if we acknowledge, as we should, that Agesilaus was suddenly ordered by the Spartan authorities to return to help with the home front, and so was unable to complete his Asian mission, we still need to know, what was it? In the *Hellenica*, Agesilaus responds to just this question, posed by Tissaphernes, in these terms: "so that the cities in Asia too be autonomous, just as they are also with us in Greece" (3.4.5). This somewhat broad statement ("the cities") is made more precise in the *Agesilaus*: Tissaphernes lied and told Agesilaus what he wanted to hear, that, if all went well, he would see to it that "the Greek cities in Asia be left autonomous" (1.10). Thus we see that Agesilaus and the Spartans were motivated after the Peloponnesian War by much the same concern they appealed to during it: to be the liberators of the Greeks, whether from the Athenian empire then, or the Persian now, whether in Greece then, or in Asia now. Accordingly, Agesilaus sometimes spoke of the men who came over to him (Greeks or not) as "free men" (1.22) and of his wish to grant them "freedom" (1.33); he and his men were "liberators" in Asia (1.33). He certainly saw to it that those Greeks who were treated with insolence before were now treated with respect (1.34), and "many" nations or cities, "in their longing for liberty," revolted in his favor (1.35).

Yet Agesilaus's initial promise to his fellow Spartans was either to "establish peace" or, failing that, to prevent the Persian from marching against "the Greeks"—in Greece (1.7); it is by no means clear that the prerequisite of the peace in question was the autonomy of the Greek cities then under the thumb of Persia. We also learn that Agesilaus intended to "rule" all such cities as had had their regimes changed after the fall of the Athenian empire (1.37) and that, at the peak of his success in Asia, Agesilaus "ruled" over many cities in fact (1.36); Lysander, whose idea the mission was, clearly wished only to reinstate the pro-Spartan "dekarchies" or Boards of Ten, a poor sort of liberty (consider, e.g., *Hellenica* 3.5.13). What is more, Agesilaus not only intended but even expected "to dissolve the empire" (1.36), a fact Xenophon mentions as if in passing: Agesilaus hoped to destroy the Persian empire altogether (see also *Hellenica* 4.1.41). The grandeur of his hope from the very beginning is confirmed by a startling episode that Xenophon omits from the *Agesilaus*. Just after setting out from Sparta, Agesilaus stopped in Aulis in order to conduct sacrifices there, "the very place where Agamemnon sacrificed when he was sailing for Troy" (*Hellenica* 3.4.3 end). In other words, Agesilaus understood himself to be a new Agamemnon, setting out as the new general-king of a united Greek force so as to wage a new Trojan War. Let us hope he did not have a daughter.[97]

In accord with all of this, when Agesilaus obeyed the order to return immediately to Sparta, he thus chose, "instead of his being the greatest in Asia," to rule and be ruled in turn at home (2.16): had he stayed, he would have sought to become "greatest in Asia"! No wonder, then, that, from boyhood, Agesilaus desired to be "famous" (*eukleēs*: 10.4). If Agesilaus clearly preferred the fatherland, friends of long standing, and just and noble profits gained at some risk to "the whole earth," newly acquired friends, and not-so-noble, low-risk profits (1.36), he nonetheless evinced some interest also in the whole earth, newly acquired friends, and not-so-noble, low-risk profits (e.g., 1.18–19). Agesilaus seems to have dreamed of bringing "peace" to Asia by destroying the Persian empire and placing himself at its head: "And when Agesilaus heard [the order to return], he took it hard, reflecting on the sorts of honors and the sorts of hopes he was being deprived of" (*Hellenica* 4.2.3; also 3.5.1). As for rendering the Greek cities of Asia autonomous, that goal recedes to the vanishing point. The Spartans' ballyhooed title to be the liberators of the Greeks remained as empty as it had been during the Peloponnesian War; at the age of eighty, Agesilaus was still talking about liberating the Greeks in Asia (2.29). However one conceives of Agesilaus's political goals in Asia, from the least to the most ambitious, Agesilaus accomplished little.

∽ The Deeds of Agesilaus: Europe and Greece ∽

The account in the encomium of Agesilaus's subsequent deeds largely accords with the account of them in the *Hellenica*, but is of course much more compressed than the latter. For this section of the *Agesilaus* covers almost thirty-five years, from about 394 to 360, the year of the king's death,[98] in roughly as many pages as were devoted to the two years in Persia. That lengthy period may be divided in two: the events that precede (2.1–22) and those that follow (2.23–31) the disastrous Spartan defeat at the battle of Leuctra in 371 (mentioned at 2.23 and 24). The events that precede that defeat also fall into two parts: the skirmishes Agesilaus fought in making his way back to Sparta once he crossed the Hellespont—the first in Thessaly (2.2–5), the second the battle of Coronea in Boeotia (2.6–16)—and those he fought once back in Sparta (2.17–22). Following Xenophon's lead, we focus first on the battle of Coronea, "for it was unlike any other in our time" (2.9; *Hellenica* 4.3.16).

In both the history and the encomium, Xenophon gives an account of the peoples that made up Agesilaus's army at Coronea: the troops he brought back from Asia, including both his own men and foreign mercenaries; some of the troops who fought with Cyrus (it is on this basis widely assumed that Xenophon, being among these troops, was present at the battle of Coronea); Spartans from home; and, of the local allies, the Phocians and Orchomenians. The account in the *Hellenica*, however, is slightly longer or more complete (compare 2.6 with *Hellenica* 4.3.15), and only there does Xenophon indicate that although the numbers on both sides were roughly comparable, Agesilaus enjoyed superiority in point of peltasts or light-shieldsmen. What takes the place in the *Agesilaus* of this somewhat longer accounting is the following remark of Xenophon: "I am not going to say this, that though his forces were both much smaller and much worse, he nonetheless joined in fight; for should I say these things, I think Agesilaus would come to sight as senseless, and I myself as a fool, if I were to praise someone who takes risks haphazardly when the greatest things are at stake" (2.7). After the main battle, in which the Spartans were victorious, the Thebans rushed the Spartans head-on in a desperate attempt to rejoin those of their men who had fled to Mount Helicon. And at this Xenophon comments: "Here it is possible to say indisputably that Agesilaus was courageous, and indeed [*ou mentoi . . . ge*] what he chose for himself were not the safest things: although it was possible for him to let pass the men charging and then to pursue and defeat their rear, he did not do this but came to blows with the Thebans head-on" (2.12; consider note 31, this chapter). If we put together the remark quoted above that appears only in the encomium with the description of the Theban-Spartan clash that appears in both sources, we come to these conclusions: Agesilaus's courage may be disputable in other cases, but not in this one; courage here means choosing for oneself the least safe, the most dangerous, things; Agesilaus chose to meet the Thebans head-on rather than attack after they had passed, as he could have done. That this is a risky strategy is confirmed (if confirmation is needed) in the immediately prior chapter of the *Hellenica*: when the Spartans attack the Argives at the battle of Nemea, the Spartan polemarch intends to meet the enemy head-on, but "someone" suggests that they should instead let the Argive front pass by, thus allowing the Spartans to strike the enemy as it ran past. This the Spartans do, killing many Argives in the process (see *Hellenica* 4.2.22). That Agesilaus's strategy here is not just risky but also costly in the event, Xenophon indicates as clearly as he can in an encomium: "Now that the battle was over, it was possible to observe the earth made damp with blood, there where they fell upon one another, corpses of friend and enemy lying with one another, shields smashed to pieces, spears broken, daggers stripped of their sheaths, some on the ground, some in bodies, others still in men's hands" (2.14).[99] We conclude that Agesilaus took risks haphazardly when the greatest things were at stake and so comes to sight as "senseless" (*aphrona*). Courage so understood, the kind Agesilaus indisputably possessed, is a sort of senselessness, not to say madness (compare 11.9 end and 6.3 end).[100]

Of the many battles Agesilaus fought once he returned to Sparta, we can comment on only a few episodes. In 390, Agesilaus launched an attack on Corinth and Peiraeum, the latter being used by the Corinthians to graze their cattle. As both the encomium and the history agree, Agesilaus seized Peiraeum after a feigned attack on Corinth proper drew the enemies' forces there, thus leaving Peiraeum vulnerable. Only in the *Hellenica*, however, do we learn of a certain "small but timely bit of reasoning" (*enthymēmati*: 4.5.4) on Agesilaus's part that brought him good repute: his men, occupying the heights near Peiraeum, were cold (the weather was harsh), and so Agesilaus had ten men bring up pots of fire. When the inhabitants of Peiraeum saw the fires above—and someone, no one knows who, set the temple of Poseidon on fire—they panicked and fled the city. Perhaps a happy unintended consequence is not properly included in an encomium. Certainly an unhappy unintended consequence is not: the *Hellenica* tells us that Agesilaus subsequently rejected with "great arrogance" or "disdain" (*mala megalophronōs*: 4.5.6; see also *Agesilaus* 11.11) the many embassies that approached him from Boeotia, including Thebes, embassies whom Agesilaus insulted by pretending not even to see them, as he sat "exulting in" what had happened (*Hellenica* 4.5.7; see also *Agesilaus* 9.1 and 9.4). Only once Agesilaus received the news of the slaughter of some 250 of the Spartan forces at Lechaeum, the port of Corinth (see 2.17), did he change his tune: "When the embassies of the Boeotians were summoned and asked what they had come for, they no longer made mention of peace" (*Hellenica* 4.5.9). The Spartans managed to hang on to Lechaeum, but Agesilaus and the defeated regiment slunk back home under the cover of evening and early morning darkness (4.5.18). Xenophon the encomiast limits himself to saying, after relating only the fact of the capture of Peiraeum, that Agesilaus "withdrew toward home" (2.19 end).

As regards the highly compressed account in the encomium of Agesilaus's aid of the Achaeans against the Acarnanians, we note only that Xenophon declines to mention the dangerous location that Agesilaus chose to set up camp (*Hellenica* 4.6.7; consider also 6.5.17) or that, after much fighting against cities in Acarnania, he "failed to take a single one of them": the Achaeans are of the view that he "accomplished nothing" (4.6.12–13). Later, when the Spartan Antalcidas brokered an important peace with Persia and the Athenian allies, including the Corinthians and Thebans, Agesilaus insisted that the cities of Boeotia be placed outside of Theban control, not because he was concerned with their autonomy, but "on account of his enmity toward the Thebans." Agesilaus hated the Thebans, it turns out, because they had impiously interrupted and then prevented altogether his sacrifice at Aulis before heading to Asia, an act he could not forgive (3.4.4; 7.1.34); this hatred was responsible also for his bloody clash with the Thebans that demonstrated his brand of courage. And when alluding to the steps Agesilaus took to aid the oligarchic elements in Corinth, Thebes, and Phliasia, Xenophon is compelled to admit that "someone may reproach these things for some other reason" —but at least Agesilaus acted out of friendship for his comrades (*philetairia*). That is, he meant well. In the case of Phliasia, for example, Agesilaus ended up besieging that democratic city for one year and eight months, in an attempt to install the pro-Spartan faction in power; as a result, "many Lacedaemonians said that, for the sake of a few human beings, they were hated by a city of more than five thousand men" (5.3.16).

The most important example of such comradely concern is the one Xenophon mentions next: when his enemies were "killing the partisans of the Lacedaemonians in Thebes," Agesilaus came to their aid (2.22). This bland formulation conceals the following facts. In 382, a pro-Spartan faction in Thebes persuaded the Spartan commander Phoebidas to occupy the Cadmea, the acropolis of Thebes. This Phoebidas did, without approval from home and in clear violation of the terms of the Peace of Antalcidas, which called for the autonomy of cities (see, above all, *Hellenica* 5.4.1 as well as 6.3.9). Now Phoebidas had "a much greater love of doing something spectacular than he did of living," and he was "held not to be skilled at thinking things through (*logistikos*) and not very prudent" (5.2.28). As a result of his rash act in Thebes, he incurred the anger of the ephors and the majority of the Spartan citizens (5.2.36). Yet Agesilaus vigorously defended him. Once the hoped-for revolution in Thebes failed to materialize, however, the Spartans were stranded in the heart of enemy territory and were subsequently killed when they attempted to leave the acropolis (5.4.10–12). Sparta then declared war on Thebes, but Agesilaus refused to lead out the army, claiming his advanced age as an excuse.[101] (So much for never using his age as an excuse: 7.1 as well as 11.13.) "Yet this was not the reason he remained behind. Rather, he knew well that, if he should campaign, the citizens would say that he caused troubles for the city in order to bring aid to tyrants" (*Hellenica* 5.4.13). This is Agesilaus's love of his comrades in action. In place of Agesilaus, Cleombrotus was sent out on his first and wholly ineffective military campaign as king (5.4.14–18). Only later did Agesilaus lead an army out against Thebes, though he had grown no younger, first in 378 and again in the spring of 377. For these deeds Agesilaus could boast of a trophy but little else (compare 6.3). Agesilaus's inveterate hatred of Thebes, which scuttled any rapprochement, together with his inability to conquer them, contributed much to the decisive defeat of Sparta at Leuctra.

As a final example of Xenophon's art of understatement in this section of the *Agesilaus*, we note the way he presents the aftermath of Leuctra: "After this [in 370], all the Arcadians, Argives, Elians, and Boeotians campaigned against Lacedaemon, together with the Phocians, both Locrians, the Thessalians, Aenianians, Acarnanians, and Euboeans" (2.24). What Xenophon here mentions is the daring march, led by the great general Epaminondas of Thebes, against Sparta that succeeded in crossing the Eurotas River at Sparta's doorstep: never before had the Spartan women seen the smoke of an enemy camp (*Hellenica* 6.5.28). One would hardly know from Xenophon's description that Sparta was hanging by a thread. In the *Agesilaus* Xenophon stresses Agesilaus's skill in defending the city (2.24); in the *Hellenica* he mentions only that the enemies themselves withdrew, in part because winter had come (6.5.50). We note also that, when Agesilaus is victorious over the Thebans, Xenophon does him the favor of mentioning them by name (see 2.9–16), but when they have the upper hand, as here, he has them disappear among "the Boeotians."

∾ The Virtues of Agesilaus and
the Admiration of Xenophon ∾

That Xenophon deems it necessary to detail the virtues of the soul
of Agesilaus is surprising. Evidently the long account of his character, brought to light by his public deeds, is insufficient for that purpose. Did those deeds not stem from virtue? At all events, Xenophon
here too is concerned to rely on facts known the world over, so to
speak: he gives only "the most conspicuous" (3.2) examples of Agesilaus's trustworthiness; the very city of the Lacedaemonians bears
witness to his justice (4.5 end); nobody knows of Agesilaus's having
been conquered by pleasure (5.1.), and "we all know" the doings
of famous people especially (5.6); the "eyes of everyone" were witnesses to the man's moderation (5.7); the proofs of his courage are
"not immanifest" (6.1); and "we all of us know" of Agesilaus's love
of Sparta (7.1). It is as if Xenophon expects the arguments he makes
to be greeted with some skepticism and so feels compelled to rely
solely on the least controversial evidence in order to make his case.

Such skepticism becomes explicit twice, once in the enumeration of Agesilaus's virtues, once in the course of Xenophon's own
praise of the man. We limit our treatment of these two sections to
the statements of skepticism recorded by Xenophon. To turn then
to the first: in the context of a praise of Agesilaus's mastery over
pleasure—of food, drink, and rest or ease—Xenophon raises the
delicate matter of Agesilaus's "continence regarding sexual matters" (5.4): "Is it not worthwhile to call it to mind, if for no other
reason than for the wonder of it?" To wonder at something amaz-
ing (*thaumadzō/thauma*) is not necessarily to admire it (*agamai*: 1.36;
2.7; 8.4, 6). So much a cause for wonder is this continence that Xenophon feels the need to add: "As for what some people suppose
about these things, I am not ignorant of it" (5.6). And what "some
suppose" seems to have a foundation in fact. For example, one reason Agesilaus sincerely lamented the death of his fellow king Ag-
esipolis is that, when they shared a tent, they liked to speak about
(among other things) *ta paidika*, "beloved boyfriends" (*Hellenica*
5.3.20). Xenophon later limits himself to mentioning the ease with
which Agesilaus satisfied his desire for food and drink and rest

(9.3)—these three only—and he fails to speak of continence at all in the handy summary with which the encomium ends (11.1–16). To take the specific example here, Agesilaus was in love with Megabates, the son of Spithridates the Persian (Agesilaus: "Have you seen how beautiful his son is?" [*Hellenica* 4.1.6]). The story Xenophon tells in the encomium, of Agesilaus's having "fought mightily"—and successfully—"against being kissed" by the boy, despite being in love with him, is indeed impressive in its way. Or, as Xenophon puts it, "is not *this* instance of moderation also overly crazy?" (5.4, reading *lian manikon* with all the MSS). We recall that Xenophon had said, in the discussion of courage, that if Agesilaus is in truth "senseless," then Xenophon himself is a "fool" for praising him (2.7): Xenophon there in effect affirms the protasis of the condition. On one additional occasion, which happens to concern the subject of kissing, Xenophon was called a "fool" by no less than Socrates (*Memorabilia* 1.3.9–13). Xenophon was sometimes willing to play the fool. Not so Agesilaus! If Agesilaus made a showy, and to Xenophon's way of thinking completely crazy, refusal to kiss someone he loved, he was also far from enjoying either freedom from desire, on the one hand, or the contentment of a desire satisfied, on the other. "And if I am lying about these things, when Greece knows contrary things about him, then I offer no praise at all but blame myself" (5.7; consider Plutarch, *Agesilaus* 20.6).

Here we should pause to record two examples of the extent to which Agesilaus's private concerns clouded his political judgment. When Agesilaus encouraged Pharnabazus to revolt from the King, Pharnabazus replied that, if the King should make him subordinate to another, he would revolt; if not, he would fight to the utmost against Agesilaus. This Agesilaus takes to be such a sign of honor on Pharnabazus's part—the profession, that is, that the satrap will do what is best for himself in either circumstance—that he promises to do no further harm to Pharnabazus's territory. This reaction has something to do, as the encomium suggests, with Agesilaus' "pious reverence" (see 3.5) that made him "trustworthy." There is no reason to doubt this. But only in the immediate sequel as related in the *Hellenica* do we learn that Pharnabazus also had a young son, "still beautiful," with whom Agesilaus establishes a formal guest-friendship and for whose own erotic interests Agesilaus later on bent some rules (4.1.34–40). Agesilaus was not so consistently a hater of all things Persian, it turns out (7.7).

The second example of Agesilaus's poor judgment concerns Sphodrias, the Spartan *harmost* or governor of Thespiae. Sphodrias was persuaded (read: bribed) by the Thebans, then at war with Sparta, to attack the Piraeus, port of the Athenians, with whom the Spartans were not then at war (*Hellenica* 5.4.20). This sneak attack failed, and Sphodrias was indicted and tried in absentia by Sparta—but acquitted through the direct intervention of Agesilaus: "In the opinion of many, this was the most unjustly decided case in Lacedaemon" (5.4.24 end). Agesilaus took this outrageous step in order to please his son, who was in love with Sphodrias's son, he being "both the most beautiful and most well-regarded of those of his age" (5.4.25). "And the errors of private persons [Agesilaus] bore gently, whereas those of rulers he regarded as great, judging the former to bring about few ills, but the latter, many" (11.6): Agesilaus failed to apply this fine judgment to Sphodrias—or to himself, in his shameful defense of him.

Xenophon turns, at 8.4, to praise and to admire Agesilaus, and to do so very much in his own name. The soul of Agesilaus, Xenophon implies, was unassailable by money, pleasure, or fear (8.8). Xenophon's only point of comparison here is the Persian King, the richest man on the planet, who evidently lived amid unimaginable splendor. Agesilaus certainly did not so live. A more telling point of comparison might have been Agesilaus's fellow Spartans. Perhaps Xenophon wishes to divert the reader's attention from the fact that other Spartans—Spartan kings included—were not so impressive: this much is suggested by the sorry cases of the deposed and traitorous king Demaratus (*Hellenica* 3.1.6), Sphodrias (5.4.24–26), and Phoebidas. If Agesilaus, then, was more restrained than the Persian King, which amounts to modest praise, he was surely better than some Spartans too. Still, we have already seen reasons to doubt whether Agesilaus was altogether unmoved by money and pleasure in particular. To those reasons we add the second expression of skepticism about the man, this one concerning Agesilaus's frugality or indifference to wealth. The Persian King, but not the Spartan one, "attempted to collect for himself all the gold there is among human beings" (8.6). Xenophon then adds: "And if somebody distrusts these things, let him see the sort of house that satisfied [Agesilaus] and let him observe its [decrepit] gates" (8.7). In the context of the skepticism concerning Agesilaus's sexual continence—to bring the two instances together—we hear of this episode: when an intermediary tried to reconcile Megabates to him, by securing in advance Agesilaus's agreement not to dishonor the boy again by refusing to kiss him, Agesilaus had said: "I swear by all the gods that I much prefer to fight the same battle again than that all that I see turn to gold for me" (5.5 end). The prospect of everything turning to gold for himself is regarded by Agesilaus too as a very great good. At any rate, Agesilaus was able to tithe one hundred talents to Apollo, after two years' labor in Asia, presumably leaving another nine hundred to spend (1.34 end).

∾ Xenophon and Agesilaus ∾

In detailing examples of the defects of Agesilaus that are recorded in the *Hellenica* but covered over in the encomium, we may seem to some to be kicking in an unlocked door. For "everyone" knows that Xenophon the encomiast smoothed off the rough edges that he left more or less intact in the *Hellenica*. Yet what would have been obvious to Xenophon's contemporary readers ("when Greece knows contrary things about him") must be recovered by many of us today. Hence the bulk of the preceding remarks. But let us now grant that Xenophon was aware of Agesilaus's shortcomings, since he recorded them. Our assessment of Xenophon in this context will rest ultimately on Xenophon's assessment of Agesilaus. Did the two men see eye to eye on matters of importance? As it seems to me, they did not.

The most important difference between Xenophon and Agesilaus, between their respective understandings of the world, is revealed early on in the encomium. Once Tissaphernes violates the oaths he swore to Agesilaus, we see Agesilaus deeply pleased by the fact: he went about with a "brightly beaming face" and made known to Tissaphernes his gratitude on the grounds that, "by betraying his oaths, [Tissaphernes] had acquired the gods as enemies but made them allies of the Greeks" (1.13). Immediately before, Xenophon had given his own assessment: "To me this seems to be the first noble thing he accomplished, for by showing Tissaphernes to be a breaker of oaths, he made him untrustworthy in the eyes of everyone; and by showing himself, by contrast, to be someone who abides by his oaths, in the first place, and, second, one who does not betray his compacts, he encouraged everyone . . . to enter into compacts with him" (1.12). In other words, Agesilaus believes that the gods will punish Tissaphernes for his deception and befriend the Greeks; Xenophon limits himself to the political, the this-worldly effects, of Tissaphernes' treachery. In that part of the *Hellenica* that is most his own (as distinguished from that which is apparently the continuation of another's work), Xenophon takes pains to record the ritual sacrifices of Agesilaus and others;[102] he is all but silent on such acts in the *Agesilaus* (for the exception, see 1.31, which reproduces *Hellenica* 3.4.23). Perhaps it is the case that, from Xenophon's point of view, this suppression of Agesilaus's zealous piety belongs to the laudatory, the embellishing, character of the encomium.

Xenophon always treats piety and justice together in the *Agesilaus*.[103] For example, in wartime, Xenophon says, deception becomes "both pious and just" (1.17). But if this is true, then Xenophon himself could hardly blame Tissaphernes for having deceived Agesilaus: neither gods nor human beings condemn—both evidently approve of—deception of enemies in war, at least in the absence of sworn oaths (consider also *Education of Cyrus* 1.6.27). And if this is true, in turn, it supplies a reason why Xenophon could not share and did not share Agesilaus's firm conviction that the gods will punish Tissaphernes: they would have no reason for doing so. Oddly enough, Agesilaus himself "heaped blame entire on those deceived by enemies"—yet he did not blame himself for being deceived by Tissaphernes—"and he judged it to be wise to deceive those who were distrustful, but impious to do so with the trusting" (11.4). Either Agesilaus was distrustful of Tissaphernes, in which case he should have applauded the wisdom of the satrap, or Agesilaus was trusting of him and so should have condemned his impiety. He did condemn his impiety. But should he then not have heaped "blame entire" on himself for having foolishly trusted an avowed enemy by whom he was of course deceived? Agesilaus is somehow confused. He seems both to accept in speech and to deny in practice the proposition that deception in war is "pious and just"—although, as we noted, he deceived his own troops to their benefit. In speech he condemns not the deceiver but the deceived, while in practice he condemns not himself but Tissaphernes. Agesilaus wishes to act on the proposition that one must *always* keep one's sworn oaths. We note in passing that, unless Agesilaus is willing to concede that deceiving the trusting may be both impious and wise, or that wisdom and piety may point in opposite directions, he here seems to bring wisdom and piety together; at any rate, what he here calls wise, Xenophon had called pious and just (compare 1.17 with 11.4 end). Xenophon understands wisdom differently than does Agesilaus.[104] This example also permits one to surmise what Xenophon thought of *the* example of Agesilaus's piety in the encomium, namely, his command to release eighty armed Theban—Theban!—cavalrymen who had sought refuge in a temple and, in addition, to give them an armed escort anywhere they liked (2.13 and 11.1, although the second part of the command is absent from the recapitulation of things to be remembered about the man).

In the first of the two discussions of piety and justice in the final chapter, Xenophon states that Agesilaus delighted in impoverishing those who made shameful gains and in enriching those who were just, "in his wish to make justice more profitable than injustice" (11.3). Agesilaus held, then, that justice is not always better than injustice, even if he clearly deplored this fact. In the second discussion, we learn that Agesilaus was always fearful of the divine because he believed that "those who live nobly are not yet happy" (11.8); for the fatherland to be happy it is enough according to Agesilaus if its citizens live quietly within the law (7.3)—but this is no guarantee that the citizens, as distinguished from the fatherland, will be happy. To live in accord with justice and virtue, then, to live nobly, is not yet to be happy. Happiness requires the intervention (or the benevolent nonintervention) of the divine, of which one should maintain a fearful respect, and it is this that seems to have guided Agesilaus in everything. Only the divine can see to it that one meet one's end accompanied by fame or renown (11.8). Agesilaus evidently regarded virtue as everything, so to speak, and as very much in need of some supplement in order to make it good or "profitable." To take another example: eager as he was to take less than his share of the good and more than his share of the bad, Agesilaus was not ashamed to take more than others of the heat in summer and cold in winter, for these harsh things require the "endurance" that should characterize a ruler (5.2–3). Such heat and cold, we learn later, are arranged for us by the gods, and Agesilaus knew that he could deal with these extremes "painlessly" (9.5). Yet Xenophon also reports: "He seemed to me to believe (*nomidzein*) virtue to be a matter not of endurance, but of enjoyment" (11.9). To be virtuous (in this case) is to endure such pain as one must; or, rather, to be such as to feel no pain, in accepting what comes from the gods; or, rather, to be such as positively to enjoy the exercise of virtue, as one believes. If virtue is pleasant or enjoyable, it would seem to need no supplement; if it is painful, if it requires "endurance," it may well need the intervention of gods to make what is in itself painful or unprofitable, profitable and pleasant. Only here, and never in the Socratic writings, for example, does Xenophon speak of the "eternal home" that awaits the virtuous (11.16; compare *Oeconomicus* 21.12). Agesilaus seems to have regarded the practice of virtue as something good in itself and as a painful but necessary means to something better than virtue.

It remains true that Xenophon began by calling Agesilaus a "perfectly good man" (1.1). Xenophon uses this phrase on only one other occasion in the *Agesilaus*: he contends that one who is first in point of endurance in toil, of stoutness in contests, and of judgment in deed would justly be held to be a "perfectly (*teleōs*) good man (*anēr*)" (10.1 end). That these three qualities—endurance, stoutness, and judgment—cannot be exhaustive of Xenophon's understanding of goodness becomes clear in the sequel, for there he speaks also of piety, justice, moderation, and continence (10.2). Do these four virtues not belong to the "perfectly good man"? That is hard to credit. A way out of the difficulty is suggested by the remark Xenophon makes immediately after speaking of the "perfectly good man" but before he expands the list of virtues in the way we have just noted: "If the carpenter's rule and measure are a noble invention for human beings to produce good works, then in my opinion the virtue of Agesilaus is a noble model for those wishing to make a practice of manly goodness" (10.2). This suggests that the "perfect" goodness of Agesilaus is as man-made or conventional as the carpenter's rule—it is not natural but invented—and is useful only for those wishing to imitate, not human goodness or goodness unmodified, but "manly goodness" (*andragathia*). Accordingly, Xenophon is here silent about wisdom. As for what Agesilaus may mean by "manly goodness," a partial answer is suggested by the fact that, according to him, raising hunting dogs and war horses, rather than horses for chariot racing (as he had his sister do, to prove the point), is indicative of "manly goodness" (9.6 end). A fuller answer is suggested by the final sentence of the encomium: "So perfectly (*teleōs*) advantageous for the fatherland did the man (*anēr*) continue to be that, even once he had met his end and was led down to his eternal home, he was still magnificently advantageous to the city, having acquired memorials of his own virtue the world over and attaining a kingly burial in the fatherland" (11.16). What is justly "held to be" perfect manly goodness consists in being "perfectly," "magnificently" advantageous for the fatherland. It is with a view to this end above all others that Agesilaus deserves praise—to the extent that he does. For Xenophon's portrait as a whole suggests that in fact Agesilaus did very little good to Sparta and even some harm, and his signal contributions seem bound up with his permanent departure from Sparta. As for the worth of manly goodness understood as being advantageous to the fatherland, it depends on the worth of the fatherland in question—a judgment Xenophon has rendered in his analysis of the *politeia* of the Spartans. It is partly for this reason that that work is rightly taken to be the pair of the *Agesilaus*.

That Agesilaus himself sensed the limits of the goodness or virtue embodied by Sparta is suggested, at least, by the "Panhellenism" for which he is well known (7.4–6), to say nothing of his "philanthropy" (1.20–22): why look beyond Sparta if Sparta is all? Something prompted Agesilaus not to be satisfied with complete devotion to the city he regarded as greatest. There may well be reasons to regret or deplore Xenophon's departure from Athens and his service first to a Persian and then to a Spartan cause. But the fact that Agesilaus, even he, looked beyond the limits of Sparta may lead some to judge Xenophon less harshly: Xenophon may have become a bad Athenian, but Athens was very bad indeed to the truly best human being he knew, Socrates, a man of superlative (though not of course perfect) goodness and

happiness (*Memorabilia* 4.8.11; Xenophon never speaks of Agesilaus as happy: compare 6.3; 7.3 end; and 11.8).

Given how much is generally made of Xenophon's friendship
with Agesilaus, a friendship that allegedly skewed his judgment of
the man, it is surprising that Xenophon never presents himself in the
company of Agesilaus, not in the encomium and not in the history.
He does not record a single conversation between them. He does
not present himself as an eye- or ear-witness to anything pertaining
directly to Agesilaus, although in both writings he speaks in the first
person singular. The most that Xenophon does, in the *Hellenica*, is
mention the soldiers who marched upcountry with Cyrus (3.1.2, 6;
3.2.6–7, 18; 3.4.2; 6.1.12), among whom, we may assume, was Xenophon himself; and he mentions the author of the *Anabasis of Cyrus*:
"Themistogenes of Syracuse" (3.1.2)![105] This self-effacing procedure
must be contrasted with the character of his Socratic writings, in
which he does record a conversation between himself and Socrates
(*Memorabilia* 1.3.9–13; see also *Anabasis of Cyrus* 3.1.5–9) and states
with some frequency either that he was present at a certain gathering with Socrates (*Symposium* 1.1) or that he himself heard Socrates
converse about or say something (e.g., *Oeconomicus* 1.1; *Memorabilia*
1.2.53, 1.4.2; 2.4.1, 2.5.1, 2.9.1, 2.10.1; 3.3.1; 4.2.1). In this way Xenophon suggests that he had a closer connection to Socrates than to
Agesilaus.

One might contend that Xenophon here declines to put himself
forward because he wishes not to seem "biased" in favor of Agesilaus, but instead to be conveying objective reportage. These are just
the facts that "everyone" knows; here are the proper conclusions to
draw from them. But then again "everyone" knows also that Xenophon was probably with the troops in the employ of Sparta, at least
for a time (consider above all *Hellenica* 3.2.7), that he surely fought
under Agesilaus's command, and that Agesilaus may have become
Xenophon's patron or sponsor at some point (e.g., Plutarch, *Agesilaus* 20.2). In any case, Xenophon's plan not to seem "biased," if
he had such a plan, has failed miserably. Perhaps then Xenophon
wished to shine the light on Agesilaus and away from himself the
better to praise the man. Hence he declined to present himself in
conversation with the man or even in his company. This suggestion
admits of more than one interpretation. For example, Xenophon's

reserve may be not so much modesty as honesty concealed as modesty: Xenophon was not close to Agesilaus in fact and was unwilling to present himself as being such. This suggests also why it was "not easy" for Xenophon to write the encomium of Agesilaus that his "virtue and reputation" truly deserved. For if Agesilaus was a "perfectly good man," he was also a deeply flawed human being. Yet Xenophon had benefited directly from the king's kindnesses or consideration, as "everyone" knew, just as he continued to benefit from Sparta after the death of their king. Xenophon therefore declined to be simply frank in publicly assessing the character and the virtue of the man in whose debt he was. Such deception can also be defended as "pious and just" if one completes Xenophon's stated principle on the matter: to deceive friends (to their benefit) is pious and just. For the *Agesilaus* is an important part of Xenophon's treatment of Sparta, and "Sparta" —the regime that gave rise to a specific way of life together with the man who most embodies that life—is *the* representative of republican political life, the life dedicated to the *polis*. And this life, as distinguished from that of grand empire, is in turn a more readily available and indeed attractive alternative to the life of Socrates for most people. The ironic or satirical presentation of "Sparta," deceptive until one begins to see it as such, is part of Xenophon's case for Socrates, a case he clearly wished to make for the benefit for his friends, actual or potential. And "all those who long for virtue still even now continue to long for [Socrates] above all others" (*Memorabilia* 4.8.11).

Over the centuries, the *Agesilaus* has been taken to be an unbalanced, extravagant, even wince-inducing praise ("morbid veneration") whose glaring lacunae should make its author blush. But the glaring character of those lacunae helped the *Agesilaus* accomplish its task or tasks: it permitted Xenophon to discharge, in the eyes of most people, any obligation he had to the Spartan king—at least Xenophon exhibited the virtue of *philetairia*—and it allowed him to indicate to some readers a path to discovering the truth of the matter, even if this required him to appear in the eyes of some people as a bit of a "fool."[106]

CHAPTER 3
Regime of the Lacedaemonians

Translated by Catherine S. Kuiper and Susan D. Collins

∾ Chapter 1 ∾

(1) But once when reflecting that Sparta, though it is among the cities with the smallest populations, appeared the most powerful as well as renowned in Hellas, I wondered how in the world this came to be.[1] When I reflected fully on the practices of the Spartans,[2] however, I wondered no longer. (2) Indeed, Lycurgus, who set down their laws,[3] in obedience to which they were happy[4]—I wonder at him too and regard him as wise in the extreme.[5] For not by imitating the other cities, but even by conceiving things that are opposed to most of them, he showed the fatherland to be outstanding in happiness.

(3) Concerning, to start with, the begetting of children (so that I may begin at the beginning): when it comes to providing nourishment to girls who are going to bear children and are held to be nobly educated, the others provide as measured an amount of basic food as is practicable and as little meat as possible. With respect to wine, furthermore, they make the girls either abstain from it entirely or take it much watered-down. And just as the majority of those who engage in the arts are sedentary, so too the rest of the Greeks deem it right that the girls sit quietly and work wool. Now then, how could one expect those reared in this way to produce any impressive offspring? (4) By contrast, Lycurgus held that female slaves are quite adequate for supplying clothes, whereas, because he believed[6] that for free females the greatest task is the begetting of children, he first prescribed that the female sex[7] exercise the body no less than the

male does. Next, just as he did for the men, he created running and strength contests also among the females, since he believed that more robust offspring come from parents who are both strong.

(5) And as to when a woman goes to a man [in marriage], seeing that others in the first part of the time would have intercourse with their wives without measure, Lycurgus conceived the opposite as regards this too. For he set it down as immodest[8] for the man to be seen coming [to her bedroom] and immodest for him to be seen leaving. Thus, the couple would necessarily have greater longing for intercourse with one another, and the one born would be more robust, if any should be engendered in this way,[9] rather than if the couple should be sated with one another. (6) But in addition to these things, he also stopped each of them from taking a wife whenever he wished, and prescribed that marriages be made when they are at their bodily prime, for he believed this too to be advantageous to fertility. (7) If it nonetheless should happen that an old man possessed a young wife, and seeing that men of such an age especially keep guard over their wives, he legislated the opposite as regards this too. For he made it such that an older man could bring in, to produce children for himself, whichever man whose body as well as soul he might admire. (8) And if, in turn, someone should not wish to live in wedlock with a woman, but should desire noteworthy children, Lycurgus also made it lawful that the fellow may beget children with whichever woman he might see who had fine offspring and was well bred, if he persuades the man who possesses her. (9) And indeed Lycurgus made many concessions of this sort. For the women wish to control two households, and the men to acquire for their children brothers who share in kinship and power but do not lay claim to their property.

(10) Let anyone who wishes, then, investigate whether, by his thus conceiving things opposite to those done by others regarding the begetting of children, Lycurgus perfected men in Sparta as excelling in both size and strength.

∽ CHAPTER 2 ∽

(1) I, however, having already discussed the question of generation, wish to make clear also the education of each.[10] So then, as

regards those of the other Greeks who profess to educate their sons most nobly: as soon as the children[11] understand what is said to them, they immediately assign pedagogues[12] as attendants over them and immediately send them to teachers to learn letters, music, and the exercises of the wrestling school. In addition to these things, they make their children's feet tender with sandals and pamper their bodies with changes of cloaks; as for their food, furthermore, they believe the measure of how much they may eat to be the size of their paunch. (2) But Lycurgus, instead of having each privately assign slaves as pedagogues, assigned a man from among those who hold the greatest offices to preside over the children; and he gave this man, who is in fact called a *paidonomos*,[13] authority both to assemble the children and, upon inspection, to chastise severely anyone who might be taking it easy. Lycurgus also gave him whip bearers from among the young men so that they could mete out punishment whenever it should be needed, with the result that there prevails among them at the same time much modesty,[14] on the one hand, and much obedience, on the other. (3) Furthermore, instead of softening their feet with sandals, he prescribed that they harden them by going barefoot, for he believed that if they should exercise in this way, they would climb uphill more easily and be steadier going downhill, and that they would be quicker in leaping, springing, and running if they should have exercised barefoot than would those who wear shoes. (4) And instead of pampering them with cloaks, he legislated that they should become accustomed to a single cloak through the year, for he believed that in this way they should be better prepared against the cold and the heat. (5) Regarding food, he prescribed that a male[15] contribute to the common mess such an amount that he would never be weighed down by surfeit nor be without experience of want. For he believed that those who were educated in this way would be better able, if the need should arise, to toil while going without food, and, if commanded, would better endure on the same food for a longer time, and that they would be less in need of meat and more accommodating with respect to all food, and they would go through life in a healthier state. And he held that the nourishment that makes bodies slender would be more conducive to growth in height than one that fattens them up with food. (6) Yet, so that they would not, in turn, be very much oppressed by hunger, while he did not permit them to take whatever else they needed without trouble, he did allow them to steal that which would alleviate their hunger. (7) And that it is not because he was at a loss[16] regarding what to allot them that he permitted them to procure food through craftiness—no one, I suppose, is ignorant of this. But it is clear that one who is going to steal must both lie awake at night and, by day, use deceit and wait in ambush, and that one who is going to capture something must prepare spies. Regarding all these things, it is therefore surely clear that he educated the children in this manner because he wished to make them craftier in procuring provisions and more skillful in war.

(8) But, someone might say, if indeed he believed stealing to be a good thing, why then inflict many lashes on anyone who was caught? Because, I contend, as with all the other things human beings teach, they chastise the one who does not perform his service nobly, so [the Spartans] punish those who are caught on the grounds that they steal badly.[17] (9) And indeed, although he set it down as a noble thing to snatch away as many cheeses as possible from Orthia,[18] he ordered others to whip those who did so, because he wished to make clear also in this case that by enduring bodily pain for a short time, one is able to rejoice in a good reputation for a long time. It is clear in this case, too, that whenever swiftness is needed, the sluggard benefits himself the least and obtains the most troubles.

(10) And so that the children would never be in want of a ruler even if the *paidonomos* should go away, he gave whoever of the citizens was present authority both to order whatever might seem to be good for the children and to chastise someone if he should miss the mark. By doing this, he made the children also more modest, for nothing makes either men or children so modest as rulers do. (11) And in fact so that the children would not be in want of a ruler if it should ever happen that no man was present, he set down that the keenest one of the males[19] of each band[20] rule. The result is that the children there are at no time in want of a ruler.

(12) But it seems that I must speak also of pederasty.[21] For this too pertains in some way to education. So then, the other Greeks are either like the Boeotians, among whom a man and boy are paired off as a couple, or like the Eleans, who enjoy the boy in the bloom of youth in return for favors; but there are also some who absolutely prevent the lovers even from conversing with the boys.[22] (13) But

Lycurgus conceived also the opposite of all these things: if someone who was himself as he ought to be, and, admiring the soul of a boy, should endeavor to perfect him as a friend beyond reproach and to consort with him, Lycurgus praised this and believed it to be the noblest education. But if someone should be manifestly seeking after the body of a boy, Lycurgus established this as most shameful and in Lacedaemon made it so that lovers stay away from boys no less than parents from children and siblings from siblings when it comes to sexual relations. (14) To be sure, I do not wonder that this is distrusted by some; for in many cities, the laws do not set themselves against the desires directed toward boys.

So then, the education both of the Laconians and of the other Greeks has been spoken of. As for which of the two renders men more obedient, more modest, and more continent with respect to their needs, let he who wishes to do so investigate these things also.

ᴥ CHAPTER 3 ᴥ

(1) Now, when they move from being children into puberty, at that age others release them from pedagogues and release them from teachers, and no one further rules over them; rather, they are let loose to live by their own law. But Lycurgus conceived the opposite of these things too. (2) For, observing that a great spiritedness is naturally implanted in those of such an age, hubris is especially uppermost, and the strongest desires for pleasures take hold of them, he laid upon those at that age the most toils and contrived for them the greatest lack of leisure. (3) But since he also further imposed the penalty that if someone should flee these difficulties, he would obtain nothing of the noble things,[23] he made it so that not only those holding public office, but also those in charge of[24] each [youth] take care that they not become altogether disreputable in the city on the grounds of cowardly shirking. (4) In addition to these things, because he wished to implant in them a strong sense of modesty, he ordered that even in the streets, they keep both hands inside their cloak, walk along in silence, and not look about here and there but keep their gaze on what is before their feet. Here too, indeed, it became clear

that the male sex is stronger also at being moderate than is the female nature. (5) At any rate, you would hear a sound less from them than from stone statues; you would less turn their eyes than you would those of bronze statues; and you would hold them to be more modest than even maidens in their bridal chambers.[25] And whenever they come to the common mess,[26] you must be content to hear them only when they are asked something.

And of the beloved boys[27] then, Lycurgus took care in this manner.

～ CHAPTER 4 ～

(1) About the young men, he was indeed the most serious by far, because he believed that, if they should become such as they ought to be, they would have the greatest influence on the city's good. (2) So, seeing that among those in whom the love of victory is most ingrained, their choruses are most worth hearing and gymnastic contests most worth seeing, he believed that if he set the young men contending in rivalry against one another concerning virtue,[28] then they would attain manly goodness[29] to the greatest degree. So I will fully relate how, in turn, he set these to contending with one another. (3) Accordingly, the ephors[30] choose three men from those in the prime of life, and these are called *hippagretai*.[31] And each of these enlists a hundred men, making clear on what account he honors some and rejects others. (4) Those, then, who do not obtain the noble things are at war both with those who dismissed them and with those who were chosen instead of them, and they watch one another closely, if they should take it easy, contrary to any of the things deemed noble. (5) And this in fact is the rivalry dearest to the gods and most befitting a citizen, in which is displayed what a good man must do. But each exercises separately as well, in order that they will always be at their strongest, and, if there be any need to do so, will individually give aid to the city with all their strength.[32] (6) And it is also necessary that they take care to be in good condition, for indeed, because of their rivalry, they spar whenever they encounter one another. To be sure, any bystander has authority to separate the combatants. And if someone disobeys the one separating them,

the *paidonomos* leads him up to the ephors; and they punish him severely, wishing to impress on him that passion must never gain mastery over obedience to the laws.

(7) As for those who have passed from the age of young men and are now to hold the greatest offices: the other Greeks relieve them from focusing their attention on their physical strength, though they still order them to serve on campaign. Lycurgus, by contrast, made it customary that hunting is noblest for people of that age, unless some public office should prevent them, so that these too, no less than the young men, would be able to bear the toils of campaigning.

~ CHAPTER 5 ~

(1) So then, the practices that Lycurgus legislated for each age have nearly been stated; and now I will try to go through also the mode of life[33] he arranged for everyone. (2) So then, Lycurgus found the Spartans taking their meals at home, just as the other Greeks did, and, recognizing that a great deal of easy living occurs in homes, he brought the messes out into the open, because he held that in this way his commands would be least transgressed. (3) As for food, he prescribed a diet such that they were left neither gorged nor wanting. Still, many unreckoned extras also come from what has been caught in the hunt, and sometimes in exchange for these, the wealthy contribute wheat bread,[34] so that then, until they separately retire, the table is neither devoid of things to eat nor extravagant. (4) And further, stopping the unnecessary drinking, which trips up bodies and trips up judgment, he permitted each to drink whenever thirsty, for he believed that drink thus becomes most harmless as well as most pleasant. So indeed, by participating in the common mess in this way, how would anyone utterly destroy himself or his household by gluttony or drunkenness?

(5) In addition, in the other cities, people mostly consort with others of the same age, and among these separate cohorts modesty least prevails. But Lycurgus mingled [the age cohorts] in Sparta [since] in most things the young are educated by the experience of the old.[35] (6) It is also local custom in the common messes to speak of anything

noble that someone does in the city. In that place, consequently, there is ingrained the least hubris, the least drunken behavior, and the least shameful conduct or shameful speech. (7) Eating outside, furthermore, brings about the following good things: they are compelled to walk on their return homeward and so have to take care not to be tripped up by wine, since they know that they will not remain where they dined and must find their way by night just as by day. For one still liable to military service is not allowed to proceed by torchlight.

(8) Furthermore, since Lycurgus also observed that those who toil hard after taking their food have a good complexion, firm flesh, and strength, whereas those who do not toil appear puffy, ugly, and weak, he did not neglect even this. Rather, reflecting that even when someone himself, through his own willing love of toil, appears to have an adequate body, Lycurgus ordered the elder in each gymnasium still always to take care so that [their labors] never be less than the food apportioned to them.[36] (9) And to me it seems that Lycurgus was not tripped up in this. In fact, one would not easily find either healthier or more able-bodied people than the Spartans: for they train similarly with their legs, arms, and neck.

∾ CHAPTER 6 ∾

(1) Furthermore, he conceived opposite things to what most do also in the following matters. For in the other cities, each man rules over his own children, household slaves, and property; but because Lycurgus wished to arrange it such that citizens should enjoy some good from one another, while in no way doing harm, he made it so that each man rule alike over his own children and those of others. (2) And whenever someone knows that these [other men] are the fathers of the children over whom he rules, he necessarily rules their children in the way he would wish his own to be ruled. And if any child ever receives lashes from someone else and reports this to his father, it is shameful for the father not to inflict additional lashes on his son. In this way, they trust one another not to give any shameful order to the children.

(3) And with respect to household slaves, too, he made it so that, if someone should have need of them, he could also make use of those that belong to others. He introduced the sharing of hunting dogs as well, so that while those who have need of them call for the hunt, one who is not himself at leisure to go sends the dogs out with pleasure. And horses, too, he made use of in like manner. For whoever is sick or in need of transport or wishing to reach somewhere swiftly, if he should see a horse anywhere, he takes it and after making fine use of it, returns it.[37] (4) Nor yet again did he make a practice of what is customary, at least among others. For sometimes those who have returned late from the hunt may have need of provisions, if they happen not to have prepared them for themselves. In this case, then, he established that those who have finished up[38] should leave what had been prepared, and those who are in need should open the seals and, taking as much as they may need, leave the rest resealed.

(5) Accordingly, by their sharing in this way with one another, even those of small means partake of all the things in the land, whenever they may have need of anything.

∾ CHAPTER 7 ∾

(1) Furthermore, Lycurgus established in Sparta also the following customs opposite to those of the other Greeks. For presumably in the other cities, all engage in moneymaking as much as they are able: one is a farmer, another a shipowner, another a merchant, and still others support themselves from the arts. (2) But in Sparta, Lycurgus prohibited free men from engaging in anything connected with moneymaking; rather, he prescribed that they believe their only works to be those that secure freedom for cities. (3) And further, why need wealth be seriously sought after in a place where, by prescribing that they contribute equally to the provisions and lead a similar way of life, he made it so that they do not grasp after money for the sake of luxurious pleasure? But not even for cloaks need they engage in moneymaking, for they are adorned not by expensive clothing, but by the good condition of the body. (4) Nor even for the sake of being able to spend on their messmates need they amass money, for

he made it more reputable to benefit one's intimates through bodily toil than by spending money on them, pointing out that the former is a work of the soul, and the latter, a work of wealth. (5) Furthermore, he hindered their making money by unjust means also in ways such as these: First, he established a sort of currency such that if a sum worth only ten minae should come into a household, it could never escape the notice of either the masters or the household slaves, for it would require both a great amount of space and a wagon for hauling. (6) Moreover, there is a search for gold and silver, and if any appears somewhere, its possessor is punished.

Why, therefore, would anyone be serious about moneymaking in a place where its acquisition brings more pains than its use yields good cheer?

~ CHAPTER 8 ~

(1) But really, we all know that in Sparta most of all, they obey the rulers as well as the laws. I, however, suppose that Lycurgus did not first attempt to establish this good condition[39] until he made it so that the strongest[40] persons in the city were of the same mind. (2) I take as evidence these things: In the other cities, the more powerful do not wish even to seem to fear the rulers, but believe this to be servile.[41] In Sparta, by contrast, the strongest both defer most of all to the rulers and take great pride in being submissive and in answering whenever they are called, running, not walking; for they believe that if they themselves take the lead in zealously obeying, so too others will follow. And this very thing has come about.

(3) It is also likely that these same people helped to establish the power of the ephorate,[42] since indeed they understood obedience to be the greatest good in the city and in the army as well as in the household: so much greater the power that the ruling office possesses, so much the more, they held, will it also terrify the citizens into submission.[43] (4) The ephors, accordingly, are competent to punish whomever they wish and have authority to accomplish this on the spot; and in fact, they have authority to terminate rulers in the midst of their office and even to imprison them and to place them on

trial for their life.[44] In possessing so much power, they do not permit, as do the other cities, that those elected rule however they wish continuously through the year, but, just like tyrants and officiators at gymnastic contests, if they perceive anyone breaking the law in any way, they immediately chastise him on the spot.

(5) While there are also many other noble contrivances by Lycurgus with a view to the citizens' willing obedience to the laws, among the noblest also seems to me to be this: that he did not deliver his laws to the populace until, going with the strongest citizens to Delphi, he asked the god whether it would be more desirable and better for Sparta to obey the laws he set down. And when the god replied that it would be better in every way, then Lycurgus delivered them, establishing that disobedience to laws sanctioned by the Pythia is not only illegal but also impious.[45]

✑ CHAPTER 9 ✑

(1) And the following, too, is worthy of being admired in Lycurgus: that he prevailed in the city in making a noble death preferred to a shameful life; and in fact, should someone investigate this, he would find that fewer of these die than do those who choose to retreat out of fear. (2) To speak truly, safety even follows upon virtue more of the time than upon vice,[46] for indeed virtue is easier, more pleasant, more resourceful, and stronger. It is clear too that glory most often follows upon virtue; for in fact, all men wish to fight in some way alongside those who are good.

(3) Indeed, the way that he contrived to bring these things about— this too, it is noble not to omit. Accordingly, he plainly prepared happiness for the good [courageous], on the one hand, and unhappiness for the bad [cowards], on the other hand. (4) For in other cities, whenever someone proves to be a coward, he possesses only the reputation of cowardice; and if he wishes, the coward goes to the market and sits and trains in the same place as the courageous man; but in Lacedaemon, every one would be ashamed to accept a coward as a messmate or as a training partner in the wrestling bouts. (5) And often, even when they are dividing up teams to play ball, such a man

is left over without a position; and in choruses, he is led away to the positions of disgrace; and further, in the roads, he must give way of his own accord; and he must give up his seat, even for younger persons; and as for his female relations, he must maintain the girls at home, and they must bear the responsibility for his [lack of] manliness;[47] and he must endure a hearth empty of a wife and at the same time pay the penalty for this; and he must not stroll about anointed, or imitate the blameless, lest he suffer lashes from his betters.

(6) So indeed, given the sort of dishonor laid on those who are cowards, I in no way wonder that death is preferred there instead of a life thus dishonored and disgraced.

~ CHAPTER 10 ~

(1) And it seems to me that Lycurgus also nobly legislated how, even as far as old age, virtue should be exercised. For by placing the decision regarding the *gerousia*[48] toward the end of life, he made it so that not even in old age are nobility and goodness neglected.[49] (2) Also worthy of admiration is the support he gave to good men in their old age: by establishing that the old have authority over capital trials,[50] he made old age more honorable than the full vigor of those in their prime. (3) It is fitting, to be sure, that this contest most of all is taken seriously among human beings. For gymnastic contests are also noble, but they have to do with bodies; by contrast, the contest involving the *gerousia* renders a judgment regarding the souls of the good. As much, then, as the soul is better than the body, so much too are the contests that concern souls more worthy of seriousness than those of bodies.

(4) How is not the following greatly worthy of being admired in Lycurgus? Since he observed that wherever those who wish to do so take care for virtue, they are not sufficient to make their fatherlands greater, he compelled everyone in Sparta to exercise all the virtues in public. Just as, then, private individuals differ from one another when it comes to virtue—those who exercise it from those who do not take care for it—so too Sparta fittingly differs from all cities when it comes to virtue, since she alone makes the practice of nobility and

goodness a public affair. (5) For is this not a noble thing: that while the other cities chastise someone if he does some injustice to another, Lycurgus imposed a penalty no less if someone should be manifestly neglecting to be the best possible? (6) For he believed, as it seems, that by those who sell others into slavery or who rob something or steal, only the ones harmed are done injustice; whereas by the bad and unmanly, whole cities are betrayed. Thus, fittingly it seems to me at least, he imposed the greatest penalties on these latter ones. (7) And in fact he imposed an irresistible necessity to exercise the whole of political virtue. For he made the city belong to all those alike who fulfill the customary laws,[51] and he did not take into account deficiency either of body or of money. By contrast, if someone should shirk in cowardly fashion from toiling hard according to the customary laws, he ordained that this one would no longer be deemed to belong to the peers.[52]

(8) But that these laws are most ancient is clear; for Lycurgus is said to have been born at the time of the *Heracleidai.*[53] Yet, although they are thus ancient, to others even now they are most novel; and in fact, the most wonderful thing of all is that while everyone praises such practices, not a single city is willing to imitate them.

∿ CHAPTER 11 ∿

(1) And these are indeed common goods both in peace and in war. But if someone wishes to observe also what Lycurgus contrived for the army, better than others did, it is possible to hear of these things as well. (2) Accordingly, first the ephors publicly proclaim the years in which it is necessary to serve on campaign, both for horsemen and for hoplites, and then for handicraftsmen. Thus, all the things that people use in the city, the Lacedaemonians have in abundance also in the army. And it is commanded that all the equipment the army may need in common is to be supplied, some equipment brought by carts and some by beasts of burden; for in this way, anything left behind might least escape notice. (3) Furthermore, as regards the contest at arms, he contrived the following: that they be equipped with a crimson cloak—for he believed this to share least in common

with feminine dress and to be most warlike—as well as a brass shield, since it is both quick to polish and slow to dirty. And he also permitted long hair to those past the age of the young men, for he believed that in this way they would appear bigger, freer, and more terrible. (4) When they were thus arranged, he divided them into six *morai*,[54] both horsemen and hoplites. And each of the citizen *morai* has one *polemarchos*, four *lochagoi*, eight *pentēkostēres*, and sixteen *enoōmotarchai*.[55] And out of these *morai*, they are deployed by word of command into *enoōmotiai*: sometimes by one, sometimes by three, sometimes by six.[56]

(5) But as to that which most people suppose—that the Laconian ordering of arms is convoluted—they assume the opposite of what is really the case. For in the Laconian ordering, the leaders are first in line, and each file has all that needs to be provided. (6) And this ordering is so easy to learn that anyone able to recognize human beings would not err. For it is given to some to lead while others are ordered to follow. Changes in movement are made clear by word from the *enoōmotarchēs*, just as from a herald, [and] the phalanxes become either shallow or deep. None of this is in any way difficult to learn. (7) To be sure, to fight in the same way alongside of whoever happens to be near even when they are thrown into confusion—this ordering is not easy to learn, except for those educated by the laws of Lycurgus. (8) And the Lacedaemonians carry out most easily even those things that seem to be altogether difficult to those practiced in the use of heavy arms. For when they march by column, of course, *enoōmotia* follows behind *enoōmotia*. And if, in such an arrangement, an enemy phalanx should appear in front, word is passed along to the *enoōmotarchēs* to deploy his line in the front on the shield side, and so through all the columns until the phalanx is standing opposite the enemy. Further, if the enemy appears in the back while they are situated thus, each file wheels about, so that the strongest will always face the enemy. (9) But though the leader is on the left, they do not regard themselves as falling short in this, and it is at times even an advantage. For if any of the enemy should attempt to encircle them, they would flank them not on the naked but on the shield side.[57] Yet if at some time, for some reason, it seems beneficial to have the leader on the right wing, the troop, turning, wheels the phalanx about to that wing, until the leader is on the right, and the

rear becomes the left.[58] (10) And in turn, if an ordering of the enemy appears on the wing from the right as they are marching, they do nothing other than turn each *lochos* just like a trireme confronting the opponents, and thus again the *lochos* in the rear is on the spear side. Further, if the enemy comes near the left, they do not permit this, but either dash forward or turn the *lochoi* to match the opponents, and thus again the *lochos* in the rear is placed on the shield side.[59]

∼ CHAPTER 12 ∼

(1) I will explain also what Lycurgus legislated as to how a camp needs to be set up. Because the angles of a quadrilateral are useless,[60] he would set up the camp in a circle, unless there were a mountain or wall as protection, or they should have a river behind them. (2) Furthermore, by day he posted guards, some alongside the weapons, looking inward; for these are put in place not on account of enemies but on account of friends.[61] Against enemies, furthermore, horsemen stand guard in positions from which they may see to the furthest extent whether someone approaches. (3) By night, he legislated, guard was to be kept by the Skiritai in forward positions outside the phalanx (though nowadays also by foreigners . . . any of these being present).[62] (4) As for their always going about with their spears in hand, one should know well, too, that they do this for the same reason that they also bar the slaves from the weapons. And one need not wonder that when they attend to the [bodily] necessities, they go no further from either the weapons or one another than they must so as not to distress one another. For even these things, they do on account of security. (5) Furthermore, they change camp frequently, both for the sake of harassing their enemies and for the sake of benefiting their friends. As well, it is announced that by law all the Lacedaemonians undertake gymnastic exercise as long as they are serving on campaign, so that they become more magnificent to themselves and appear freer than the others. And neither a walking nor a running course should be made greater than the space covered by the *mora*, in order that no one ends up far from his weapons. (6) After gymnastic exercises, the first *polemarchos* makes the proclamation that they are

to sit down—this is like an inspection—and after this to get their breakfast and quickly relieve the outpost. After this, in turn, there are pastimes and recreations until the evening gymnastic exercises. (7) Further, after these things, the proclamation is made that they are to get their dinner and, whenever they have sung to the gods to whom they have sacrificed with favorable omens, to take their rest upon their weapons.

That I write so much of these things, one ought not to wonder, for one would find that the Lacedaemonians least of all have neglected to take care for any of the things that are needed in military campaigns.

⮌ Chapter 13 ⮍

(1) I will go through also the power and honor that Lycurgus arranged for the king while on campaign.[63] First, then, the city provides nourishment for the king, and those with him, while he is on expedition. The *polemarchoi* pitch their tents with him, in order that, always consorting with him, they may also better deliberate in common, if they have any need. In addition, three other men of the peers pitch their tents with him; these latter take care of all the provisions, so that neither the king nor the *polemarchoi* lack the leisure to take care of the affairs of war.

(2) I will go back and take up how the king is sent forth to war together with the army. For first, while at home, he sacrifices to Zeus Agētōr and to the gods with him.[64] If he sacrifices with fine omens there, then the fire bearer takes the fire from the altar and leads the way to the borders of the country; at that place, the king offers sacrifices again, to Zeus and Athena.[65] (3) When he sacrifices to both these gods with good omens, then he crosses over the borders of the country. And the fire from these sacrificial offerings, which is never extinguished, leads the way, and all sorts of sacrificial animals follow. Whenever the king sacrifices, he always begins this deed while it is still dark, for he wishes to attract the favorable notice of the god. (4) Present around the sacrifice are the *polemarchoi, lochagoi, pentēkostēres, stratiarchoi* of foreign troops, those who lead the army's

baggage train, and any of the generals (*stratēgoi*) from the cities who wishes to be there. (5) Also present are two of the ephors, who in no way meddle unless the king summons them, yet by seeing what each person does, they moderate them all, as is fitting. When the sacrificial offerings are complete, the king, summoning all, declares what is to be done. The result is that, seeing these things, you would regard the others to be mere improvisers[66] when it comes to military affairs, and the Lacedaemonians alone the real craftsmen in the affairs of war.

(6) Furthermore, whenever the king takes the lead, provided no opposition appears, no one marches before him except the Skiritai and the horsemen who are scouts. But whenever they suppose that a battle will ensue, then, taking the troop of the first *mora*, the king leads, turning to the spearhand, until he is between two *morai* and two *polemarchoi*.[67] (7) The eldest of the public officials organizes those who must be stationed alongside of these: the peers who are the king's messmates, the diviners, the physicians, and the aulos players who lead the army, as well as any volunteers who may be present.[68] The result is that, regarding the things that are needed, there is nothing left unprovided for; for nothing is unforeseen.

(8) And Lycurgus contrived also the following noble and beneficial[69] things, as it seems to me, with respect to contests at arms. For whenever a she-goat is sacrificed as a victim, the enemy already being in sight, it is a law both that all the aulos players who are present play and that no Lacedaemonian be without a garland; also, it is announced that weapons are to be polished. (9) And even a young man is allowed to go into battle anointed with oil, and to be brightly beaming[70] and glorious. And they call out the order[71] to the *enoōmotarchēs*, for it cannot be heard across every entire *enoōmotia* by the *enoōmotarchai* on the outside. To take care that it comes out finely is the obligation of the *polemarchos*.

(10) Further, as to when it seems the opportune moment to make camp, indeed the Lycurgus with regard to this is the king,[72] and, as well, over pointing out where it must be made. Likewise, as to the sending of an embassy, whether to friends or to enemies, this in turn belongs to the king.[73] And everyone begins with the king, whenever they wish to do something. (11) If someone arrives who wants justice, the king sends him to the Hellanodikai;[74] if he is in need of money, to the treasurer; and

if he brings spoils, to those in charge of the spoils. Since things are done in this way, there is no other work for the king on expedition but to be a priest in the affairs that have to do with the gods and a general in the affairs that have to do with human beings.

∾ CHAPTER 14 ∾

(1) But if someone should ask me whether, even now, the laws of Lycurgus seem to me to remain unchanged—this, by Zeus, I would no longer boldly say![75] (2) For I know that formerly the Lacedaemonians chose to live with one another at home, possessing means within measure, rather than, by acting as harmosts[76] in the cities and being flattered, to become utterly corrupted. (3) And I know that before, they were afraid of being seen in the possession of gold; but now there are those who show off their possession of it. (4) I also know that before, there were expulsions of foreigners[77] and travel abroad was not permitted for this reason: so that the citizens might not take to easy living through the influence of foreigners. But I know that now, those thought to be first among them are seriously intent on never ceasing to act as harmosts over a foreign land. (5) And there was a time when they took care that they would be worthy to lead; but now they would much more exert themselves so as to rule rather than to be worthy of these things. (6) Accordingly, in former times, the Greeks would go to Lacedaemon and beg them to take the lead against those thought to be unjust; but now many are calling on one another to hinder them from ruling again. (7) To be sure, one need not wonder that these reproaches have arisen against them, when they are manifestly obeying neither the god nor the laws of Lycurgus.

∾ CHAPTER 15 ∾

(1) But I wish also to describe what compacts Lycurgus made for the king in relation to the city. For indeed this ruling office alone continues just as it was established in the beginning; whereas the

other regimes one would find changed and still changing even now. (2) For he established that the king should offer all the public sacrifices for the city, on the grounds that he is from the god, and that he lead the army wherever the city should send it. (3) And he granted that the king take the honorary portions from the sacrifices, and he assigned him land in many of the surrounding subject cities—land that is choice enough that he should neither want for means within measure nor be outstanding as regards wealth. (4) And so that the kings[78] too might take their meals outside, he assigned them a public tent, and he even honored them with a double portion from the meal, not so that they might devour twice as much, but so that they might be able to honor someone if they should wish. (5) And again, he also granted that each of the kings pick out two messmates, who indeed are called Pythioi.[79] He also granted that each king take a young pig from the brood of every sow, so that he might never lack sacrificial offerings, if he should need to consult with the gods about something. (6) And near his dwelling, a pool supplies an abundance of water—that this, too, is useful for many things, those who are without it well know. And all rise from their seats for the king, except the ephors from the seats of the ephorate. (7) And every month, they make oaths to each other: the ephors on behalf of the city; the king on behalf of himself. The oath for the king is that he will reign in accordance with the established laws of the city; for the city, that if he keeps his oath, it will maintain the kingship undisturbed. (8) These are the honors, then, that have been given to the king at home during his lifetime, none of them greatly surpassing those of private individuals. For he did not wish to infuse the kings with a tyrannical turn of mind or to make the citizens envious of their power. (9) Yet through the honors given to the king who has met his end, the laws of Lycurgus wish to make clear that it is not as human beings, but as heroes that they honor the kings of the Lacedaemonians.[80]

An Introduction to the Regime of the Lacedaemonians

Susan D. Collins

Xenophon's *Regime of the Lacedaemonians* is the only extant full treatise written by an ancient author that provides an account of the Spartan *politeia* ("regime" or "constitution").[81] It is therefore of interest to students of classics, history, and political philosophy alike. Yet it is a strange work, which has been subject to a wide variety of readings. The two poles between which these readings range could hardly be more distant: On one side, the treatise is seen to be a naïve encomium of Sparta by an unreserved Laconophile, a gentleman possessed of soldierly virtue but lacking in philosophical depth and sophistication. On the other side, it proves an ironical and wonderfully wrought satire of Sparta, penned by a topflight student of Socrates and in the philosophical spirit of a committed Socratic.[82] I am sympathetic to the latter view, but in the present introduction, I aim most simply to offer guidance in reading this admittedly puzzling work.[83]

After outlining the treatise, then, I consider the question that generally divides commentators, namely, Xenophon's pro-Spartan bias. Both the surface impression of the treatise, especially its prologue, and certain facts about Xenophon's own life are typically adduced as evidence for this bias. Yet, I argue, if we take Xenophon's life and work as a whole into account, we have good reason to be alert to the ways in which otherwise perplexing features of the treatise undermine this initial impression. We are not without aid, moreover, in making sense of the treatise, since Xenophon provides indications regarding how to read it. By considering a few important examples,

I illustrate how Xenophon's criticisms of Sparta emerge when we take our bearings by these indications. Finally, I examine Xenophon's treatment of what he suggests in the prologue is the aim of the law and political wisdom: the happiness of the Spartans and of their *patris* (or "fatherland"). For if we read the treatise in the manner indicated by Xenophon, we see that he examines the Spartan regime in light of necessities inherent in political life, namely, the extraordinary power of human desire and passion, the ever-present problem of war, and the natural human fear of death. In presenting Sparta as he does, Xenophon points to the limits inherent in law and political virtue in addressing these necessities, and he opens up the path that our education must take if we are to acquire wisdom regarding the question about which the law itself claims to be authoritative: the question of how best to live. That he undertakes this education with a certain politic reserve as well as playful wit will, I hope, become clear as our discussion unfolds.

Now, with a notable exception, the fifteen chapters of the treatise proceed in an orderly way. Its prologue seems to indicate straightforwardly enough Xenophon's intention: to describe the practices that conduced to the power and renown of Sparta, the happiness of the Spartans, and the outstanding happiness of their *patris* (1.1). Xenophon indicates that he seeks to explain by way of an account of these practices his admiration for the wisdom of the legendary Lycurgus, who set down the laws "in obedience to which the Spartans were happy" (1.2). In the discussion of the regime that follows, Xenophon begins "at the beginning," with the procreation of children (chapter 1), after which he takes up the education (*paideia*) of the children (chapter 2), the training of the young men (chapters 3–4), the mode of life (*diaita*) of the Spartans (chapters 5–7), the peak of the Lycurgan education in political virtue, understood as courage and law-abidingness, including the role of the offices of the Spartan ephorate and *gerousia* (or senate) in securing this virtue (chapters 8–10). As Xenophon indicates, these first ten chapters form a whole regarding the common goods of the Spartans in both peace and war (11.1)—in a word, the happiness of those who abide by the laws laid down by Lycurgus (cf. 1.1 with 9.3). In the last five chapters, he then takes up the provisions Lycurgus set down for the army on campaign (chapters 11–12), and for the kings, both on campaign and at home (chapters 13 and 15). He also addresses the problem of the decline of the Spartans in the present day (chapter 14).

What, then, is so strange about the treatise that a few prominent commentators even doubt its authenticity?[84] Not much attentiveness is required to notice the most obvious oddity, and the one that causes the greatest consternation: the role and place of chapter 14. After thirteen chapters seemingly in praise of Sparta and its lawgiver, Xenophon is provoked by an anonymous questioner to acknowledge the poor condition of Spartan virtue in the present day. Xenophon's abrupt turn from an encomium of Sparta to a lament about its present state is made especially puzzling because this lament appears in the penultimate chapter of the treatise—wedged between a concluding discussion of the power and honors Lycurgus provided the kings on campaign (chapter 13) and the honors he provided them at home (chapter 15). Why should Xenophon turn without any obvious preparation to the question of Spartan virtue at present? Why should the problem of Sparta's decline arise not in the final chapter of the treatise, as the logic of the presentation would more neatly dictate, but in the penultimate chapter, between the two that treat the Spartan kingship? Short of excising or explaining away this chapter, as some commentators attempt to do, readers are forced to puzzle out Xenophon's intention in introducing the question of Sparta's present condition where he does.[85] That this condition is a matter of serious concern, especially from the point of view of piety, is indicated by the fact that Xenophon's response to the anonymous questioner is punctuated by the only oath of the treatise (14.1).

In its context in the treatise, chapter 14 raises the question of whether the present condition of Sparta has its source in the Lycurgan regime as such—as defective from the beginning, so to speak—or whether the Spartans have declined from what was once their peak for reasons that have nothing to do with the regime strictly speaking.[86] If only by placing in a new and critical light Xenophon's opening praise of the Lycurgan regime, then, this chapter challenges us to retrace our steps to see if we have overlooked anything that prepares for it. Xenophon thereby raises the very question of *how* we are to read his treatise.

In settling this question, however, many commentators take their bearings from certain facts of Xenophon's life—some well established, some speculative—as evidence that he writes with a pro-Spartan bias.[87] If one takes one's bearings from Xenophon's close relationship with the Spartans, that is, it seems sensible enough to read the treatise as an encomium of the Lycurgan regime and chapter 14 as a lament, if awkwardly placed, about the decline of the Spartans from what was once their peak, when they lived fully in accord with that regime.

What, then, can be said with confidence about the facts of Xenophon's life? He was born in Athens around 430 BC. As a child and young man, he lived through the Peloponnesian War, which saw Athens fall from the height of its imperial power to ignominious defeat in 404. He subsequently experienced the oligarchic regime of the Thirty Tyrants, supported by the Spartans, in 404–403, the brutal civil war and the restoration of the democracy in 403, as well as the amnesty that followed. By his own account in the *Anabasis of Cyrus*, Xenophon then left Athens for Asia Minor in 401 to join his Boeotian friend Proxenus and ten thousand Greek mercenaries in the expedition of Cyrus the Younger to overthrow his brother, the Persian king Artaxerxes.[88] This expedition collapsed with Cyrus's death at the battle of Cunaxa, in the aftermath of which Xenophon rose to prominence as a leader of the Greeks, who had to make their way home through hostile barbarian lands. Having helped lead the bulk of the Greeks to safety, he remained with these mercenaries in support of Spartan action in Asia Minor from 399 to 395. In the course of this campaign, he became a friend of the Spartan king Agesilaus, whose patronage proved especially propitious since at some point the Athenians had exiled Xenophon.[89] Under the protection of Agesilaus, he lived out his exile mainly in the Peloponnese, on an estate in Skillous,[90] for a period of twenty years or so. He had two sons, the older of which, Gryllus, died in the battle of Mantinea fighting on behalf of Athens.[91] As the result of this fact not least, we know that at a certain point the Athenians had lifted the decree of exile against Xenophon. Sometime after 371, he left Skillous, but where he went is uncertain. Sometime after 362, he died, though we know not exactly when or where.[92]

Now, if these are the most significant facts of Xenophon's life, there may be a plausible, if not a knock-down, case for attributing to him a pro-Spartan bias and hence for accepting at face value what is for the most part on the surface of the relevant treatises: his praise of Sparta and Spartans in the *Regime of the Lacedaemonians, Agesilaus,* and *Hellenica.* For even if such praise does not reflect a wholly uncritical admiration for all things Spartan—a bias in the strict sense—his view of Sparta may be heavily influenced by his gratitude toward the Spartans, and Agesilaus in particular, for the protection they afforded him during his exile from Athens. In some form or fashion, that is, Xenophon's treatise reflects Spartan sympathies.

Yet, if we leave the story here, we neglect other significant facts of Xenophon's life, which is marked not only by his deeds in war but also, like the life of Thucydides, by the use he made of his exile to study and write. His remarkable works have come down to us without loss and cover an array of topics, from hunting, horsemanship, and war to household management, politics, and philosophy. Over the generations, his readers have been charmed by a range of "heroes": military and political men of Xenophon's own time, such as his friend King Agesilaus, as well as legendary founders of regimes, such as Cyrus the Great of Persia and the "wise Lycurgus." Not least among these heroes is Xenophon himself. Indeed, much more so than does Plato or Thucydides, Xenophon draws attention to himself: to his deeds in war, to be sure, but also to his deeds in peace and to his own reflections. In drawing attention to himself, Xenophon alerts his readers to a fact of his life that is central to his self-understanding: For he makes clear that he was a student and admirer of a man who was arguably the greatest of his heroes, the philosopher, and Athenian, Socrates. The significance of Socrates for Xenophon, and for the perspective from which he writes, is indicated most simply by the fact that Xenophon's work entitled *Memorabilia* or *Recollections* is given over entirely to recollections of Socrates.[93]

Now, this fact of Xenophon's life, central as it is, does not by itself settle the question of his view of Sparta,[94] yet it cautions us against assuming this view in light of other facts of his life. A full accounting of Xenophon's life and works, that is, encourages us not simply to begin with an open mind regarding his understanding of the Spartan regime, but to read the treatise in light of its possible philosophical or Socratic character. By considering the work in this light, we can begin to see that what one commentator calls a "seemingly eccentric collection of information about the Spartan *politeia*"[95] is not simply eccentric—but that it presents important clues to Xenophon's full thought about Sparta.

One of the first things we see is that the treatise itself provides guidance as to how to read it. Its opening line, even its first word—*alla* (but)—points immediately to the kind of self-reflection and second thought that will distinguish Xenophon's inquiry: "But once when reflecting that Sparta, though it is among the cities with the smallest populations, appeared the most powerful as well as renowned in Hellas, I wondered how in the world this came to be" (1.1). The treatise thus begins midstream in Xenophon's own thinking, as if he is considering or reconsidering his own or someone else's claim about Sparta. He then proceeds to recount the train of his initial reflections. In thinking about the Spartan practices that conduced to the city's power and renown, he then turned his attention to Lycurgus, who had laid down the laws in obedience to which the Spartans were happy. Lycurgus's feat aroused Xenophon's wonder, and he regarded the lawgiver as "wise in the extreme(s)."[96] For Lycurgus did not imitate the practices of other cities. To the contrary, he put in place practices that opposed those of most cities, and, in laying down such laws, he "showed the fatherland to be outstanding in happiness" (1.1). From the very beginning, Xenophon thus indicates, his thought is in motion, and the treatise presents the path of his reflections on the Lacedaemonian regime.

In the body of the treatise, Xenophon further guides readers along this path. For example, in ostensibly seeking to show the innovative, not to say radical, character of the practices Lycurgus set down—and hence the lawgiver's remarkable wisdom—Xenophon contrasts certain of these practices with those of other cities. But he does not always make parallel contrasts, leaving us to wonder about the equivalent practice in Sparta of which he omits to speak (cf., e.g., 1.3 with 1.4; 2.1 with 2.2–5; 3.1 with 3.2–4). Twice, he explicitly invites his audience to undertake an independent investigation of his claims about the Spartans (1.10; 2.14), and twice again he introduces anonymous objectors, who, puzzled by Xenophon's presentation of a matter, raise a serious question about it (2.8; 14.1). He signals his own reluctance to speak openly about the role of pederasty in the Lycurgan education (2.12), and he acknowledges that at least some in his audience will be skeptical about his gloss on the matter (2.14). He is not above addressing some issues by way of a rhetorical question (1.3; 5.4; 7.6; cf. 9.1 with 10.4–5), in contrast to those about which he more or less states his own view (cf. 5.4 with 5.9; 7.6 with 9.6; 10.1–2 with 10.4–5; see also 8.1–2, 5; 9.1–2, 6; 10.6; 14.1–4). In one instance, he contends that what most people suppose is true about the Spartans is not in fact the case (11.5) and, in another, that the Spartans are willing to do things simply for the sake of appearances (11.3; 12.5). He thus cautions students of the regime to be wary of what appears or is said to be true about the Spartans. In these ways, then, Xenophon invites his readers to engage the text as active interlocutors: to notice and make sense of its apparent disjunctions or inconsistencies, silences or omissions, rhetorical questions and objections. These textual indications encourage readers to balance Xenophon's praise of Sparta—as up-front as it is in the prologue—with a more nuanced and considered inquiry into his view of the Lycurgan regime.

The prologue immediately raises a series of questions. After initially taking his bearings from the power and renown that Spartan practices secured for the city, Xenophon is moved to focus not on this power and renown, but on the wisdom of the lawgiver in setting down the practices that conduced to the happiness of the Spartans and the "outstanding happiness" of their *patris*. Are the practices that secured the city's power and renown, then, to be equated with those that conduced to the Spartans' happiness and that of their *patris*? Or is the latter question regarding happiness broader than that of the city's power and renown, and more fully an object of the lawgiver's wisdom? Is, for that matter, Lycurgus truly wise? Or is the measure of his wisdom to be the success of his laws in achieving the happiness of the Spartans and of their *patris*? Are the two kinds of happiness equivalent, or does Xenophon mean to indicate an important distinction by speaking of the "outstanding" happiness of the latter? In the account of Sparta that follows the prologue, Xenophon encourages and even provokes his readers to reflect on these and other questions that are fundamental to understanding the Lycurgan regime and the status of that regime in Xenophon's own thought.

A few important examples from the chapters that lead up to the explicit criticisms of Sparta in chapter 14 illustrate the character and potential of such an engagement with the text. In his prologue, Xenophon attributes the Spartan laws to their legendary lawgiver Lycurgus, praising him for the wisdom with which he laid down the practices that redounded to the Spartans' happiness and the happiness of their *patris* (1.1–2). But later, in chapter 8, he indicates that there is less to the legend than meets the eye—or at least that Lycurgus had "help" from the strongest of his contemporaries when it came to at least one important political institution (8.1, 3). For these Spartans, whom Lycurgus had to win over to his cause (8.1), helped to establish the extremely powerful office of the ephorate, and they accompanied Lycurgus to Delphi to request the oracle's sanction of the laws (8.1, 3, 5). We are thus permitted to wonder, if provisionally, whether Lycurgus is something of a figurehead, a mask that covers a less perfect or less wise founding. Indeed, Xenophon indicates in chapter 8 that it is not, strictly speaking, the wise ancestral laws that the Spartans obey with a view to their happiness. Rather, in the face of no little resistance, the ephors secure that obedience as only "tyrants" can "on the spot" (8.1, 4).[97]

After praising Lycurgus's unparalleled wisdom at the outset, furthermore, Xenophon ostensibly proves this claim in the body of the treatise by drawing contrasts between what the Spartans do and what others do. But why, in some cases, does Xenophon remain silent about the parallel practice in Sparta, for example, regarding the dietary habits of the Spartan girls, as contrasted with those of the other Greeks, or the status of "letters and music" in Spartan education (cf. 1.3 with 1.4; 2.1 with 2.2–5)? In supplying what is omitted, we see that Xenophon's praise of Lycurgus's provisions disguises serious defects or even understandable failures of the early education. Xenophon himself later raises the question of the "moderation" of Spartan women (3.4; see also 1.9), whose appetites are not, in the final analysis, adequately educated or governed. Further, his emphasis on the harsh physical training through which Lycurgus aimed to control the natural spiritedness, hubris, and desire for pleasure of the young raises the question of whether the neglect of letters and music in favor of this training leads to a certain brutishness and to an obedience grounded in fear rather than in understanding (3.2, 4; 4.1, 6).[98]

It is true that Xenophon generally appears to laud the education laid down by Lycurgus, especially the education of Spartan males in modesty or a sense of shame (*aidōs*) and continence (*enkrateia*) with respect to the bodily appetites as well as money. He also describes as "worthy of admiration" the measures by which Lycurgus establishes the peak or completion of Spartan virtue in courage and lawfulness (see, e.g., 9.1, 3; 10.4–7). But upon closer inspection, we see that he nonetheless acknowledges, even underscores, troubling aspects of the education of children: the questionable character of certain pedagogic provisions, such as the encouragement of stealing and the arrangements regarding pederasty (2.7–8, 12–14).[99] We see also that the Lycurgan regimen is distinguished by severe harshness, not only in its education of the children, as compared with that of the other Greeks (cf. 2.1 with 2.3–6 and esp. 2.2), but also in the punishments that await any Spartan who proves a coward or who fails to obey either the law or the rulers (8.3–4; 9.4–6; 10.4–7). Only once, in fact, does Xenophon explicitly describe Spartan obedience to the law as "willing" — when he speaks of Lycurgus's use of the Delphic Oracle in securing this obedience (8.5). This observation serves to highlight the compulsion under which the Spartans generally acted. It also puts in a new light Xenophon's frequent references in the last chapters of the treatise to the sacrifices the Spartans undertook in the preparation for war (12.7; 13.2–5, 8), and, at the same time, underscores the strange absence of any explicit consideration, let alone praise, of piety in his account of Spartan virtue.[100]

In pointing to these difficulties regarding the Lycurgan regime, Xenophon gives his readers warrant to wonder about the extent to which Lycurgus's laws were able to transform the Spartans (see, e.g., 5.2; cf. 1.7–9), or whether there were necessary limits to what could be accomplished by law and the Lycurgan education. By giving us a picture of the Spartans as Lycurgus first found them, in fact, Xenophon underscores the gluttony and drunkenness — "easy living" — in which they then indulged. He also points to the fact that such vices can generally be hidden from the public eye in the privacy of the household (5.2, 7). Seeking to instill continence with respect to the bodily appetites, Lycurgus brought eating and drinking "out into the open" into the common messes, and he contrived many obstacles to prevent the Spartans from overindulging the pleasures associated with food and wine (5.2–7). He made similar provisions with respect to money by freeing the Spartans from moneymaking and its attendant temptations, establishing the common use of private property, and making difficult the accumulation of wealth (chapters 6–7). Yet, given his actual starting point and the power of the desire for pleasure that even Lycurgus acknowledges, how successful could we reasonably expect even or especially his most radical provisions to be? For all of Lycurgus's efforts to tamp down the love of money, for example, the Spartans had to rely on spies and undertake searches of their fellow citizens' homes to root out the gold and silver hidden there (7.5–6; see also 2.7). And Xenophon indicates that, like the love of wealth, the love of pleasure was less tamed than it was satisfied behind closed doors (cf. 1.5 with 1.7–8; 3.1 with 3.4–5; 3.7; 6.2).

Such difficulties point to the resistance confronted by any law, let alone a regime as demanding as the one laid down by Lycurgus, that seeks to tame or manage the desires and passions. Certainly, the original circumstances themselves dictate to some degree the character and limits of the laws. But even if such a strict regime could be implemented in the beginning, could it truly endure over time, given the power of the desires and passions, always clamoring for satiation? In the first thirteen chapters of the treatise, Xenophon appears to speak indiscriminately of Spartan practices in the past and present tenses, as if the laws of Lycurgus continue as they were set down from the beginning, while those of other cities constantly change (cf., e.g., 1.3 and 1.10 with 1.4–9; 2.10 with 2.11; 3.1–4 with 3.5; 15.1). But then chapter 14 abruptly makes clear just how far the Spartans of the present day have deviated from the letter as well as the spirit of the Lycurgan laws. By considering the difficulties that have emerged in a rereading of the preceding chapters, we have warrant to raise the question of when precisely the Spartans began to do so. Given the Spartans' original condition and then their continued resistance to and even covert disobedience of the laws, we may begin to wonder whether they were ever so perfectly formed in virtue as to constitute a peak. If we are so immodest as to look behind Sparta's closed doors, we become hard pressed to defend the regime laid down by Lycurgus as a stellar success in the education to virtue, at any point in time.

Chapter 14, then, is only one puzzle in a set of puzzles presented by Xenophon. Given the rhetorical power of the opening and closing statements of the treatise, and Xenophon's appeals to Lycurgus's wisdom and innovativeness, we might almost be forgiven for passing over those puzzles without a second thought. But we see that Xenophon actively encourages his readers to give the question of the regime more thought. As compared with the Lycurgan education, which cultivates virtue at the end of the lash with a view to securing the Spartans' unquestioning obedience to the laws,[101] Xenophon encourages his readers to weigh their doubts about what appears or is said to be true, take the measure of highly rhetorical claims or arguments from authority, supply for themselves what is left unstated, and raise the necessary questions and objections. With his praise and not his criticisms of Sparta at the forefront, it is true, Xenophon writes with a certain reserve. But not least in the face of the power and renown of Sparta, if not for other and higher reasons, such reserve is demanded of those who would act and speak judiciously in political life, as well as write well about it.

In this light, we begin to see how Xenophon offers an education not simply in the art of reading, but also in political wisdom or prudence. One final example of Xenophon's artfulness in this regard may suffice to indicate how deeply his critique of Sparta goes and with what care he presents it: his treatment of the relation between the Lycurgan laws and the happiness of the Spartans and of their *patris*—the proposition with which he opens the work and to which he returns in chapter 9. In returning to this proposition, Xenophon remarks that Lycurgus is worthy of admiration for his success in making "a noble death preferred to a shameful life" in Sparta, a feat the lawgiver accomplishes by "plainly prepar[ing] happiness for the good [courageous], on the one hand, and unhappiness for the bad [cowards], on the other hand" (9.1, 3). The context of Xenophon's return to the question of happiness is thus the virtue that may be said to constitute a peak of the Spartan education: *andreia*, "manliness" or courage in war.[102] He then proceeds to offer a stark enumeration of the penalties Lycurgus laid down for the one who proves cowardly in battle: forms of shunning, including exclusion from the common messes; public marks of disgrace, some of which extend to the coward's female relations; the absence of a wife at his own hearth, as well as the penalty for remaining a bachelor; and even "lashes from his betters" should he try to claim the privileges of a courageous man. So severe is the disgrace suffered by cowards that Xenophon ends chapter 9 by saying: "So indeed, given the sort of dishonor laid on those who are cowards, I in no way wonder that death is preferred there instead of a life thus dishonored and disgraced" (9.6). Upon consideration of Lycurgus's various provisions in this regard, we can surely see how the lawgiver prepared unhappiness for cowards or "the bad." But when it comes to the happiness of "the good"—those who risk death in defense of Sparta—Xenophon maintains an audible silence.

Now, it might be argued that the other side of the penalties enumerated in chapter 9 are the goods that the Spartans share as a community (*koinonia*)—a possibility that Xenophon himself seems to invoke at the beginning of chapter 11 in speaking of their "common goods in both peace and war" (11.1). A review of the treatise suggests that these goods include their common messes, the first aspect of the Spartan mode of life that Xenophon highlights (5.1, 5–6; see also 3.5), as well as other activities that he mentions in passing, such as their gymnastic contests, hunting, and choruses (1.4; 4.1, 7–8; 9.3–5). In seeking to make Sparta a unified whole, moreover, Lycurgus "wished to arrange it such that citizens should enjoy some good from one another, while in no way doing harm" (6.1). He thus made provision not only for the common use of private property, but also for the Spartans' common rule over one another's children and household slaves (6.1–3)—under certain circumstances, even wives fall into the category of common goods, if they have the potential to produce robust offspring with men other than their husbands (see again 1.7–9). In freeing up the Spartans from the work of moneymaking, in favor of their common defense of the freedom of the city, he also wished to reduce the usefulness and divisiveness of a key instrument in the pleasant or easy living associated with private households (7.3). The Spartans' communal mode of life may require that they forgo the private pleasures that money makes available, but it replaces these pleasures with the benefits associated with the freedom, power, and renown of their city (7.2; 1.1; 10.4–7), with the comradeship forged by war, and with their communal sacrifices (11.1, 7–8; 12.5–7; 13.1).

Even as Xenophon underscores the harsher aspects of the Spartan regime, then, he gives us enough to stitch together a picture of the common way of life of the Spartans. Instrumental to this life are the very virtues to which Xenophon draws our attention, Spartan modesty and continence, and at its peak, Spartan courage and lawfulness. If the former virtues make their common life possible; the latter complete the "whole of political virtue" that is the distinctive happiness of the Spartans.

Yet, if this argument is true, then all the more remarkable are the myriad ways in which the Spartans, from the beginning, resist or subvert the very laws that are said to make them happy (see again 1.2). Indeed, as we have seen, immediately following Xenophon's praise of Lycurgus's wisdom in setting down these laws, he begins to call this wisdom into doubt by exposing the pitfalls of Lycurgus's efforts to manipulate erotic desire with a view to producing robust offspring for the city—the greatest work for a free woman (1.4). Xenophon is surprisingly frank, in fact, about Lycurgus's failures in controlling this desire and other aspects of the Spartan household: the lawgiver is forced to make "many concessions" to both Spartan women and men, particularly with a view to erotic and family matters (1.7–9). In then underscoring the markedly punitive and morally ambiguous character of the education of the children and youth, Xenophon also makes increasingly clear that this education aims to prepare the Spartan young not for a life of communal peace and happiness, but for war. When he treats in particular the education of the young men (*hēbontes*)—about whom Lycurgus was the "most serious" because they would have "the greatest influence on the city's good" (4.1)—Xenophon goes out of his way to emphasize the rivalry that Lycurgus intentionally introduced into this education (4.2–6). To be sure, this rivalry is "dearest to the gods and most befitting a citizen" (4.5), for it is concerned with "manly goodness" (*andragathia*) and is fueled by a "love of victory" and ambition for the honors that are customarily deemed noble (4.1, 4). Yet, however instrumental it may be in the training for war—when giving aid to the city is most necessary and serious—such rivalry far from cultivates peaceful communal life. To the contrary, it arouses the Spartans' jealous regard of one another's honors and fuels factions based on differences of privilege (4.4–5); it also necessitates the constant vigilance of the ephors and other rulers lest the young men visit violence on one another or their fellow citizens and, as a result of their anger, undercut the rule of law and the unity of the city (4.6).

What of the peaceful practices by which Lycurgus aimed at making the city ever more communal by bringing out into the public those activities, such as eating and drinking, that are ordinarily reserved for the household? Even regarding the adults, whose education to virtue should make them such as to cherish the happiness associated with a life of virtue, Xenophon emphasizes that in doing everything in his power to make normally private practices as wholly public as possible, Lycurgus acted for reasons other than the goods or the virtues of a common way of life. Rather, in setting down the arrangements he did, he believed that "his commands would be least transgressed" (5.2). That they are nonetheless still transgressed is indicated both by the draconian measures that Lycurgus puts in place to enforce correct public speech and conduct and by his own acknowledgment, noted early in the treatise, that the household and its property remain a central concern of the Spartans (2.10).

This difficulty is connected with a fact that also becomes clear as the treatise proceeds: Lycurgus is able to blunt the influence of wealth in the regime, but in no way to eliminate it. In the end, Xenophon's description of Lycurgus's provisions regarding common property and money concludes with a rhetorical question: "Why would anyone, then, be serious about moneymaking in a place where its acquisition brings more pains than its use yields good cheer? (7.6; cf. 9.6). With but a brief backward glance, we see that he has just answered his own question. Apparently *some* Spartans are still serious about moneymaking, given the need to institute searches for gold and silver, not to mention the reliance on household spies (7.5–6). A reader may even wonder about the measures that the "strongest" in the city may have taken to protect or leverage their wealth in the beginning: the account of their participation in establishing the Spartan regime follows directly on the heels of the discussion of money, and Xenophon indicates in several places that there remain differences of wealth even among the *homoioi* or peers (2.9; 5.3; 6.3, 5; 10.7; 15.8).

Just how unified a city is Sparta, then, or to what degree is it held together by the devices Lycurgus and the strongest citizens put in place to ensure obedience to the laws and to the rulers? If we reflect on the details of Xenophon's account of the Spartan education and mode of life—especially regarding the desires and passions that this education aims either to manipulate or to tame, and the powerful resistance it confronts—we cannot be wholly surprised by his description of the tyrannical character of the office of the ephorate or the belief of the people who helped Lycurgus establish it, that "so much greater the power that the ruling office possesses, so much the more . . . will it also terrify the citizens into submission" (8.3; see also 8.4). In this condition, the Spartans are not much different than their Helots, the class of Spartan slaves about whom Xenophon is notably silent.[103] Leaving little to the voluntary or willing pursuit of virtue, which distinguishes only a few people (10.4), Lycurgus seeks to ensure what he and the strongest men of Sparta considered to be "the greatest good in the city and in the army as well as in the household": obedience not only to the laws but most especially to the rulers (8.3, 1). For all of Lycurgus's attention to education, then, Spartan adults prove to resemble their children, under the constant vigilance of the ephors and subjection to their rulers. As Xenophon remarks in his discussion of the children, "Nothing makes either men or children so modest as rulers do" (2.10).

When we come to the final chapter of the first part of the treatise, chapter 10, we are thus prepared to grasp more fully the substance and significance of the second of Lycurgus's accomplishments that Xenophon calls "worthy of admiration": that he "compelled everyone in Sparta to exercise all the virtues in public," making "the practice of nobility and goodness a public affair" and "the exercise of the whole of political virtue" "an irresistible necessity" (10.4, 7). As Xenophon makes clear in this chapter, "the whole of political virtue" and "nobility and goodness" (*kalokagathia*)—he uses here and only here the Greek term for "gentlemanliness"—are equated in Lycurgus's regime with obedience to the "customary laws" (10.7). That the sum of Spartan virtue should finally be so characterized makes sense of the fact that this chapter begins from a consideration of the *gerousia*. The *gerousia* is the council of Spartan elders who represent the traditional order and who are rewarded near the end of their lives *for* their nobility and goodness: for their adherence to the laws. They are also awarded *with* the power to judge capital crimes, even over those who are in "the full vigor" of "their prime" (10.2; cf. 8.4). Tradition in Sparta, in other words, rules with an iron fist.

Xenophon ends the tenth chapter by underscoring the "ancient" lineage of the laws, "for Lycurgus is said to have been born at the time of the *Heracleidai*." But he then remarks on their novelty at present. Despite their ancient lineage, that is, the practices that constitute

Lycurgus's regime remain a novelty to most other human beings, and "the most wonderful thing of all is that while everyone praises the practices of the Spartans, not a single city is willing to imitate them" (10.8). Yet, not only has Xenophon cast doubt on what "is said" about Lycurgus; he also has shown that the Spartans themselves are not particularly enamored of their own ancient tradition. As the resistance and covert disobedience of the Spartans themselves indicate, the other cities are not willing to imitate the laws of Lycurgus, because they grate so harshly against the desire for pleasure and the love of wealth that is prevalent and powerful among human beings.

Still, when Lycurgus asks the god "whether it would be more desirable and better for Sparta to obey the laws he set down," the god replies "that it would be better in every way" (8.5). Even if the aim of the laws is not a life of communal peace and happiness for the Spartans, perhaps they nonetheless achieve the "outstanding happiness" of the *patris*: the unity of the city and its power and renown especially on the battlefield (see again 1.2). In the words of the god, are the laws not "better in every way" in this sense for Sparta? The very order of Xenophon's discussion underscores what becomes increasingly clear in his treatment of the Spartan education and mode of life, that the Lycurgan regime seeks to ensure the obedience of its citizens and the success of the city in war. So it is that the first ten chapters are followed directly by his account of Lycurgus's provisions for the army on campaign: its abundant supplies and outfitting of its soldiers; its phalanx tactics; and the arrangements of its encampment (chapters 11–12). Not the shared goods of peace, let alone the playful activities of leisure, such as communal feasts and choruses, but civic unity and success in war—these are the aims of the Lycurgan regime. Indeed, the final of only three mentions of leisure (*scholē*) in Xenophon's treatise occurs in its account of the king on campaign, who, together with his polemarchs, requires leisure "to take care of the affairs of war" (13.1; cf. *Symposium* 1.1).[104]

Soldier though he was, however, Xenophon himself proves less interested in or impressed by Lycurgan military arrangements than we might expect. He takes them up as something of an afterthought, acknowledging that someone in his audience may wish "to observe also what Lycurgus contrived for the army, better than others did"

(11.1), and he suggests at a certain point that, contrary to common belief, Spartan tactics are "easy to learn" (11.6).[105] Yet Xenophon does call attention to and is impressed by the provisions Lycurgus laid down regarding the sacrifices. After he has completed his review of the mundane details of the army on campaign and in camp, Xenophon begins again, as it were, to describe in some detail "how the king is sent forth to war together with the army" (13.1). For the king performs the *diabateria*, or border-crossing sacrifices, the fire from which leads the army on its way and is never extinguished (13.2–3). In clear sight of the enemy, moreover, he also performs the sacrifices before battles, to the music of the aulos players and with the troops standing at the ready, adorned with garlands and with weapons polished (13.3–4). Whenever the king sacrifices, he does so while it is still dark, for he aims to attract "the favorable notice of the god" (13.3). Xenophon insists that in seeing the manner in which the king undertakes these sacrifices and sends the army to its battle stations, "you would regard the others to be mere improvisers [or bunglers] when it comes to military affairs, and the Lacedaemonians alone the real craftsmen in the affairs of war" (13.5; see also 13.8–9). It is no small thing, then, that the king should keep his diviners close as he marches into battle (13.7). The Spartans may choose death on the battlefield in preference to a painful life of reproach, but if the sacrifices are right, they can fight with some confidence or hope in the god's favor. In this sense, their obedience to the laws may be more willing than coerced (8.3; cf. again 8.5).

Yet, by Xenophon's own account, such confidence or hope—such manner of piety—cannot compensate for the defects of the Lycurgan education to virtue. Given what we have seen of these defects, the specific character of the Spartans' condition at present ceases to be surprising: the Spartans are not willing to stay at home, content with moderate means; they actively seek out the corruption and flatteries that come with foreign governorships; they show off the gold and silver they once feared to be seen to possess; and they rule without regard to justice (14.2–6). As Xenophon pointedly concludes, "They are manifestly obeying neither the god nor the laws of Lycurgus" (14.7). The good or happiness promised by obedience to the laws is clearly not reward enough for the other losses such obedience entails, however good this lawfulness may be for the city as a whole.

Immediately following his sharp criticism of the Spartans, Xenophon opens chapter 15 of the treatise by speaking of the "compacts" Lycurgus set down for the king in relation to the city and by remarking that only the office of the kingship "continues just as it was established in the beginning" (15.1). Obscuring the fact that Sparta was not a simple monarchy but a diarchy—and so obscuring the rivalry inherent in the office itself—Xenophon then tells us of the oaths exchanged between the city and the king: "The oath for the king is that he will reign in accordance with the established laws of the city; for the city, that if he keeps his oath, it will maintain the kingship undisturbed" (15.7). Yet, as chapter 14 clearly acknowledges, the ancestral laws are not now obeyed (15.1; see also 15.6–7), and, as the criticisms of the earlier chapters indicate, the established laws of the city always reflected in deed the rule of the strongest, in the beginning and over time. On what basis and by what rightful authority, then, does the kingship endure? Given what Xenophon has indicated in his account of the regime, it is not hard to see that the power of the ephors is key in maintaining the office of the king both at present and at the beginning.[106] The kingship, "just as it was established in the beginning," as much manifests the poor condition of Sparta as do the actions of the present-day Spartans.[107] In this sense, then, the discussion of the king or kings at home in chapter 15 follows naturally from the concerns of chapter 14.

As many commentators have noted, the treatise concludes on a solemn note, with a "solemn spondaic hexameter":[108] "Yet through the honors given to the king who has met his end, the laws of Lycurgus wish to make clear that it is not as human beings, but as heroes that they honor the kings of the Lacedaemonians" (15.9). These honors, however, cover over the decidedly unheroic—all too human—regime of the Spartans. That Xenophon should dress up the Spartans in such solemn clothing, in a treatise in which there proves to be more than a little humor at their expense, is most obviously connected with what he first points to in the prologue: Sparta's power and renown, particularly as it shines on the battlefield. And yet, it would seem, neither this education nor the Spartan mode of life achieves the happiness of the Spartans themselves or even, in the end, the outstanding happiness of their *patris*.

The decline of Sparta's power and renown occurs after the Peloponnesian War, when its battlefield prowess becomes markedly less impressive; the Spartans ultimately suffer humiliating defeats at the battles of Leuctra and Mantinea, and even an invasion of Laconia itself (see especially *Hellenica* 6.4.3–16; 7.5.18–24; 6.4.25–28). After prevailing over Athens in the Peloponnesian War, Sparta attempts to expand her rule, and, as Xenophon notes, the Spartans become more and more exposed to foreign ways (14.4). One might thus blame their decline on the introduction of ways alien to Sparta's ancestral regime. But Xenophon's account of that regime shows that the Lycurgan education is defective from the beginning in forming or reforming the desires and passions of the Spartans. In fact, in orienting this education toward success in war, the Spartan regime not only inadequately habituates the desires and passions; in some cases, it also perverts or magnifies them, by manipulating erotic desire with a view to the needs of the city, introducing rivalry into the relations among both the young and the old, and driving into hidden spaces the desire for pleasure and love of lucre. Even regarding the peak of Spartan virtue in manly courage, Xenophon indicates that the Spartans naturally fear death as much as the next mortal does: they typically seek safety when it is to be had, and they are happy to put others—that is, non-Spartans—out in front when it comes to forward action on the battlefield (cf. 12.2–4 with *Cyropaedia* 4.2.1). It would also appear that since they are now so "*manifestly* obeying neither the god nor the laws of Lycurgus," the present-day Spartans can hardly enter into battle with the requisite confidence or hope regarding the god's favor. With that hope taken from them, they must be moved to risk death on the city's behalf only for fear of a greater evil—a powerful motive but not the highest or noblest one.

In following Xenophon's reflections on the Spartan regime, then, a reader comes to see that the defects of this regime, so evident in its present condition, are inherent in its very constitution. Hence, it is all the more curious that Xenophon should couch his treatment of these defects between the praise of the prologue and the solemnity of the ending. The care that Xenophon takes in this regard could well be traced to the debt of gratitude he owed to the Spartans and to King Agesilaus in particular. Surely it belongs to a person of refinement not to show open disrespect to those to whom he owes such a debt, and in other works, Xenophon emphasizes the importance of gratitude in the education to virtue and as a sign of lawfulness.[109] Yet in this treatise, he indicates other reasons why he writes in such a way that his criticisms of the Spartan regime should come fully to light only with the active participation and independent thought of his reader.[110] Among these reasons is the fact that although the power of Sparta is obviously on the wane, praise of its ancestral laws lives on: even though not a single city is willing to imitate the practices of the Spartans, nevertheless "everyone" praises them. Xenophon may well be exaggerating the extent of this praise for effect—he himself did not wholeheartedly belong to the Spartan fan club. But he certainly knew and knew of many a powerful person who did belong, including his fellow "Socratic," Critias.

Leader of the Thirty Tyrants, and an especially brutal one, Critias wrote two treatises in praise of Sparta, one in verse and one in prose. Only fragments of these writings survive, but enough to see that Critias deserved to be called a Laconophile.[111] The difference between Critias and Xenophon, in this as well as other respects, may be most plainly seen in their choice of lives: when given a chance, in the lawlessness of postwar Athens, Critias sought to impose on his fellow citizens a reign of terror so brutal that Xenophon himself described the Thirty as acting like "tyrants without fear" (*Hellenica* 2.4.1). By comparison, while Xenophon could hardly be called an Athenian patriot, neither did he long to rule over his fellow citizens, even when they had forcibly exiled him (cf. *Hellenica* 2.3.15). If we judge by his actions, that is, he ultimately preferred a life removed from politics, making use of the leisure afforded by his exile to think and to write.

From his reflections in the *Anabasis*, we see that the reasons for this choice are complicated, as Xenophon was not without political ambition himself (see especially *Anabasis* 3.1.4–10; 6.1.20–21). Yet among these reasons is one that may finally undergird the politic reserve with which he writes the *Regime of the Lacedaemonians*. For he makes clear in this treatise that Sparta represents virtue understood as obedience to law, or political virtue simply (see again 10.4–7). Even though there is much to criticize in the real Spartan regime, Xenophon indicates in this and other writings that we should hesitate to undermine justice understood as lawful obedience and dedication to the *patris*.[112] The indication of this treatise is that the willing obedience of citizens is best and most nobly secured not by fear of pain or punishment, but by reverence for the laws and for the city understood as holy.[113] Is it, then, the possibility, and even nobility, of such reverence that Xenophon was unwilling to disturb by too plain a critique of the city that was held most to exemplify it?

This reflection is admittedly speculative, and much careful reading of Xenophon's corpus would be required to substantiate it.[114] Taken on its own terms, however, the treatise shows that Xenophon reflected on fundamental problems of political life, especially the limits of law and political virtue in containing human desire and passion, the ever-present problem of war in human affairs, and the powerful fear that is natural to all human beings, the fear of death. These are necessities with which every human life must contend, including the one that Xenophon himself finally chose—a life close to, if not in simple imitation of, the life led by his admired teacher. While the education in reading and thinking that Xenophon provides is clearly valuable to political virtue and the community dependent on it, this education proves crucial for the question that Xenophon raises in the prologue with respect to Lycurgus's wisdom and returns to in chapter 9: the question of happiness. Not least for the defects in Lycurgus's wisdom that come to light in this treatise, Xenophon turns not to the lawgiver regarding the question of happiness but to Socrates, whose life was such that, as we see in the works that portray it, Xenophon was more than once moved to call him "blessed" (*Memorabilia* 1.6.14; *Apologia Socratis* 34).

Xenophon's admired teacher makes only two appearances in his non-Socratic works. In the *Hellenica*, Xenophon draws attention to Socrates' actions as a member of the Prytany when the Athenians are angrily calling for the mass prosecution of the generals involved in the battle of Arginousai for failing to rescue all the survivors or retrieve the dead. Much to the Athenians' displeasure, Socrates insists that they abide by the law they had set down to try individuals separately—the law they now wish to break (*Hellenica* 1.7.15). In the *Anabasis*, Socrates advises a young Xenophon to ask the oracle at Delphi whether he should undertake the expedition with Cyrus (*Anabasis* 3.1.5–7). In neither case is Socrates very successful: the Athenians do prosecute and execute the generals en masse, though they feel remorse in the aftermath of their unlawful deed (*Hellenica*

1.7.35). Xenophon does go to Delphi, but he asks a somewhat different question of the oracle than his teacher had intended him to ask (*Anabasis* 3.1.7). Still, perhaps the most important difference between the Athenians and Xenophon in their relation to Socrates is the following: in the former case, the Athenians eventually saw to Socrates' own prosecution and execution; in the latter, a grateful student left behind recollections of his teacher that have educated generations of other grateful students, from then until now.

CHAPTER 4
Regime of the Athenians

TRANSLATED BY GREGORY A. McBRAYER

∼ CHAPTER 1 ∼

(1) But concerning the regime of the Athenians,[1] that they chose this character of regime I do not praise, for the following reason: in choosing these things, they chose to make the vulgar better than the worthy.[2] That, then, is why I do not praise. Since, however, their opinion favored things in this way, I will show that they preserve their regime well and accomplish other things by which they seem to err in the eyes of the other Greeks.

(2) First, then, I will say this: that both the poor and the people[3] there justly have more than the well-born and the wealthy—and for this reason, that it is the people who row the ships and bestow power on the city, along with the pilots and the boatswains and the ensigns[4] and the lookouts and shipbuilders—it is these who bestow power on the city, much more than do the hoplites[5] and the well-born and the worthy. So since this is how things are, it seems to be just for everyone to participate in the offices, both those drawn by lot and those elected by vote, and to allow any citizen who wishes, to speak.

(3) Next, as for those offices that bring safety to the whole people, when they are in the hands of the worthy—and bring danger when in the hands of the unworthy—the people do not request to participate in any of these offices; they do not suppose that they should participate by lot in the offices of general or cavalry commander: for the people recognize that it benefits them more not to hold these

offices, and instead to let the most capable hold them. On the other hand, as many offices as are for pay, or as benefit one's household, these the people do seek to hold.

(4) Next, as to what some wonder at, that everywhere they assign more to the vulgar and to the poor and to the democrats[6] than to the worthy; it is in this very thing that they will manifestly be seen to be preserving the democracy. For when the poor and the commoners and the inferior fare well and become numerous, they increase the democracy. But if the wealthy and the worthy fare well, the democrats establish a strong opposition for themselves. (5) And everywhere on earth, that which is best is opposed to democracy. For among the best persons there is the least licentiousness and injustice, and the greatest exactitude in worthy things; but among the people, there is the greatest lack of learning, lack of order, and vulgarity.[7] For poverty draws them more toward shameful things, as do lack of education and that ignorance that stems, for some human beings, from want of money.

(6) But someone might say that they should not let everyone speak one after another, and deliberate,[8] but the cleverest and best men.[9] But even in this matter they deliberated excellently, in allowing even the vulgar to speak. For if the worthy were to speak and deliberate, it would be good for them and those like them, but it would not be good for the democrats. But as things stand, anyone desiring to speak, however vulgar a human being, stands up and discovers the good both for himself and for those like him. (7) Someone might say, "What good, then, could such a human being recognize, either for himself or for the people?" But they recognize that this fellow's lack of learning, and baseness, and goodwill are more profitable than the virtue, and wisdom, and ill will of a worthy one.

(8) So, a city would not be the best from such practices; but democracy would be kept especially safe in this way. For the people do not want to be enslaved in a city with good laws, but to be free and to rule, and care little if the city has bad laws.[10] For from what you believe[11] to be not ruled by good laws, the people itself is strong and free. (9) But if you seek good, lawful order, you will first see the cleverest establishing laws for themselves. Next, the worthy will punish the vulgar, and the worthy will deliberate about the city, and they will not allow crazy human beings to deliberate or to speak or

to serve in the Assembly. Now from these good things, the people would fall very quickly into slavery.

(10) Again, among the slaves and the resident aliens, there is very great licentiousness in Athens, and neither are blows possible there, nor will a slave make way for you. Why this is characteristic of that country, I will tell you. If the law were that a slave—or a resident alien or a freedman—could be struck by one who is free, one would frequently hit an Athenian, supposing him a slave. For the people there are dressed no better than the slaves and the resident aliens, nor do they have any better looks. (11) And if someone is amazed at this too, that they let the slaves enjoy luxuries there and that some lead their daily lives in magnificent fashion, they would come to sight as doing even this with judgment. For wherever there is a naval power, it is necessary, out of compelling need for money, to be slaves to the slaves,[12] so that we might take portions from what they make, and even to let them go about freely. And where there are wealthy slaves, it is no longer profitable there for my slave to fear you—but in Lacedaemonia, my slave would fear you—but if your slave fears me, he will risk giving up his money so as not to have to risk what concerns himself. (12) This, then, is why we have made equality between the slaves and the free—and between the resident aliens and the townsmen, since the city needs resident aliens on account of the multitude of arts and on account of the navy; so this is why we fittingly made equality for the resident aliens.

(13) The people have dismissed those engaged in gymnastics and those who practice music, regarding this not to be noble, since they know it is impossible for the people to practice these things. Again, as regards equipping choruses, managing gymnasia, and fitting out triremes, they know that the wealthy equip the choruses, while the people have choruses equipped, and that the wealthy manage gymnasia and outfit triremes, while the people have outfitted triremes and managed gymnasia. At any rate, the people think they deserve to take money for singing and racing and dancing and sailing in ships, so that they might acquire some and the wealthy become poorer. And in the courts, they do not care more about the just than their own advantage.

(14) And concerning allies, when they sail to them they bring slanderous charges against the worthy, it seems, and hate them, know-

ing that it is necessary for the ruler to be hated by the ruled, and if the wealthy and the worthy are strong in the cities, the rule of the people in Athens will be for a very short time. This is why they dishonor the worthy, take away their money, drive them out, and kill them, but augment the vulgar. But the worthy Athenians keep the worthy in the allied cities safe, knowing that it is always good for them to keep the best in these cities safe.

(15) But someone might say that it would be a strength of Athens, if its allies were able to contribute money. But, to the democrats, it seems to be a greater good for each individual Athenian to have the money of the allies, and for the allies to have only enough to live on, and to work so that they are unable to plot.

(16) And the Athenian people seem to have deliberated badly in this matter, namely, that they compel their allies to sail to Athens for trials. But in response, they count how much good this does for the people of Athens. In the first place, they receive wages from the court deposits[13] throughout the year. Next, they manage their allied cities while sitting at home, without setting out in ships; and, in courtrooms, they save those among the people and destroy the opposite types. But if each [of the allied cities] had its own domestic courts, they, because they are hostile to the Athenians, would destroy those among them who are most friendly to the Athenian people.

(17) In addition to these things, the people of Athens also profit in the following ways from their allies' trials being held in Athens. First, the 1 percent duty in the Piraeus brings in more for the city. (18) Next, if someone has lodging to offer, he fares better—as does someone who has a pair of yoked beasts or a slave[14] for hire. Next, the heralds fare better because of the allies' visits. And in addition to these things, if the allies did not come to court, they would honor only the Athenians who sail to them—the generals, the trierarchs,[15] and the ambassadors. But now each one of the allies is compelled to flatter the people of Athens, because he knows that if one goes to Athens, paying a penalty and punishing is necessarily in the hands of none other than the people, which is the law in Athens. And he is compelled to beg in the courtrooms, and to grasp the hand of the ones entering. This, then, is how the allies have been established more as slaves of the Athenian people.

(19) In addition to these things, on account of their possessions abroad, and on account of the offices they hold abroad, they are, without noticing it, learning to row with oars—both they and their followers. For a human being who frequently sails necessarily takes up an oar—both he himself and his domestic servant—and learns the terms associated with the naval art. (20) They also become good pilots both through experience with voyages and through practice. Some practice piloting small vessels, others merchant ships, and others were subsequently stationed in triremes. And the many are able to row as soon as they board a ship, because they have been preparing for it for their whole lives.

∼ CHAPTER 2 ∼

(1) And their hoplite force, which least of all seems to be in good condition in Athens, has been established in this way: they consider theirs to be weaker even though more numerous than their enemies, but stronger on land than their allies who pay tribute. And they believe that their hoplite force suffices, if it is stronger than their allies.

(2) Additionally, by chance something like the following has been established for them: for those who are ruled on land, it is possible to come together, from small cities, and to do battle assembled; but for those who are ruled by the sea, as many as are islanders, it is not possible for their cities to unite in the same place. For the sea is between them, and their superiors are masters of the sea. And even if it were possible for the islanders to come together in the same place on one island unnoticed, they would die of hunger. (3) And as many cities as are ruled by the Athenians on the mainland, the large ones are ruled by fear, and the small ones very much by need. For there is no city that does not need to import or export something. And these will not be possible for [a city] unless it subordinates itself to the rulers of the sea. (4) Next, for the rulers of the sea it is possible to do the things that the rulers of the land do on occasion—to lay waste the land of those who are stronger. For it is possible for them to sail to where there are either no enemies or where there are few, and if

the enemy approaches, they can embark and sail away. And the one who does this is at less of a loss than the one who comes to the rescue with infantry. (5) Next, for the rulers by sea it is also possible to sail away from their home on however great a voyage you wish, but for those who rule by land it is not possible to leave their home for a journey of many days. For marches are slow, and it is not possible, going by foot, to have provisions for a long period of time. And it is necessary for the one going by foot to go through friendly territory, or to be victorious battling. But for the one sailing it is possible to disembark where he is stronger and wherever he is not stronger, he is able not to disembark, but sail along until he comes to friendly territory or someone weaker than he is. (6) Next, as regards diseases on crops that come from Zeus, those who are strongest on the land bear them with difficulty, but those who are strongest on the sea bear them easily. For the entire earth is not sick at the same time; so food can come to the rulers of the sea from land that is flourishing.

(7) And if smaller matters should also be recalled, on account of the rule over the sea, they in the first place by mingling with others have discovered various types of luxuries. So whenever there is something pleasant in Sicily or in Italy or in Cyprus or in Egypt, or in Lydia, or in the Pontus, or in the Peloponnesus, or in some other place, all these things can be collected in a single place on account of the ruler over the sea. (8) Next, since they hear every language, they pick for themselves this from one language and that from another. And the other Greeks rather use their own peculiar language and way of life and manner of dress, but the Athenians have mixed theirs from all the Greeks and barbarians.

(9) And, with respect to sacrifices, temples, festivals, and sacred spaces, since the people know that it is impossible for each poor person to sacrifice and to hold feasts and to establish temples and to inhabit a beautiful and great city, they have discovered a way for these things to exist. The city sacrifices many victims at the public expense. And it is the people who are feasted, dividing by lot the sacrificial victims. (10) And some of the wealthy have their own gymnasia and baths and dressing rooms, but the people itself builds for itself many wrestling schools, dressing rooms, and baths of its own. And the mob enjoys these things more than the few and the happy do.

(11) And they are the only ones among the Greeks and the barbarians able to possess wealth. For if some city is rich in wood that is used for shipbuilding, where will they dispose of it if they do not persuade the ruler of the sea? And what if some city is rich in iron or copper or flax, where will they dispose of it if they do not persuade the ruler of the sea? In fact my ships are made from these very things; wood from one place, iron from another, copper from another, flax from another, and wax from another. (12) In addition to these things, our rivals, whoever they are, will not allow export except where they proclaim control of the sea. And I, by doing nothing, have all these things from the land as a result of the sea, but no other city has two of them—there is not wood and flax in the same place, but wherever there is an abundance of flax, the land is flat and woodless. Nor is there copper and iron from the same city, or any two or three of the other things in one city, but one thing is found in one city, and another is found in another.

(13) And moreover, in addition to these things, near every part of the mainland there is either a tract of land jutting out, or an island nearby, or some strait; consequently, the rulers of the sea can anchor there and pillage those inhabiting the mainland. (14) But they are deficient in one regard. For if the Athenians were masters of the sea who inhabited an island, they could undertake to do evil to others, if they wished, and suffer nothing, as long as they ruled the sea, nor would they have their land laid to waste nor would they expect enemies to come. But now the farmers and the wealthy Athenians rather ingratiate themselves with their enemies, but the people, since they know well that nothing of theirs will be burned or laid waste, live without fear and do not ingratiate themselves with the enemies. (15) In addition to these things, they would have escaped also another fear if they inhabited an island: their city would never be betrayed by a few, nor would the gates be opened, nor would enemies burst in on them.[16] For how would these things come about if they inhabited an island? Nor would any factions form among the people, if they inhabited an island. For now if there is factious strife, those forming the faction put their hope in bringing the enemies in by land. But if they inhabited an island, they would bear even this without fear. (16) Since, then, they did not happen to inhabit an island from the beginning, these are the things they now do: they put away all of their

substance[17] in their islands, trusting in the rule over the sea, and they allow the Attic land to be laid to waste, recognizing that if they have pity for it, they will be deprived of other, greater goods.

(17) And moreover, it is necessary for the oligarchic cities to maintain their alliances and oaths. And if they do not abide by their treaties, or if any injustice is done, the names of the few who made the treaty are there. But when the people make some sort of treaty, it is possible for anyone to place the blame on the one who spoke [on behalf of the treaty] and brought it to a vote, and to deny his own responsibility to others [saying], "I was not present and I was not in favor" —which they learned about only when it was being agreed upon by the entire people.[18] And if things do not seem best, they have discovered ten thousand excuses not to do whatever they do not want to do. And if some evil arises from what the people have deliberated, the people blame a few human beings who are opposed to them for corrupting them, but if it is something good for them, they take the credit themselves.

(18) And they do not allow making comedies about the people or speaking badly about them, so that they do not hear themselves spoken about badly. But if someone wants to ridicule an individual, they encourage him, knowing full well that the one ridiculed in a comedy will not, for the most part, be from among the people or the multitude, but he will be wealthy or well-born or powerful; only a few of the poor and democratic will be ridiculed in a comedy, and not these, except if they are busybodies and seek to do better than the people in some way. So they are not vexed by these types being ridiculed in comedies.

(19) I, for my part, declare that the people of Athens recognize which citizens are worthy and which ones are vulgar. And recognizing the ones who are helpful and advantageous to them, they love them, even if they are vulgar, and they rather hate the worthy.[19] For they do not believe that the virtue of the latter is by nature for their good, but for their detriment. On the other side, there are some who, despite truly being of the people, are not democratic by nature.

(20) But with respect to the democracy, I excuse the people themselves. For it is pardonable for everyone to treat himself well. But whoever is not of the people but chooses to live in a democratic city rather than in an oligarchic one is preparing to do injustice and

recognizes that there is a greater possibility of escaping notice being bad in a democratic city than in an oligarchic one.

∾ CHAPTER 3 ∾

(1) And concerning the regime of the Athenians, I do not praise its character. But since in fact it seemed best to them to be ruled democratically, they seem to me to preserve their democracy well, employing its character in the way that I have shown.

Moreover, I see some who blame the Athenians for the following things: because sometimes it is not possible to conduct business with either the Council[20] or with the people, even for a human being who has sat and waited a year. (2) And this comes about in Athens for no other reason than that the volume of their affairs makes it so that they are unable to conduct business before having to send people away. For how could they be able? They for whom, in the first place, it is necessary to celebrate more festivals than any other of the Greek cities (and during these times it is even less possible to conduct the city's affairs)? Next, they decide more trials and indictments and public examinations of officials than all other human beings put together decide, and their Council deliberates often about war, and often about acquiring wealth, and often about establishing laws, and often concerning things that always come up in the city, and also often about affairs among their allies; and it receives tribute, and it takes care of the dockyards and temples. Is it any wonder, if, in undertaking so many affairs, they are not able to conduct business with all humans? (3) But some say, "If someone has money and goes to the Council or the people, he will conduct business." I would agree with them that much gets accomplished in Athens with money, and still more would get accomplished if even more people gave money. However, I know well that the city is not capable of accomplishing everything for those who need it, no matter how much gold and silver someone should give them.[21] (4) It is necessary to settle disputes also in these things: if someone does not equip a ship, or builds something on public land. In addition to these things, they settle disputes every year on who will be the chorus equippers in the

Dionysia, the Thargelia, the Panathenaia, the Promethia, and the He-
phaestia.[22] And four hundred trierarchs[23] are established each year,
and every year [the Athenians] have to settle disputes for those [tri-
erarchs] who want [to bring a dispute].[24] In addition to these things,
they have to audit offices and settle disputes on offices, and audit orphans, and establish guards for the prisons. (5) These are the things
that are done every year. Sometimes they have to settle disputes in
cases involving military service as well as any other unexpected unjust act that might happen, whether persons commit an unusual act
of insolence or commit impiety. There is still a lot that I am leaving
out. The greatest part has been spoken about, except for the assess-
ments of tribute. And this happens, for the most part, every four
years. Come, then, should it not be considered that they have to settle disputes in all these matters? So let someone say on what matters
they should not settle disputes there. (6) And further, if it should
be agreed that they have to settle disputes on all these matters, the
entire year is necessary. For now, even though they judge during the
entire year, they cannot undertake to stop those who commit injustice, on account of the number of human beings involved. (7) Come
then, someone will say that they do need to judge, but that fewer
persons should judge. But unless they create only a few courts, there
will necessarily be only a few persons in each courtroom. The result
will be that it will be both easier to intrigue with a few jurors and to
bribe them to judge much less justly. (8) In addition to these things,
it should also be considered that Athens has to lead festivals, during
which it is not possible to judge. And they lead twice as many festivals as the others. But I will assume that they have the same number
as the city who leads the fewest. Were things like this, I deny that it
would be possible for matters in Athens to be different from what
they are now, except that it would be possible to make a small addition or subtraction here and there. But it is not possible to make a
great change without taking something away from the democracy.
(9) It is possible to discover many ways for the regime to be better,
but it is not easy to discover satisfactorily how they could be governed better in a way that the democracy continues to exist—except,
as I just said, by making a small addition or subtraction.

   (10) And it seems to me that the Athenians do not deliberate correctly in that they join the inferior side in cities engaged in factional

conflict. But they do this advisedly. For if they joined the better side, they would be joining those who are not of the same judgment as they. For in no city is the best part well disposed toward the people, but the worst part in each city is well disposed toward the people. For like are well disposed to like. Because of these things, then, the Athenians choose those who are suitable for them. (11) And whenever they tried to join the best, it was not advantageous for them—in a short time the people were enslaved in Boeotia. And when they joined the best of the Milesians, in a short time they revolted and massacred the people. And then when they joined the Lacedaemonians against the Messenians, shortly after the Lacedaemonians subdued the Messenians they waged war against the Athenians.[25]

(12) Someone might then suspect that no one is unjustly dishonored in Athens. But I assert that there are some who have been unjustly dishonored—though only a few. But it would take not a few to attack the democracy in Athens; and, things being as they are, those human beings who have been justly dishonored do not take it to heart; only those who were dishonored unjustly do so. (13) How, then, could someone believe that the many are dishonored in Athens, where the people are the ones holding the offices? Not ruling justly or not saying the just things or not doing them—dishonor comes from these things in Athens. He who has calculated these matters should not expect any danger, from those who have been dishonored, to Athens.

An Introduction to the Regime of the Athenians

Gregory A. McBrayer

The *Regime of the Athenians* is worthy of study because it is the only sustained investigation into the virtues and vices of Athenian democracy that lays claim to being written by a student of Socrates. And although the secondary literature in political theory, for example, abounds with analysis of the political thought of Socrates and his students concerning Athenian democracy especially, the *Regime of the Athenians* has yet to receive serious treatment by historians of political thought or political theorists. The primary reason for this neglect is that the *Regime of the Athenians* is no longer thought to be the work of Xenophon, but is instead attributed either to Pseudo-Xenophon or to the "Old Oligarch," which amounts to anonymity. As a result, the majority of scholarship devoted to the *Regime of the Athenians* focuses on identifying the author of the work and its likely date of composition rather than investigating its political and philosophical content.[26] Moreover, as the epithet "Old Oligarch" suggests, the work admittedly evinces a clear oligarchic, or antidemocratic, prejudice. Therefore, it has been deemed to be the product of a lesser mind than Xenophon's. And yet, the arguments adduced in support of this denial of Xenophontic authorship, however, do not rise to the level of demonstration and are in fact questionable.[27]

The case against Xenophon's authorship rests on four contentions. First, Diogenes Laertius (2.57) reports that, according to Demetrius the Magnesian, a work called the *Regime of the Lacedaemonians and Athenians* is not by Xenophon. Diogenes thus has Demetrius refer by a single title to what has come down to us as two works. And while modern scholars mostly accept Demetrius's opinion, they gloss over the fact that they in effect reject his opinion as to there being a single work entitled the *Regime of the Lacedaemonians and Athenians*.[28] Moreover, Diogenes points to Demetrius as the exception to the rule; by singling Demetrius out, Diogenes implies that most ancient scholars accepted the *Regime of the Athenians* as Xenophon's.[29] Such was the consensus, so far as one can judge, from antiquity until the nineteenth century: the manuscript tradition attributes the *Regime of the Athenians* to Xenophon the Orator, and major thinkers such as David Hume and Montesquieu accept Xenophon's authorship of the work.[30]

Two other arguments against Xenophon's authorship are based on the work's date of composition and style.[31] The two grounds are interrelated. It is widely believed that the treatise could not be by Xenophon because its author refers to events that would have occurred before or during Xenophon's youth.[32] Yet scholars rightly admit that their attempts to date the work are "suggestions," "open to debate," and that "any attempts to speculate [precisely about the date] must be pure hypothesis."[33] Even if we grant that the work refers to events that occurred before Xenophon was an adult, this alone is insufficient for rejecting his authorship, since the dramatic date of his *Symposium,* for example, an event that Xenophon stresses he attended, is about 422, when Xenophon was about eight years old. It is possible, in other words, that such anachronisms are intentional. Xenophon certainly could have affected a voice from an earlier time; he could have, in other words, pretended to be someone other than who he was. In fact, Xenophon frequently plays with his own voice and authorship. In the *Hellenica* (3.1.2), Xenophon suppresses his authorship of the *Anabasis of Cyrus* and gives credit instead to one Themistogenes of Syracuse.[34] Yet Xenophon's authorship of the *Anabasis* is not seriously doubted. And in the *Anabasis*, scholars generally recognize that Theopompus (roughly "Godsend") is likely a character invented by Xenophon.[35] And in the *Education of Cyrus*, the character of Tigranes is generally taken to represent Xenophon himself.[36] If Xenophon is thus willing to put his own voice and opinions into the mouth of a minor or even invented character, it is plausible that he could do the reverse: play the part of someone with whose opinion he is not altogether in accord.

The *Regime of the Athenians* admittedly differs in style from the other writings we have of Xenophon. But Xenophon wrote in many different styles and genres, the full range of which is underappreciated. The *Education of Cyrus* is often likened to a novel, for example, and the *Hellenica* is a work of history. Xenophon also wrote dialogues, as well as treatises on skills befitting gentlemen. He wrote in the voice of a poet, a tyrant, a statesman, a gentleman, and Socrates. Moreover, Xenophon can even change his manner of writing within the same work. It is widely recognized,[37] for example, that Xenophon alters his style in the *Hellenica* at about 2.3.10, when the war ends.[38] He there changes his use of particles, and he begins to report sacrifices, something he had not done up to this point. As Vivienne Gray says, "Xenophon writes in so many different genres that require different styles that it is impossible to speak of any one style as characteristic."[39]

The remaining argument against Xenophon's authorship rests on interpretations of the work. The *Regime of the Athenians* has been rejected as Xenophon's because the content does not seem to fit with Xenophon's political thought generally, and in particular what he says elsewhere about democracy.[40] To question or rebut this argument compels another attempt at textual interpretation. And while I cannot claim to have demonstrated that the *Regime of the Athenians* was written by Xenophon, I have shown, I believe, that any argument against its authenticity must proceed through a careful analysis of its content, that the claim stands or falls by our interpretation of the work as a whole.

This essay, then, in contrast to the majority of the scholarly literature on the work, investigates the political and philosophical content of the *Regime of the Athenians* on the basis of the assumption that it was written by Xenophon. This assumption will allow for a novel interpretation, providing new avenues for understanding its teaching. Comparing and contrasting the *Regime of the Athenians* with Xenophon's other works,[41] and recognizing Xenophon's careful, even ironic manner of writing, enable the reader to call into question the common scholarly opinion that the *Regime of the Athenians* is an uncritically prejudicial criticism of the Athenian regime from the point of view of a rather narrow oligarch. I argue instead that Xenophon advances a disorderly and unsatisfactory critique of democracy in order to show the limits of such a critique, and that he ultimately shows Athens to be a tolerably decent regime, no doubt imperfect, but nonetheless superior to many available alternatives; he thus shows that Athens is deserving of qualified respect because of its (limited) justice and stability. What appears on the surface to be an uncritical castigation of Athens, then, is in fact much more ambivalent. To be sure, the treatise does not voice full support of the regime. Athenian democracy, like any actual regime, does not deserve the highest praise or allegiance of a student of Socrates, but neither does Athens deserve the severest blame—as Xenophon will show us.

The *Regime of the Athenians* begins rather abruptly, as though Xenophon wanted it to appear to be the continuation of a thought or part of a larger work. In that way, it resembles the *Oeconomicus, Hellenica, Symposium,* and the *Regime of the Lacedaemonians.* And like this last work, the *Regime of the Athenians* fits into the tradition of constitutional praise and blame, which could indicate that it is a companion to that treatise. Unlike the *Regime of the Lacedaemonians,* however, the beginning of this treatise is rather inelegant and clumsily repetitious, and this graceless start undoubtedly gives weight to the claim that the work is not by Xenophon. In the first lines, the author informs us that he will not praise the regime of the Athenians because, in choosing this type of regime, they have elected to make the vulgar citizens fare better than the worthy citizens. This opening remark is often submitted as evidence of the author's oligarchic prejudice, insofar as he implies that he would prefer that the worthy citizens fare better than the vulgar. Moreover, the terms he uses to describe the better (*chrēstoi*) and worse (*ponēroi*) citizens imply an identity between wealth and moral superiority, on the one hand, and economic and moral poverty, on the other.[42] It is possible, however, that, in employing terms with clear economic overtones, the author invites the reader to question this simple identification of moral excellence with wealth; he may thus quietly call into question the prejudice of the oligarchs that they are morally superior. Whatever we make of this, we can be certain that Xenophon does not hold to the simple opinion that excellence is the preserve of the wealthy: Xenophon reserves his highest praise for Socrates, who, Xenophon tells us, lived in utmost poverty.[43]

Moreover, even while he withholds praise for the Athenians' choice of regime, the author repeatedly calls their political order a "regime" (*politeia*).[44] By comparison, in the body (as distinguished from the title) of the *Regime of the Lacedaemonians*, Xenophon fails to call the Lacedaemonian political order a "regime." Xenophon thus appears to use the word *politeia* in an equivocal way. The general meaning refers to the entire way of life of a given people, including its political constitution, and in this sense all political communities possess a regime. But at times *politeia* refers more narrowly to a sort of republicanism, as opposed to, say, tyranny or empire.[45] Tyranny and empire would both qualify as *politeiai* in the general sense of the term, but fail to qualify in the narrow one.

While designating Athens a regime in the narrow sense may not rise to the level of praise, the author next promises to show us how well the Athenians preserve their regime and how they also accomplish other things well—things that look like mistakes to other Greeks, but are not such in fact. This seems to get to the heart of the matter; the Athenians are very good at figuring out how to look after their self-interest. It is easy to glide over this seemingly unimportant remark, but the perpetuation of a political order is no easy task.[46] Indeed, Xenophon indicates in the *Education of Cyrus* (1.1) that the fundamental political problem is stability; everywhere regimes are constantly being overturned, democracies included. By the end of the work, Xenophon will have made clear what he believes to be the source of Athens' stability as well as his reason for focusing on it.

Xenophon indicates that the first source of the stability of the Athenian democracy is its justice (1.2). The Athenian regime, according to Xenophon, justly accords the lower classes more influence because they are indeed the ones responsible for Athens' great power (*dunamis*). The people (*dēmos*) chiefly man the ships, and the navy is a far greater source of Athens' power than the heavy infantry or hoplites, who, because of the expense of providing their own armor, are wealthier citizens. The pilots, boatswains, ensigns, lookouts, and shipbuilders are all drawn from the people (i.e., the poor). Political power, offices, burdens, and wealth are distributed according to the principle that those who are more responsible for the success of the city should partake of greater rewards, and this, Xenophon affirms, is just (1.2). Next, the people make an exception to this general rule, and this exception also preserves the regime. Those offices that require expertise, such as the generalships and commands of the cavalry, they adroitly reserve for those with the requisite skill. Offices that do not require such skill, but carry a large stipend or in some way benefit their households, the people do seek. But there seems to be no harm to the preservation of the regime from this profit seeking.

Next, even by giving themselves more (presumably more money), the people increase their number, strengthen the regime, and render it more stable. The lower class is self-interested, Xenophon concedes, but as it grows relative to the other classes, democracy is better preserved. By contrast, if the poor were to allow the upper class to prosper, such prosperity would magnify dissension and undermine the stability of the democratic regime. These remarks convey doubt that a genuine common good is achievable. As he stresses in the next sentence, the better classes everywhere oppose democracy, so by enlarging the people and helping them prosper, the Athenians mitigate class strife. The reason for this class opposition, he indicates, is the superior moral virtue of the better class; the better are less prone to licentiousness and injustice, and are most exacting in financial matters. This sounds like high praise for the upper class, but Xenophon proves to be much more ambivalent about the moral superiority of the upper class. First, honesty and justice in financial matters are clearly in the interest of the upper class—this is not praise for a self-sacrificial devotion to the common good. Second, Xenophon makes clear that the well-off are less inclined to licentiousness and injustice thanks to their wealth. Similarly, the lower class may indeed be more inclined to shameful deeds, but this inclination is a product of ignorance and poverty, not some intrinsic inferiority. Why Xenophon would choose to flatter the upper class will become clearer once he indicates the audience of the treatise. At any rate, by justly distributing political power, offices (within reason), and wealth, the Athenian people skillfully perpetuate their democracy.

Xenophon next turns to a series of anonymous objections to the Athenian regime (1.6–7). Because the people are of a lesser moral character, as Xenophon seems to concede, surely the Athenians are mistaken to allow just anyone to speak on public matters and to advise the Assembly. Yet Xenophon asserts that even in this regard the Athenians deliberated excellently, because at least the people are well disposed toward their peers. Although the objector might be amazed, wondering how any ordinary person could possibly be of any benefit to the city, Xenophon assures him that the Athenians recognize that a person's goodwill, even if coupled with ignorance and worthlessness, is more profitable for them than the wisdom and virtue of a worthy citizen, if that wisdom and virtue are accompanied by ill will. An ever-expanding democratic class, comprising citizens who are well disposed toward one another, is a great source of stability.

Xenophon admits that the best city would not come about as a result of these practices, and, coupling this with the previous sentence, we get an indication of a contender for the best city: one ruled by a wise, virtuous ruler who is well disposed toward (all) the citizens. However, the rule of wise, virtuous, benevolent leaders is not likely to come about, and, even if it could, it would not be stable.[47] The unlikeliness of the best regime coming into being helps explain Xenophon's muted praise of an otherwise imperfect—but stable and relatively just—regime. The people, Xenophon tells us, have no desire to live as slaves in a so-called well-ordered city. (The term "well-ordered" [*eunomeisthai*] has clear oligarchic overtones and was even synonymous with the Spartan way of life.)[48] We see more clearly, then, that the Athenian demos had no desire to imitate the Spartan way of life.[49] In discussing the "well-ordered" city, Xenophon also reveals something about the character of the direct addressee of the work. Here (1.8–9), Xenophon addresses in the second person singular an anonymous advocate of a well-ordered regime. The addressee is then someone with oligarchic, pro-Spartan sympathies who would like to see Athens similarly well ordered. It would appear, then, that the addressee is an Athenian who is discontent with his current regime, someone who views freedom as disorderliness and who would like to see Athens become more like Sparta. Our author does not share the view of the addressee; rather he seems to have reconciled himself to democratic rule and aims similarly to reconcile the addressee to it. Xenophon explains to the addressee that making Athens well ordered—giving it good laws, allowing the worthy citizens to punish the vulgar ones, preventing "mad" human beings from public deliberation—these things would, very quickly, amount to nothing short of total enslavement of the people.

Xenophon aims to show that one cannot make Athens well ordered without fundamentally changing the nature of the regime or overthrowing the democracy. Only an Athenian of lapsing allegiance to his regime would need this speech, for Xenophon gives the subtly qualified praise and blame designed to keep such a person in the fold.

Understanding the character of the addressee of the treatise allows us to revisit a possibility alluded to earlier, namely, that in the *Regime of the Athenians* Xenophon plays the part of someone with whose opinion he is not altogether in accord. For if the *Regime of the Athenians* is indeed by Xenophon, it undeniably does not sound like him. Apart from questions of style, Xenophon presents himself from the start as someone highly critical of the political order in Athens, just as the *Regime of the Lacedaemonians* appears to praise Sparta. To criticize openly, however, is out of character for Xenophon, who believed it was noble, just, pious, and more pleasant to recall good things than bad.[50] Xenophon's choice of direct addressee — an Athenian, presumably a wealthy or aristocratic Athenian, with an affinity for Sparta — gives an indication of the broader audience he hoped to reach: those who were inclined to assume the superiority of Sparta to Athens and who viewed democracy as bad. So, in order to reach such people, Xenophon invented a persona through whom he speaks, and this persona has come to be called the "Old Oligarch," as we noted.[51] We can infer that the persona Xenophon creates is Athenian (1.11–12) as well as a shipowner (2.11). And, while he is as such likely wealthy, he curiously presents himself as a member of neither the upper nor the lower class. Rather, our speaker presents himself as a kind of arbiter between the two classes throughout the treatise, declining to identify himself explicitly as a member of either class despite the frequency of first person singular and plural pronouns in the treatise. Moreover, the speaker has an interest in persuading a dissident that Athens does some things fairly well, and is not as foolishly governed as it appears to be in the eyes of other Greeks (1.1). Xenophon invented this persona to appeal to those who were critical of the Athenian regime, because a direct appeal would not have been convincing and probably would have even been taken to be disingenuous. His connection to Athens would have tainted the reception of a treatise on its regime. After all, Xenophon had been exiled from Athens for serving under the Spartan king Agesilaus, and he retired to Elis, outside of Sparta. In order for the treatise to receive a fair hearing, Xenophon needed to take himself out of the equation. Now, Xenophon could have assumed the persona of a partisan democrat to defend Athenian democracy, but an unqualified praise of Athenian democracy by an Athenian democrat could easily be dismissed by an opponent—if it were even regarded at all. Additionally, Xenophon had reasons of his own not to praise Athens unqualifiedly, especially in light of what Athens did to Socrates. By contrast, a defense of Athenian democracy that begins by acknowledging the addressee's basic premise that democracy, as such, is a bad regime might receive a hearing.

After speaking directly to his addressee, Xenophon—or rather, his invented persona—changes topics quite abruptly, turning to a discussion of the status of slaves and resident aliens in Athens (1.10–12), as though the mere mention of slavery in 1.9 had reminded him of the actual slaves in Athens. In what seems to be a minor digression, Xenophon laments the near equality between citizens, slaves, and resident aliens in Athens. Many have taken this series of remarks as another indication of the viciousness of the Athenian regime, but again Xenophon argues that the good treatment of slaves and resident aliens is a sign of their good judgment. The slaves are actually more profitable if they are well treated and are allowed to live a comfortable life—indeed some slaves even live luxuriously (thus in a not very slave-like manner). Where slaves are well-off, it is no longer expedient to make them fear you, to say nothing of the decency of not having them fear you. So in Athens, the slaves do not fear the citizens, but in Sparta they do. Xenophon fails to mention another obvious benefit of treating slaves well—you have less reason to fear them.[52]

The next criticism of Athens is that the people have dismissed those engaged in music and gymnastics (1.13). This is a strange passage, as there were indeed music and gymnastics in Athens, and its meaning has accordingly eluded scholars.[53] Moreover, this criticism of the Athenian regime is not offered, as the others are, by an otherwise anonymous "someone" (*tis*) or by "you," the addressee. Rather, Xenophon's silence regarding the source of this criticism suggests that the speaker raises it himself. Now, Greeks understood education to be composed principally of music and gymnastics, and so this objection underscores the fact that Xenophon does not treat Athenian education in this treatise. This is a surprising omission considering how much attention he devotes to Spartan education in his treatise on that regime.[54]

This criticism of Athens is followed by a series of seemingly minor criticisms concerning the role that the rich played in furnishing choruses, gymnasia, and triremes; the rich often furnished these things, but the poor received the benefit of them. While this is no doubt true, there is evidence that the wealthy enjoyed great honor in thus furnishing the city.[55] Xenophon concludes this section with another serious criticism, namely, that the Athenians are more interested in their own advantage than in injustice in the law courts. So far, these are the only criticisms of Athens that do not meet with a rebuttal. At any rate, Xenophon focuses on only one aspect of the Athenian court system: how it treats its allies in court cases (1.14). Just as they run things at home, so too the Athenians tend to favor the interests of the popular classes in other cities. They could go to extremes in these matters, but the upper-class Athenians tend to balance this preference by protecting the upper-class citizens in other cities. Someone might object that Athens is plundering its allies, but in so doing, Athens is able to keep its allies relatively poor and ward off rebellion. Moreover, the Athenians compel their allies to come to Athens for court cases, and while they seem to have deliberated badly in this, Xenophon explains how the Athenians consider only the benefits to operating in this manner, which are many. Xenophon has returned to defending Athens because it does things that other Greeks view as mistakes.

Xenophon's last topic in the first chapter regards the naval expertise of the citizens (1.19). Because of their possessions abroad, the Athenians learn, almost imperceptibly, to become expert in naval matters. This, in turn, became a self-perpetuating way to maintain naval superiority over others. By virtue of their expert seamanship, they remain superior, insofar as it is almost compulsory for all citizens to take part in naval matters in one fashion or another. Moreover, the citizens become expert in technical nautical terms.

In the next part of the treatise (2.1–17) Xenophon continues to discuss Athens' ability to preserve its regime, but now he does so principally with regard to what today is referred to as foreign affairs. Though Athens does not possess a large hoplite force, it is nevertheless large enough to maintain superiority over tribute-paying allies. A larger army is unnecessary because of Athens' superior navy. This opening remark paves the way for a more general discussion of the advantages of naval superiority to land power.

Xenophon proceeds to list several advantages that he says are established by chance or fortune (2.2); these advantages are connected to being masters of the sea (*thalassokratores*). (Does this mean that the advantages enumerated in the first chapter are not from chance?) The repetition of the phrases "masters of the sea" and "rulers of the sea" leaves the impression that our author is speaking of imperial Athens, and, given the absence of any reference to the Peloponnesian War, he is likely referring to the empire prior to the war's outbreak in 431. With regard to the advantages of sea mastery, Athens' subjects—island-bound cities—cannot easily unite to revolt. Athens is able to subdue its smaller allies because they fear its naval power, and Athens can subdue larger allies because of the latter's need to import goods. Next, it is easy for Athens, being a naval power, to ravage its more powerful enemies' land. And the Athenians can sail away easily if enemies approach them. A sea power can move more quickly than an army, and can more easily face food shortages because it can procure goods abroad. To these advantages, Xenophon adds the following smaller advantages: Athens can import luxuries, including food, and it can draw what we might call "social capital" from the plethora of languages spoken in its marketplaces and docks. Indeed, while other Greeks tended to prefer their own dialects, ways of life, and manner of dress, the Athenians, because they have heard and seen much as a result of their naval supremacy, adopt a mixture of practices from all Greeks and even barbarians. The commercial character of their republic enables them to choose from among the best practices at home and abroad rather than relying on the simple conflation of "the best" with "one's own."

Another advantage is that the city has become large and beautiful, providing temples, sacrifices, shrines, gymnasia, baths, and wrestling rooms for its citizens from the wealth the sea power accords it (2.9–10). Indeed, Xenophon tells us that Athens alone among Greek and barbarian cities is capable of amassing wealth. All of this is a result of Athens' naval power. Clearly Xenophon recognizes that naval power enables commerce, which, in turn, provides the things that beautify a city. Further, our author, who now presents himself as a wealthy shipowner (2.11), brags that his ships are made from wood, iron, copper, flax, and wax from all over Greece and that he imports all sorts of goods.

Xenophon repeats another advantage of naval supremacy, the ability to attack enemies who are close to the coast, before turning to speak of Athens' disadvantages in foreign policy, which flow, it would seem, from one unfortunate fact: Athens is not an island. First, Athens cannot avoid having its land ravaged; second, Athens cannot prevent betrayal by oligarchic elements of its populace to its enemies. Xenophon assures the reader that Athens has solved the problem of the first disadvantage: Athens has abandoned the city and taken to the sea before. But regarding the second disadvantage, his silence seems to confirm the risk of oligarchic revolution.

Xenophon then mentions another advantage, this one stemming from the character of democracy rather than anything specific to naval supremacy (2.17): a democracy, unlike an aristocracy, can make and break treaties with greater impunity because it is difficult to assign blame to the people as a whole. If something bad arises from what the people have deliberated, they find individuals to blame; there can always be a scapegoat. The people as a whole is always blameless.

Next, in the same chapter, Xenophon discusses the political aspect of comedy in Athens (2.18–20). This part of the chapter seems to be out of place, since Xenophon departs from so-called high politics to delve into seemingly lesser matters, at least from the point of view of the city's ability to preserve itself in the face of external threats. But it can be connected with the preceding remarks insofar as Athens forbids blaming the entire people. Speaking badly about the people as a whole (*dēmos*) or satirizing them in a comedy is not allowed. While the people collectively may not be satirized in comedy, it is allowed, encouraged even, to satirize individuals. The reason for this allowance is that the people are confident that the person satirized will not be of the people, but rather someone rich, well-born, or powerful. Very few poor people will ever be satirized on stage, and the only ones who will be are those among them who are busybodies and those who think they are in some way superior to the people.[56] And the Athenian people, our speaker tells us, can recognize which of the citizens are useful and which are not. The vulgar are in fact useful to democracy, while the "worthy" are least useful. The indication, then, is that those who are called worthy are not useful to democracy. There are also, on the other side, members of the demos who are not by nature democratic. Xenophon does not identify anyone who meets this description, but Socrates seems to fit the profile.

Xenophon's speaker concludes the chapter (2.20) by telling his audience that he understands the Athenian people's preference for democracy, or even that he excuses or sympathizes with (sungignōskō) their preference. Everyone, he says, is to be pardoned for wanting to treat himself well. Finally, he says that anyone who is not a member of the demos but nevertheless chooses to live under a democracy plans to do injustice guided by the recognition that is easier to do so inconspicuously in a democracy than in an oligarchy.

But the treatise does not end there, and Xenophon takes up a series of what seem like minor criticisms of the regime again voiced by an anonymous "someone" (3.1–9). The first criticism is that the Athenian regime prevents Athens from acting quickly. The speaker concedes this is so, but proceeds to dismiss proposals for remedying this problem (bribes, smaller courts); the remedies would be worse than the disease. Among the many matters that Athens must take up are cases regarding hubris and impiety, again reminding us of Socrates.[57] Despite these and other flaws in the city, Xenophon does not advocate radical change in Athens. The classical political philosophers in general, however radical they may have been in speech or in their thought, were not revolutionary in deed. Changes to Athens, or to any existing regime, would have to be small and gradual, and thus Xenophon attempts to moderate the hopes of an oligarchic Athenian. Xenophon further dashes such hopes by recalling three times that the Athenians had supported the better, oligarchic element in foreign cities in the past (against the Boeotians, Milesians, and with the Lacedaemonians against the Messenians) (3.10–11). In each of these instances, things did not turn out well for Athens. Athenian support for the oligarchs in Boeotia led to the enslavement of the people; in Milesia, the oligarchs subsequently massacred the people; and when the Athenians aided the Lacedaemonians against the Messenians, the Lacedaemonians, after having subdued the Messenians, waged war directly against Athens. These are the only historical events to which Xenophon refers in the treatise. They offer only marginal guidance in determining the dramatic date, so to speak, of the treatise. All of the events are thought to have occurred in the middle of the fifth century, between 467 and 443, during Athens' so-called golden age. But the speaker does not indicate how long ago these events took place, so we can only say that the remarks are offered at some unspecified time thereafter.

Xenophon discusses last the question of being dishonored (*atimia*) by the city, which covers a range of penalties including exile (3.12–13). Xenophon asserts that some, though very few, have been unjustly dishonored (there is a high concentration of the words relating to justice in these final two sections). Athens has nothing to fear from such a small group. Moreover, those who have been justly dishonored will harbor no ill will toward the regime either. So, Athens has nothing to fear from those it has dishonored—regardless of whether they were dishonored justly or unjustly. This would include Xenophon (Diogenes Laertius 2.58).

The treatise then ends and leaves one with the impression that there is much that is in fact praiseworthy in Athens. Athens' democracy is tolerably just, and, as a result, it is quite stable. Slaves are treated well, commerce brings certain luxuries as well as toleration of foreign practices, and the city can accumulate wealth. Moreover, Athens allows a degree of private education in music, unlike, say, Sparta. Athens produced, or at least did not arrest the production of, a Xenophon and a Socrates. Athens tolerated Socrates for nearly seventy years, and he was executed only after the democracy had been overthrown and reinstated, and fear of antidemocratic sentiment was understandable, if not excusable.

If the *Regime of the Athenians* is indeed by Xenophon, it shows that Xenophon was not Athens' harshest critic. Even if he assumes the role of an adopted persona in the treatise, as I have suggested, Xenophon's willingness to advance this treatise nevertheless illustrates some level of fondness for his native city. To be sure, Athens was not without its flaws, but I suggest that, by focusing his praise on imperial Athens, Xenophon raises the possibility that this was Athens at its most praiseworthy. Elsewhere, Xenophon gently criticizes the later democracy for being unrestrained by law,[58] and he would surely disapprove of the restored democracy that executed his teacher Socrates in 399 and exiled himself sometime between 399 and 394. Thus, Xenophon's views on the Athenian regime are ambivalent. No city can perfectly accept philosophy, and hence no city receives the complete loyalty of philosophy and philosophers. But an actual city can expect the guarded loyalty of a thoughtful citizen, the kind of loyalty Xenophon here evinces for his native regime.

The contributions of the *Regime of the Athenians* to our understanding of ancient democracy are deserving of greater scholarly attention. Easily mistaken as a piece blaming the Athenian regime, the treatise actually aims to attract those like Xenophon's invented addressee, who are sympathetic to critiques of democracy, and by the end to have reconciled them to it. Xenophon recognizes the oligarchic, even revolutionary inclination to blame one's native democracy and appeals to such antidemocratic prejudices in order to moderate them. He can do so only by accepting some of the blame of the regime, showing that it is not really as destructive as the addressee believes, and pointing to the praiseworthy qualities of democratic rule. Indeed, Athens, in Xenophon's view, is just in a qualified sense and is relatively stable. By virtue of this approach to such criticisms, Xenophon has led his addressee and reader alike not just to such estimation, but more importantly he has pointed to fundamental questions of political philosophy: the question of justice and the common good, the nature of regimes and cities, and the proper role of education. Insofar as this treatise aims to moderate and educate its readers, the *Regime of the Athenians* is an important contribution to the tradition of political philosophy.

CHAPTER 5
Ways and Means, or On Revenues[1]

Translated by Wayne Ambler

∽ Chapter 1 ∽

(1) I, for my part, hold to this belief: whatever sort the leaders may be, such also the regimes become.[2] And since some of the leaders of Athens used to say that they knew what the just is no less than other people,[3] but that because of the poverty of the multitude they were compelled, they claimed, to be more unjust regarding the cities,[4] I on account of this undertook to consider whether the citizens would in any way be able to feed themselves from their own [land], which is also the most just way, believing that if this could happen, it would aid them with respect both to their poverty and to their being held in suspicion by the Greeks.

(2) As I considered my reflections further, this immediately became clear: that the country is naturally such as to produce a great deal of revenue. In order that what I say may be known to be true, I will first narrate the nature of Attica. (3) Now, that the seasons here are most mild, even the very things that grow testify. At any rate, things that would not even be able to sprout in many places bear fruit here. And as is the earth, so also the sea that surrounds the land is most productive. And as many of the good things as the gods provide in seasons, all these get started here at the earliest moments and cease only at the latest. (4) The land's strength is not only in the things that bloom and grow old in a single year, but also in that it has good things that last forever. For building stone is naturally abun-

dant in it, out of which most beautiful[5] temples and most beautiful altars come to be, and the most fitting statues to the gods. And many are in need of it, both Greeks and barbarians. (5) There is also earth that does not bear fruit when sown, but when quarried feeds many times more than if it brought forth grain. Indeed, it is clearly owing to a divine fate that there is silver underground. At any rate, of the many cities dwelling nearby, both by land and by sea, not even a small vein of silver extends as far as any one of them.

(6) One might not unreasonably think that the city is situated near the center of Greece and, indeed, of the entire inhabited world. For by the extent to which anyone is farther from it, to this extent he encounters more severe cold or heat. And for those who may wish to depart from one extreme limit of Greece and arrive at its other extreme limit, they all must either sail or travel past Athens, like the center of a circle. (7) And although it is not surrounded with water, nevertheless, like an island, all winds bring in what it needs and send out what it wishes; for it has the sea on two sides. And it receives many things by trade on land as well; for it is on the mainland. Moreover, for most cities there are barbarians dwelling adjacent to them who make trouble for them, but even the cities that are neighbors with Athens are themselves very distant from the barbarians.

~ CHAPTER 2 ~

(1) Of all these things, as I said, I believe the land is itself the cause. But what if, in addition to the naturally present goods, attentive care should be taken of the resident aliens first? For the revenue they bring seems to me to be among the finest things, since even though they maintain themselves and benefit their cities in many ways, they do not receive a wage; rather, they pay their special tax.[6] (2) Now it seems to me that it would be sufficient to take attentive care of them like this, namely, if we should stop imposing anything that seems to dishonor the resident aliens without benefiting the city, and if we should also cease having resident aliens be hoplites along with townsmen[7] on military campaigns; for the danger for one who is away on campaign is great, and to be away from one's children[8]

and houses is a considerable burden. (3) And the city would also be benefited if the citizens should go on military campaigns with one another rather than have, as we do now, Lydians, Phrygians, Syrians, and all other sorts of barbarians marshaled for battle with them in their military formations; for many of the resident aliens are such. (4) In addition to its being good that these would be exempted from being marshaled for battle, it would also be an adornment for the city if the Athenians should be thought to trust themselves in battle rather than trusting others from all sorts of places. (5) And if we should allow the resident aliens to share in other matters in which it is noble for them to share, including the cavalry, it seems to me we would make them more well-disposed and, at the same time, show the city to be both stronger and greater.[9]

(6) Moreover, since many houses inside the walls are vacant, as are also house-building sites, if the city should grant ownership of houses to those who would build them, after they asked and were deemed worthy of doing so, I think that many more and better [people] would desire to take up residence at Athens because of this. (7) And if we should establish an office of protectors of resident aliens just as we do protectors of orphans, and if there should be an honor for those who would enroll the most resident aliens, this too would make the resident aliens more well-disposed, and, as is likely, all those without a city would desire to become resident aliens at Athens and would augment our revenue.

∼ CHAPTER 3 ∼

(1) I will now explain how the city is most pleasant and profitable for commerce as well. For first, surely, it has the most beautiful and safest harbors for ships, where it is possible for them to be moored, laying up without fear when there is a storm. (2) Now in most cities it is necessary for the merchants to take something away as a return cargo; for the local currency[10] is not useful elsewhere. But at Athens it is possible to carry away in exchange most things that people need; and if merchants do not wish to take away a return cargo, they can carry out fine merchandise by

carrying out silver; for no matter where they sell it, they will get more than their original cost. (3) If someone should bestow prizes on the magistrate over commerce who resolves disputes in the most just and quickest way, so that the merchant who wanted to sail away was not detained, on account of this many more would travel here for commerce and would do so with greater pleasure. (4) It is good and noble[11] also that merchants and shipowners be honored with front-row seats, and, sometimes, that hospitality be extended to them, when they seem to benefit the city with worthy ships and merchandise. For when they are honored in these ways, they would hurry to us as to friends, not only for gain but also for honor. (5) To the extent that more [people] come to settle or visit, it is clear that to this same extent more [goods] would also be imported, exported, paid out, bought, earned, and paid in customs.

(6) Now such increases in our revenues do not require advance spending but only humane[12] policies and attentive care. But as regards other sources of revenue as seem to me to be possible, I know that a capital fund will be needed. (7) I am not without hope, however, that the citizens would contribute[13] eagerly for such things, since I have in mind that the city contributed a great deal when it gave aid to the Arcadians at the time Lysistratus was in command, and a great deal also at the time of Hegesilaus.[14] (8) And I know that triremes have often been sent out at great expense and that this has occurred even when it was not clear whether it would be for better or worse, and yet it *was* clear that they would never recover what they contributed nor even get a share of it.

(9) Contributors could acquire no acquisition so fine as the one for which they spend to establish a capital fund. For he who makes a ten-minae contribution, as [he might if he were investing] in a ship, receives almost a fifth, since he receives three obols per day.[15] He who makes a five-minae contribution would take more than a third. (10) And most of the Athenians would receive more in a year than they contribute.[16] Those spending a mina in advance will receive almost two minae in revenue, and all this investing is in the city, which seems to be the safest and longest lived of the human things.[17] (11) And I think, if they were going to be listed as benefactors for all time, many foreigners would contribute as well; and it is possible that there would also be cities that would want to be listed. I expect

also that there are some kings and tyrants and satraps who would desire to share in this [mark of] gratitude.[18]

(12) When the capital fund should be sufficient, it would be fine and good[19] to build additional lodgings for shipowners around the harbors, and fine also to build fitting places for merchants to buy and sell, and public lodgings for those who visit. (13) And if houses and shops were made ready in the market areas, both in the Piraeus and in the city center, this would at the same time be an adornment for the city, and a great deal of revenue would be derived from them. (14) It seems to me to be good to try whether, just as the city possesses public warships, it might thus be possible to acquire public merchant ships as well, and to rent them out if guaranteed by securities, just as also with other public things. For if this too should appear to be possible, a great revenue would be derived from them.

~ CHAPTER 4 ~

(1) As for the silver mines, if they were prepared as they ought to be, I believe a great deal of money would come in from them even without the other sources of revenue. I wish to show their potential to those who do not know it; for if you do know it, you would deliberate better about how you should use them.

(2) Now it is clear to everyone that they have been active for a very long time; at any rate, no one even tries to say when they were first begun. Although they have been mined and have had silver ore extracted for such a long time, consider how small a fraction the mounds [of slag] that have been heaped up amount to when compared to the natural and silver-laden hills. (3) And it is manifest that the silver-yielding area is not contracting into a smaller zone but is always stretching out further. In the time when the greatest number of people[20] was in them, no one ever was at a loss for work, but the work to be done always exceeded the number of those working. (4) And now, regarding those who possess slaves in their mines, no one reduces their number but always adds as many as he is able. For whenever few dig and seek, I think few things[21] are found. But when many do so, the silver vein is revealed to be many times as

great. (5) So that of the kinds of work I know, it is only in this one that no one envies those who expand their operations. Further, all those who own fields would be able to say how many yoked teams suffice to work their land, and how many workers as well. And if anyone introduces more than enough, they calculate it a loss. But in working on silver mines, all say they are in need of more workers. (6) It is not the same as when there are many bronze-smiths and works in bronze become inexpensive, so the bronze-smiths quit; and so too with those who work in iron. And when there is a great deal of grain and wine, and crops become inexpensive, farming becomes unprofitable, so that many cease to work the earth and turn to commerce, retail trade, and moneylending. But to the extent that more silver ore comes to light and there is more silver, to this extent more take up this line of work. (7) For also with regard to household utensils, whenever someone has acquired a sufficient amount for his house, he will certainly not purchase still more. But no one ever yet acquired so much silver that he no longer needs more. But if any have a vast amount, they take no less pleasure in burying the excess than in using it. (8) And when cities fare well, people strongly desire silver; for men wish to spend it on beautiful armor, good horses, houses, and magnificent furnishings, while women turn to expensive clothes and golden adornments. (9) And when, in turn, cities are suffering, either from the dearth of crops or from war, and with their land becoming idle, they need currency still more for provisions and for military aid. (10) If someone should say that gold is no less useful than silver, I will not disagree with him; nevertheless, I know that even gold itself becomes less expensive whenever it appears abundant, but this makes silver more expensive. (11) Now I am showing this so that we may be confident in leading as many people as possible to the silver mines and also so that we may be confident in making preparations in them, on the grounds that the vein of silver will never run out and that silver will never lose its value. (12) It seems to me that the city came to know this before I did; at least it provides equality in taxes for any foreigner who wishes to work in the mines.

(13) In order that I might speak even more clearly about this way of making a living, I will now explain how the silver mines might be prepared in the way most beneficial for the city. Now in what I am about to say, I do not think there is anything worthy of wonder,

as if I had found out something difficult to discover; for we all still even now observe some of the things I will say, and we all hear of the rest, the things of the past, that they were about the same. (14) It is, however, very much worthy of wonder that even though the city perceives that many private individuals have grown rich from her, by working the mines, she does not imitate them. For surely we who have given attentive care have long ago heard that Nicias, the son of Niceratus,[22] once acquired a thousand people in the silver mines, whom he leased out to Sosias the Thracian, on the conditions that he give him an obol net per day for each and maintain the total number always constant. (15) Hipponicus also had six hundred slaves whom he leased out in the same way, and they brought him a mina per day net. Philemonides had three hundred and received a half a mina; and others too, I think, received profits in proportion to their investment.[23] (16) But why should I speak of days gone by? For even now there are many people leased out in the silver mines in just this way.

(17) If the measures I am speaking about were put into effect, the only novelty would be that just as private individuals secured an everlasting revenue by acquiring slaves, so also the city might acquire public slaves until there were three for each of the Athenians. (18) As to whether the points we are making is possible, let whoever wishes consider each of them one by one and then judge them. It is certainly clear that the public would be more able to provide the cost of people than private individuals are. Moreover, it is quite easy for the Council to announce that whoever wishes to import slaves may do so and for it to purchase those that are imported. (19) And when they have been purchased, why would anyone be less inclined to hire from the public than from private individuals, if he were going to get them on the same terms? At any rate, [people] now rent sacred spaces, temples, houses, and tax-farming privileges from the city. (20) Now to see to it that what is purchased is kept safe, it is possible for the public to receive sureties from those who lease [the purchased slaves], just as is done also with those who purchase tax-farming privileges. And surely it is easier for one who has bought tax-farming privileges to do injustice than for one who leases slaves. (21) Because the silver belonging to the public is similar to the silver of a private individual, how would anyone detect that it was the public's that was being carried off? But because public slaves are branded with a mark and

there is a penalty set for both the seller and whoever carries them off, how would anyone steal them? Up to this point, then, it seems possible for the city both to acquire and to protect people.

(22) Now if someone should next take this question to heart—when there are many workers, why will many others show up to pay their wages?—let him reflect on this and be confident: many of the contractors already on hand will hire the additional public [slaves], for they already have substantial resources, and many of their current workers are growing old. Moreover, there are many others, both Athenians and foreigners, who would neither wish to nor be able to work with their bodies but who would be pleased to provide their livelihood by using their judgment and supervising.[24] (23) Now if at first there were twelve hundred slaves, it is likely that from the revenue [they bring in] there could be at least six thousand in five or six years. And from this number, if each brings in one obol net each day, the annual revenue would be sixty talents.[25] (24) And if twenty of these are paid for other slaves, it will be possible for the city to use forty talents for anything else it needs. When a total of ten thousand is reached, the revenue will be one hundred talents. (25) If there are any who still remember how much tax revenue [the city] gained from slaves before the events at Decelea,[26] they would testify for me that [the city] will receive many times as much. And this too offers useful testimony, that although countless people have worked in the silver mines for time immemorial, the mines are now no different from how our ancestors remember them. (26) And events now occurring, all of them, testify that there would never be more slaves there than the works require; for the miners find no limit either to the depth or to the lateral galleries. (27) And indeed, it is no less possible to cut new shafts now than it was before. Nor could anyone speak with knowledge about whether there is more silver ore in the mines that have already been dug or in those that are still to be dug. (28) Why then, one might say, are there not many who are digging in new areas now, as there were before? It is because those occupied with the mines are poorer now; for only recently are they again making their preparations, and there is a great risk for one who digs in a new place. (29) For he who finds good production becomes rich; he who does not find anything loses everything he spent. So [people] now are not very willing to pursue this risk.

(30) I, however, think I am able to offer counsel about how new digging might be done in the greatest safety. For of the Athenians, of course, there are ten tribes. Suppose the city should grant to each of them an equal number of slaves, and the tribes would share in taking their chances in doing new digging. (31) Then, if one should find something, this would return a profit for all; and if two, three, four, or half of them found something, these works would clearly be more profitable. Yet that all should fail of their chance would be unlike anything that has happened in the past. (32) And it is possible also for private individuals to associate, share in taking their chances, and run the risk with greater security. Do not fear, however, either that the public, if it is prepared to act in this way, will interfere with private individuals, or that private individuals will interfere with the public. Rather, just as allies make each other stronger to the extent that they are more numerous, so also in the silver mines they will find and extract more good things from the mines to the extent that more are working them.

(33) I have now said how, if the city is prepared, I believe a sufficient livelihood for all Athenians could be derived from the commons.[27] (34) If some calculate that a very great capital fund would be necessary for all these things and do not believe that sufficient money would ever be contributed, let them not be discouraged. (35) For it is not the case that necessity compels all these things to be done at the same time or, if they are not, deprives them of all benefit. Rather, whatever the number of houses built, ships constructed, or slaves purchased, they will be beneficial immediately. (36) Indeed, doing things in stages is more advantageous in one respect than doing everything all at once: for if we should build many houses all at once, we would finish our work at greater cost and more poorly than when we build in stages; and if we were to seek a great number of slaves all at once, we would be compelled to purchase ones that were both inferior and more expensive. (37) Now if to the extent possible we carry out and accomplish what we know to be fine, [we can persist in it[28]]. But if something goes awry, we could then refrain from it. (38) Moreover, if all measures were to be put into place at the same time, it would be necessary for us to provide all funds at once; but if some should be completed and others postponed, the initial revenue would help provide what was required.

(39) But what perhaps seems most frightening to everyone is that if the city should acquire too many slaves, they would overcrowd the works. We could free ourselves from this fear if we did not introduce more people than the works themselves required each year. (40) It seems to me, at least, that in whatever way it is easiest to do these things, this way is also best.

And, next, if you believe that you would not be able to contribute anything else at all, because of the contributions that arose in the recent war,[29] then manage the city in the coming year with the same amount of money the taxes raised before the peace; but then take whatever additional money is raised because of the peace, and because of the care taken of resident aliens and merchants, and because of increased imports and exports owing to there being more people, and because of the increase of the harbor and market dues—taking all this—prepare things so that your revenue would become as great as possible. (41) And if any fear that this preparation should prove in vain if war should be awakened, let them consider that if these measures are put into place, war will be much more frightening for the attackers than for the city. (42) For what possession is more useful for war than people? For they would be sufficient to fill many ships for the public; and a numerous infantry[30] for the public would have the power to be burdensome to the enemy, if someone should care for them attentively.

(43) I calculate that even if a war does break out, the mines would not need to be abandoned. For of course there is a fort in the area of the mines at the sea to the south at Anaphlystus, and there is a fort in the area to the north in Thoricus.[31] These are about sixty stadia apart from each other.[32] (44) If there were also a third fort in the middle between them on the highest point of Besa, the works would be united into one by all the forts; and if anything hostile were perceived, it would be a short distance for each to retreat into safety. (45) Further, if the enemy should come in larger numbers it is clear that they would carry off any grain, wine, or cattle they should find outside. But if they become masters of silver ore, how would they be able to use it any more than rocks? (46) How indeed would the enemy ever even set out for the mines? For surely the city nearest to the silver mines, Megara, is much more than five hundred stadia away. And Thebes, the nearest city after this, is much more than six hundred

stadia away.[33] (47) If they march to our silver mines from some such place, they will need to pass beside our city. And if there are few of them, it is likely that they would be destroyed by our horsemen and our city guards. On the other hand, it will be difficult for them to march by us with a large force, since they then must abandon their own property [at home]. For the city center of the Athenians would be much nearer to their cities than they themselves would be when they are at the mines. (48) But even if they should come, how would they be able to stay if they do not have provisions? If they seek food with part of their force, there are risks both for those going out after it and for that over which they contend. But if they all go out after provisions, they would become the besieged rather than the besiegers.

(49) Not only will the tax from renting the slaves increase the sustenance and support for the city; but if there were an increased population collected in the area of the mines, there would also be great increases in revenue from the market there, from public housing around the mines, from the furnaces, and from all other such sources. (50) For this too would become a densely populated city if it were established in this way; and plots of land there would be no less valuable for their owners than they are in the city center. (51) If the measures I have spoken of are enacted, I agree[34] that the city would not only be better provided with money, but it would also become more obedient, better ordered, and more prepared for war. (52) For those assigned to do physical training would do it with much greater care if they get more nourishment in the exercise areas than when leading the exercises in the torch-race festivals.[35] And those assigned to stand watch in the guard posts, to serve as light-armed troops, and to patrol the country will do all these things with much greater care when their livelihood is granted them for each of their works.

~ CHAPTER 5 ~

(1) If it seems clear that there must be peace for all revenues to come in fully, then is it not worthwhile also to establish a board of peace guardians? For having this office elected would make the city

much friendlier and thickly settled[36] for all people to come to. (2) But if some think that if the city keeps a lasting peace, she will become less powerful, less highly reputed, and less renowned in Greece, they too, as it seems to me, are incorrect.[37] For surely cities that spend the most time in peace are said to be happiest. And of all cities, Athens is especially suited by nature to grow greater when there is peace. (3) For when the city stays at rest, what shipowners and merchants, first of all, would not be in need of her? Will not those with lots of grain, those with lots of wine, and those who take pleasure in wine[38]? What about those with lots of olives, those with lots of cattle, and those able to make money with their judgment and their capital[39]? (4) And what about the craftsmen, the sophists, and philosophers; what about the poets; what about those who take up these things;[40] what about those who desire what is worth seeing or worth hearing, sacred or profane? And what about those also who need to sell or buy many things quickly: where would they obtain what they need more than at Athens? (5) If no one contradicts this, but if those who wish the city to recover her leadership[41] hold that this would be achieved better through war than peace, let them reflect first on the events concerning Persia,[42] whether we obtained our leadership over the [combined Greek] fleet and over the Greek treasury by using violence or by benefiting the Greeks. (6) Moreover, when the city was deprived of its empire, having been thought to preside over it with excessive cruelty, did we not even then become, after we abstained from being unjust, the leaders of the fleet by the islanders' voluntary action?[43] (7) And did not also the Thebans grant that the Athenians would be their leaders because they found it to be beneficial?[44] Indeed, even the Lacedaemonians turned the leadership over to the Athenians to arrange in whatever way they wished, not because we forced them to but because they were being treated well.[45] (8) But now, because of the confusion in Greece,[46] events seem to me to have turned out so that the city might regain the Greeks even without hard work, risk, or expense. For it is possible to try to reconcile the warring cities with each other, and if any are in faction with themselves, it is possible to reconcile them as well. (9) And if you should be manifest in your care that the temple at Delphi be autonomous as it was before, not by making war but by sending embassies throughout Greece, I do not think it would be wondrous if you would get all the Greeks to share your opinion, swear oaths, and become allies against whoever should seek to take over the temple if the Phocians should abandon it.[47] (10) If you should be manifest in your care that there be peace over all the earth and sea, I think everyone would pray that, after their own fatherland, Athens be preserved above all.

(11) If someone believes that war for the city is more profitable in monetary terms than peace is, I do not know how this could be judged better than by considering how prior events turned out for the city. (12) For he will find that during the more distant past much more money was carried into the city when there was peace, while in war all this was spent. He will come to know, if he considers it, that also in the present, because of the war, many of our revenues have fallen off and those that come in have been exhausted on numerous and varied expenses. But when there has been peace at sea, he will realize both that the revenues have increased and that it is possible for the citizens to use them in whatever way they wish. (13) If someone should ask me further, "Then do you mean that if someone is unjust to the city, it is necessary to keep peace also with him?" I would say, "No!" But I say rather that we could take our vengeance against them much more quickly if we have been unjust to no one; for then they would not have any ally.

∾ CHAPTER 6 ∾

(1) But if, then, there is nothing either impossible or difficult among the measures proposed, and if, when they are done, we will have more friendly relations with the Greeks, we will dwell more safely, we will be more illustrious, the people will be better provided with a livelihood while the rich will be free from the expenses of war; and since there will be great abundance, we will conduct our festivals still more magnificently than now, we will refurbish our temples, we will repair our walls and harbors, we will restore the ancestral [payments and privileges] to priests, the Council, magistrates, and horsemen, how is it not worthwhile to act on these measures as quickly as possible so that we may look upon the city happy in safety in our time?

(2) But if you should resolve to do these things, I would counsel you to send to both Dodona and Delphi and ask the gods whether it is more agreeable and better for the city to prepare itself in this way both at the moment and for the longer term. (3) And if they should consent, then I would say that next we need to ask which of the gods we should win over to carry them out in the noblest and best way. After there are sacrifices with good omens to the gods they ordain, it is fitting that the work should begin. For when actions are taken with god,[48] it is fitting[49] that these actions advance toward what is always more agreeable and better for the city.

An Introduction to the Ways and Means

Abram N. Shulsky

In Xenophon's *Oeconomicus*, Ischomachus, Socrates' interlocutor, explains how he and his father buy run-down farms, improve them, and then sell them at a profit.[50] The two men thus appear to combine farming, an activity that is not only compatible with their status as gentlemen, but is also the preeminently "natural" form of acquisition according to book 1 of Aristotle's *Politics*, with business or "moneymaking," the preeminently "unnatural" form. Xenophon thus blurs the qualitative distinction between "natural" and "unnatural" ways of earning a living, a distinction to which Aristotle appears to attribute political importance.[51] Leo Strauss describes this account as an "experiment" (i.e., the development of "an economics which is about to become pure chrematistics [i.e., moneymaking]") by means of which Xenophon "paves the way for certain post-Machiavellian thinkers."[52]

Strauss's hint leads us to consider the possibility that Xenophon's *Poroi*, being the work in which he discusses topics recognizable as part of the modern discipline of "economics," would contain his reflections on the economic concepts characteristic of our own time, including that of economic growth. For various reasons, this possibility is not borne out. Nevertheless, the study of this work illustrates some of the obstacles that had to be overcome in order for economics to become an autonomous subject, as well as the seemingly paradoxical role that some aspects of Socratic thought could play in its development.

This essay is divided into three sections. The first provides a commentary on Xenophon's *Poroi*. The second considers a particularly revealing discussion of economic matters in Xenophon's *Memorabilia* (2.7) in which Socrates solves his friend Aristarchus's financial problem by ignoring the distinction between free persons and slaves and, instead, viewing individuals in economic terms as producers and consumers.[53] Finally, the essay discusses Xenophon's intention in writing the *Poroi*.

⁓ COMMENTARY ON XENOPHON'S *POROI* ⁓

As suggested by its title, Xenophon's treatise concentrates on increasing the revenues of the city of Athens. He means to do so, however, even while abandoning Athenian imperialism, which had been a major source of revenue. His timing is good: he is writing at the close of the "Social War," in which Athens attempted, but failed, to keep several of its most important "allies" in subjection.[54] The focus on revenues differentiates Xenophon's work from a work like Isocrates' oration *On the Peace*, which also makes an anti-imperialist argument. However, Isocrates fails to address a key objection to a pacific policy, that is, the loss of the revenue (tribute) Athens had collected from its "allies."

Xenophon wishes to propose a new nonimperialist policy that will be equally profitable to Athens, but that will avoid both the injustice of reducing "allied" cities to subject status and the resulting ill will the imperialist policy generated within the Greek world.

Xenophon begins by stating his belief that the constitution or regime of a city (*polis*) reflects the character of its leaders (1.1).[55] In context, this appears as a criticism of the Athenian leaders—since the injustice of Athens' imperialism is taken for granted, Athens' imperial rule over other cities suggests that the leaders themselves are deficient in justice.

Some of the Athenian leaders, however, defend themselves by asserting that they recognize justice no less than other men,[56] but that the poverty of the multitude of citizens requires them to deal somewhat unjustly with other cities; they take for granted that the city must contribute to the livelihood of the mass of citizens. (Other leaders, presumably, do not recognize any injustice in Athenian imperialism.) The "poverty" of the many does not necessarily imply destitution; rather it implies the absence of independent wealth. The "poor" are those who must work for a living; if such a person is to be a full participant in the city's affairs (as would be required by the ancient understanding of democracy as "direct" rather than "representative" democracy) then the city must compensate him for his time. As Aristotle notes in his *Politics*, providing payment for the performance of public duties is a characteristic of democracy.[57] The degree of public participation is determined by the amount of money available:

> Of the offices the most popular [i.e., democratic] is the council, when there is not a ready supply of pay for all—when there is, the power even of this office is eliminated, for if the people are well supplied with pay they have all decisions referred to themselves.[58]

Aristotle traced the economic reliance of the common people on the gains of empire back to the great Athenian leader Aristeides, in the period immediately following the Persian War.[59] Aristeides advised the Athenians to leave the countryside and settle in town, obtaining their sustenance by serving in the army or as guards (on the city's walls) or by taking care of the city's business (e.g., as jurors or assemblymen). Athens' revenues, swollen by the contributions (or tribute) of other Greek cities, were sufficient to maintain twenty thousand citizens in this manner. This revenue was the result of Athens having achieved leadership or hegemony over the Greeks; Aristeides advised Athens to maintain this hegemony by enabling the bulk of the citizenry to devote themselves to public affairs, including warfare.

The apparent injustice of imperialism leads Xenophon to wonder whether the common people of Athens would be able to feed themselves while relying exclusively on the city's own resources. He believes that this way, which would be the most just, would suffice to support the population and would quiet the other Greeks' suspicions of Athens. Thus, justice is not only an independent goal for

Xenophon; it is also instrumental to the goal of reducing the enmity felt by other Greek cities toward Athens.

Xenophon, in effect, counters Aristeides' advice and tries to convince the Athenians that they can afford to give up hegemony. By posing the problem as one of finding an alternative source of revenue, Xenophon accepts not only Athenian democracy, but its particular reliance on public funding to enable the common man to participate in public affairs in person on a frequent basis. He thus accepts a type of democratic government that was in bad odor among ancient "conservatives," as may be seen from Aristotle's discussion of the various kinds of democracy.

In his thematic discussion of the types of democracy,[60] Aristotle emphasizes the importance of the city's revenues. When the revenues are large, the poorer citizens can be paid for performance of public duties (such as serving as jurors or participating in assemblies). However, the result of this situation, from Aristotle's point of view, is pernicious—the multitude rules by specific decisions and decrees, rather than being bound by law. For Aristotle, the best forms of democracy are those in which the multitude, although having ultimate authority (as expressed, for example, in infrequent assemblies, called only when necessary), is willing to be ruled by the relatively unchanging laws, with the actual work of government carried on by those who have the leisure to do so.[61]

To support his contention that Athens can live off its own resources, Xenophon begins by enumerating the natural advantages of Attica, the peninsula on which Athens, and the surrounding countryside it controlled, are located. In the first instance, Xenophon mentions the mildness of its climate, which he implies makes the land very productive.[62] The sea around Attica is likewise said to be productive.

This looks at first like a "conservative" position—increasing agricultural production would require the Athenians to go back to their rural roots, thereby dispersing the common people away from the city itself and thereby making them less powerful politically. It would also seem to be in accord with Aristotle's views as expressed in book 1 of the *Politics*—agriculture is the preeminently "natural" mode of acquisition, taking from nature (not from other men) the nourishment it seems ready and willing to give.[63]

Xenophon begins to inch away from this position almost immediately by noting that Attica is also rich in building stone and silver.[64] He notes in passing that a quarry can feed more people than a similar acreage of farmland could (and the same would be true a fortiori of a silver mine). We note the germ of the modern economic notion of comparative advantage. While Xenophon speaks explicitly of nonarable land (thereby correcting, in passing, his earlier implication that the territory of Attica was especially productive agriculturally), it is not hard to see that, even if the land in question were arable, it would be economically advantageous to use it as a quarry. By treating it as a matter of comparative advantage, however, Xenophon ignores the traditional "conservative" argument according to which agriculture was the best economic basis for building a sound democratic political order.[65]

Next, Xenophon praises Athens in terms of its location. While Athens is not, as Xenophon implies, on the land route from anywhere to anywhere, it is, however, well located in terms of sea routes: though it is not an island,[66] it is in a sense surrounded by the sea. Xenophon's praise of Athens' central location, implicitly as a commercial asset, raises another issue on which he parts company with ancient "conservative" views. While Aristotle, for example, understands the importance of foreign trade for a city, he treats it as a politically and morally sensitive issue.[67] He gives credence to the argument that the presence of people brought up under other laws is detrimental to the good order of the city, and that a large number of foreigners would make it harder for the city to be governed well.

Aristotle therefore strives to balance the potential for political and moral corruption caused by the presence of foreigners with the necessity to engage in foreign trade to obtain items that the city cannot produce for itself. One solution he recommends reflects (and improves upon) Athenian reality: an inland city (Athens proper) connected to, but geographically separate from, a port (the Piraeus). The "corruption" of foreign influence is limited to the port and can be kept at a distance from the city itself: laws can regulate the interactions between people in the port and people in the city.[68]

Aristotle understands that a great commercial port can be a profitable asset, independently of the city's need for specific imports, but, considering the political and moral sensitivities, he rejects this option:

> Those who set themselves up as a market for all do so for the sake of revenue; a city that should not be party to this sort of aggrandizement should not possess a trading center of this sort.[69]

For Aristotle, it would be better to design the city's institutions so as not to require such revenues. Xenophon, by contrast, dispenses with Aristotle's concerns about corrupting foreign influences in his search for the necessary revenues.

After this review of Athens' "natural goods," that is, the good things due to the land itself, Xenophon turns in chapter 2 to a consideration of the resident aliens, non-Athenians who were allowed to live in Athens but who did not become citizens. Rather than see them as a threat to the city's good order, Xenophon regards them as among the "finest" sources of revenue, since, unlike the citizens, they support themselves economically, do not receive compensation from the city, and even pay a special tax. As noncitizens, the resident aliens can, of course, devote themselves entirely to their trades, since they do not perform the civic services for which citizens receive payment from the city. (The implicit comparison between citizens and aliens is not necessarily to the former's advantage.)

Viewing the aliens as a source of revenue, Xenophon lists steps Athens can take to attract more of them. In general, Xenophon recommends steps to improve the status of the aliens and what we would call the "business climate" in order to maximize the amount of commerce transacted and hence Athenian tax revenues. He emphasizes, for example, the importance of the just[70] and rapid adjudication of commercial disputes; he recommends that prizes be given to the magistrates who settle such disputes most justly and most rapidly (3.3).

Of greatest interest are his superficially contradictory recommendations with respect to military service. On the one hand, Xenophon would exempt aliens from military service as hoplites (heavy infantry). Aside from the obvious benefit to the aliens themselves, Xenophon stresses that the city will gain as well: it would be an adornment for the city if it appeared that the Athenians relied on themselves rather than others to fight their battles. He also implies that morale, solidarity, and perhaps even military efficiency would improve if the citizens did not have to serve alongside "barbarians" — Xenophon mentions in particular three non-Greek ethnic groups represented among the Athenian resident alien population (2.3).

Once again, Xenophon appears at first to be taking a "conservative" tack — he praises the citizen hoplite force and implies that it could serve as a school for old-fashioned patriotism and honor. However, he quickly shifts tack, recommending that aliens be allowed to serve in the cavalry. Given that the cavalry was a preserve of the aristocracy (for one thing, a cavalryman had to supply his own horse, thus making service an expensive proposition), this is a radical position to take.[71] Forgotten is the glory that would accrue to Athens for not relying on foreigners to fight its battles, or the improvements in morale, solidarity, and military efficiency thought to come from a military unit's ethnic homogeneity. Xenophon's initial "conservatism" gives way again, and quickly, to a very radical suggestion.

Here (and elsewhere) Xenophon appears to believe that providing a "good business climate" will not be sufficient to attract resident aliens and other foreigners in the numbers he wishes. At least among the economically more successful, a desire for honor is likely to arise alongside the (partly fulfilled) desire for profit. Xenophon is willing to accommodate this desire — allowing aliens to join the cavalry is perhaps the accommodation that would be most shocking to conventional Athenian opinion — but Xenophon also recommends such things as offering foreign merchants and shipowners seats of honor at the theatrical festivals as well as other forms of hospitality (3.4) and allowing aliens to own land and houses in Athens (2.6). As a general principle, Xenophon states that all rules that discriminate against resident aliens should be abolished, except, to be sure, for those that directly benefit the city itself (such as the requirement to pay the special tax) (2.2).

Xenophon's initial recommendations for attracting resident aliens and improving Athens' "business climate" would not, according to him, cost any money. Other possibilities, however, involve public undertakings of various kinds, whose implementation would require raising capital (3.6).

The term "capital fund," although perhaps the best translation for the Greek word used in the text, can nevertheless mislead the reader into believing that Xenophon is proposing that Athenians voluntarily "invest" in the public undertakings he recommends. He further compounds the confusion by talking about the "return" (complete with calculations of interest rates) that individuals could expect to receive on their "investment." In fact, however, Xenophon is proposing the levying of a special direct tax on property, although, for reasons of political prudence, he is not as explicit as he might have been. Over the preceding years of warfare, Athenians, especially rich Athenians, had been hit with a succession of such taxes—proposing additional taxation would have been as popular in Xenophon's time as it is now.[72]

That Xenophon is not talking about anything like a normal investment is clear from his discussion of the "returns." It appears that whether one contributes ten, five, or only one mina, one receives the same "return"—three obols per day. In other words, the amount an individual citizen would pay is not a matter of how much he wishes to "invest," but of how much property he possesses; the more property, the more he is compelled to pay.

It is not of course an accident that the three obols mentioned by Xenophon was the daily pay for an Athenian citizen serving as a juror or participating in an assembly. Xenophon tries to make the prospect of paying yet another special tax more palatable to the Athenian citizenry (who would have to vote for it in the Assembly) by pointing out that, whereas past taxes paid for military expeditions whose results were uncertain, and, in any case, never benefited the taxpayers directly and personally, the proceeds of this special tax would be used to enhance Athens' revenues over the long run, thus helping assure its ability to pay the wage that citizens received for performing their civic responsibilities.[73]

Xenophon neglects to point out, not surprisingly, that the tribute Athens collected from its allies, which supported the payments to its citizens, was due ultimately to the military capabilities and activities supported by those very wartime taxes. In that sense, these taxes also produced benefits for individual Athenians. His real argument, of course, is that the capital fund he proposes will be a more reliable source of revenues than was the older imperial system. Given that he is writing at the end of an unsuccessful war, his argument is not unpersuasive.

Xenophon proposes various uses for the capital fund, for example, the construction of hotels for foreign shipowners near the harbor, of convenient marketplaces, and of houses and shops for retail traders.[74] He also suggests that the city build and lease out merchant vessels.

The longest section of the *Poroi* is devoted to the proper management of the silver mines at Laurion in southern Attica; Xenophon claims that revenues from the mines alone would be sufficient to enrich Athens. Exploitation of the silver mines had apparently been lax since the time when the Lacedaemonians attacked them during the second half of the Peloponnesian War, and Xenophon proposes to rebuild them into a major source of revenue.

He asserts that one can be confident that the silver ore will never be exhausted (4.11), noting that, although the mines have been worked from time immemorial, there is no indication that the veins of silver ore are being exhausted. In fact, as one commentator notes, Athens was able to continue exploiting the silver mines throughout the following centuries, losing its political independence before they ran out.[75]

Of greater theoretical interest is Xenophon's claim that the *demand* for silver is likewise infinite. Unlike directly useful items such as the furnishings of a house, no one, he says, has so much silver that he does not seek to have more; if someone has a huge amount, Xenophon claims, he takes as much pleasure in burying the surplus as in using it (4.7).

It was just this potentially infinite acquisition that Aristotle criticized in his treatment of economic issues in book 1 of the *Politics*. Wealth, Aristotle argues, consists of those possessions that are necessary for life or that heads of households or cities (exercising what Aristotle calls the art of household management or politics) find useful for the well-being of the household or city for which they are responsible. He then reasons as follows:

For sufficiency in possessions of this sort with a view to a good life is not limitless, as Solon asserts it to be in his poem: "of wealth no boundary lies revealed to men." There is such a boundary, just as in the other arts; for there is no art that has an instrument that is without limit either in number or in size, and wealth is the aggregate of instruments belonging to household managers and political rulers.[76]

Thus, for Aristotle property is seen as a support for the "good life" — once one has sufficient property to live well, continued acquisition can be seen only as irrational and as a sign of foolish immoderation. Thus, a well-governed city will discourage it.

Xenophon, however, while agreeing that the desire for ordinary useful things is limited, sketches out the reasons why people in fact pursue infinite wealth: in good times, they want luxuries, and, in times of war[77] or famine, individuals and the city need silver to buy necessities and pay the troops (4.8–9).

Many of the luxuries that people want in fact derive their desirability from the fact that they enable the owner to overawe his fellows; thus, people will always want to outspend each other, and hence there can be no upper limit on the amount of wealth that can be used in pursuit of this goal. Similarly, the search for the security of the sort that wealth can provide (i.e., that one will not lack for necessities in the future) is also infinite: one cannot know ahead of time how much might be necessary, so more is always better. While Aristotle would have recognized the persuasiveness of this motive for infinite accumulation, he would also have argued that taking action to mitigate possible future catastrophes has, at some point, to give way to living well now.

Xenophon argues not only that the demand for wealth (in the form of silver) is infinite, but also that, unlike in the case of other items — he specifically mentions bronze work, iron, corn, and wine — no increase in the supply of silver will lead to a decrease in its value (4.6). He also specifically notes that an increase in the supply of gold leads to a fall in its value relative to that of silver, while implying that an increase in the supply of silver will not lead to a fall in its value relative to that of gold (4.10). The difference, of course, was that silver (often in the form of Athenian coins) was used as currency throughout the Greek world.

A modern economist would, by contrast, argue that an increase in the supply of currency would be expected, in general, to lead to inflation, that is, a relative fall in the value of money (in this case, silver) as compared to other goods. As a practical matter, however, it is likely that the amount of silver Athens could produce, which would circulate throughout the Mediterranean basin, would be insufficient to produce a noticeable inflation; indeed, it is more likely that an increase in the amount of silver would rather lead to the monetization of trade with and among tribes that were accustomed to barter.[78]

Xenophon proposes that Athens imitate those private individuals who have grown rich by renting out slaves to entrepreneurs in the silver mines. The famous general Nicias is one example: he is said to have rented out one thousand slaves at the rate of one obol per day per slave (4.14). Xenophon envisions that Athens might eventually own three slaves for each Athenian (4.17),[79] thus realizing the three obols per day that he had referred to earlier (3.9) as the "return" on the special tax to create the capital fund.[80]

Xenophon's claim is that the Laurion area is so rich in silver ore that there is no limit to the number of workers who could be profitably employed in mining it. Thus, he has to explain why the actual exploitation of the mines is so limited. Why aren't more entrepreneurs actively engaged in mining the known veins of silver ore and opening up new ones?

His answer is that although mining, especially opening up new areas to exploitation, can be extremely profitable, it is also risky. One cannot be sure one will find good ore, and, if one does not, one's entire expenditure is lost. Xenophon proposes to reduce this risk by spreading it around, either through partnerships of individual entrepreneurs or by having each Athenian "tribe"[81] undertake to open new areas for exploitation while sharing the profits among them.

Given that Athens may have had twenty to thirty thousand citizens, obtaining the three-to-one ratio of slaves to citizens would seem unlikely.[82] Indeed, Xenophon soon backtracks from this goal.[83] He also argues that the goal needn't be achieved all at once and that, indeed, it would be advantageous for various reasons to proceed on a gradual basis. He even accepts the possibility that no new taxes will be possible, given the financial demands imposed on the Athenians by the war that is drawing to a close. His fallback proposal is that Athens limit its expenditures in the coming several years to the amount that was expended for nonwar-related purposes in the

last year of the war; since regular revenues (e.g., from taxes levied
on various commercial transactions) would presumably rise with
the peace (and the revival of foreign trade), the excess could be invested as Xenophon proposed, and the return on that investment
reinvested as well.[84]

The expansion of mining necessarily leads to an expansion of various auxiliary activities, such as separating out the silver ore and
smelting it. Xenophon envisages the development of a populous
area (what we might call an "industrial zone")[85] devoted to these activities. Presumably, in addition to the publicly owned slaves, many
free individuals would be engaged in work related to the various
mills and furnaces. Xenophon does not fail to note that this would
also yield revenues to Athens, such as taxes on commercial activity
in the new or expanded markets or ports.

However, Xenophon has one last objection to dispose of: in case
of war, would not this entire effort be rendered useless? Xenophon's
audience would of course have been aware that during the Peloponnesian War, in 413 BC, the Spartans and their allies invaded Attica
and established a fortress at Decelea, essentially shutting down mining operations.[86] The enemy presence also facilitated the escape of
twenty thousand Athenian slaves (presumably many, if not all, employed in the silver mines).[87] Even during the early years of the Peloponnesian War, well before the fortification of Decelea, the Spartans'
invasion of Attica took them all the way south to the Laurion mines.[88]
(The city of Athens is located in the western part of the peninsula of
Attica, all of which was Athenian territory. An invader, coming from
the north, would have crossed most of Attica, with Athens on his
right flank, in order to reach the mines, which were in the southern
part of Attica.)

Xenophon's response seems inadequate; indeed, given his military experience, it seems surprising that he did not treat this objection more seriously. His first point in response (4.41–42) is that the
slaves themselves could be used in the war effort, as rowers in the
navy[89] and as light infantrymen, assuming they were well treated.
Although there was precedent for using slaves as rowers, the result
presumably would have been their emancipation, at great cost to
the city. As for using slaves in the infantry, this seems a heroic assumption; one would imagine that the slaves would rather take the

opportunity presented by an invasion of Attica to try to escape. Xenophon does not explain what kind of treatment of the slaves would be sufficiently good to negate a desire to escape; perhaps he imagines allowing them to have wives and children.

Second, Xenophon notes (4.43–45) that there were already two fortresses in the mining region, separated by about 60 stadia (roughly 7.5 miles). He recommends that a third fortress be built on high ground between them. This would, he claims, allow everyone to take shelter in one of the fortresses in case of an invasion. All the enemy would be able to do, Xenophon asserts, would be to take any unprocessed silver ore it found, something that would not be of any use to him. Xenophon does not consider that the enemy could destroy the processing mills and furnaces.

Finally, Xenophon claims (4.46–48) that the enemy would not likely be able to reach the mines, since that would leave Athens itself on his lines of communication back to his home city. Athens could either attack the enemy army en route or threaten its now-unprotected home city or harass it in the field (especially its foraging parties). The unstated assumption appears to be that, unlike the situation in the Peloponnesian War, Athens would not be faced with a large enemy coalition; rather its likely enemy would be a single city.

The implicit rationale for this assumption appears to be that, once Athens gave up its imperial ambitions, its potential enemies would no longer have a common motive sufficiently strong to sustain an alliance against it.[90] (Indeed, Athens owed its survival after being defeated in the Peloponnesian War to the rift that had already begun to develop between Sparta and its Theban allies.) In addition, the assumption seems to be that Athens' overall military posture and strategy would be different from that of the Peloponnesian War; Athens would devote more effort to its army (including its cavalry) and not leave the territory of Attica undefended while concentrating the bulk of its military effort on the navy.[91]

Xenophon's goal, as he stated at the beginning, was to devise a way in which the Athenian populace could be supported without resorting to its previous imperialist policy of extracting tribute from subject and "allied" cities (a policy whose injustice is tacitly admitted by some of the "leading men" who implement it). By attracting productive foreigners to Athens, making Athens a more attractive commercial center in which to do business, and expanding the exploitation of the Laurion silver mines, Xenophon claims this can be done. (He is, of course, silent about the dubious justice of his proposed significant increase in the slave population.)

These economic benefits would be threatened by war, and Xenophon ends with a more explicit explanation and defense of his "peace policy." To announce this policy to the rest of the world, he proposes the establishment of a new magistracy, the "peace guardians," although it is not at all clear what its responsibilities would be; indeed, it seems to be totally a matter of public relations (5.1).

Xenophon then attempts to reassure those who believe that a peace policy would cause Athens to lose power, glory, and renown. He paints a picture of a peaceful, flourishing Athens to which all sorts of people from throughout the Greek world are drawn—that is, he portrays Athens as a cultural as well as a commercial center. This resembles the picture of Athens painted by Pericles in his funeral oration, without, of course, the military adventurousness.[92]

But even those who accept that a peaceful Athens could flourish commercially and culturally might still wish to regain Athens' former leadership (or hegemony), something they might believe would require war. Xenophon responds (5.5–7) by arguing from history that Athens gained hegemony not by subjugating other Greek cities but by benefiting them. He ignores, however, the fact that the "benefit" in question was Athens' taking a leading role in the common military effort to defend Greece against the Persians. In other words, Athens' former hegemony was far from being a result of its pursuit of a "peace policy"; rather it was in fact due to Athens' military strength and its willingness to fight on behalf of the Greek world as a whole. Thus, while it is true that the other cities voluntarily accepted Athenian hegemony at first, this reflected their need for Athenian military (primarily naval) prowess; once that need no longer existed, they resented Athenian primacy, and eventually Athenian hegemony could be maintained only by force.

In the absence of an external threat, Xenophon suggests (5.8–9) that the current state of "confusion" in the Greek world provides a similar opportunity for Athens to regain hegemony, but this time without military effort, risk, or expense. Essentially, Xenophon argues, a militarily capable[93] but nonaggressive (and therefore not distrusted) Athens could, through adroit diplomacy, establish itself as a sort of arbiter of the Greek world. Athens' first diplomatic project could be to promote the recovery of the traditional independence of the Delphic oracle, currently held by the Phocians. Whether active diplomacy could be as successful in securing a leadership role as Athens' military strength had been is doubtful.

Xenophon closes with an appealing description of a peaceful and prosperous Athens (6.1). To the people he promises an adequate livelihood, that is, many opportunities to perform public duties and be recompensed for them, and to the wealthy he promises relief from the financial burdens of war. He also claims that his project will enable the city to restore to the priests, councillors, magistrates, and knights (cavalrymen)[94] their traditional privileges.

The first of these promises helps cement Athenian democracy in the sense that the common people will have the opportunity to partake in civic life fully. Xenophon, however, appears to rely on the belief that if the people are satisfied that they can continue to draw their livelihoods from the city, they will not insist on their previously preferred policy of naval imperialism, nor will they be averse to the city's return to a more traditional manner of life. The likelihood of this is hard to determine.

Although Xenophon claims to have demonstrated the feasibility and advisability of his project, he ends by advising the Athenians to inquire of the gods at Dodona and Delphi whether it would be profitable, and, if so, which gods should be propitiated. He thus implicitly admits his foresight is necessarily imperfect with respect to the political and economic issues with which he is dealing.[95]

ᐧᔛ SOCRATES'S ADVICE TO ARISTARCHUS
(XENOPHON, *MEMORABILIA* 2.7) ᐧᔛ

We may gather some insight into Xenophon's overall approach to Athens' economic difficulties by reflecting on a discussion in which Xenophon claims to show how Socrates usefully advised a friend concerning economic matters. The Socratic advice turns on ignoring the distinction between free men and slaves, a distinction that is of course of paramount political importance. As we have seen, Xenophon similarly downplays the importance of political distinctions (such as that between Athenian citizens and foreigners) in his economic proposals.

Socrates' friend Aristarchus is at his wit's end because, as a result of war and political unrest, a large number of his female relatives have taken shelter with him in his house, and he is without the financial means to support them. Socrates responds by adducing the example of a certain Ceramon, who also has many mouths to feed, but who is enriched, rather than impoverished, by them. This elicits the response from Aristarchus that, "by Zeus," Ceramon's dependents are slaves, while his (Aristarchus's) are free. In the course of this discussion, Aristarchus swears by Zeus three times; in each case the oath emphasizes the difference between slaves and his free relatives.

The second difference Aristarchus notes is that Ceramon's slaves are artisans, and hence have useful skills, while his relatives are liberally educated. Aristarchus appears to assume that liberal education is incompatible with usefulness, but Socrates obtains his agreement that his relatives have nevertheless learned some useful skills, such as baking bread and tailoring; Socrates mentions some individuals who have prospered in these trades.

Aristarchus's final response is that those individuals can compel their dependents (barbarian slaves who have been purchased for the purpose) to work, whereas his dependents are free and are relatives to boot (and hence cannot be compelled). Thus, Socrates must try to demonstrate to Aristarchus that his relatives can be induced to work willingly.

This leads Socrates to praise work and diligence as opposed to idleness and carelessness. The supposed moral advantages of work include moderation and justice. Having his relatives work will also lead to greater affection between Aristarchus and them—he will no longer resent them as costly, and they will no longer react to his suppressed anger.

Aristarchus borrows money and buys some wool, and his relatives, despite working long hours spinning and weaving, are cheerful. They complain, however, that Aristarchus alone eats without working; the women now appear to believe that justice requires that one earn one's keep. Aristarchus appears to be stung by this reproach; at least, he does not, on his own, seem to have an answer to it.

Socrates suggests that Aristarchus reply by recounting a fable in which a guard dog, swearing by Zeus, explains to the sheep that, although he does not provide the shepherd with wool, lambs, or cheese, he nevertheless performs an important function by protecting them from wolves and other humans. The result of the dog's explanation is that the sheep concede that the dog should be preferred in honor.

We note that the dog's speech could have been interpreted as meaning that the dog has a job to do, just as the sheep do. In modern terms, the dog is management, and the sheep are labor. Executives and workers are compensated differently, but they both work for the corporation. In this way, the dog's guarding activity could be seen as merely another cost of doing business; he and the sheep have different jobs to do, but the jobs are fundamentally of equal dignity.

Instead, the fact that the dog swears by Zeus—as we noted, Aristarchus's oaths by Zeus were associated with the difference in status between beings—helps us see the significance of the sheep's acquiescence in the dog's primacy in terms of honor. In other words, the dog introduces a notion of difference in status between him and the sheep. (Of course, this difference is more visible in the case of the dog and the sheep than with respect to Aristarchus and his relatives, who are members of the same species.)

The key to Socrates' initial advice to Aristarchus had been to ignore the difference in status between free individuals and slaves. Socrates helps Aristarchus deal with his problem by seeing people, not in terms of their legal or political status, but in economic terms as (to use modern language) consumers and (potential or actual) producers. Viewed in this optic, the solution to Aristarchus's problem becomes obvious.

The analogy between the sheep and Aristarchus's relatives raises more questions than we can address, let alone answer. Nevertheless, the Socratic approach, as reported by Xenophon, of ignoring certain conventional distinctions among people (in this case, the difference between free and slave status) is not inconsistent with Xenophon's approach in the *Poroi*. He too ignores certain conventional status distinctions that are politically important—most notably that between

Athenians and foreigners. He praises the foreigners for their usefulness—they contribute to the city's coffers while earning their own
keep; to attract more of them, he breaks down the distinctions in
(conventional) honor between them and the citizens.

∾ Xenophon's Intention ∾

Returning to the *Poroi*, we note that, despite its apparently practical character, Xenophon's treatise is marked by at least two glaring
omissions. First of all, there is no explicit discussion of the citizens'
own economic activities; although presumably at least some of the
concessionaires at the silver mines and some of the merchants and
ship captains would be citizens. Thus, Xenophon does not focus on
what is the major practical concern of modern economics, that is,
determining how to raise the standard of living of the population. (If
anything, he proposes that the city compete with its citizens, by renting out slaves, merchant ships, and, perhaps, real estate properties
such as hotels or residences for foreign visitors to Athens.)

Indeed, the general thrust of Xenophon's proposal is to render
most of the economic activity of the ordinary citizens superfluous.
He also appeals to the richer citizens' private economic interests
rarely, and almost never in terms of their economic activity. His
main appeal to the richer citizens is that his proposal will provide
adequate funds for paying the poor while relieving the rich of the
burden of special war taxes (which had been especially frequent
and burdensome during the "Social War"). When discussing his
own proposal for a peacetime special tax, he attempts to sugarcoat
the pill by suggesting that even the rich citizens would be appro-
priately recompensed. However, it becomes clear in the course
of the rest of the treatise that the promised compensation—three
obols per day year-round—will be possible only far in the future,
if ever.

Xenophon's consistency in ignoring the citizens' ordinary economic activities highlights the anomalous character of a remark he
makes in passing in his discussion of increased exploitation of the
silver mines—he notes that the additional development would make

building lots in the area as valuable as those near the center of Athens (4.50). One possible implication of this apparent throw-away line is that Xenophon's policies, if successful, will produce an increase in the general level of prosperity in Athens, something that will redound to the benefit of many of its citizens, especially the savvier, richer ones (whom Xenophon may be inviting to speculate in real estate in the Laurion area).

Xenophon's second glaring omission is the absence of any discussion of the navy (except that the Laurion slaves could serve as rowers in case of war).[96] A commercial city would presumably need a navy as a defensive measure, to make sure no enemy could blockade it. Would it also need a navy to keep the passage to the Black Sea open to the grain trade? (Consider that it was the destruction of the Athenian fleet in the Dardanelles that signaled Athens' defeat at the end of Peloponnesian War. On the other hand, an Athens that was not facing a coalition of the Spartans, their allies including the Syracusans, and the Persians, might have alternative sources of grain.)[97]

It is hard to assess to what extent these deficiencies would affect the political feasibility of Xenophon's proposals, in terms of policy choices to be made at the time. Reflecting on the longer-term effects of Xenophon's proposals and their meaning, we can note that he appears to describe his goals for Athens in terms of two possible "ideal types," which do not, however, seem to go together very well.

The first "ideal type" is that of a democratic and cultured Sparta. As in Sparta, the citizens would be devoted entirely to the public good. They would have minimal private interests and spend essentially every day in public pursuits, for which they would receive three obols per day, enabling them to live austerely. (Unlike in Sparta, however, the public activity could involve attendance at festivals, including performances of tragedies and comedies.)

The standard "conservative" objection to this arrangement is that it would lead to an overpoliticized polity, and especially that the common people would become addicted to the lawsuits that gave rise to the need for large numbers of jurors (service on a jury being one source of pay). As the orator Isocrates explains,[98] to the extent that the poor lived from pay for attendance at assemblies and jury service, this led them to support the demagogues, who multiplied the number of assemblies by urging the common people to rule by means of specific decrees in the Assembly,[99] and the sycophants (essentially, extortionists who sued the wealthy in the hopes of being bought off), who increased the number of court cases. It would also lead the people to support naval imperialism as a way of raising the required revenue.

Xenophon's solution seems to be to steal the demagogues' thunder not only by expanding other sources of revenue but also by proposing other tasks for the poor to perform to earn their daily wage. One important possibility would be military training and peacetime guard duty. In particular, the young Athenians undergoing their mandatory period of military training and service would be compensated, leading them, Xenophon claims, to do their work better. (Presumably, naval service, that is, rowing, would be another possibility; however, as noted, Xenophon ignores the navy because of its association with the imperialist policy. However, some navy would be required even for the pacific policy that Xenophon favors.) This possibility helps explain how Xenophon can claim that his proposals will make the city better prepared for war (4.51).

Xenophon's manner of proceeding thus seems similar in spirit to that of such nineteenth-century conservatives as Disraeli and Bismarck, who stole the radicals' and socialists' thunder by such actions as expanding the suffrage and instituting forms of social insurance, relying on what they saw as the lower classes' inherent conservatism. It also resembles the ancient Roman policy of managing the plebeians by means of "bread and circuses."

This democratic Sparta, however, has to coexist with, and, indeed, rest upon, a vigorous commercial economy, in which all forms of entrepreneurship, including commerce and silver mining, are actively promoted and encouraged.

As in Sparta, most of the economically productive work would be done by noncitizens, resident aliens, and other foreigners with respect to commerce, and slaves with respect to silver mining. These groups take the place of the Spartan Helots. Whereas Sparta devoted a great deal of attention to keeping down the Helots (who were a homogeneous population living in their ancestral lands), Xenophon evidently figures that Athens can dispense with this kind of oppression, which had a great deal to do with the dour character of the Spartan education and regime. Instead, the aliens will be made generally content with their lot, while the slaves will presumably be a heterogeneous population kept under conditions that would make organized resistance more difficult.[100]

However, whereas Sparta was known for the limitations it placed on its citizens' contact with foreigners, Athens' commercial character requires that the city be opened up to foreigners on a grand scale, even allowing the richer aliens to hobnob with the native aristocrats in cavalry service. As opposed to Sparta, Athens will be not only open, but positively welcoming, to foreigners.

Sparta closed itself off from foreigners because it feared that contact with those who had not undergone its rigorous education to martial virtue would corrupt its citizens. Xenophon, by contrast, does not discuss education and appears to believe that the citizen's daily wage can take the place of the stringent Spartan education. The effectiveness of such education as Athenians would receive (e.g., the military training required of the young) is determined by the availability of the wage (4.52).

As a commercial society, Athens will not prohibit but instead honor the private pursuit of wealth. If the financially successful resident aliens and other foreigners are to be honored, as Xenophon suggests, what would prevent the Athenian citizens from pursuing wealth? The Laurion "industrial zone" would offer a great scope for entrepreneurship (as well as land speculation, as already noted). Would some of this commercially driven wealth trickle down to the common people? If ordinary Athenians are able to secure for themselves a moderate amount of prosperity, will they lose interest in the fee, and the public service that enables them to earn it? Would Athens' commercial success subvert the democratic Sparta that Xenophon appears to be proposing?[101]

Xenophon's proposals point toward two possible futures for Athens—either as a rentier republic in which the citizens live (albeit austerely) on the labor of others, or a commercial republic in which trade and entrepreneurship replace naval imperialism as the predominant source of the city's wealth. Either alternative would probably have looked attractive to the impoverished and defeated Athens of 355.

CHAPTER 6
The Skilled Cavalry Commander[1]

TRANSLATED BY WAYNE AMBLER

∽ CHAPTER 1 ∽

(1) First you must offer sacrifice and ask the gods to grant that you think, say, and do such things that you would rule in the manner most gratifying to the gods, and—as for yourself, your friends, and the city—in the manner most friendly, most illustrious, and most beneficial.

(2) The gods being propitious,[2] you must have your horsemen[3] take their mount and in such a way that they reach the full number set by law[4] and that the existing cavalry does not get smaller. Unless new horsemen mount up, the cavalry will grow ever smaller; for it is necessary that some retire because of old age and others quit or cease for other reasons.

(3) While the cavalry is being brought up to size, care must be taken first that the horses are nourished such that they are able to endure toils; for those that are overcome by their toils would not be able either to capture others or to escape. Care must also be taken that they be easily managed; for the disobedient are allies more to enemies than to friends. (4) And horses that kick when mounted must be removed; for such often do more harm than enemies. Their feet also ought to be taken care of, to enable them to be ridden even on rough ground, in the knowledge that horses are useless wherever it is painful for them to be ridden.

(5) When the horses are as they ought to be, one must next train the horsemen: first, that they will be able to leap up onto their horses; for from this [skill] salvation has already come to many. Second, that they will be able to ride in all sorts of terrain; for enemies turn up at different times in different sorts of places. (6) As soon as they can keep themselves well seated, one must next consider how as many as possible will both throw their javelins from their horses and be able to do the other things skilled horsemen must.[5] After this, one must arm both horses and horsemen in such a way that they would suffer the fewest wounds and yet be most able to harm the enemy. (7) After this one must take measures so that the men be obedient; for failing this, neither good horses, nor well-seated horsemen, nor beautiful[6] armor are of any benefit. Now it is fitting[7] that the cavalry commander be the leader in all of this to see to it that it be done in a fine manner. (8) But also, since the city—having decided that it is difficult for the cavalry commander to accomplish all this on his own—chooses colonels[8] to be coworkers with him, and in addition has ordered the Council to help take care of the cavalry, it seems to me a good thing for you to take measures so that the colonels join in your desire for what is noble for the cavalry and so that you have suitable speakers in the Council, whose speeches might put fear in the cavalry—for your troops would be better, if they were frightened[9]—and might make the Council gentle, if it should turn harsh on the wrong occasion.

(9) These, then, are notes[10] of things you must take care of. But how each of them could be carried out in the best way, this, indeed, I shall try to say.

As for the horsemen, then, it is clear that one must, in keeping with the law, enroll the most powerful in both wealth and body, either by taking them to court or by persuading them. (10) And I think one must take those to court who, if left unprosecuted, would most make one appear to have acted for the sake of gain; for unless you compel the most powerful first, there would soon be a refuge for the less powerful as well.[11]

(11) There are also youths, it seems to me, in whom someone might stimulate a desire to ride in the cavalry by speaking of the illustrious aspects of horsemanship. And one might make their guardians[12] less opposed by teaching them that they will be compelled to maintain

horses in any event, if not by you, then by someone else, because of their wealth; (12) and that if their sons mount up during your term, you will turn them away from the expensive and mad fascination with buying horses,[13] and you will take care that they quickly become skilled horsemen. After speaking like this, one must also try to accomplish it.

(13) As for the existing horsemen, it seems to me that the Council would incite them to rear their horses better and care for them more, if it would announce that in the future it will require twice the current amount of exercise and will reject upon scrutiny any horse that is not able to keep up. (14) It also seems to me good to announce that violent horses will be rejected upon scrutiny; for this threat would further encourage owners to sell such horses and to purchase their horses more moderately.[14] (15) It is good to announce also that horses kicking during exercises will be rejected upon scrutiny; for it is impossible even to keep such horses in order. Rather, it is necessary, if at some point one must charge the enemy, for them to follow last, so that because of the vice of his horse the horseman too is rendered useless.

(16) As for making the horses' feet strongest, if anyone has an easier and cheaper sort of exercise, use it. If not, I say with my experience that it is useful to throw down a heap of paving stones, more or less a pound in weight,[15] and to curry the horse on these and make it stand on them when it goes away from its manger. For the horse will never cease walking on these stones either when it is curried or when it is bothered by flies. Whoever tries this will both trust what I say in other respects and will see the feet of his horse become curved at the hoof.[16]

(17) When, then, the horses are as they need to be, how the horsemen would themselves become best, this I shall now explain. We would of course persuade the youths among them to learn for themselves how to leap up onto their horses; but if you provided someone who would teach this, you would justly obtain praise. As for the older ones, you would benefit these too by habituating them to be helped up by others in the Persian manner. (18) In order that the horsemen be able to keep a good seat when riding in all sorts of terrain, it is perhaps burdensome to lead them out often when there is no war. But one must assemble the horsemen and counsel them to

practice, whenever they go to the country or anywhere else, how to go off the roads and gallop quickly in all sorts of places; for this is nearly as beneficial as leading them out in a group, but it is not as burdensome.

(19) It is suitable to remind them that the city bears an expense of nearly forty talents per year for the cavalry,[17] so that if there should be a war, it need not then go seek a cavalry but is able to use one already prepared and on the ready. By taking this to heart, it is likely that the horsemen will exercise horsemanship more frequently in order that, if war is awakened, they will not be unpracticed when they need to contend over the city, glory, and their lives.

(20) It is also good to tell the horsemen that you too are going to lead them out sometime in the future and that you are going to lead them across all sorts of terrain. And in the practices before the mock cavalry combat, it is a fine thing to lead them out at different times into different sorts of places; for this is better both for the horsemen and for the horses.

(21) As for throwing the javelin from their horses, it seems to me that the greatest number will practice it if you announce to the colonels that they will need to ride to the javelin exercises and lead the javelin throwers from their tribe. Thus, as is likely, each of them would be ambitious to display to the city as many javelin throwers as possible.[18] (22) But as for having the horsemen be beautifully armed, the colonels would contribute the most to this, it seems to me, if they should be persuaded that in the eyes of the city it is much more glorious for them to be adorned by the illustriousness of their tribe than by their own equipment alone. (23) It is likely that those who desired to become colonels out of a longing for reputation and honor would not be hard to persuade in such matters; and they are also able to provide what the law requires even without spending anything themselves, by compelling their troops to use their wages to arm themselves in accord with the law.[19]

(24) Now for the ruled to be obedient, it helps a great deal to teach them by reasoned speech how many good things are included in obedience to rule. But it also helps a great deal to make it work out in deed that those in good order get greater advantages, in keeping with the law, and that those in disorder get less in all respects.

(25) But the strongest incitement, it seems to me, for each of the colonels to be ambitious to be the leader of a finely prepared tribe is for you to adorn your own forerunners[20] with weapons as beautifully as possible, to compel them to practice throwing their javelins as much as possible, and to lead them to javelin practice only after you yourself have practiced extremely well.

(26) And if someone were able also to award prizes to the tribes for as many of the qualities as it is believed good that the cavalry train for in the spectacles,[21] I think this would especially turn all Athenians toward the love of victory. This is clear also in the choruses: for the sake of small prizes much hard work and great expense are invested.[22] One must find the sort of judges, however, in whose presence the victors would feel especially glorified.

~ CHAPTER 2 ~

(1) If your horsemen have been well trained in all these things, they surely need to know also the particular order in which they will conduct the most beautiful processions for the gods, will ride most beautifully, will fight best, if need be, and will most easily and with least confusion travel over the roads and execute river crossings. So by the use of what order, as it seems to me, they would accomplish these things in the most beautiful way, this I will now try to make clear.

(2) Now the city is already separated into tribes. Within these, I say one must first with the advice of each of the colonels appoint leaders of ten from those who are in their prime and are most ambitious both to do and to hear something noble. And these must form the front rank. (3) After these, and equal in number to them, one must choose from among the eldest and the most prudent those who will be at the rear of the files of ten. If an image is needed, iron cuts through iron best when the leading part of the blade is strong and the posterior part is sufficient. (4) As for those in the middle between the first and the last ranks, if the leaders of ten should choose those who stand behind them, and then the rest should follow, it would then be

likely that each would have a most trusted soldier positioned behind him. (5) Of course for the rearguard leader one must appoint a man competent in every respect. For being good, if it should ever be necessary to charge forward against the enemy, his encouraging shouts would impart strength to those in front; and again, if ever it should happen that there is a critical occasion for retreat, he would, as is likely—by leading back prudently—keep his fellow tribesmen safe. (6) Of course when there is an even number of the leaders of ten, it allows them to be divided into more equal parts than if their number were odd. This is why this order pleases me: first, all those in the front rank become rulers. And the same men, when they are ruling, somehow think it is more fitting for them to do something noble than when they are private individuals. Next, whenever something must be done, it is far more effective to pass orders to rulers than to private individuals. (7) Now when in this order, just as the cavalry commander announces the position where each colonel must ride, so also the colonels must give orders where each leader of ten must ride. For when positions are announced in advance in this way, there is much better order than if, as people do when they leave a theater in whatever way they chance to do so, they hinder one another. (8) And those in the front ranks are more willing to fight, if ever there is an attack from the front, when they know that this is their assigned position; and so too the rear guard, if anything ever appears from behind, because they know it is shameful to abandon the order. (9) But when they are out of order, they cause confusion to one another both on narrow roads and at river crossings, and no one willingly puts himself in order to fight the enemy. All these things must be present and ingrained through hard work in all the horsemen, if they are going to be coworkers with their leader without excuses.

∽ CHAPTER 3 ∽

(1) The following things, surely, the cavalry commander must himself take care of: first, how he will obtain fine omens when he sacrifices to the gods on behalf of the cavalry; then, how he will make the processions in the festivals most worthy of being seen; next, how

he will make all the other displays that must be made to the city as beautiful as possible—those in the Academy, those in the Lyceum, those at Phaleron, and those in the hippodrome. These too are other notes; but how each of these displays would be executed as beautifully as possible, these are the things I will now say.

(2) As for the processions, I think they would be most gratifying to both the gods and the spectators if [the horsemen] were to start from the busts of Hermes and ride in a circle around the marketplace and the temples, honoring the gods whose temples and statues are in the marketplace. (And at the Dionysia the choruses gratify by their dancing both the other gods and the Twelve.[23]) When the riders have circled around and are back again at the Herms, it seems to me to be beautiful to let the horses go from this point at top speed, tribe by tribe, as far as the Eleusinion.[24] (3) Nor will I leave aside how the riders' lances might least interfere with one another: each must hold it between his horse's ears, if they are going to be both frightening and kept separated, while at the same time appearing to be numerous. (4) When they stop charging at top speed, it is then beautiful for them to ride at a slow pace the rest of the way back to the temple, by the path they took before. And in this way everything possible to see performed by a mounted horse will be put on display for both gods and human beings.

(5) Of course I know that our horsemen are not habituated to do these things, but I also recognize that they will be good and beautiful and for the spectators pleasant. And I perceive that the horsemen introduced innovations also in other contests when the cavalry commanders were sufficient to persuade them of what they wished.

(6) Now when they ride through the Lyceum, before the javelin throwing, it is beautiful for them to ride on a broad front in two divisions of five tribes each,[25] as though in battle, with the cavalry commander and the colonels in the lead, in an order such that they fill the breadth of the course. (7) Then, as soon as they surmount the summit looking down on the theater facing them, I think it would be manifestly useful if you would display in groups of limited numbers those of your horsemen who are able to ride swiftly downhill. (8) I am certainly not ignorant of this, that if they trust that they are able to ride fast, they would take great pleasure in making this display. But if they do not practice it, one must see to it that the enemy does not compel them to do it.

(9) Now in reviews the order in which they would ride most beautifully has already been stated. But if the leader—if he has a powerful horse—always rides on the outside rank, he would thus always be riding fast; and those who are at any time with him on the outside would also ride fast in their turn. Thus the Council will always see the part that is riding fast, while the horses, resting in turns, will not get worn out.

(10) Now whenever the display takes place in the hippodrome, it would be beautiful to arrange the order first so that by filling the hippodrome with horses on a broad front, they drive the people[26] out of the center. (11) And whenever in mock cavalry combat the tribes pursue and flee from each other at high speed, it is beautiful for them also to ride through each other's lines, with the cavalry commanders each leading five tribes.[27] In this spectacle, their riding toward each other, face to face, is terrifying; and after they have ridden across the hippodrome, their halting once again, opposite one another, is imposing; (12) and their charging toward each other a second time, even faster and at the sound of the trumpet, is beautiful. And after halting again, then for the third time, at the sound of the trumpet they must charge each other at the fastest pace; and after riding through each other's lines, they must ride up to the Council, all coming to a halt in a phalanx for dismissal, just as you are accustomed to do. (13) It seems to me that these exercises would appear to be both very warlike and very innovative. But as for riding more slowly than the colonels, and riding in the same way they do, this is not worthy of the office of cavalry commander.

(14) Whenever one must ride on the hard-trodden ground in the Academy, I advise as follows. To keep from being thrown from their horses, the horsemen should lean back while charging. To keep their horses from falling, they should rein them in on the turns. On straight courses, however, they must ride fast, for in this way the Council will see both safety and beauty.

~ CHAPTER 4 ~

(1) On marches, surely, the cavalry commander must always think ahead about how by walking he might rest the horses' backs on the

one hand and rest the horsemen on the other, by having them ride a measured amount and go on foot a measured amount. If you think about "a measured amount," you will not err; for each is himself a measure, and he will not fail to notice it if he is working too hard.[28] (2) But when you are on the march somewhere, and it is unclear whether you will chance upon enemy troops, you must rest your tribes in relays; for it would be difficult if the enemy should approach when all were dismounted. (3) And if you are riding on narrow roads, you must pass the word and lead them in a column. But if you chance upon broad roads, you must pass the word and then broaden the front of each tribe. And when you arrive upon an open plain, you must form all the tribes into a phalanx. It is a good thing to do all this both for the sake of practice and also for the sake of traversing the roads with greater pleasure, giving variety to the march with different cavalry orders. (4) But whenever you are riding across difficult country away from roads, it is very useful in both hostile and friendly territory to send subordinates forward from each tribe. If they chance upon impassable forests or ravines, they will go forward to easier passages and show the horsemen where they must make their advance, so that whole orders do not go astray. (5) If you are running risks while riding somewhere, it is characteristic of the prudent cavalry commander to send forward other advance parties, ahead of the usual ones, in order to search things out; for perceiving the enemy from as far away as possible is useful for both attacking and defending. So too he must wait at river crossings so those at the rear do not fatigue their horses trying to catch up to the leader. Nearly everyone knows these things, of course, but not many are willing to take care and be steadfast in doing them.

(6) It is fitting for a cavalry commander, while there is still peace, to take care to become experienced in both hostile and friendly country. And if he himself is inexperienced, it is fitting to get others who know the most about each of the various places; for when it comes to leading, one who knows the roads is far superior to one who does not, and when it comes to plotting against the enemy, one who knows the different places is far superior to one who does not.

(7) And regarding spies, one must take care to get them before war, both from cities friendly to both sides and from merchants; for all cities always accept as well disposed those who bring them

something. And there are times when fake deserters are also use-ful.[29] (8) However, one must never let down one's guard because of trust in one's spies. Rather, one must always be prepared just as if an enemy's immanent attack had been announced; for even if spies are highly trustworthy, it is difficult for them to report on critical occasions: many are the obstacles that arise in war.

(9) The enemy would be less likely to perceive your cavalry's advances if the order to begin should be passed along from one soldier to another rather than by herald or by written notice. With a view to advancing by passing orders along, it is good also to appoint leaders of ten, and "rulers of five" for these leaders of ten, in order that each soldier pass the order to as few others as possible. (10) In this way the rulers of five could lengthen the front line of the order without confusion, by riding up alongside, whenever a critical occasion for this should arise.[30] And when one must send an advance guard, I always praise having hidden lookouts and guard posts. For in this way they become guard posts for friends, and at the same time they furnish places of ambush against the enemy. (11) And since the soldiers themselves are out of sight, they are harder to plot against, and they are more frightening to the enemy. For knowing that there are guard posts, but not knowing where or how numerous they are, the enemy is prevented from being confident and is compelled to be suspicious of all places. But open guard posts make clear both where to be afraid and where to be confident. (12) Moreover, if one has hidden guard posts, it is possible to try, by putting a few guard posts out in the open and in front of the hidden ones, to lure the enemy into ambushes. And there are also times when it shows a hunter's skill to put other guard posts out in the open, but behind the ones that are hidden. For this too is as prone to deceive the enemy as the plan mentioned earlier.

(13) But it is also characteristic of the prudent ruler never to run risks voluntarily, except wherever it may be clear in advance that he will get the advantage over his enemies. Serving up what is most pleasant to the enemy would justly be judged to be betrayal of one's allies rather than courage. (14) And it is a moderate act to rush to the enemy's weak points wherever they are, even if they happen to be far away; for working extremely hard is less risky than contending against those who are stronger. (15) If the enemy somewhere enters

in between strongpoints friendly to you, even if he is much stronger, it is a fine thing to attack from whichever side you may get to him unseen; and it is also a fine thing to attack from both sides at once. For whenever either of your two groups retreats, those pursuing from the other side could throw the enemy into confusion, and they could save their friends.

(16) As for trying to know about the enemy by using spies, it was said before that this is good. But I believe that it is best of all, if there is a place from which it may be done safely, to try on one's own to observe the enemy and see if he ever makes a mistake. (17) One must send out suitable troops to steal whatever it is possible to steal, and one must dispatch others to seize whatever admits of being seized.[31] And when the enemy is marching somewhere, if a part gets detached that is weaker than one's own force, or if a part disperses out of overconfidence, this too must not go unnoticed. Surely it is for the stronger always to hunt the weaker. (18) It is possible for one who pays attention to learn this well, since even in the case of wild animals, which have more limited intelligence than a human being, hawks are able to seize whatever may be left unguarded and retreat to safety before getting caught, and wolves both hunt whatever is left unguarded and steal what is in hard-to-see places. (19) And if some dog comes running up after him, the wolf attacks it if it is weaker; but if it is stronger, the wolf slaughters whatever it has[32] and retreats. And whenever wolves hold a guard in contempt, they put themselves in order, and some of them drive off the guard while others make the seizure, and in this way they provide what they need. (20) Since beasts are able to plunder such things prudently, how is it not fitting for a human being to be manifestly wiser than these beasts, which are themselves captured by a human being with his art?

∼ CHAPTER 5 ∼

(1) Now every skilled horseman should know the distance from which a horse could overtake a foot soldier and that from which slow horses could escape fast ones. It is for the skilled cavalry commander to know also the terrain where infantry would be stronger

than horsemen and where horsemen would be stronger than infantry. (2) He must also be a contriver who can make a few horsemen appear to be many, and, conversely, can make many appear to be few; can seem to be absent when he is present, and can seem to be present when he is absent; can know not only how to steal by stealth what belongs to the enemy but also how at the same time to conceal by stealth his own horsemen so as to attack the enemy unexpectedly. (3) It is a good contrivance also to be able, whenever his own position is weak, to fill the enemy with fear so they do not attack, and whenever his own position is strong, to fill them with boldness so they make an attempt. In this way you would suffer least harm yourself, and you would catch the enemy making the most mistakes.

(4) In order that I not seem to command the impossible, I will also write how the challenges that seem most difficult might come to be [met]. Experience of the capacity of horses is what makes it possible, then, to avoid mistakes when attempting to pursue or retreat. But how would you gain this experience? If, during the mock cavalry combat that occurs in friendship, you should pay attention to the horses' condition after all their pursuits and escapes. (5) And whenever you wish your horsemen to appear to be numerous, let this one thing be first: if possible do not attempt to deceive when up close to the enemy; for what is far off is safer and more deceptive. Second, one must know that horses in a crowded group appear to be more numerous because of the size of the animal, but they are easily counted when scattered. (6) Further, your cavalry would appear greater than it really is if you were to position grooms among the horsemen—especially if they hold spears, but if not, then things like spears—whether you display your cavalry at a halt or whether you wheel them into line.[33] For it is necessary that the bulk of the order appear greater and denser in this way. (7) And if in turn you wish many to seem to be few, if the terrain is such as to help you hide them, it is obvious that by keeping some out in the open, and hiding others in parts unseen, you would conceal your horsemen. But if the whole terrain is exposed, one must have the groups of ten wheel and form into rows, leaving gaps between the rows, and the horsemen of each group of ten who are closest to the enemy must hold their spears upright, while the others keep theirs low and inconspicuous.

(8) Surely one must put fear in the enemy by such things as making false ambushes, false rescues, and false reinforcements. Conversely, enemies become especially confident when they hear those on the other side are having difficulties and are preoccupied.

(9) These points having been written down, one must oneself always contrive to deceive with a view to present circumstances; for really nothing is more profitable than deception in war. (10) For since even boys, when they are playing the game "How Many?" are able to deceive— when they hold out a few, they seem to have many; and when they hold out many, they seem to have few—how would not men, if they pay attention to deception, be able to contrive such things? (11) And if one should reflect on what brings extra advantages in war, one would find that the most and the greatest of such occur with the help of deception. On account of this, either one must not attempt to rule, or along with the rest of his preparation, he must ask the gods that he be capable of doing this, [deceiving,] and he himself must be a contriver of [new ways to do] it. (12) And for those near the sea, it is an additional deception to get ships ready and then make a move on foot, and while pretending to attack on foot, to make an attempt by sea.

(13) It is for the skilled cavalry commander also to teach the city how weak a cavalry without infantry is when compared to a cavalry that includes infantry attached to it. If he receives infantry, it is for the skilled cavalry commander also to use them. It is possible to hide infantry not only among but also behind horsemen; for a mounted horseman is much larger than an infantry soldier.

(14) Now regarding all these things, along with whatever else someone will contrive involving force or art out of the wish to capture his opponents, I advise one to do them with [the help of] the god,[34] in order that chance too may show favor, the gods being propitious.[35]

(15) There are times when it is very deceptive to pretend to be exceedingly on your guard and in no way willing to take risks; for this often leads the enemy to make the mistake of letting their guard down. And if one once seems to be a lover of risks, it is possible that even if he keeps quiet but pretends to do something, he will cause problems for his enemy.

∼ CHAPTER 6 ∼

(1) But one would not be able to fashion anything in the way he wished unless the materials provided, from which he will do his fashioning, were such as to obey the judgment of the artisan. Nor would [a ruler succeed] with a project to be fashioned out of men, unless they will have been prepared with [the help of] god so that they are friendly to the ruler and believe that he is more prudent than they are concerning contests against the enemy.

(2) Now it is from the following that those who are ruled are likely to be well disposed [toward their ruler]: when he is both friendly toward them and manifestly thinks in advance about how they will have food and how they will both retreat safely and be well guarded when they rest. (3) In the guard posts, regarding fodder, tents, water, firewood, and all other necessities, he must be manifest in his care, forethought, and sleeplessness for the sake of those he rules. And whenever he has something extra, sharing it is profitable for the one who stands foremost. (4) And they would least have contempt for their ruler, to put it in general terms, if he himself would be manifestly superior to them in doing everything he exhorts and advises them to do. (5) He must, then, starting from how he mounts horses, practice all aspects of horsemanship in order that [his troops] see that their ruler is able to cross ditches safely on his horse, jump walls, rush down from hills, and throw his javelin competently. For all these things contribute something to not being held in contempt. (6) If they judge that he also knows how to put troops in order and is able to make preparations so that they would get the advantage over the enemy, and if in addition to this they also embrace the notion that he would not lead them against the enemy carelessly, without [the help of] the gods, or contrary to the sacrifices, this would all make the ruled more obedient to their ruler.

∼ CHAPTER 7 ∼

(1) Certainly it is fitting for every ruler to be prudent, but the cavalry commander of the Athenians must be far superior also

in serving the gods and in being warlike; for right on the border he faces not only rival cavalry of similar numbers but many
hoplites[36] as well. (2) And if he should attempt to invade enemy
territory without the rest of the city, he would run the risk of
confronting both of these with only his cavalry. And if the enemy
should invade the territory of the Athenians, in the first place he
would not do this unless he were bringing along other horsemen
in addition to his own and, in addition to the horsemen, hoplites
in such numbers as he would think not even all Athenians would
suffice to do battle. (3) Against so numerous an enemy, if the entire city should go out in order to defend its territory, the hopes
are fair. For with [the help of] god, the horsemen will be better,
if someone takes care of them as need be, and the hoplites will
be no fewer and will have bodies no worse, and souls more loving of honor, if they have been led to exercise correctly, with [the
help of] god. And with regard to ancestors, at least, the Athenians
think they are no worse than Boeotians.

(4) But if the city should turn to its navy and is content to keep
its walls safe, just as when the Lacedaemonians invaded with all
the Greeks, and if she expects its cavalry to protect what is outside
of the walls, having them alone run the whole risk against all the
city's opponents—here, I think, first, the gods are needed to be
strong allies. Second, it is fitting also that the cavalry commander
be a fully accomplished man,[37] for he needs great prudence
against those who are far more numerous, and he needs daring as
well, whenever a critical occasion arises. (5) He also, as it seems
to me, needs to be capable of working hard.[38] For if he runs the
risk of the invading army, against which not even the entire city
is willing to take a stand, it is clear that he would suffer whatever
the stronger would wish, and not be able to do anything. (6) But if
he should keep watch over what is outside the walls with enough
troops to observe the enemy and, from as far away as possible,
to bring back into safety what they need to. . . .[39] Few are no less
capable of keeping a lookout than many, and those who do not
trust either themselves or their horses are no less suited to keep
watch over and bring back into safety what belongs to friends. (7)
For fear seems to me to be a terrific fellow guard. And one who
makes his guards out of [the fearful] would perhaps plan cor-

rectly. But as regards the troops above and beyond those used to keep watch, if anyone believes that he has an army, it will appear small to him; for it will be lacking in all respects when it comes to running risks out in the open. But if he uses them as plunderers, it is likely he would have a force quite sufficient to accomplish this. (8) But even as he keeps them always at the ready to do something, and while staying out of sight, he must, it seems to me, be on the lookout in case the army of the enemy makes a mistake in anything. (9) To just the extent that they are more numerous, soldiers are somehow wont to make more mistakes; for either they scatter out of concern for provisions, or when on the march, out of disorder, some go far forward, while others lag back more than is opportune. (10) Accordingly, one must not let such mistakes go unpunished (otherwise, the entire country will become [the enemy's] camp), though he must also pay attention to this in fine fashion, that after he acts, he be the first to retreat, before the main body of the enemy comes up to help. (11) An army on the march often comes to roads where the many are no more powerful than the few; and at crossings it is possible for one who pays attention, following behind in safety, to count out the enemy so that he engages just as many of them as he wishes. (12) And there are times when it is a fine thing to attack those who are making camp, having breakfast, making dinner, or also those who are getting up out of bed; for in all these cases, soldiers are disarmed—hoplites for a shorter period of time, horsemen for longer. (13) One must never cease plotting against scouts and advance guards; for these are always few, but they sometimes are stationed far from the main strength. (14) But when the enemy guards in fine fashion against such efforts, it is a fine thing, with [the help of] god, to sneak unseen into enemy territory, after first taking care [to learn][40] how many advance guards they have and where in each part of the country they have them; for there is no plunder so fine as guards, if they may be overcome. And guards are easily deceived; (15) for they pursue whatever little thing they see, believing that this is their assignment. Escape routes, however, must be considered so they don't lead directly toward the troops who will be coming to help [the guards when they are attacked].

∼ CHAPTER 8 ∼

(1) As for those who are going to be able to harm a much stronger army, and to do so safely, they clearly need to be so far superior that they appear to be experts trained in the warlike deeds of horsemanship, while their enemies appear to be mere amateurs.[41] (2) Now this could be the case, first, if those who intend to become plunderers have worked hard at riding, so that they are able to endure the hard work of a military campaign; for those who are negligent in this regard, whether horses or men, would likely compete like women against men.

(3) Those who have been taught and habituated to leap across ditches, jump over walls, bound up steep hills, descend safely from high places, ride swiftly downward—these would surpass those who neglected these things to the same degree that winged creatures surpass those on foot. Also, those who have worked hard to toughen their [horses'] feet will surpass those unpracticed on rough and rocky ground to the same degree that the healthy surpass the lame. And, when it comes to advances and retreats, those who are experienced in various places, compared to those who are inexperienced, would surpass them to the same degree that the sighted surpass the blind.

(4) One must know this too, that well-prepared horses are ones that have been well fed and have exercised so much that they do not get winded in their hard work.[42] Since the bridles and the saddlecloths are usable when attached by straps, the cavalry commander must never be without straps; for with a small expense he would render his troops useful when they would otherwise be at a loss.[43]

(5) But if someone should believe that it is a lot of trouble if he needs to train in horsemanship like this, he should reflect that those training for athletic contests have a lot more trouble and difficulty than those who practice horsemanship to the highest degree. (6) In athletic exercises, athletes must work hard at the majority of them with the sweat of the brow, whereas in horsemanship exercises are done for the most part with pleasure. As for that very thing that one might pray for, to become winged,

there is nothing more like it among mere human deeds [than rid-ing]. (7) Moreover, being victorious in war is far more esteemed than in boxing; for the city also has a certain share in this esteem. And in the majority of cases the gods crown cities with happiness for victory in war, so I do not know what it is fitting to train in more than in the arts of war.

(8) One must keep in mind that also those who plunder at sea, because they have trained at working hard, are able to live off even those who are much stronger. And on land as well, it is fitting for those who do not have harvests of their own but are deprived of nourishment to turn to plunder; for one must either work or be nourished from what others have worked on. Otherwise, it is not at all easy either to stay alive or to obtain peace.

(9) One must also remember never to charge those who are stronger if you leave in your rear places that are hard for horses to traverse. To make a mistake is not the same thing for one who is trying to get away and one who is in pursuit. (10) I wish moreover to mention guarding against the following mistake too. For there are some who, whenever they think they are stronger than those they are attacking, attack with a force that is weak in all respects. As a result, they have often suffered what they thought they would inflict. And, whenever they know clearly that they are weaker, they engage their entire force, however great it may be. (11) But I say one must do the opposite of this. Whenever one attacks thinking he will prove stronger, let him not spare his power, however great it may be; for being victorious by a wide margin has never yet proved a matter of regret for anyone. (12) But when he attacks those who are stronger by far and he knows in advance that he must flee after doing whatever he can, I say it is much better in such cases to attack with few rather than many—though these few should be selected, both horses and men, for being the best; for if they are, they would be able both to accomplish something and to retreat more safely. (13) But when he has led all his troops against a stronger foe and he wishes to retreat, it is necessary that those on the slowest horses be captured, that others fall off because of poor horsemanship, and that others get cut off because of rough terrain; for it is difficult to find much ground such as one would pray for. (14) And because of their large numbers they would bump into one another, and hinder and harm

each other in many ways. But good horses and horsemen are able to escape even on their own, especially if one uses the rest of the horsemen to contrive something frightening for their pursuers. (15) False ambushes are also advantageous for this. This too is useful: find places where friends, appearing from positions of safety, would make those in pursuit go more slowly. (16) But this too is clear, that when it comes to hard work and speed, the few would surpass the many much more than the many surpass the few. I do not mean that because they are few they will also be able to work harder and be swifter, but that it is easier to find few than many who will take care of their horses as one ought and will themselves practice horsemanship prudently.

(17) If ever one should happen to contend against horsemen that are about equal in number, I think it would not be worse if [each colonel] should make two orders out of his tribe, and the colonel should lead one and whoever is thought best should lead the other; (18) and this one, then, should follow in the rear, behind the order with the colonel. And just when their opponents were near, he should ride out against the enemy when the order was passed. For in this way I think they would be both more startling to the enemy and harder to fight against. (19) And if each of the two orders had infantry troops and these too were hidden behind the horsemen, and if they appeared suddenly and came to close quarters, it seems to me they would contribute far more to achieving a victory. For I see that what is unexpected, if good, is more cheering to human beings; and if terrible, is more stunning to them. (20) One could recognize this especially by considering how those who fall into ambushes are stunned, even if they are far more numerous; and how, when enemies are positioned opposite one another, they suffer the greatest fears in the first few days.

(21) Now to arrange one's troops in these orders is not difficult; but to find those who will prudently, faithfully, eagerly, and with good spirit ride forward against the enemy, this belongs to the good cavalry commander. (22) For he must himself be sufficient both to say and to do such things that the ruled will recognize that it is good to obey, follow, and ride to close quarters against the enemy, will desire to hear something noble, and will be able to endure steadfastly in what they know.

(23) To take another case, if ever there are either phalanxes arranged opposite one another, or each side has taken a position and cavalry skirmishing takes place in between them—routs, pursuits, and retreats—[cavalry troops] are then accustomed in most cases to start slowly after such maneuvers, while they ride fastest in between. (24) If after making a feint of this sort, someone should then come out of his turns and rapidly give chase and rapidly retreat, he would be able to harm his enemy the most and, as is likely, get though the contest in the safest way, rapidly pursuing when near his own force and rapidly retreating from the enemy's forces. (25) And if he were also able to escape notice while leaving aside four or five of the best horses and men from each order, they would have a great advantage in falling upon the enemy when they were turning around.

∾ CHAPTER 9 ∾

(1) It is sufficient to read these things even just a few times; but one must always reflect on one's own chance situation, and while considering the present circumstances, one must work hard for what is advantageous. To write down everything that must be done is no more possible than to know the entire future. (2) Of all these notes it seems to me the best is this: take care that everything one knows to be good gets done. Things that are correctly known do not bear fruit in farming, managing a ship, or ruling, unless someone takes care that they are also carried out thoroughly.

(3) I say also, with [the help of] the gods,[44] that the full complement of cavalry would be filled out to one thousand horsemen far more quickly and far more easily for the citizens if they should enroll two hundred foreign horsemen.[45] For it seems to me that if these were added, it would make the whole cavalry both more obedient and more ambitious toward each other to excel in manly goodness. (4) And I know that the Lacedaemonian cavalry is beginning to win a good reputation since they included foreign horsemen. And in other cities everywhere I see the foreign elements winning a good reputation; for need contributes to great zeal. (5) To offset the cost of the horses, I believe there are funds available from those who

vehemently resist serving in the cavalry—because even the troops who are now enrolled in the cavalry are willing to spend their silver so as not to do so[46]—from those wealthy but in body unable, and also, I think, from orphans of those having powerful households.[47] (6) I believe that also some of the resident aliens would be ambitious if they were enrolled in the cavalry. For I see that in whatever other honors the citizens share with them, some are willing to carry out their assignment ambitiously. (7) It seems to me also that infantry would be most active along with the horses, if it should be composed of men most opposed to the enemy.[48] (8) All these things would come to pass if the gods are willing as well.

And if anyone wonders at this, that it has often been written to act "with [the help of] god," let him know well that if he runs risks often, he will wonder at it less; and so too if he considers that whenever there is war, opponents plot against each other, but they rarely know how the plots will turn out. (9) In such matters, then, it is impossible to find anyone from whom to seek counsel, except gods. For they know all things and they give signs in advance to whomever they wish, in sacrifices, in omens, in voices, and in dreams. It is likely they are more willing to give counsel to people who ask what they must do not only when they are in need but who also do the gods whatever service they can in times of good fortune.[49]

An *Introduction to* The Skilled Cavalry Commander

Wayne Ambler

The Skilled Cavalry Commander is regarded as one of Xenophon's lesser works. Several considerations support this categorization: it is short, neither Socrates nor his characteristically probing dialogue appears in it, and it presents no brilliant examples of any speeches or deeds of political or military leadership. It never refers to a Cyrus or a Xenophon, for example. Nor is its vocabulary elevated by terms like "wisdom," "philosophy," or "virtue."[50] It is also limited in scope and time. At least in several important passages, the cavalry commander primarily under consideration is an Athenian officer subordinate to the city, to its laws, and to other political and military authorities, at a particular moment in Athens' history (7.1–8; 3.1–14; 9.3–7).[51] Even Xenophon himself announces limits to the importance of his essay. He indicates that it does not readily provide all the knowledge needed to command well and that knowledge is insufficient in any event. On the former point, he insists that no book can teach how best to perform all the duties of a cavalry commander: circumstances are always changing and cannot be known in advance, but it is on the basis of what is advantageous in light of them that decisions must be made (9.1).[52] Second, the challenge of leadership is not entirely one of knowledge; it lies as much in doing what we know to be good as in knowing what is good in the first place (9.2; 4.5). Finally, the scope of this essay may seem narrow because its first sentence addresses a single (unnamed) individual,[53] and the essay discusses a very specific task or skill, commanding a cavalry.[54] This said, and even while noting limits to what it can achieve, Xenophon nevertheless recommends reading his essay several times (9.1); and if after comparing it to Xenophon's other works one should judge the *Commander* to be a lesser one, we will see that it is both a useful and a provocative essay.

The *Commander* is in the first place an essay intended to help a cavalry commander discharge his responsibilities well. Toward this end, it includes lessons on such likely subjects as the training of horses as well as soldiers, the chain of command, the formations or "orders" one should use on the march and in battle, the importance of obedience and how to foster it, and how soldiers should hold their lances. Although it considers especially the situation of the cavalry commander in Athens at a time when Thebes posed a major threat and the cavalry was undermanned, the essay is broad enough to offer advice that would be useful if it were taught to aspiring officers either at West Point or in ancient Athens. Moreover, its frank acknowledgments of the challenges leaders must face would make it a sober and hence useful text for many of the leadership programs on contemporary American campuses, which often imply that everyone can be a leader and do not consider cases in which defeat and death are the price of failure. Many of its practical lessons may be called "commonsensical." Partly because my essay is to serve as an introduction but especially in the belief that such reminders are in the spirit of the original essay, I will begin by mentioning four commonsense recommendations Xenophon makes. I will thereafter turn to the deeper issues of his essay.

∾ Commonsense Advice ∾

Work hard, Train hard! Xenophon himself tells us that his most important point is that one must actually take care to do what one knows should be done (9.2). Knowledge is necessary,[55] but it is not sufficient: one cannot lead cavalry troops, or anyone else, if one does not *do* anything. One might know a lot about farming, but if one never stoops to plant a seed, there will be no harvest. Xenophon stresses that his advice is in this regard not hard to understand: every athlete knows that hard work and training are essential to victory (8.5–7), but not every athlete trains with equal zeal. Knowledge is not the whole of the ruler's virtue; it must be supplemented by active caring.[56] Consider this passage: "Nearly everyone knows these things [such as making sure the troops in the rear of a march do not get separated from those in the front], of course, but not many are willing to take care and be steadfast in doing them" (4.5). It is easier to know, for example, that one ought to practice riding under all conditions than it is to go riding in cold and wet weather; and perhaps it is easier to know that sharing one's possessions will win goodwill than it is to actually part with them (6.2–3).

Hard work is required in part because long training is required. The commander and his troops must work hard to acquire such skills as riding over varied terrain, changing formations, remounting, and throwing the javelin. Their hard work must thus be properly directed, and it must come long before the critical moments in which it is likely to pay off (2.9; 8.2–3, 8, 16; 7.4; cf. 1.26). There are ways to reduce the tedium of regular exercise or stimulate zeal for it (1.18–20, 26), but regular training is essential. The cavalry commander thus must not only work hard and train hard; he must also stimulate others to do the same.

Practice what you preach! A second straightforward but important point is that the cavalry commander must be an excellent horseman: he must in the first place be an excellent rider in all respects and must throw the javelin well (1.25; 6.5–6). Of course being an excellent horseman might save his life and enable him to defeat a rival, but Xenophon stresses the need for excellence especially because of its effect on the soldiers he leads, at least when this excellence is made manifest. This is one of several cases in which Xenophon puts his point in general terms. He never actually says "cavalry" or "cavalry commander" in chapter 6, where this point is made, but speaks rather of the "ruler" and the "ruled," as if all rulers must begin by being supremely good in the skills they demand of others (6.4).[57] By this presentation, rank alone will not reliably win one obedience or protect one against contempt.

Broaden your gaze! Third, the *Commander* teaches that the scope or range of military leadership is vast. The commander can take no detail for granted but must attend to such seemingly minor matters as the condition of the hooves of his soldiers' horses and the need to carry enough straps—for battles may be lost owing to sore feet or the absence of some seemingly insignificant gear (1.16; 8.4).[58] As the commander must look down to the details and preconditions of his rule, so he must also look up to the political context of his position. Sometimes the Council or city as a whole will make decisions that will have a powerful effect on the Athenian military commander. The size of his force, its training, the chosen wartime strategy, and even the quality of his soldiers' horses will be powerfully affected or even determined by decisions made by political bodies (1.8–10, 13–14; 3.5, 9; 7.3–4). While it is imperative for the ruler to be aware of this dependency, Xenophon does not counsel that it be simply accepted. The commander must seek political influence as well: he must win support from the Council, for example, and Xenophon never teaches blind acceptance of the city's decisions. To the contrary, he implies that the city might act adversely to the interests of the cavalry, of its commander, or even of the city itself (1.8; 5.13; 7.15). The power of the city is noted, but not its wisdom, justice, or loving care. Rulers in subordinate positions must consider not only how to rule their primary subjects but also how to influence—or even to "teach" (5.13)—those who rule over them. To us today it might seem to challenge the civilian control of the military for West Point to teach cadets how to influence Congress, but Xenophon does not neglect the importance of trying to use and to guide the Council and the city in general. Xenophon appears to follow his own advice, for his essay ends with a radically innovative suggestion about how to build up the numbers of the cavalry, the opposite of complacent fidelity to traditional policy (9.3–7).

Practice trickery! Deceive! Fourth, the commander must be an expert in deception. He must be able to make a small force seem large, a large force seem small; a distant force seem close, a close force seem distant; a vulnerable force seem threatening, a threatening force seem vulnerable. He must be able to watch the enemy so as to choose the right moment to attack them directly or steal from them surreptitiously. He must employ spies as well as scouts and forward scouts ahead of his ordinary scouts. He must be able to either frighten or embolden the enemy by the way he uses the forts and observation posts he allows them to see, and he must catch them by surprise by having strongpoints they cannot see. After making these and related points, and after offering examples of how to achieve such deception (see especially 4.7–12, 16–20; 5.2–12), Xenophon concludes: "Although these points are in writing, one must always contrive on one's own to deceive with a view to present circumstances; for nothing in war is more profitable than deception" (5.9).[59] That is, one must be creative in one's deceptiveness: one must be, as it were, a "poet" of new tricks (*Education of Cyrus* 1.6.38). Xenophon makes this point not only without apology but even with an enthusiasm I confess to find contagious.

A final point by way of introduction is that the essay includes a good supply of sententious or gnomic sentences. Even in support of ostensibly simple points, Xenophon's summaries are often succinct and memorable. Here are a few examples:

No one willingly puts himself in a position to fight the enemy. (2.9)
Men think it is more fitting to act nobly when in positions of responsibility than when they are mere private individuals. (2.6)
Many are the obstacles that arise in war. (4.8)
Doing what is most pleasant for the enemy [by launching bold attacks] would justly be judged to be betrayal of one's allies, not courage. (4.13)
It is at all times necessary for the stronger to hunt the weaker. (4.17)
Nothing in war is more profitable than deception. (5.9)
Understanding things correctly does not bear fruit in farming, shipbuilding, or ruling, unless one also takes care to bring into effect what one knows. (9.2)

⁓ On the Gods ⁓

If the *Commander* would make a useful handbook on leadership even or especially in our day, it also includes subjects that contemporary leadership classes would be embarrassed to raise. Chief among these is the gods. Over all, the *Commander* includes twenty-five uses of "god" or "gods," and these occur in every chapter except chapter 4. They are the subject of the essay's very first and last paragraphs:

the essay begins by advocating prayer and sacrifice, and it ends by advocating service to the gods in good times as well as when in need (1.1; 9.8–9).[60] "Gods" is even the essay's very last word. One might be tempted to pass over this theme on the grounds that it shows Xenophon to have unthinkingly accepted beliefs commonly held in his own day but that are of no importance for today's more enlightened audience. This case for neglect might go further: If Xenophon could not break free from the superstitious religious prejudices of his day—not even with the benefit of having had Socrates as his teacher and Aristophanes as a public inspiration—then how probing are his thoughts on any issue likely to be? But, to proceed more slowly, do his comments really reflect the religious prejudices of his day? Note in the first place that Xenophon himself volunteers that his frequent uses of "act with god" may prompt surprise even in his contemporary readers (9.8). Since he sees his references to the gods as a stumbling block even for his immediate audience, they cannot be a mere reflex of the pious sentiments of the time.

Xenophon's treatment of the gods here invites patient reflection also because key passages, and especially the essay's concluding section, invite comparison with remarks Xenophon attributes to his Socrates.[61] Taking note of the real or apparent piety of the *Commander* is a useful preparation for pondering the real or apparent piety of Xenophon's Socrates. My suggestions here will stay closer to the practical purposes of his essay.

How, then, does Xenophon respond to the "someone" who wonders at his repeated advocacy of acting "with god"? As follows:

Let him know that if he faces danger often, he will wonder less [at my references to the gods]; and so too if he considers that whenever there is war, opponents plot against each other, but they rarely know how the plots will turn out. In such matters, then, it is impossible to find anyone from whom to seek counsel, except gods. (9.8–9)[62]

The experience of danger helps to open one to Xenophon's treatment of the gods. So too does the awareness that one cannot learn on one's own how a future fraught with danger will turn out. The sense of danger and ignorance open one to appeals to the gods, who are the only possible helpers in the face of such grave challenges. Conversely, writing of the importance of acting with the gods is a way of making one's readers more alert to their ignorance and vulnerability.

On the other hand, Xenophon does not promise much in the way of divine aid. He denies that there is any way for us to persuade or compel the gods to reveal what they know. In this relatively pious conclusion he adds only that the gods give signs and that it is more likely that they would share their wisdom with someone who serves them even when he is enjoying good fortune and does not come crawling to them only in times of need.[63] Xenophon recommends a policy of consistent piety, not sudden piety when at the brink, but he also discourages one from expecting that any particular line of conduct toward the gods can guarantee their aid.[64] In the end, the gods do what they want, regardless of human concerns. The commander's focus is clearly on his own troops and on the enemy. If he acts "with god," he does not act "for god."

Other passages also suggest that the felt need of the gods increases with increasing danger. When Xenophon stresses the threat facing Athens from its powerful neighbor Thebes, he stresses that the commander must excel not only in being warlike but also in serving the gods (7.1). And if the Athenians should want the cavalry on its own to face the entire Theban enemy, then in this case, "the gods are needed first, to be strong allies" (7.4). Xenophon's emphasis on the gods is at least partly an acknowledgment of the inability of the commander to ensure victory on his own, no matter what his merits. It reminds us of the limits of our power, as the passage discussed above reminds us of the limits of our knowledge.

But if acting "with god" might bring one some advantage, Xenophon does not lead the commander to expect miracles. Note Xenophon's very first sentence, which calls for sacrifice and prayer to seek divine aid in thinking, speaking, and acting so as to rule in the best way possible. As at its conclusion, the essay begins on a pious note, but the ruler should invoke the gods to help him to rule well; he is not advised to ask for miracles. Xenophon's religious education, if I can call it that, begins by emphasizing the commander's responsibility to learn, speak, and do everything he can to rule well. If the gods help him to do what he should, so much the better.

As if in further elaboration of the first sentence of the essay, a passage in the center gives a more specific example of what to pray for when seeking to rule well. After discussing ways of deceiving enemies, Xenophon concludes, "either one must not attempt to rule, or . . . he must ask the gods that he be capable of deception, and he himself must be a contriver of it" (5.11). If one is not willing to do everything he can to become an arch-deceiver, including asking the gods to help him perfect this skill, he should not even seek to rule. As implied by the first sentence of the essay, the commander should ask for help in being as he should be, not for help that simply dissolves the problems rulers must face. Moreover, the knowable demands of ruling, including especially the need to turn deception into a high art, should guide the commander's requests of the gods; he is not to guide his rule by the imagined demands of the gods—this may also help explain why the essay is silent about justice.[65] Pious acts, ultimately, are to help the ruler deceive and defeat his enemies (9.8–9); their goal is not to win divine love for its own sake.

If the commander's recommended prayers ask only that the gods help him to think, speak, and act as he should, other passages go a little further in holding out the hope that the gods will offer some aid beyond helping the commander be all he can be. We have already seen that the last sentences of the essay suggest that the gods might share their all-knowing counsel. And in the essay's only use of "chance" (*tuchē*, the noun), Xenophon advises the commander to act "with god, in order that chance too may show favor, if the gods are propitious" (5.14). Again, Xenophon promises no miracles, but perhaps—just perhaps—the gods may be induced to influence chance. But even this is beyond our control, so Xenophon's saying "act with god" is not so distant from our saying, "God be with you." It is not a summons to follow a transcendent morality but a reminder of the uncertainties of war and of human life in general.

Whatever effect it may have on the gods themselves, the ruler's attentiveness to them is important for the effect it has on his subjects. Pious conduct helps confirm the troops in the belief that "[the ruler] would not lead them against the enemy carelessly, without [the help of] the gods, or contrary to the sacrifices," and this in turn helps to render them more obedient (6.6). That is, the commander must appear pious to his troops, no matter what his understanding of the gods may be, for such an appearance helps him solve one of his main challenges, that of making his troops obedient in the face of mortal danger. To say this is not to embrace the cynical advice that princes should appear to be religious while carefully guarding against this weakness; but Xenophon indicates that the ruler has no choice but to cultivate a reputation for attentiveness to the gods: a ruler's reputation is essential to his rule. If we ever come to know that a ruler holds the reputation for piety to be important, however, then the reason behind his every expression of piety becomes open to question. This would be true not only for rulers but also for a thinker like Xenophon himself (if a reputation for piety should for some reason be important to him).

The chapter describing how the cavalry should honor the gods by participating in religious processions also notes some practical benefits. These processions will contribute to their training whether the gods are actually spectators of the events or not (3.2, 8),[66] and they may further lead the troops to think they might earn the gods' support.

∾ Challenges and Risks Facing the Commander: Four Cases ∾

Xenophon defends the importance of acting "with god" by calling attention to limits on human knowledge and power and hence on rulers' ability to secure the ends they seek. What, then, are these limits? With regard to what challenges and risks do they most show themselves?

1. Recruitment

Commanders need troops, and Xenophon's essay considers a situation in which they are not in abundant supply. Under Athens' current circumstances,[67] at least, the commander cannot rely on top-quality volunteers coming to him: he must seek them out. Indeed, compulsion and deceptiveness are essential for the commander not only when he faces the enemy; they are also employed in the recruiting, outfitting, and training of his troops, though of course they are to be used in accord with the law (1.9–11, 23–25).

So vigorously do Athenians resist service in the cavalry that the commander must expect them to offer bribes to avoid it (1.9–10; see also 9.5). As difficult as it is to recruit troops, constant attrition requires that one must always be seeking new ones (1.2). Surely the particular issues facing Athens at this time aggravate this challenge, but the general point is that leaders will not succeed unless they find followers in sufficient numbers.

To help address this challenge, Xenophon suggests that "someone" might move young recruits by speaking of "the brilliant aspects of horsemanship," but these "brilliant aspects" are clearly not the whole story, which is something a commander in need of recruits cannot afford to tell (1.11). It appears the commander should be happy to have someone else stress the brilliant aspects of cavalry service, perhaps to protect him against a possible loss of credibility in case such high hopes are not met.[68] It does not appear that either Xenophon or his cavalry commander shares this youthful focus on the allure of galloping into battle. The need for the commander to tailor his speech to suit his addressee is further shown in the immediate sequel. When he speaks to the parents or guardians of these young men, the commander is advised to substitute the language of profit, loss, and safety for that of glory (1.11–12). Reminding them of their financial interests will help lead fathers to accept their sons' enlistments, and professing care in the teaching of horsemanship may alleviate their concerns for their sons' safety. Sons may often think of their patrimony more than of their fathers, but fathers' concerns for their sons do not exclude consideration of their own possessions (as the case of Strepsiades indicated, which Xenophon alludes to here).

It is a sign of the challenges facing the Athenian commander that Xenophon does not exhort his addressee to seek only troops of the highest quality. He mentions youths moved by "the brilliant aspects of horsemanship" because they might be induced to enlist, not because they are especially well suited to be good soldiers in the most important respects. As he notes later, it is easier to find a few good troops than it is to find many (8.4). That recruitment cannot be guided exclusively by questions of quality raises an important question to which we will turn below: to what extent can training make up for limitations in the quality of the incoming troops?

Finally, in the penultimate point of the entire essay, Xenophon recommends a highly unconventional approach to help solve the problem of recruitment, one that undercuts the traditional prestige of the cavalry. He there recommends beefing up the cavalry's numbers by the addition of mercenary and resident alien troops (up to 20 percent of the total size, 9.3–6). These, he suggests, will not only help boost the bulk of the Athenian cavalry but will also improve its quality. He claims in particular that mercenary troops will be both more obedient and more ambitious than native troops are, and he supports this surprising affirmation with frequent and emphatic uses of the first person singular. Once a bulwark of aristocratic elements in Athens, the cavalry now needs support even from foreign mercenary riders. In making this recommendation, which is potentially offensive to Athenian pride, Xenophon increases its appeal, at least to a certain sort of audience, by noting that it will be "easier" for the citizens if they bring in others to serve in their cavalry. Some young Athenians think service in the cavalry will be glorious, but many appear content to let others serve in their place.

2. Training and its limits

I highlighted above Xenophon's stress on the importance of hard work and training: the commander must train both his horses and riders so as to bring them into the best condition of which they are capable. But to stress the essential importance of training is not to advance the claim that it can overcome all weaknesses in the quality of recruits.

Xenophon makes his most memorable statement about the limits of training at the beginning of chapter 6:

> But an artisan would not be able to fashion anything in the way he wished unless the materials provided, from which he will do his fashioning, were such as to obey his judgment. (6.1)

If Michelangelo had carved his *David* from sandstone instead of from Carrara marble, it would be an inferior statue: the same training will not "take" equally well on all recruits. The commander will be able to fashion better troops if he starts with better raw materials. Not only are the current Athenians so lacking in public spirit as to resist enlistment, but Xenophon claims that adding mercenary troops would increase the cavalry's ambition in "manly goodness." It is a challenge to recruit a cavalry of sufficient size, but it is no less a challenge to field one of sufficient quality.[69]

When Xenophon introduces the topic of seeing to it that the horsemen become "best" (1.17), for example, his very first point acknowledges that some will be too old to leap up on their horses and so will not be able to mount without assistance from others. As he has already indicated, this will put them in greater peril should they fall from their horses in battle (1.5). This vulnerability is a liability both for the older men subject to it and for the cavalry as a whole, but Xenophon does not pretend that even the skilled cavalry commander can rely exclusively on young and athletic troops or can make the old as nimble as the young. The commander will go into battle with some troops who, if they fall from their horses, will likely be left to the mercy of the enemy.

Perhaps another sign of the difficulty of filling the cavalry with worthy troops is that Xenophon's partly parallel treatment of men and horses is not wholly parallel. Both horses and horsemen must be trained and rendered obedient, for example, but only in the case of the horses does Xenophon explicitly recommend getting rid of the truly bad ones (1.4, 13–15). I suspect Xenophon intends his addressee to infer that bad soldiers must be treated as bad horses are, and perhaps this is gently suggested at the end of 1.2. After all, Xenophon's Cyrus found it important to purge his army of soldiers who were not carrying their weight, and his defense of this policy was compelling.[70] Still, Cyrus had a vast pool of soldiers eager to win greater rewards, whereas the Athenian commander here in view has fewer rewards to offer and a smaller group of citizens from whom to recruit. Xenophon is now advising a commander while Thebes is threatening Athens, no rich new conquests are in view, and foreign troops are needed to increase the size of the cavalry. Armies need soldiers even when they are not likely to be of the highest quality. Xenophon stresses the importance of training, but he shows less emphatically that it cannot overcome every difficulty.

3. Obedience

Obedience is a subject of special importance and sensitivity, and Xenophon takes it up more than once and in different ways.[71] As in the discussion of recruitment, the main underlying problem is that what is beneficial for the city or the army often appears harmful for the soldier.

Xenophon first stresses the necessity of obedience in his preliminary review of the subjects he will address. The precise wording of this brief passage is worth noting:

> After this, one must take measures so that the men (*andres*) be obedient; for failing this, neither good horses, nor well-seated horsemen, nor beautiful weapons are of any benefit. (1.7)

The goodness of the horses and the beauty of the weapons persist even if they are not beneficial; they are not dependent upon the obedience of the men who wield them. Goodness and beauty, at least for horses and weapons, are independent of any benefit they might produce. What about men? Is their goodness or nobility independent of their being beneficial? Moreover, whose benefit is being considered? That of the cavalry (or cavalry commander) or the city, I presume. But while making their horses, their weapons, and their own riding skills useful to the cavalry or city by being obedient, do obedient men also do what is beneficial for themselves? The importance of obedience for the cavalry and city is clear, but it is not clear that the goodness, nobility, or interest of men requires it.

If obedience is of questionable goodness for the individual, then how should the commander try to instill this quality? Consider the following passage:

> Now for the ruled to be obedient, it helps a great deal to teach them by reasoned speech how many good things are included in obedience to rule. But it also helps a great deal to make it work out in deed that those in good order get greater advantages . . . and that those in disorder get less in all respects. (1.24)

The commander, then, must explain to his troops that their obedience will bring good things, including good things for them, I presume. The commander might teach, for example, that their obedience can help save their lives in battle, bring victory to the city in which they and their friends live, and win them honor. Or, he might take Socrates' approach: we obey the doctor in the belief that he knows how to cure our illnesses better than we do (*Memorabilia* 3.3.9). But perhaps in part because all arts can be used for different ends, and because the art of rule, if there is one, does not seem guided above all by the goal of benefiting the ruled, reasoned speech is not sufficient to secure obedience in one's troops. The problem is not with the weakness of the soldiers' reasoning powers but with the case reasoned speech is asked to defend. Some soldiers will see the costs obedience entails, if only when in the line of fire, so strengthening this quality is an enduring challenge.[72]

Since teaching the goodness of obedience is not sufficient to instill it, the commander must also arrange things such that his troops are led by experience to expect that they will "get more" by being obedient than by being disorderly. So long as the commander has rewards to distribute, this would be a manageable goal under the circumstances of regular training. Even if he lacks abundant resources, the honor that attaches to smaller prizes, like medals, can help to compensate (1.26). In battle, however, the rewards and punishments are not entirely under the commander's control: he cannot guide the enemy's arrows and javelins, so the most obedient may suffer more than others. Indeed, the circumstances of battle often tend to see to it that the best do not "get more" but rather suffer most, unless their noble conduct itself or the honor it may win is somehow included in the "more" they earn.[73]

Xenophon's remarks on love of honor (or "ambition," *philotimia*) both clarify and help overcome the problem that the good of the soldier may not perfectly correspond with the good of the army. Several considerations influence how the commander should organize his cavalry, and love of honor is one of these. In discussing the choice of the forward and rearguard leaders, Xenophon indicates that those in the front should be chosen from among those in their prime and "most honor-loving [or "ambitious"] to do and to hear something noble" (2.2). Those in the back should be chosen from among the

oldest and most prudent (2.3). Love of honor and prudence are distinct qualities: Are they also opposed to one another, like youth and
age, as this passage implies? Must the prudent soldier overcome
the love of honor, and must the honor-loving soldier disregard the
counsel of prudence? Moreover, Xenophon adds that prudent leadership of the rear guard would save the lives of retreating troops (or
would do so, at least, "as is likely"). No such reassuring statement
suggests that safety is a likely consequence of having honor-loving
troops lead the vanguard. Surely obedience sometimes reduces the
risk of death or wounds, for it serves to keep the troops organized
and fighting together, but obedience to the honor-loving may also
increase exposure to risk. The commander needs the most honor-loving soldiers to lead precisely because the victory that is beneficial for the city entails risks for those who fight to secure it. Love
of honor is useful as a powerful motive and can help lead troops to
enlist, furnish themselves with worthy weapons, train, and face the
enemy,[74] but there are reasons some soldiers will doubt that honor is
their greatest good.[75]

Military formations can help compensate for deficiencies of ambition and obedience. To begin with a point in the negative, Xenophon
does not give any indication that the troops in the rear must compel
their fellow Athenians in the front to fight, so he is not accusing the
Athenians of an utter lack of discipline.[76] However, he does recommend choosing the formation of the cavalry not only for its suitability
for the immediate terrain and circumstances—columns for a narrow
road, for example, and a broad front when confronting an enemy
on a plain. The formation also has an effect on the state of mind and
behavior of the soldiers who make it up. Having trusted soldiers in
the rear increases the confidence of those in front (2.4). Being visibly
in positions of leadership helps soldiers act a little more like leaders
(2.6). Being in the van increases soldiers' willingness to fight enemies
up front, for they know that this is their assignment; and the same is
true for the rear guard when there is an attack in the rear: changing
the order of the troops affects what they consider to be shameful
for themselves (2.8). Xenophon concludes his discussion with this
memorable point: "No one willingly puts himself in position to fight
the enemy"; left to their own devices, many would be eager to station themselves in the safest possible positions (2.9). A formation is

in part a way of inducing one's own soldiers to fight. It mitigates a problem, however; it does not solve it.

For the reasons indicated, promoting obedience in war is especially difficult, and Xenophon returns to this challenge again in chapter 6 and in 8.21–22.

Recall the opening sentence of chapter 6, which I quoted above. Soldiers are the commander's raw materials, and they must obey him, as materials "obey" the artisans who use them. But the commander can also prepare his "materials." The sentence that follows in 6.1 explains further how:

> Nor would [a ruler succeed] with a project to be fashioned out of men, unless they will have been prepared with [the help of] god so that they are friendly to the ruler and believe that he is more prudent than they are concerning contests against the enemy.

Xenophon has added three new points: a god's help is somehow needed, the troops must be friendly or well disposed toward the ruler, and they must consider him to be more prudent than they are in the decisive respect. The rest of chapter 6 is devoted to these or related ways of making the ruled "more obedient" (6.6).

Xenophon stresses that the ruler must show himself not only to be prudent but also to be well disposed toward those he rules. By working tirelessly to satisfy such of their needs as food, safety in retreat, and protection when resting, for example, he can come to seem as devoted to them as doctors are to their patients, at least if he *shows* that he is taking care of them in these ways.[77] If it was not already clear, Xenophon indicates that the ruler's sleepless concern for his subjects is driven by the ruler's concern for himself or for his rule: sharing of his own possessions with his troops is defended as "profitable" for him, not as generous to his subjects (6.3). Xenophon also shows again why obedience is such a challenge by mentioning "safety in retreat" (6.2): can a ruler show safety to be his primary concern when he attacks?

The ruler's manifest friendliness promotes a degree of trust or gratitude among the ruled that fosters obedience in the face of danger. Such friendliness is not sufficient, however: what good is friendliness if not accompanied by an admirable competence? As noted above, rulers must also show that they are better than their troops in the skills they demand of them.

Finally, in concluding the chapter, Xenophon says,

> If they judge that he also knows how to put troops in order and is able to make preparations so that they would get the advantage over the enemy, and if in addition to this they also embrace the notion that he would not lead them against the enemy carelessly, without [the help of] the gods, or contrary to the sacrifices, this would all make the ruled more obedient to their ruler. (6.6)

That is, it is also necessary for the ruler to be seen as knowing how to dispose his troops and prepare them to get the better of the enemy, but neither is this sufficient. Because of the uncertainties of war, I presume, it contributes further to obedience if subjects are convinced that their ruler would not lead them into battle without having done everything possible to secure the aid of the gods. Their increased obedience is increased even further to the extent the troops believe the gods are likely to respond favorably to their ruler's attentiveness. So important is it to have obedient troops when their lives are at risk, and so difficult is it to secure them, that the ruler must be conspicuous in enlisting the gods' support.

Xenophon's third and last discussion of obedience appears in chapter 8, in a summary of the properties of the good cavalry commander. He concludes,

> It is characteristic of the good cavalry commander to find those who will prudently, faithfully, eagerly, and with good spirit ride forward against the enemy. For he must himself be sufficient both to say and to do such things that the ruled will recognize that it is good to obey, follow, and ride to close quarters against the enemy, will desire to hear something noble, and will be able to endure steadfastly in what they know. (8.21–22)

Even if one has spirited troops who recognize that it is good to obey, follow, and go to close quarters with the enemy, it is still necessary that they "be able to endure steadfastly in what they know" (8.22). The shock of battle sometimes leads soldiers to forget their prior resolutions, training, and knowledge, it seems. Or, rather, is it that the shock of battle leads some to remember what they had been able to forget when danger was not at hand? However this may be, even the best commanders will find it a constant challenge to encourage obedience and ambition when adverse circumstances are at hand.[78]

These challenges are traceable to the fact that soldiers have more than one goal. As Xenophon put it earlier, war is a contest concerning the city, fame, and life (1.19). He intended this formulation in the first place to encourage assiduous training by appealing to the high stakes in war, but he also shows that these three goals may diverge once the fighting starts. The desire to win honor and to avoid shame are allies in the battle against the fear of death, but the shocks of war pose obstacles that do not exist on the practice field or in the boardroom. Not surprisingly, the chapter on the ceremonial functions of the cavalry, where there are no enemies on hand and dangers are limited, does not mention obedience. Obedience is a special challenge when the goals of safety and nobility diverge, not when they go together (3.14).

4. The enemy

Xenophon is at pains to explore the grave challenges of ruling while yet not discouraging his reader. As it seems to me, at least, and as already indicated, Xenophon's encouraging suggestions are sometimes strained. For example, he shows the need for divine aid more clearly than its likelihood. He also tries to encourage his reader by likening training in horsemanship to athletic training (8.5–7). If anyone thinks it is difficult to practice horsemanship, just consider how hard boxers train! And boxers train hard for relatively low stakes — certainly not for a victory in which the whole city participates! Training in horsemanship, on the other hand, is mostly pleasant, for riding makes one as close to being a winged creature as is humanly possible, and what would be better than to be able to fly! But if practicing horsemanship were as consistently pleasant as soaring like a bird,

Xenophon would not have suggested so many ways to make it more bearable. It makes sense to use the example of athletes at practice to encourage soldiers to quit complaining, do their push-ups, and ride their ponies, but the great athlete may win more glory than a single horseman, and he does not fight to the death. Xenophon's attempt to mitigate a problem is also a way of exposing the problem.

Other comparisons that raise doubts include the five metaphors that begin chapter 8. All five stress the need to be superior to the opposing forces in particular respects, and all raise the hope of victory even against an ostensibly stronger army. The proper training may bring such superiority that the two forces are related as trained athletes to rookies, men to women, swift and winged creatures to walkers, healthy soldiers to lame ones, and ones with good vision to the blind. These metaphors are hopeful in that they hold out the possibility of achieving decisive superiority, and they are instructive in calling attention to training—and to particular areas of training—as the means by which to achieve this superiority. But they also convey the more quiet reminder that achieving this superiority also requires that one's rival not train with equal ardor and good sense. If one's enemy neglects to practice, one can prevail over him as men would over women, but how does one ensure that one's rival be lazy or lack ambition and foresight? The *Commander* includes lessons on how to prepare one's own troops, but it recognizes that one's enemy may also be formidable (chapters 7–8). Military capacity cannot be measured in absolute terms; it also requires an eye on the opposing force. Xenophon's five metaphors can help inspirit a commander who is outnumbered, for they make vivid the extent to which training and other forms of preparation can trump numbers, but all five encouraging metaphors presume an enemy who is not well prepared.

∼ Back to the Beginning ∼

The *Commander* is useful first for its practical advice, which I have called "commonsensical" only because it ought to be commonly understood. Most impressive in this regard is its emphasis on the importance of deception. But beyond this, the *Commander* helps one understand the several reasons ruling is so difficult, especially when one lacks subjects well prepared to act as they should, when political circumstances may not support one's efforts, and when a powerful enemy is threatening. In light of these challenges, the question of possible divine aid naturally arises, along with the observation that there are important advantages in having one's troops believe such aid is possible and that their leader might help secure it. It may make sense to place the *Commander* among Xenophon's *Scripta Minora*, but its few pages offer a probing account of how to understand and address the problems of rule.

One begins to see this in the captivating complexity of the essay's very first sentence:

> First you must offer sacrifice and ask the gods to grant that you think, say, and do such things that you would rule in the manner most gratifying to the gods, and—as for yourself, your friends, and the city—in the manner most friendly, most illustrious, and most beneficial.

Xenophon's pious beginning offers a sweeping indication of a problem of rule in general; he does not here limit his remarks to the case of the cavalry commander. Rule has multiple goals or criteria and multiple constituencies. The ruler must rule with an eye on both gods and mortals; and the mortals are subdivided into the city, friends, and the ruler himself. He is to rule so as to gratify the gods and, with regard to mortals, to rule in a way that is most friendly (or "most productive of friendly feelings"), most illustrious, and most beneficial. But are these different goals and groups harmonious?

Real tensions exist among the ways the ruler is to rule for these three categories of mortals. What is illustrious is not always beneficial, and what is most friendly (to some) may not be most beneficial to others. Ruling concerns or distributes very different goods or apparent goods, and it distributes them to different groups who will not reap the same harvest. This is one reason why, as we noted earlier, the ruler faces challenges regarding recruitment and obedience, for example.

This sentence also asks about the effect of the ruler's rule on himself. What is his motivation?[79] Is what is beneficial to the city beneficial also to him? Does he seek honor in return for thinking of the city's benefit rather than his own? In a passage that emphasizes the honors available to the cavalry commander, Xenophon adds, "In the majority of cases, the gods crown cities with happiness for victory in war" (8.7). Commanders sometimes win happiness for their cities and honor for themselves, but Xenophon never says they win happiness for themselves.

Whereas the essay as a whole explores the tensions among different groups of mortals, it says little about what sort of rule would gratify the gods. Xenophon's relative silence in this regard nevertheless implies an answer: the immediate concerns of the commander concern his troops and their horses, not divine gratification. Xenophon begins and ends his essay with emphatic but general statements about the gods, but he does not allow them to distort the ruler's proper focus on his human constituents and enemies. The ruler must sacrifice and pray that he gratifies the gods, but Xenophon never suggests that this effort should guide or in any way be allowed to interfere with a ruler's actions toward his city, subjects, friends, or enemies. Never in Xenophon's account do the gods incite war, demand peace, insist on justice, or dictate any other sort of policy. To the contrary, the challenges of rule require and guide Xenophon's counsel about rulers' words and deeds with regard to the gods. The ruler must demonstrate his concern with the gods to his troops, and he is advised to seek divine aid to assist his rule; he does not do the opposite and craft his policy based on what he imagines might gratify the gods. One might say his concerns flow from the bottom up, not from the top down.

The *Commander* offers excellent advice on how to rule and a probing account of the challenges of ruling, especially, but not only, as a cavalry commander. So great are these challenges that rulers are well advised to seek the help of the gods, in one way or another. But in advising the commander to seek this help, Xenophon is careful not to foster any more than is absolutely necessary the thought that the commander should imagine his role to be that of serving those whose help he needs.

CHAPTER 7
On Horsemanship

TRANSLATED BY AMY L. BONNETTE

～ CHAPTER 1 ～

(1) Since we suppose that we have become experienced in horse-manship because we happened to have been in the cavalry for a long time, we also wish to clarify for the younger of our friends how we believe they would behave most correctly toward horses.[1]

Of course Simon too wrote a treatise about horsemanship. He is also the one who dedicated the bronze horse at the Eleusinion in Athens and engraved his own deeds on its pedestal.[2] For our part, where our judgments happen to be the same as his, we will not omit any of them from our [writings] but will convey them to our friends with far greater pleasure, believing them more trustworthy because he too, a skilled horseman, judged the same as we. We will also try to make clear what he left out.

First, we will write how one might be deceived least in horse buying.[3]

As for a yet untamed colt, it is clear that one must assess the body, for a horse furnishes no very clear signs of its soul before it has been mounted.[4]

(2) As for the body, we say that first one ought to examine the feet. For just as there would be no benefit from a house if it had very beautiful upper parts without its underlying foundations being as they should, so also there would be no benefit from a warhorse with bad feet even if everything else were good, since one would not be able to make any use of those good things.[5]

(3) The feet one would assess by first examining the horn of its hoof, for thick ones are far superior to thin ones for having sound feet.[6] Next, one must not fail to notice whether its hooves are high or low to the ground, both in front and behind, or whether they are flat.[7] For high hooves keep the so-called swallow far from the ground, while low hooves put the same weight on both the hardest and softest part of the foot, as occurs in knock-kneed human beings.[8] And Simon, speaking beautifully, says that the ones with good feet are made clear by their sound, for the hollow hoof sounds like a cymbal against the ground.

(4) Since we began from here, we will also ascend in this way to the rest of the body. Accordingly, the bones above the hooves and below the fetlocks must not be excessively upright like a goat's, because legs of this type, being rigid, jar the rider and also become more inflamed.[9] But the bones must not be excessively low to the ground either, for the fetlocks would be exposed and lacerated should the horse be made to gallop over clods of earth or over stones.

(5) As for the cannon bones, they ought to be thick because these are the supports of the body, but not thick with veins or with flesh. Otherwise, when ridden over hard terrain they will necessarily fill with blood and become knotty, then the legs swell and the skin recedes, and when it loosens, frequently the ligament also recedes and renders the horse lame.[10]

(6) As for the knees, if the colt bends them flexibly when walking, you may conjecture that its legs will also be flexible when it is ridden.[11] For over time they all bend at the knees more flexibly. And flexible legs are justly held in high regard, since they make the horse less prone to stumble and to weary than stiff legs.

(7) Furthermore, when the thighs under the shoulder blades are thick they appear stronger and more fitting, just as do those of a man.[12]

Moreover, broader chests are naturally better for beauty, for strength, and for keeping the legs apart so as not to cross over one another.

(8) The horse's neck should not naturally incline forward from the chest like a boar's but rather be upright to the crown like a cock's. It should narrow in at the joint, and the head should be bony and have a small jaw. Thus the throat would be in front of the rider, and the

eye would see in front of the feet. And a horse with such a shape, even a very spirited one, would be least able to act up, since the horses that try to act up do not bend their throat and head but rather extend them out.[13]

(9) One ought to examine also whether the jaws are both soft, or both hard, or whether they are dissimilar. For those with differently sensitive jaws usually come to be horses with jaws of uneven sensitivity.[14]

Then, having protruding eyes appears more alert than having sunken eyes, and this type would see further.[15]

(10) And nostrils that are flared open rather than contracted are better for breathing and at the same time show the horse as more fierce. For a horse flares its nostrils more whenever it is angry at another horse or when its spirit is heightened during a ride.

(11) A bigger crown of the head and smaller ears present a more horse-like head.

In turn, high shoulder points provide a safer seat for the rider and also a stronger point of attachment for the shoulders and the body.[16] [As for the back,] one that is two-ply is softer to sit on and more pleasing to look at than a simple one.[17]

(12) And a rib cage that is deeper and more round in relation to the stomach usually makes the horse at the same time better to sit on, stronger, and have better digestion. As for the loins, insofar as they are wider and shorter, the horse more easily lifts its forequarters and more easily brings forward the hindquarters.[18] In this way the flank appears smallest, which, when it is large, makes the horse ugly on the one hand, and on the other hand renders it both rather weak and ungainly.[19]

(13) As for the hip joints, they ought to be broad and muscular so as to be in conformity with the rib cage and chest; and if they are all solid, the parts for running would be lighter, and it would make the horse more swift.[20]

(14) As for the thighs under the tail, if these are separated by a wide gap, the horse will thus also plant its hind legs a distance apart.[21] When it does so, it will be at the same time fiercer and stronger at crouching as well as riding and be better at everything else.[22] You may gather evidence for this also from human beings, for whenever they wish to lift anything from the ground they all try to lift with their legs set apart rather than set together.

(15) As for testicles, the horse must not have large ones, a thing not possible to observe in a colt. Concerning the parts below—the hocks, cannons, fetlocks, and hooves—we say the same things as about the front parts.[23]

(16) I wish to write also about how one may least make a mistake concerning height. For the one with the tallest cannon bones right from birth will be the tallest: over time the cannon bones of all quadrupeds do not increase much in height, and the rest of the body grows so as to be symmetrical with these.

(17) By assessing the form of the colt in this way they will most likely obtain, in our opinion, one that is sure-footed, strong, muscular, well shaped, and of good height. Although some change as they grow, we may nevertheless in this way make a confident assessment, since far more become good from ugly than become ugly from these types.[24]

∾ Chapter 2 ∾

(1) In our opinion we should write about how one must manage a colt. For those in the cities who are ordered to be horsemen are the most sufficient in wealth and have no very small level of participation in the city. And, rather than taming colts, it is far better for a youth to take care concerning his own good character, and to practice horsemanship, if he already knows how to ride; and [it is far better] for an elder [man] to take care concerning his household, friends, affairs of politics, and affairs of war rather than pass time in breaking colts.[25]

(2) He who judges as I do about the management of colts will clearly send the colt out [for training]. When he does send it out, however, he ought to put down in writing what he needs it to know when he gets it back, just as when he sends out his child for [training in] an art.[26] These will be notes concerning what the colt tamer must take care of, if he intends to receive his pay.[27]

(3) Care should be taken that the colt sent out to the colt tamer be gentle, accustomed to being handled, and friendly to human beings. This is the sort of thing in fact accomplished mostly at home and

through the horse groom, if he knows how to provide that hunger, thirst, and being bothered by flies happen to the colt when in solitude, and that eating, drinking, and being free from pains happens through human beings.[28] Under these conditions it is necessary that human beings will not only be loved but even longed for by colts. (4) And he ought to touch the horse where it is most pleased when stroked, that is, where the horse is hairiest and itself least able to help itself if something pains it. (5) Let the horse groom also be commanded to lead it into a crowd and make it approach a variety of sights and a variety of sounds.[29] And if the colt is afraid of any of these, the groom should not be harsh but be gentle and teach that these things are not terrible.

About the management of colts, it suffices, in my opinion, to tell a private individual to do this much.[30]

∾ Chapter 3 ∾

(1) As for when one buys a horse that has been trained for riding, we will write notes on what the one who is not going to be deceived must notice when horse buying. First, then, let him not overlook what its age is, for if it no longer has milk teeth, it will neither delight one with hope nor likewise be easy to sell.[31]

(2) When its youth is clear, one must not then fail to notice how it accepts the bridle-bit into its mouth, and how it accepts the headpiece around its ears. And one would least fail to notice these if the bridle is put on while the buyer is looking and removed while the buyer is looking.

(3) Next, one must pay attention to how it accepts the rider on its back. For many horses are difficult about accepting whatever indicates to them beforehand that they will be compelled to toil if they accept it.

(4) One should also consider this: whether, once mounted, it is willing to keep away from other horses, or whether while riding it bolts toward horses standing nearby. There are some that, because of bad rearing, even escape from riding grounds to the roads heading home.

(5) As for horses with unevenly sensitive jaws, they are indicated by the so-called fettered riding exercise, and, far more, by changing direction in exercise as well.[32] For many do not attempt to bolt unless the obstinate jaw coincides with an escape route toward home. One must also know whether it can be quickly checked after being let loose at top speed, and whether it is willing to be turned around.

(6) It is also good not to fail to test whether even when roused by a blow it is willing similarly to obey. To be sure, a disobedient household servant or army is useless; but a disobedient horse is not only useless but often accomplishes the very same results as a traitor.

(7) Since we have presupposed the purchase of a warhorse, one should undertake to test it in everything that the war too will test it; and these are leaping across trenches, jumping over walls, bounding up onto hills, bounding down off hills; and one should also undertake to test it galloping up, down, and sideways on hills.[33] For all these things assess the soul, whether it is strong, and the body, whether it is sound.[34]

(8) If the horse does not perform these things very beautifully, however, one need not reject it. For many fall short in these not because of inability but because of inexperience, and—once they learn, become habituated, and practice—they may do them all beautifully if otherwise they are sound and not bad.

(9) One should guard, however, against those that are shy by nature. For overly fearful horses do not allow harming the enemies from horseback, and they often throw the rider and put him in most grievous circumstances.[35]

(10) One must observe also whether the horse is very difficult in any way, whether toward horses or toward human beings, and also whether it is skittish, for these are all difficulties for their owners.

(11) One would be far more likely to notice behavior that hinders bridling and mounting and other signs of willfulness if, just after the horse has toiled, he tries again to make the very same preparations as before he began the ride.[36] Those willing to take up again the toils just endured offer this as sufficient evidence of a strong soul.

(12) To sum up, a horse that is sure footed, gentle, sufficiently swift-footed, willing and able to undergo toils, and above all obedient would likely cause the least grief and most likely save its rider in hostilities. And those in need either of much driving due to laziness,

or of much fuss and bother due to over-spiritedness, in the latter case cause busyness for the hands of the rider, and in the former dispirit-edness in dangers.[37]

~ CHAPTER 4 ~

(1) Once one admires a horse, buys it, and brings it home, it is a fine thing if its stable be in a location on the estate where the master will see the horse most frequently; and it is good to furnish it a stall so that stealing the horse's food from its trough is no more possi-ble than stealing the master's food from his storeroom.[38] One who neglects this neglects himself, in my opinion, for it is clear that the master entrusts his own body to the horse in dangers.[39]

(2) A secure stall is good not only so that its food is not stolen but also because it will be obvious when the horse isn't throwing its food out [of the manger].[40] And one perceiving this might know that its body needs care because it is overfilled with blood, or it needs a rest if it is fatigued, or it is overfed on barley, or some other such weak-ness is coming on.[41] Just as for a human being, it is the case also for a horse that diseases are all easier to cure at the beginning than once hardened and mismanaged.

(3) Just as one should take care of the horse's food and exercises so that its body is strengthened, so also one should exercise its feet. Now, wet and smooth stables will ruin even naturally good hooves. But stables that are drained so as not to be wet, and not smooth but instead having stones that are close to the size of hooves set in the ground against one another—these in fact harden their feet as they stand on them.

(4) Next, the horse groom should lead the horse out where he will brush it down, and he should untie it from the trough after breakfast in order that it might approach dinner with more pleasure. And in the following way the horse's stableyard would be best and would strengthen its feet: if one pours randomly four or five wagonloads of round stones as large as can be grasped, about a mina, after making an edge around with iron so that they do not scatter.[42] For, if the horse stands on these, it would be as if it were continually walking on a rocky road for a portion of its day.

(5) When it is being brushed down or bothered by flies, it would necessarily make use of its hooves just as when it is on march.[43] Rocks poured out in this way will also toughen the "swallows" of the feet.[44]

Just as one must take care that the hooves will be hardened, so also one must take care that the mouth will be soft. And the same things soften the flesh of a human being and the mouth of a horse.[45]

∼ Chapter 5 ∼

(1) In our opinion it is also the role of a man skilled in horsemanship to educate his horse groom in what he must do regarding the horse.[46] First, then, he must know that the manger halter should never be tied in the same spot where one puts the headpiece. For if the manger halter is not safely positioned around the ears it may cause wounds often, since the horse often scrapes its head against the feeding trough.[47] If these wounds are present the horse will necessarily be more peevish at being bridled as well as at being brushed down.[48]

(2) It is good also if the horse groom is commanded to remove the manure and bedding to a single spot each day. For by doing this the groom himself would change it most easily and would benefit the horse at the same time.

(3) The horse groom ought also to know how to put the muzzle on the horse both when he leads it out for brushing and for its roll. For he must always use a muzzle wherever he leads it without a bridle. For the muzzle does not hinder breathing and does not permit biting; and when in place it forestalls horses from even contriving mischief.

(4) And he must tie the horse from above its head, for the horse naturally tosses back its head if there is anything troublesome around its face. And if tied in this way, the horse loosens the bond rather than breaks it when tossing its head.

(5) And when he brushes it down [he must] begin from the head and mane, for he cleans the lower parts in vain if the upper parts are not clean. Next, he must clear away the dust down along the rest of the body, lifting up the hair with all the cleaning tools in

the direction of the natural growth of the hair. He must not touch the hair on the spine with any other tool but must brush it with his hands and smooth it in the direction it is naturally inclined, for this would cause the least harm to the seat of the horse.[49]

(6) And he ought to wash the head by pouring water over it, for, since it is bony, if he cleaned it with iron or wood, he would cause the horse pain. And he ought to wet the forelock also, for even if this hair is long it does not hinder the horse from seeing and keeps painful things away from its eyes. And one ought to think that the gods gave this hair to the horse instead of the big ears they gave to donkeys and mules as protectors in front of their eyes.[50]

(7) He ought to wash the tail and mane also, since the hair should grow on the tail, so that the horse might reach as far as possible to keep away that which pains it, and on the neck, so that the grip be as abundant as possible for the rider.[51] (8) And the mane as well as the forelock and the tail are bestowed by the gods upon the horse also for splendor. And there is evidence. For as long as they have long hair, mares in herds of horses do not submit to donkeys for breeding in the same way. That is why all mule breeders clip the hair of the mares for breeding.

(9) We rule out washing the legs down with water; for it has no benefit, and getting the hooves wet every day harms them.[52] One ought also to minimize excessive cleaning under the stomach, for it particularly pains the horse, and, the cleaner these parts are, the more likely it is that painful things collect under the stomach. (10) Even if one works very hard at it, no sooner is the horse brought out than it is straightaway the same as those that have not been cleaned. So, he ought to let this go. In fact, a brushing down of the legs with one's hands suffices.

∼ CHAPTER 6 ∼

(1) We will also make clear the way in which one might brush it down with the least harm to himself and the greatest benefit to the horse.[53] For if he cleans it while looking in the same direction as the horse, there is a risk of being struck in the face by the knee or hoof.

262]   Amy L. Bonnette

(2) But if he cleans it looking opposite to the horse and positioned outside of the leg, he could thus brush it down while sitting alongside the shoulder blade and suffer nothing, and he might even care for the swallow of the horse by bending back the hoof. Let him also clean the hind legs in the same way.

(3) The one who does this and everything else that must be done around the horse ought to know that he should approach the horse as little as possible while putting himself directly opposite its face or tail. For if it tries to act wrongly,[54] the horse is stronger than a human being in both these positions. But one who approaches from the side would do so with the least harm to himself and be able to best deal with the horse.

(4) Whenever one must lead the horse, we do not recommend leading it behind [oneself], for the following reasons: because this way makes it least possible for the one who leads to protect himself, and it makes it most possible for the horse to do whatever it wishes.

(5) And for the following reasons we also censure teaching a horse to go in front and be conducted with a long leading rein: for the horse is permitted to do mischief on whichever side it wishes, and it is permitted to turn about and be face to face with the one who leads. (6) And how could horses in close order ever be kept apart from one another if led in that way?[55] But a horse habituated to being led from the side would be least able to cause mischief to horses or human beings, and it would be most beautifully prepared for the rider, if ever he must mount rapidly.

(7) So that the horse groom also places the bridle correctly, first let him approach along the left side of the horse; next let him throw the reins around its head and put them down on its withers, and let him lift up the headpiece with his right hand and apply the mouthpiece with his left hand.[56]

(8) And if the mouthpiece is accepted, it is clear that the headstall must be put on; but if the horse does not open its mouth a little, the groom must hold the bridle-bit near the teeth and put the big finger of his left hand inside the jaw of the horse.[57] For many slacken their mouths when this happens. But if the horse does not even accept it in this way, let the groom press the lip against the canine tooth. Indeed there are very few who do not accept the bridle-bit when they suffer this.

(9) Let the horse groom be taught also the following. First, he should never lead the horse by the rein, for this produces horses with jaws of uneven sensitivity.[58] Then, how far he must keep the bridle-bit away from the jaws. For too close to them makes the mouth callous, so that it does not readily feel; but too much toward the front of the mouth gives it the license to disobey by clenching the bit in its teeth.

(10) The horse groom ought to watch closely also for such things as the following: whether the horse easily accepts the bridle-bit when it perceives that it must toil—for the horse being thus willing to accept the bridle is so important that a horse that refuses it is altogether useless. (11) If the horse is bridled not only when it is about to toil, but also when it is led to food or from riding to home, it would be no wonder if it grabbed the bridle-bit of its own accord when it was offered.

(12) It is good if the horse groom also knows how to give a lift-up, in the Persian manner, so that the master himself will have someone to make mounting easy if he at some point lacks strength or is elderly, or if he wishes to do a favor for someone else by having [the groom] give a lift-up.[59]

(13) Moreover, never behaving in anger toward the horse is the single best teaching and habit regarding a horse. For anger is lacking forethought and frequently results in what it is necessary to regret.

(14) Further, whenever a horse is suspicious of something and unwilling to approach it, one must teach it that it is not terrible, particularly with the help of a stouthearted horse, or, if not that, then by oneself touching the thing that seems terrible and leading the horse to it gently. (15) Those who try to compel it with blows only provide even more fear. For, whenever horses experience anything harsh in such a circumstance, they suppose that the suspicious things are also the cause of the harshness.

(16) When the groom hands the horse over to the rider, we do not censure his knowing how to make the horse crouch down so as to be easy to mount. We do believe, however, that the horseman ought to practice being able to mount without the horse thus cooperating; for different types of horses will fall to him at different times, and the same horse serves him in different ways at different times.[60]

∼ CHAPTER 7 ∼

(1) As for when he receives the horse in order to mount it, we will now write what the horseman does in his horsemanship that would be most beneficial both for himself and for the horse. First, then, he ought to grasp with the left hand either the halter rope from the chin strap or the rope hanging ready from the curb chain so as not to jerk on the horse, whether he is going to mount by grasping the hair near the ears or by leaping up from one's spear.[61] With the right hand, he should grasp the reins near the withers together with the mane so as not to jerk the horse's mouth to one side with the bridle-bit when mounting.

(2) When lifting himself up for mounting, he should draw up the body with the left hand while extending the right hand, and help lift himself up—for by mounting in this way he will furnish no ugly sight from behind by bending a leg in—and he should also not put the knee on the backbone of the horse but instead bring the shin up and over to the right side.[62] And when he has brought his foot around, he should at that point also sit his buttocks down on the horse.

(3) And in case the horseman happens to lead the horse with the left hand while holding the spear in the right hand, it is good in our opinion to practice also leaping up from the right side. And he must learn nothing other than doing with the left parts what he did then with the right parts of the body, and doing with the right what he did then with the left.

(4) We also recommend this way of mounting because as soon as mounted he would be prepared if he must suddenly contest against enemies.

(5) Once seated, whether on a bare back or on a saddlecloth, we do not recommend a seat as if on a chair, but rather as he would be if standing up straight with legs set apart. He would thus hold onto the horse better with his thighs and, being upright, would be able to more vigorously hurl a javelin or strike from the horse, if need be.

(6) And he ought to let his shin, together with the foot, be slack from the knee. For if he keeps the leg rigid, and it knocks against something, it would be shattered. But when the shin is flexible and

something falls against it, it would yield without making the thigh shift at all.

(7) The horseman must also accustom his body above his hips to be as flexible as possible. For thus he would be able to toil even longer, and also he would be less likely to fall if someone pulls or pushes him.

(8) Once he is seated, he must first teach the horse to keep still while he arranges what is beneath (if there is any need), he equalizes the reins, and he gets hold of the spear in the way easiest to carry. Then, he should hold his left arm against his ribs, for thus the horseman will be best equipped and his hand will be most powerful.

(9) As for reins, we recommend the sort that are equal and neither weak, nor slippery, nor thick, so that the hand is able to accept a spear too when needed.

(10) When he signals the horse to go forward, let him begin at a walk, for walking causes the least confusion. Let him hold the reins higher with his hands if the horse holds its neck too arched; and hold the reins lower if it has its head and neck too much up and back. For in this way its shape will be especially comely.

(11) After this, by going at its natural trot the horse may loosen its body most painlessly, and it will most pleasantly arrive to the point of being urged to gallop. And since it is thought to be better to begin from the left side, he may best begin from this side as follows: if it is trotting, signal the horse to go faster at the moment when it reaches up with the right foot,[63] (12) because, since the horse will be about to raise the left foot, it will begin with that foot; and at the moment it turns to the left, then let it begin its first bound of the gallop.[64] For the horse naturally, in turning to the right, leads with the right, and, in turning to the left, leads with the left.

(13) And we recommend the riding exercise called fettering [riding in figure eights], for it habituates the horse to be turned in the direction of both jaws. And reversing the riding exercise is good, so that both jaws are equally used in each of the rides.

(14) We also recommend fettering at different lengths rather than in a circle. For the horse would turn around more gladly if it already has its fill of the straight, and it would practice at the same time running straight and wheeling about.

(15) And he must also give a check to the horse in its turns, for it is neither easy for the horse, nor safe, to wheel in a small space when going quickly, especially if the terrain is hard trodden or slippery.

(16) When checking the horse he ought to turn it sideways with the bridle as little as possible, and he ought to turn himself sideways as little as possible. If not, he ought to know well that a small pretext suffices for both him and his horse to fall.

(17) When the horse looks straight ahead, coming out of the turn, he should urge it on to speed at that point—for, clearly in hostilities too, turns are for the sake of pursuing or retreating. So it is good to practice being quick after turning.

(18) When it seems the exercise is already enough for the horse, it is also good, after resting a bit, to urge it on again[65] to top speed, but away from horses, not toward horses; and from speed again to come as soon as possible to rest; and from standing he must, turning, urge it on again. For it is clear beforehand that there will be a time when he will need each [of these maneuvers].

(19) When it is then the moment to dismount, he should never dismount among horses, or near a gathering of human beings, or outside of the riding area, but the horse should obtain its ease at the very place where it is also compelled to toil.[66]

∽ CHAPTER 8 ∽

(1) Since in fact there will be a point where the horse must run downhill, uphill, and slantwise, and where it must leap across, and where it must also leap out, and where jump down, he must teach all of this, and he himself, as well as the horse, must thoroughly practice it.[67] For they would thus be saviors for one another and would seem to be more useful.

(2) If someone thinks that we are repeating ourselves because we speak about the same matters now as previously, this is not a repetition. For we bid him, when making the purchase, to test whether the horse would be able to do these things; but now we are saying that he ought to teach his own horse; and we will write how he must teach it.

(3) Therefore, if the horse is altogether inexperienced in leaping across, he must himself cross over the ditch before the horse, letting down the leading rein, and then he must put tension on the leading rein so that it jumps across. (4) If it is unwilling, someone with a whip or a rod should strike it as hard as possible. It will thus jump not the measured distance but far beyond what is requisite. And then there will be no need to strike it in the future, but it will jump if it merely sees someone approaching from behind.

(5) When it is accustomed to leaping across in this way, he should mount it and lead it at first to small ditches, and then also to bigger ones. And when it is about to leap, he should strike it with a spur. And he should similarly strike it with a spur to teach it both to bound uphill and to bound downhill. For the horse will act more safely for itself as well as for the rider if it does all of this with the body compact rather than if it leaves the hind parts out when it leaps across, leaps up, or leaps down.[68]

(6) As for going downhill, he ought to teach it first on soft terrain, and finally, when accustomed to this, it will be far more pleased to run downhill than to run uphill. And while some fear that the shoulders will be shattered by galloping downhill, they should learn[69] that Persians and Odrusians all vie on declines and have no less healthy horses than the Greeks.

(7) Nor will we pass over how the rider must be of service in each of these circumstances. When the horse suddenly sets forth, the rider ought to lean forward, for the horse would be less likely to slip out from underneath or unseat him. And when it is pulled up short he ought to lean back, for he would less likely be knocked off.

(8) When it leaps across a ditch, and when it sets off uphill, it is kind to hold onto the mane, lest the horse be oppressed by the terrain and by the bridle-bit all at once.[70] However, when going downhill he should position himself more backward and hold the horse back with the bridle-bit, lest either he or the horse be borne downhill precipitously.

(9) It is correct to make the rides sometimes in different places and sometimes long and sometimes short. For these will also be less hateful to the horse than always making similar rides in the same places.

(10) Since he must keep his seat on a horse galloping at full strength over all sorts of terrain, as well as be able to make fine[71] use of his weapons from horseback, practicing horsemanship on hunts is

irreproachable, where the terrain and wild prey are suitable. Where these are unavailable, it is also good practice if two horsemen make an agreement: the one will flee on horseback over all sorts of terrain and retreat, pointing his spear backward; the other will pursue holding javelins blunted with a ball and a similar spear; and when he is within javelin range he will cast at the one fleeing with the blunted javelins, and, when he is within range of the strike of a spear, he will strike the captive with the [blunted] spear.[72]

(11) It is also good, should they ever engage, to pull the enemy toward oneself and then push away suddenly; for this makes the other fall off. It is also correct for the one who is being pulled to drive his horse forward, for by doing so the one who is pulled might make the one who is doing the pulling fall, instead of falling off [himself].

(12) And when cavalry engage from opposing camps, and pursue the opponents up to the enemy phalanx, and then retreat to a friendly phalanx, it is also good to know then that, as long as he is beside his friends, it is noble and safe to turn about in the front ranks and receive the attack at full strength; but when it happens near the opponents [it is noble and safe] to have his horse under control. For in this way it is likely that he would be especially able to harm opponents without being harmed by them.

(13) Now, the gods granted to human beings [the ability] to teach a human being by rational speech what he must do, but clearly you would teach nothing to a horse by rational speech. But if you somehow gratify it when it does as you wish, and if you chastise it when it is disobedient, it would thus most learn to serve as it must.

(14) And, in brief, this follows through the whole of horsemanship. For [the horse] would take the bridle more readily if something good should happen to it whenever it accepts; and it would jump across, leap out, and serve in every other respect if it expects some ease whenever it does what is signaled.

∼ Chapter 9 ∼

(1) Now, this is what has been said: how one might be least deceived when buying a colt or a horse, and least ruin it when dealing

with it, and especially how one would produce a horse that has what a horseman needs for war.[73] Perhaps it is a suitable time to write also how, if at some point one should happen to deal with a horse that is more spirited than is suitable, or more lazy, he may deal with either most correctly.

(2) To begin with, then, one ought to understand that spiritedness in a horse is just like anger is in a human being. And so, as one would least anger a human being by neither saying nor doing anything harsh, so too with a spirited horse, one would least enrage it by not vexing it.

(3) And so, right away in mounting, he ought to take care to mount so as to cause as little pain as possible, and once mounted, after letting it remain quiet for a longer time than usual, move it forward with the gentlest possible signals. Next, by starting from a very brief walk and leading it on to a quicker pace, the horse would as much as possible be unaware that it is coming to full speed.[74]

(4) Whatever he signals suddenly will agitate a spirited horse, just as unexpected sights, sounds, and experiences agitate a human being. So one must know that in a horse, too, the unexpected produces agitation.[75]

(5) And if he wishes to check a spirited horse when it sets out at a quicker pace than is suitable, he must not pull unexpectedly, but gently draw it back with the bridle, calming and not forcing it to come to rest.

(6) And long rides calm horses more than frequent turns, and quiet rides of long duration temper, calm, and do not rouse a spirited one. (7) And if someone thinks that if he makes fast and frequent gallops he will calm the horse by wearing it out, he judges the opposite of what happens. For under such conditions the spirited horse especially tries to lead by force and with anger, like an irascible human being, and frequently does much that is irreparable to both itself and the rider.

(8) He also ought to stop a spirited horse from going at full speed, and to refrain altogether from matching it against another horse; for generally the most high-spirited among horses become also the most victory-loving.[76]

(9) And smooth bridle-bits are more suitable than rough ones; but if in fact a rough one is inserted, he must himself make it similar to

the smooth by slackening [his hold on the reins]. It is good also to accustom oneself to keep still, especially on a high-spirited horse, and to hold onto it as little as possible with anything other than that which we use for holding so as to sit securely.[77]

(10) He ought to know also that calming a horse by whistling, and rousing it by clicking, is something taught; and if someone from the beginning presented mild things with clicking and difficult things with whistling, the horse would learn to be roused by whistling and calmed by clicking.

(11) So too, he must not himself be manifest to the horse as being alarmed at the war cry or at the trumpet, nor should he present to it anything alarming, but rather rest it as far as is possible in such a situation, and bring it breakfast and dinner, if feasible.

(12) The finest advice is not to acquire an excessively spirited horse for war. As for a lazy horse, it seems to me sufficient to write that one should do everything opposite to what we advise for using a spirited one.

⌇ CHAPTER 10 ⌇

(1) If one ever wishes to manage a horse useful for war in such a manner as to make it more magnificent and spectacular to ride, he must avoid pulling back on the mouth with the bridle, or using a spur, or whipping the horse, things the many do because they think it makes horses splendid, when in fact they are doing completely the opposite of what they want.

(2) When they pull back on their mouths they make the horses blind instead of being able to see in front, and they startle them by using the spur and striking, so the horses are confused and become dangerous.[78] These are the actions of horses vexed by exercise and behaving shamefully and ignobly.

(3) But if he teaches the horse to ride in a loose bridle, and to lift up its neck, and to arch it from the head, he would thus cause the horse to do the very things by which it is itself pleased and exalted. (4) There is evidence that it is pleased by this: for whenever the horse itself wishes to posture in some way among horses, especially when

among females, it will then lift up its neck and very much arch its head, making itself fierce, and raise its legs up flexibly, and toss up its tail.[79]

(5) Accordingly, when he induces the horse to take those postures that it takes itself when it preens the most, he thereby shows it to be pleased by riding, magnificent, fierce, and spectacular. And so we will now attempt to explain how we believe these things may be accomplished.

(6) First, then, he ought to possess no less than two bridle-bits.[80] Let one of these be smooth with well-sized rings, and the other have sharp points with rings that are heavy and low, so that, whenever the horse takes hold of this one it will be vexed by its sharpness and let go because of it, but when it is changed for the smoother one, the horse will be pleased by its smoothness and will also perform in the smooth bridle-bit whatever it was educated to do by the rough bridle-bit.

(7) If, however, the horse frequently leans forward into the bridle-bit out of contempt for its smoothness, we add large rings onto the smooth bridle-bit, so that the horse is compelled by them to open its mouth and let go of the bridle-bit. It is also possible to vary the harsh one by wrapping up the parts that stretch.[81]

(8) However many the bridle-bits may be, let them all be flexible. For the horse has the whole of the stiff one against his jaws wherever he seizes it, just as a person lifts the whole of a spit wherever he grasps it. (9) The other bridle-bit behaves like a chain: only the part the horse holds remains unbent, while the remainder hangs loose. And always searching for the part that slips in its mouth, the horse lets the bit drop away from its jaws; and for this reason too rings are hung down in the middle from the axle; so that while pursuing these with its tongue and teeth it neglects to take up the bridle-bit against the jaws.

(10) In case one is unaware of what flexibility in a bridle-bit is, and what stiffness is, we will write this too. Flexibility is when the axles have wide and smooth joints so as to bend easily; and it is more flexible if everything arranged around the axles is wide mouthed and not compressed. (11) If each part of the bridle-bit runs across and goes together with difficulty, this is being stiff. Whatever sort it may be, if one wishes to display his horse as mentioned, he should do all the

same things with it as follows. (12) The mouth of the horse should be pulled up neither with excessive harshness, so that the horse jerks its head, nor with excessive gentleness, so that it takes no notice. But, on being pulled up, if it lifts its neck, the rider should immediately give on the bridle-bit. In other respects, too, he must gratify the horse whenever it serves beautifully, as we do not cease saying. (13) And when he perceives that the horse is pleased by carrying its neck high and loosely, at this point he must present nothing harsh, as though compelling it to toil, but instead pat it as though it wishes to be ridden, for it will thereby proceed most confidently to swift riding.[82]

(14) There is evidence also that a horse is pleased by fast running, for none goes at a walk when it escapes but it runs instead. For it is naturally pleased by this unless one compels it to run more than is suitable; but exceeding the suitable in anything is pleasant neither for a horse nor for a human being.

(15) When the horse has come to the point of riding with stateliness, presumably it has been habituated by us in its first riding exercises to set out at greater speed from the turns. But if, after it has learned this, one restrains it with the bridle at the same time as signaling it to set out, then, thus pressed with the bridle while being aroused by the signal to set out, it will jut forth its chest and lift up its legs in anger, but not flexibly, for horses do not employ very flexible legs when they are pained.[83] (16) But if one gives on the bridle-bit when the horse is thus excited, because of the pleasure of believing itself freed through the slackening of the bit, it will thereupon prance and bear itself in a stately posture, with flexible legs, altogether imitating its display before horses.[84] (17) And those who behold a horse of this sort call it free, willing to work, fit for riding, spirited, haughty, and at the same time both pleasant and fierce to look at.

So, if one is desirous of these things too, let it have been written by us to this extent.

∼ CHAPTER 11 ∼

(1) If one wishes, then, to manage a horse that is suitable for procession, lofty, and splendid, such characteristics are not likely to

come from every horse, but it must have a high-minded soul and a vigorous body.

(2) It is not the case, however, as some think, that the horse with flexible legs is also able to lift up its body. Instead, it is the one with a flexible, short, and strong lower back (and we do not mean the part down toward the tail, but what naturally grows between the ribs and the hip joints down the flank)—this will enable it to plant the hind legs further under the front ones.[85]

(3) So, if the rider checks the horse with the bridle when it is planting its legs underneath, it bends the hind legs at the ball of the ankle joints and raises up the front of the body, so that it shows its stomach and private parts to those in front. He must also give on the bridle when it does this, so that the onlookers may opine that the most beautiful [movements] of the horse are done voluntarily.

(4) There are, indeed, people who in fact teach these [movements], some by knocking it under the ankle joints with a rod, others bidding someone with a staff to run alongside and strike under the thighs.

(5) We, however, believe that the best thing in lessons is—as we keep saying—that it obtains ease from the rider following closely upon every instance of its acting in accord with the rider's judgment. (6) For—as Simon says as well—whatever deeds the horse does under compulsion, the horse does not understand them, and the deeds are not any more beautiful than if one whipped and used a spur on a dancer: the one suffering this, both horse and human being, is far more graceless than beautiful. Instead, it is from signals that the horse must show forth the most beautiful and most splendid things he has.[86]

(7) And if when exercised the horse is galloped to the point of much sweating and it then raises itself up beautifully into the air—if at that point one quickly dismounts and unbridles it, one ought to know well that the horse will voluntarily go on to lift itself up into the air.

(8) Now, indeed, gods and heroes are depicted as riding on such horses; and those men who manage (*chrēsthai*) them beautifully appear magnificent.[87]

(9) The horse that thus lifts itself up into the air is in fact so exceedingly beautiful or terrible or admirable or wondrous that it holds the eyes of all who see, both young and older.[88] Indeed, no one watch-

ing it leaves or gives up watching, as long as it displays itself most splendidly.

(10) If it ever befalls any owner of such a horse to hold the office of phylarch or hipparch, he must not be eager that he alone be splendid but far more that all following him be manifestly worth seeing.[89] (11) If the horse leads—in the manner people especially praise such horses— by rearing up highest, and with its body compact, taking very short steps, clearly the rest of the horses would follow him at a walk. But what splendid thing could result from this sight? (12) If, however, after rousing the horse, you lead it at neither excessive speed nor excessive slowness, but in the manner horses become as spirited, as fierce, and as graceful at toiling as possible—if you lead in this way, the collective stomping, and collective neighing and snorting of the horses, would be an accompaniment such that not only the horse itself but all those accompanying would be manifestly worth watching.

(13) If, then, one buys a horse finely, and raises it so as to be able to endure toils, and manages it correctly in the practices for war, and in the riding exercises for display, and in the contests of war, what further hindrance could there be to his making horses worth more than when received, and to having horses with good reputations, and to himself having a good reputation in horsemanship, unless some *daimonion* prevents it?

∾ Chapter 12 ∾

(1) We wish to write also how he who intends to take risks on horseback must be armed. First, then, we say that he ought to have a breastplate made proportionate to his body.[90] For the breastplate that fits beautifully is carried by the [whole] body, but the shoulders alone carry the excessively loose one. The excessively tight one is bondage, not armor.

(2) And since the neck too is one of the vital areas, we say that he ought to have also a covering for it, [shaped] like the neck, coming out of the very breastplate. For this will furnish adornment and, at the same time—if it is crafted as it should be—covers his face up to the nose when the rider wishes.

(3) As for the helmet, we believe the Boeotian style is the best; for, again, it covers very well everything above the breastplate but does not hinder sight.

As for the breastplate, in turn, let it be made so as to hinder neither sitting nor bending forward.

(4) And as for the area of the abdomen and private parts, and there-abouts, let there be flaps of a number and kind to ward off arrows.

(5) Since if the left hand suffers anything, it also disables the horse-man, we recommend the armor invented for it, the so-called hand. For it shelters the shoulder, arm, forearm, and the part holding onto the reins, and it extends as well as bends in. Additionally, it covers the gap under the armpit left by the breastplate.

(6) He must raise the right hand, however, if he wishes to hurl a javelin or strike. So, he should remove the part of the breastplate impeding this, and instead add flaps to the hinge joints so that they unfold when he lifts [the arm] just as they close when he lowers it.

(7) On the arm, it is better, in our opinion, to place a piece like a greave against it rather than something tied to the armor.[91] And the part that is bare when the right arm is raised should be covered near the breastplate, either with calfskin or with bronze. Otherwise, he will be unprotected in a very vital spot.

(8) Since the rider is in every danger too if the horse suffers any-thing, he must also arm the horse with a frontlet, a breast covering, and side protectors; for these are at the same time thigh protectors for the rider as well.[92] Most of all, he must protect the flank of the horse, for while being most vital it is also most defenseless; but he is able to protect it too with the saddlecloth. (9) The saddlecloth ought to be sewn such that both the horseman is seated very safely and the horse's back is not hurt.[93] In this way the horse and the horseman would be armed in other respects. (10) But, the [horseman's] shins and feet would likely extend beyond the thigh protectors. These too would be shielded if there were soft shoes made of the leather from which soldiers' boots are made, for these would thus be at once armor for the shins and shoes for the feet.

(11) This is the armor for avoiding being harmed—if the gods are propitious. To harm the opponents, we recommend a saber rather than sword, for since a horseman is at a height the blow of a curved knife will be more effective than a sword.[94]

(12) In the place of a cane spear, since it is weak and unwieldy, we recommend two javelins of cornel wood.[95] For indeed he who knows how can hurl one of them and be able to use the remaining one in front, to the side, or to the rear; and these are at once stronger and easier to carry than a spear.

(13) As for the throw, we recommend the furthest; for the time would more likely allow turning around and getting the other javelin. We will also write, briefly, how one might make the best throw. For if, bringing forward his left side, while drawing back the right side and being upright from his thighs, he launches it with the point tending slightly upward, the javelin will thus have the strongest impetus and go the farthest, yet with very good aim, if the point always aims at its target when launched.

(14) Let these be the notes, lessons, and practices written by us for a private citizen.[96] What is fitting for a cavalry commander to know and do has been made clear in another account.

An Introduction to On Horsemanship

AMY L. BONNETTE

Expert equestrians continue to read *On Horsemanship* (*Peri Hippēkēs*) two millennia after Xenophon wrote his advice to younger friends on how to manage their horses.[97] Aside from Xenophon's expertise, his gentle and appreciative yet unsentimental approach to the animals must account for much of the work's continued attraction (e.g., 6.13).[98] He discusses the beauty of horses' souls as well as their bodies, and he insists on using persuasion in training, reserving compulsion for circumstances that involve the safety of both horse and rider. Besides, the relation between horse and rider stands outside of political regimes in all their variety—even more than family and friendship.[99] Here, changes of regime do not cast Xenophon's opinions in an unfashionable light.

Yet this very transcendence of politics makes us wonder whether today's political scientist, as opposed to an equestrian, can read the treatise with profit.[100] The political orders that relied on a class of knights are long gone, and horsemanship, as such, has no role in military strategy. Still, Xenophon sometimes mentions horsemanship in his portrait of his teacher Socrates.[101] He also develops the theme of horsemanship at some length in his portrait of Cyrus, his exemplar of political leadership. In Xenophon's account, Socrates brought philosophy down from the heaven not only into households and cities but also onto the farm.[102] We are thus led to wonder, unlikely as it may sound, whether this treatise on horses offers any insight into Socratic political philosophy. In any case, a preliminary reading shows that *On Horsemanship* is something more than a fine contribution to

the equestrian arts. We begin by situating the treatise among Xenophon's five works addressing individual subjects of expertise, then
take a brief overview of its opening and contents. Next, we examine
two passages in some detail. One sheds light on Xenophon's general
use of the technique of repetition in his writing. The other addresses
the cultivation of horses' hooves. We conclude with a broad overview of horsemanship as it is presented in Xenophon's Socratic writings as well as in the *Education of Cyrus* and *Anabasis*.

∾ THE TITLE ∾

Peri Hippikēs (*On Horsemanship*, or *About Skill with Horses*) is one
of Xenophon's four relatively brief works addressing arts to which a
gentleman should aspire. The others are the *Oikonomikos* (*The Skilled
Household Manager*, traditionally the *Oeconomicus*), *Kunēgetikos* (*The
One Skilled at Hunting with Dogs*), and *Hipparchikos* (*The Skilled Cavalry Commander*).[103] Of these four, only the *Oeconomicus* is a Socratic
writing. The *Oeconomicus* is also a political writing, for it addresses
what Socrates comprehensively named the "royal art," the art of
managing human beings in households and cities. *The Skilled Cavalry
Commander* too is a political work, for it discusses the duties of an
important Athenian official. One might be tempted to set aside *On
Horsemanship* with *The One Skilled at Hunting with Dogs* as addressing
merely private arts, except that *On Horsemanship* and *The Skilled Cavalry Commander* are closely related by a textual link: *On Horsemanship*
ends by referring the reader to the subject matter contained in *The
Skilled Cavalry Commander* (12.14).[104] Xenophon clearly intended his
two equestrian works to be read as a pair. Indeed, *On Horsemanship*
culminates in a discussion of weaponry and armor, and is concerned
throughout with purchasing, training, and riding a warhorse (1.1).
And, when it addresses techniques of horsemanship for display, we
can presume that these displays are for civic processions to the temples of the gods (cf. *The Skilled Cavalry Commander* 3.1–2). Linking
these two treatises is in keeping with Socrates' advice to an aspiring
cavalry commander in the *Memorabilia*, where he makes it clear that
this official must not only be an expert horseman himself but also

be able to convey the expertise to others, because the success of the cavalry depends on the good condition, character, and training of its horses (*Memorabilia* 3.3.3–4).

Now, there is a fifth treatise by Xenophon, *Hiero, or The Skilled Tyrant* (*Hieron ē Turannikos*), whose title also indicates that it addresses a form of expertise, but it is expertise that is emphatically not to be learned or practiced by gentlemen, and so of course it is also not a Socratic work, even though it is in the form of a dialogue. While offering an analysis of Xenophon's titles in his essay on the *Hiero*, Leo Strauss perplexingly comments, "We cannot discuss here the question why [*Peri Hippikēs*] is not entitled *Hippikos*" (*OT* 107n2; cf. 1.1). As far as I know, Strauss does not mention *Peri Hippikēs* again in his later works on Xenophon, although he does discuss other titles (*XS* 3; *XSD* 87). It is true that the title *On Horsemanship* is unique among Xenophon's five works treating arts. While all five contain "an adjective referring to the subject" (*OT* 31), *Peri Hippikēs* alone contains the feminine form of the adjective and thus suggests that the subject of the treatise is the art itself rather than a man who is skilled in the art.[105]

❧ The Opening ❧

Xenophon begins his treatise humbly. He presents himself as a mere experienced practitioner and refers deferentially to a famous established expert, a man named Simon, with whom he only sometimes agrees (1.1, 3). His reference to Simon's dedication of a bronze horse in the Eleusinion suggests that the treatise is addressed to Athenians (1.1; *The Skilled Cavalry Commander* 3.2). It may be fitting for Xenophon to refrain from mentioning that his own extensive experience as a cavalryman came from serving under Spartans. That service apparently led to exile from his native city.[106] In spite of that exile, Xenophon remained manifestly respectable. He differs in this regard from another student of Socrates, Alcibiades, who, as it happened, was exiled for the impiety of mocking the Eleusinian mysteries.[107] Thus, Simon's pious gesture serves to remind us of Xenophon's own manifest piety, and of his frequent emphasis on the

importance of seeking guidance from the gods in any pursuit, especially ruling activities (the cavalry commander is no exception; see
The Skilled Cavalry Commander 1.1). Simon's deeds make us wonder
whether Xenophon himself could have dedicated such a statue, or
even whether he could have held the office of cavalry commander in
Athens, as it seems Simon did.[108] In spite of his respectability, Xenophon's reference to Simon may constitute a quiet acknowledgment
of the unorthodox way in which he earned his own right to disagree,
on some points, with the established Athenian expert in the art of
horsemanship.

The fact that Xenophon does not include an expression of piety of
his own at the outset of this work may result from his reflection on
Socrates' statement that it is impermissible to consult the gods about
something one can know on one's own, while one ought to consult
them about what is unclear (*Memorabilia* 1.1.7–9; cf. *Oeconomicus*
6.1). Horsemanship proper is surely less dependent upon divine
prescience and providence than cavalry command, since war is so
unpredictable (*The Skilled Cavalry Commander* 9.8–9). Moreover, the
beings ruled by this art, horses, are incapable of worshipping gods,
in spite of the gods' care for them (5.8). Still, it is curious that Xenophon begins this education of his young friends without any reference to seeking divine support. For one thing, he makes clear that
one cannot be certain how even the purchase of a horse will turn out
(1.1, 17; 3.1; 11.13). In addition, the art of riding is important for two
civic duties of a gentleman in the knightly class: military service and
public processions to the gods, processions that in turn remind us of
the role of the divine in war.[109] In any case, the reference to Simon's
statue substitutes in *On Horsemanship* for Xenophon's reminder in
The Skilled Cavalry Commander about the inadequacy of relying solely
upon one's own knowledge in the practical arts.[110]

∾ An Outline of the Argument ∾

On Horsemanship consists of twelve chapters without headings. We
can discern five sections by using Xenophon's indications of a change
of subject in the text: the acquisition of the horse (chapters 1–3),

the housing, care, and feeding of the horse at home (chapters 4–6), horsemanship proper, that is, riding (chapters 7–8), dealing with spirited horses and horses for show (chapters 9–11), and an appendix on equipment for battle with a transition to *The Skilled Cavalry Commander* (chapter 12). What follows is a brief description of these five sections.

1. Chapters 1 through 3 serve as an introduction by treating the purchase of a horse, along with its early training for being ridden. Chapter 1 contains a brief general introduction to the work as a whole before turning to the assessment of an untrained colt, which means evaluating its body, because to evaluate a horse's soul one must be able to ride it. Chapter 3 explains how to assess a horse that has already been trained for riding. Chapter 2 serves as an interlude between the two chapters on assessment by explaining why a gentleman should send a colt out for training, and what his written instructions to the trainer should be.

2. Chapters 4 through 6 discuss the housing, care, and feeding of the horse, once it is brought home, and how one should educate the groom to handle the horse in general, and in particular how to put on its bridle.[111] Although one would not allow one's son to consort with horse trainers, a gentleman must himself deal with and educate a horse groom. The groom's task is to make the horse disposed to love human beings. The method involves making pleasant things, like food, available to horses when human beings are present, and the unpleasant things, like hunger, when human beings are absent. Chapter 4 introduces Xenophon's innovation for the hardening of hooves, discussed below. He is so proud of this discovery that he repeats it in *The Skilled Cavalry Commander* (1.15).

3. Chapters 7 and 8 treat horsemanship proper, that is, the art of riding, including how one should mount, dismount, exercise the horse, and practice maneuvers for war, with an emphasis on using rewards rather than punishments. The horseman must educate his horse and know it well before he takes it to war. Chapter 8 includes a brief but important remark, also discussed below, on Xenophon's use of repetition in his writing.

4. Chapters 9 through 11 treat overly spirited horses and horsemanship for display. Chapter 9 begins with a summary of the prior arguments and then turns to dealing with a spirited horse. Chapters

10 and 11 shift to the techniques for riding a show horse so that it has a magnificent bearing, emphasizing the use of persuasion rather than force in training for graceful movement. Chapter 11 ends in what seems like a conclusion to the treatise, recapping the subject matters, from purchasing to managing horses so as to make them worth more than their purchase price, thus making the horses and oneself highly regarded "unless some *daimonion* prevents it."

5. Chapter 12 reads like an appendix. It discusses equipment for battle, defensive armor for both the rider and the horse, and offensive weaponry for the rider, ending with its own brief general conclusion and a bridge to *The Skilled Cavalry Commander*.

∾ Xenophon as a Writer ∾

Let us begin by considering a passage containing the following brief but revealing comment on Xenophon's use of repetition: "If someone thinks that we are repeating ourselves because we speak about the same matters now as previously, this is not a repetition" (8.2). Now, in *On Horsemanship*, as elsewhere, Xenophon occasionally calls attention to his being a writer by saying, "I will write," as opposed to merely "I will explain" or "give an account." Because he differed from his teacher Socrates by choosing to write, it is reasonable to assume that Xenophon thought about the advantages and disadvantages of written communication and how to navigate them. One obvious advantage, familiar to a reader of Xenophon's *Memorabilia* and *Apology of Socrates to the Jury,* is that writing allows defense of one's reputation at a distance of time or place, in case of slander or unjust accusation (*Memorabilia* 1.1–2). Writing also allows one to preserve one's discoveries for others who may benefit from them in the future.[112] Socrates' failure to write appears to be a shortcoming. On the other hand, writing is problematic because one must write the same thing to everyone, whether they are hostile or sympathetic, curious or bored. Xenophon offers his above words on repetition in order to teach the sympathetic and curious how to benefit the most from reading him. With this brief sentence, buried in the innocuous subject matter of horsemanship, Xenophon calls our attention to the difference between an author who repeats himself accidentally and one whose apparent repetition reveals more (if we are willing to compare the apparently repetitive texts).

We should consider, of course, the context of this revealing statement. Xenophon explains that a rider must train both himself and his horse to perform a variety of dangerous maneuvers in exercises, for in this way the horse and rider will save one another and be more generally useful (8.1). Then he refers to his apparent repetition and explains that it is not a repetition, because in a prior passage he was encouraging the potential buyer of a trained horse to try difficult maneuvers on his test ride, while in the present passage he will write how one ought to teach his own horse (8.2). If we turn back to the first passage on these riding maneuvers, we see that the context was how to avoid being deceived in the purchase of a grown horse (3.1), which itself was an expansion on the earlier account of how to avoid being deceived in buying a colt (1.1). In the case of the colt, one can judge only the body, whereas in the case of a trained horse, one is able to judge the soul as well, by taking it for a test ride. The horse in question is intended for war, so one must test it in all circumstances in which war also will test it, before one makes the purchase (1.2; 3.7).

Therefore, even before purchase one may try a variety of difficult and even dangerous maneuvers in order to test a horse's soul. Only when one owns the horse can one actually train it oneself for these dangerous maneuvers, as one must do before taking it into battle, where one's own life will be at stake. Xenophon thus acknowledges the politically crucial distinction between thine and mine in the realm of education. One could not very well try to rectify the defect in horse buying—the problem of being deceived—by training another man's horse before purchasing it. No owner of a horse would put up with the possibility of having his property ruined, unless he were reasonably sure of a rider's competence and intention (*Oeconomicus* 2.13). And yet a seller of a horse must allow some leeway—he must allow a test ride to prove the horse's soundness. Thus a seller and buyer are in a peculiar position. A potential purchaser may legitimately take risks with another man's horse. He may even take risks that an owner himself would be careful to avoid in his daily exercise, as we see if we compare these passages with a further repetition of this thought in the *Oeconomicus*.[113]

In between the first discussion of buying a colt and the later discussion of buying a horse ready to ride is the discussion of initial
colt training, where a third party in the education of a horse is introduced, the professional trainer, whose art overlaps with the groom.
The gentleman owner of a horse should not perform colt breaking
himself. If he is a young gentleman, he should instead be developing
his own character and his own skill in riding. And if he is an adult,
he has important private and public duties to perform: taking care
of his household, his friends, and affairs of politics and war (2.1).
Xenophon does not make explicit that the gentleman himself need
not even know how to educate a colt, just as he may not know how
to educate his son, for that matter, if he wants him to learn how to
play the flute or the lyre (*Oeconomicus* 2.12–13). Fortunately, there
are professionals for these tasks. Regarding horses, the solution is
simple: if a gentleman does not know what to require from his horse
trainer, Xenophon conveys here written notes for the owner to convey in turn (2.1–2; 12.14).

The two passages on difficult riding maneuvers—when put together with the statement on colt training—offer a hint about Xenophon's use of writing. The question of training or education more
generally is a vexed one in the Socratic circle, with explorations of
whether education in virtue is even possible, and who should be responsible for it, whether the fathers or a potential outside expert,
such as Socrates (*Memorabilia* 1.2.27–28, 49–53; *Apology of Socrates to
the Jury* 19–20, 29–31; *Symposium* 2.4–7). We also know that Socrates
was executed in part for educating, or, rather, for "corrupting" the
youth, especially young men of political ability like Critias and Alcibiades (*Memorabilia* 1.2.12). Xenophon defends his teacher partly
by claiming that Socrates was always in the open so that anyone
could hear what he had to say (*Memorabilia* 1.1.10). Writing allows
Xenophon in fact to associate with youths and others only in public.
In this treatise for his young friends "everyone" really can see and
hear what Xenophon has to say to them about horses. And if the
young friends go on to read his other writings, those too are available to the public. In this way, an educator might avoid the unreasonable suspicions and slander that proved injurious to Socrates.
Moreover, Xenophon's own manifest uprightness is evidence of his
teacher's benefit to students. Whatever may have gone wrong with

Critias and Alcibiades, Xenophon's gentlemanliness does immense credit to Socrates.

∿ Xenophon's Innovation regarding Hooves ∿

Our second passage to consider appears of interest at first only to equestrians, for it introduces an innovation for hardening horses' hooves (4.3–5). Xenophon demonstrates a peculiar attachment to this literally pedestrian discovery by repeating it in *The Skilled Cavalry Commander*, where it seems out of place, considering his statement that the two works treat separate topics (12.14; *The Skilled Cavalry Commander* 1.16). Hoof care is primarily the responsibility and concern of the individual horseman, or even his groom, and it is attended to at home.[114] As in every other instance—except for the one discussed above—Xenophon does not call attention to the apparent repetition. The suggestion for hoof care is the following. One should partially bury large round paving stones where the horse will be standing most of the day. Thus the hooves are strengthened, worn to a curved shape, and conditioned to march on roads, without the horse being aware of the training.[115]

In *On Horsemanship* the context for this hoof-hardening innovation is the beautiful as well as beneficial arrangement of the horse's stable on the estate (4.1–3). A stable placed in the line of sight of the master will be beautiful,[116] presumably because the master bought a horse he admired. Such a placement will also be good (*agathon*), for the eye of the master is important to assure that the horse receives proper care and feeding from the servants. As Xenophon explains, "One who neglects this neglects himself, in my opinion, for it is clear that the master entrusts his own body to the horse in dangers" (4.1). In *The Skilled Cavalry Commander* the context for this same hoof care is Xenophon's advising the Athenian government to encourage cavalrymen to take better care of their horses. He explains his easy and inexpensive method for making hooves strong directly after advising the rejection of horses that kick (1.15). Thus, *The Skilled Cavalry Commander* indicates the hooves' danger or liability (kicking) alongside their usefulness. By using human art to strengthen hooves as a foundation for the horse, one incidentally strengthens the horse's natural weapons—weapons that can be dangerous to friends as well as foes.[117]

In *On Horsemanship* the hoof is introduced as the support for both horse and rider, comparable to the stone foundations of houses (1.2). There is no benefit from a warhorse with bad feet, even if the rest of it is in good condition, just as a fine house is worthless if it is built on a rotten foundation. This statement, in turn, reminds us of Socratic statements on houses in the *Memorabilia*, where a general's tactics are compared to a well-constructed house (3.1.7). Houses are built primarily to be useful or good, as providing shelter from weather and safety for possessions, yet they are also beautiful or noble, for they are dwellings for a family's ancestral gods, and even serve as the dwellings for the city's gods when they are temples (*Memorabilia* 3.8.10; cf. *Oeconomicus* 9.4 and context). Horses too, the fellow warriors and exercise companions of gentlemen, have their own duality with respect to beauty and goodness. The very life of the cavalryman depends on his horse (4.1; *Memorabilia* 3.3.4). Even their hooves may mean the difference between success and failure in warfare. Horses are secondarily useful at home, by allowing the gentleman to go early and stay late in the fields, by providing him with a portion of his daily exercise, and even by helping the servant to carry produce in from the fields (*Oeconomicus* 5.6; 11.18). At the same time, they are such beautiful and graceful creatures that their statues adorn temples, and they dignify processions to the gods (1.1; *The Skilled Cavalry Commander* 3.1). *On Horsemanship* discusses the parts of the horse both with a view to their utility—either for the horse, or for the rider, or both—and with a view to their beauty. For example, the horses have the hair of the forelock, mane, and tail both for beauty and for keeping flies away (5.5–8). The mane, in particular, distinguishes the horse by providing splendor or adornment to it, even as it gives the rider something to hold onto. This adornment is a gift from the gods and provides a peculiar haughtiness, particularly to mares (5.8).[118] Indeed, the horse as a whole serves as an adornment for the gentleman, for it allows him to become a knight. As we learn from both Xenophon in *The Skilled Cavalry Commander* (8.6) and Cyrus's right-hand man, Chrysantas, in the *Education of Cyrus* (4.3.15), a knight feels superhuman, like a winged being.

These two aspects of the horse, its utility and beauty, may not be in simple harmony, or may be confused with one another. Xenophon of course does not claim that one should choose a warhorse for its beauty, yet he frequently remarks on the beauty of the animal as a desirable quality. Certainly, beauty is a requirement for show horses, and striving to please the city's gods in public processions is important for war (10.1; 11.1).

A horse can be a temperamental and even dangerous creature that requires careful selection, care, and training if it is to perform its noble and useful functions for its owner. Xenophon's focus on the pedestrian foundations of the horse at the opening of his equestrian treatise brings the owner's expectations literally down to earth, as much as he may wish to fly like a winged being. A beautiful but high-strung horse may be quite serviceable for show, but it would be foolish to take it into battle.[119] Xenophon remains aware of, and is even himself affected by, the horse's beauty. But he does not want the horseman to forget the most crucial things about the horse for the life of the rider, as well as for the life of the horse.

∾ HORSEMANSHIP AND XENOPHON'S SOCRATES ∾

An overview of horsemanship in Xenophon's other works shows that the theme plays a role in understanding his political philosophy. It certainly has some prominence in three of his four Socratic writings, the *Oeconomicus, Symposium,* and *Memorabilia.* And, although it is not mentioned in the very brief *Apology of Socrates to the Jury,* that work focuses on Socratic education, which we will see is somehow tied to horsemanship in each of Xenophon's other treatments of his teacher (cf. *Apology of Socrates to the Jury* 19–20, 29–31).

Among this group of writings, horsemanship is most prominent as a theme in the *Oeconomicus.* In the introductory part of the work, Socrates earnestly recommends proficiency in horsemanship to his primary interlocutor, Critoboulus, the undisciplined heir to the large estate of Socrates' old friend Crito.[120] In the second part of the work—a long conversation motivated by Socrates' desire to understand the connection between nobility (beauty) and goodness for human beings (*Oeconomicus* 11.11–18; 6.13–17)—horsemanship appears in a more comic light. Ischomachus has a noble reputation as being both wealthy and an expert horseman (*Oeconomicus* 11.20). Socrates, by contrast, compares himself to a famously admired horse, because he, like the horse, has no money but is good, or can hope to be. Moreover, in spite of his ostensibly teaching Critoboulus the gentlemanly art of farming (a part of household management) Socrates does not even claim to possess the skill of horsemanship, as is understandable, since it requires a good deal of land and money, both of which Socrates lacks (*Oeconomicus* 2.2–4). Accordingly, horsemanship plays a role in the contrast between Socrates' way of life and that of Ischomachus.[121]

Some light can be shed on the comic aspect of horsemanship in the *Oeconomicus* if we glance at the playful discussion among gentlemen in Xenophon's *Symposium*. There Socrates uses horsemanship as an analogy for educating human beings, as appears in a joke he makes about his manifest failure at educating his own wife, even while he exhorts other gentlemen to educate theirs (*Symposium* 2.3–13). The impetus for the remark—a display put on by a traveling showman involving two girls, a flute player and a daring acrobat—permits us to consider themes reminiscent of Plato's *Republic*. Socrates notes the real differences between men and women, while insisting that gentlemen should educate their wives. (A comedian present draws the conclusion that the female acrobat's teacher would be useful in the formation of warriors.) Then, one of the gentlemen brings up the potentially refuting example of Xanthippe. Socrates defends his own implicit boast about wifely education by comparing himself as a husband to those who wish to become skilled horsemen, for they acquire the most spirited rather than very obedient horses because they believe that if they are able to keep hold of the spirited ones they will more easily deal with every other horse (*Symposium* 2.9–10). Socrates thus suggests that he acquired his own wife as challenging practice for dealing with all types of human beings—a seemingly frivolous suggestion, considering his argument in the *Oeconomicus* that a wife is a crucial partner in household management (*Oeconomicus* 3.15).[122]

The *Oeconomicus*'s and the *Symposium*'s intriguing references to horsemanship encourage us to look for the theme in Xenophon's defense of Socrates in the *Memorabilia*. We mentioned above Socrates' conversation with a young man aspiring to be a cavalry commander in our discussion of the link between *On Horsemanship* and *The Skilled Cavalry Commander* (*Memorabilia* 3.3).[123] That conversation indicates—to the surprise of the aspiring officer—that a cavalry commander must not only know but be able to teach the art of caring for one's horse. Socrates asks him how he intends to make the horses better. The commanding officer cannot solely entrust the fitness of the cavalry's horses, on which so much depends, to the private supervision of the individual cavalrymen (*XS* 60; 3.3.3–4).

As this conversation makes clear, horsemanship is necessary for the gentleman not only for the private reasons presented to Critoboulus but for public ones as well. Xenophon himself—a man of unusual political ambition combined with an intense curiosity to understand political things—went, with some of his own horses (*Anabasis* 3.3.19), on an expedition to aid the younger Cyrus. After the latter's death, Xenophon saved the Greek contingent in part by creating a cavalry. Creating a cavalry is also key to the political accomplishments of the earlier Cyrus, the founder of the Persian empire. Xenophon's account of both the younger and the elder Cyrus provides further information on the relation between politics and horsemanship.

～ Horsemanship and Xenophon's Cyrus ～

Horses are crucial to the founder of the Persian kingdom, and hence for Xenophon's case study of a possible solution to the problem of political rule.[124] The *Education of Cyrus* recounts Cyrus's transformation of a small republican community (similar to Sparta) into a huge empire ruled by an absolute king. Cyrus, the son of a limited constitutional monarch, becomes a skilled horseman only because during his childhood he makes a long visit to his maternal grandfather, the tyrannical ruler of the neighboring Medes. Horses were rare in Persia.[125]

When he sets out to build his empire, Cyrus's first major military reform is to arm and retrain his relatively large body of light-armed commoners to become heavily armed hoplites, nearly erasing their military difference from the elite "peers." His second major step is to persuade his Persian captains to pass a unanimous resolution to form a cavalry. Horses are key to the acquisition of wealth in battle, because only the cavalry can capture those fleeing with booty after the infantry routs the enemy. Cyrus's desire to build a cavalry is almost as evident as is his desire to rule an empire. The rest of his campaign sometimes appears a constant quest to acquire more horses and cavalrymen under his personal command. In the end, no elite member of his empire is to appear in public on foot. A Persian monarchy supported by a court of wealthy knights eventually replaces his father's constitutional republic supported by heavily armed middle-class hoplites.

Cyrus's education of his captains about their need for a cavalry is especially notable (*Education of Cyrus* 4.3.4–15). He speaks of the advantages of going to war on horseback. He emphasizes the pleasure of being carried rather than carrying all the heavy equipment oneself. He downplays the difficulty grown men may have in acquiring the skill of horsemanship (although he himself acquired it when young). Accordingly, he avoids mentioning the danger of being thrown, especially in battle. With the help of a speech by his supporter, Chrysantas, Cyrus proposes and passes a law to form a cavalry (4.3.22–23). Chrysantas's almost poetic speech reinforces how important horsemanship is to Cyrus's founding enterprise.[126] Chrysantas stresses both the nobility and pleasure of riding horses. He claims that he envies centaurs because they have the speed and strength of a horse, together with the manual and prudential dexterity of a human being. In keeping with Cyrus's reticence about any possible disadvantage to riding, when Chrysantas enumerates the advantages of a horseman's being separate from the horse's body he too skips over the possibility of being thrown (cf. *Education of Cyrus* 5.3.1; *Oeconomicus* 1.8; *Anabasis* 3.2.19). He emphasizes instead that having two heads joined together for an enterprise can be an advantage, for partnership with the horse means four eyes and ears are on the task. Horses often see and hear things before human beings.

The *Anabasis*, in its turn, highlights the defensive function of the cavalry. Xenophon becomes the general of a Greek army facing a long and dangerous retreat, fleeing the Persian King's army. Orderly retreat requires a cavalry contingent guarding the rear. Thus, horsemanship as crucial to self-preservation is emphasized, rather than the acquisitive role evident in the *Education of Cyrus*. It is true that—upon first becoming a general of the trapped and frightened infantry—Xenophon gives a speech downplaying their lack of a cavalry (*Anabasis* 3.2.18–19). He emphasizes a cavalry's excellence in fleeing to safety as opposed to fighting, thus suggesting that they may prevail without horsemen. This argument is certainly prudent for bolstering the morale of his men, who are facing imminent destruction by an army possessing a huge cavalry. He does not mention what we learned from the *Education of Cyrus*, that the cavalry excels also at capturing those who flee, in other words, those in retreat. Just one day's march later, however, we see Xenophon himself making a separate case to his fellow generals that they must prepare a small force of cavalry with some slingers, in order to protect their rear. This force proves to be immediately effective (*Anabasis* 3.3.16, 3.4.4). Xenophon's few horses, supplemented with others from the baggage train—although amounting only to fifty—prove crucial to the survival of those of the ten thousand Greeks who made it back home, including that expert cavalryman Xenophon himself.

Socrates did not see any utility in horsemanship for his own continent form of home economics, yet his poverty was no hindrance, and perhaps even a help, to conversing with a gentleman's horse groom when he felt it necessary to know something about a horse (*Oeconomicus* 11.4). Xenophon, on the other hand, looks more like Ischomachus. He was himself an expert at horsemanship with extensive personal experience in the field (1.1). In spite of his great admiration of Socrates, he lived so as to possess the wherewithal for a gentlemanly way of life, and he maintained that wherewithal even as conditions grew unfavorable in his declining native Athens. Perhaps horsemanship is a skill by which Xenophon improved upon the life of Socrates through imitating also his secondary mentor, Cyrus. Whether this points to a genuine advance over Socrates' way of life or to a mere compromise with Xenophon's personal preferences cannot be discerned until we better understand, among other things, the political as well as private significance of horsemanship for Xenophon.

Now Ischomachus offers sensible practical reasons in the *Oeconomicus* for learning and practicing horsemanship. He mingles the horse's utility in war, on the farm, and for the household with his personal concern for physical fitness (*Oeconomicus* 11.8, 11–13). While his emphasis is on his private use of the horse, a fairly extensive farm is also necessary, if one wishes to contribute to the safety of one's city as a cavalryman (*Oeconomicus* 5.5). And Ischomachus prays to the gods that he obtain both "noble safety and noble increase of riches" in war (*Oeconomicus* 11.8). As we learn from our reading of the *Anabasis* and *Education of Cyrus*, horsemanship is indeed key to both safety and the noble increase of wealth (*Anabasis* 3.2.19; *Education of Cyrus* 4.3.5; *The Skilled Cavalry Commander* 7.17). Moreover, to the extent that one desires honorable safety (escape without throwing away one's weapons), as opposed to mere safety—not to mention acquisition of booty—horsemanship is a most useful skill to possess. Finally, the cavalry also has a role to play in the official cult of the city (1.1; 11.13).

The above suggests that *On Horsemanship* adds to our understanding of Xenophon's political philosophy. The horse's willingness and cooperation allow the rider to achieve superhuman feats in battle. Yet that cooperation is not gained without considerable skill and effort on the part of more than one human being. Breeders, grooms, and trainers all contribute to the formation of a horse with the requisite attributes of body and soul to make a partner for a gentleman in war. *On Horsemanship* tells us something about the roles of each of these contributors. All of this is expensive. Yet horsemanship need not carry with it the crushing debt portrayed in Aristophanes' *Clouds*. It might even bring a profit (11.13). Besides, since one's opponents most likely have cavalry forces, horsemanship would be a necessary art for a political man to know. All of the outstanding statesmen of the *Education of Cyrus* and the *Anabasis* are enthusiastic horsemen, whether the elder or younger Cyrus or Xenophon himself (*Education of Cyrus* 1.3.3, 8.3.25–26; *Anabasis* 1.9.1–5, 3.3.19). Because Xenophon speaks throughout *On Horsemanship* in his own voice, it is an especially valuable resource for filling in details left out of his other writings regarding this activity belonging to high practitioners of the royal art.

We must ultimately ask why horses are important to Xenophon as a writer. Horses differ from us in their strengths and vulnerabilities. They can be naturally beautiful not only in body but also in soul, partly because they are spirited like us, partly because they have such awesome capacities. Horses can also be frightening precisely because of their capacities combined with their spiritedness. One must be wary around horses. However, a horse is also a being susceptible to education, such that—if one adjusts oneself to it, studies it, protects oneself from its natural weapons, and trains it from the time it is young—one may entrust one's life to it as a comrade in arms. One may also perform very impressive acts of showmanship that are delightful for spectators to watch and beautiful enough for solemn processions.

CHAPTER 8
The One Skilled at Hunting with Dogs[1]

TRANSLATED BY MICHAEL EHRMANTRAUT AND
GREGORY A. MCBRAYER

⁓ CHAPTER 1 ⁓

(1) The invention of the gods, of Apollo and Artemis,[2] are the chase and dogs; and they gave this gift to Cheiron[3] and thus honored him for his justice. (2) He accepted the gift with joy and put it to use. He came to have, as students of hunting with dogs and other noble things, Cephalus,[4] Asclepius,[5] Meilanion,[6] Nestor,[7] Amphiaraus,[8] Peleus,[9] Telamon,[10] Meleager,[11] Theseus,[12] Hippolytus,[13] Palamedes,[14] Odysseus,[15] Menestheus,[16] Diomedes,[17] Castor,[18] Polydeuces, Machaon,[19] Podaleirius, Antilochus,[20] Aeneas,[21] and Achilles[22]— each of whom was in his own time honored by the gods.

(3) Let no one wonder that many of them, although pleasing to the gods, nevertheless died—for this is nature; yet their fame came to be great. Let no one wonder, either, that they were not all of the same generation, since Cheiron's life was long enough for all. Zeus and Cheiron were brothers, having the same father, yet the mother of the one was Rhea, and of the other, Nais, a nymph. (4) So Cheiron was born before his students, but died later, since he educated Achilles. (5) From their attentiveness to dogs, hunting with dogs, and the rest of education they distinguished themselves very much and were wondered at for their virtue.

(6) Cephalus was even carried off by a goddess,[23] but Asclepius acquired greater things, raising the dead and healing the sick; and for these reasons he possesses ever-remembered glory among human beings as a god.

(7) Meilanion was so superior in love of toil that, although the best men of the time were his rivals in love,[24] he alone won the hand of Atalanta in what was the greatest marriage of the time.

Accounts of the virtue of Nestor have already spread among the Greeks, so that I would be speaking to those who already know of it.

(8) Amphiaraus, in campaigning against Thebes, having acquired the most praise, attained from the gods the honor of everlasting life.[25]

Peleus prompted in even the gods the desire both to give him Thetis and to celebrate in song his marriage at the home of Cheiron.

(9) Telamon came to be so great that he married the woman he wanted, Alcathus's daughter Periboea, from the greatest city; and when the first of the Greeks, Heracles, the son of Zeus, distributed prizes to the best after having seized Troy, he gave Hesione to Telamon.

(10) The honors that Meleager won are evident; but that he suffered misfortune was not his own fault, since it was his father who, in his old age, neglected the goddess.[26]

Theseus by himself alone destroyed the enemies of all Greece, and because he made his fatherland much greater even now he is wondered at.

(11) Hippolytus was honored by Artemis and held conversation with her; and having been deemed blessed for his moderation and piety, he died.

Palamedes, for as long as he lived, was much superior to all others of his time in wisdom; but, having been killed unjustly, he obtained vengeance from the gods such as no other human being has. He did not die at the hands of those supposed by some; for, if so, the one could not have been almost the best of men, and the other the equal of the good.[27] The deed was executed by bad men.

(12) From his attentiveness to hunting with dogs, Menestheus so surpassed others in his love of toil that the first of the Greeks agreed that in matters of war they were inferior—save for Nestor; and he is said not to outdo, but to rival him.

(13) Odysseus and Diomedes were brilliant on every single occasion; and they were on the whole responsible for the taking of Troy.

Castor and Polydeuces are immortal because of the worthiness they acquired from having displayed in Greece so many of the things they learned from Cheiron.

(14) Machaon and Podaleirius, educated in all the same things, became good in the arts, in speeches, and in war.

Antilochus, in dying for his father, acquired such glory that he alone among the Greeks was proclaimed to be "Philopator."[28]

(15) Aeneas, having saved his paternal and maternal gods, and having saved his father, thus won a reputation for piety such that in fact even his enemies allowed him alone among the vanquished at Troy not to be stripped of his arms.

(16) Achilles, reared in this education, handed down such noble and great memorials that no one grows weary of speaking and hearing of him.

(17) These became such as they were from attentiveness to what they learned from Cheiron and these are things that the good passionately love[29] even now, and the bad envy, such that if calamities ever befell Greece, whether a city or a kingdom, they were delivered through these men. And if there was a dispute or war involving Greece as a whole against all the barbarians, it was through them that the Greeks prevailed, so that they made Greece invincible.

(18) I therefore advise the youth not to despise hunting with dogs nor the rest of education. For it is from these things that one becomes good both at war and at the other things as a result of which one necessarily thinks, speaks, and acts nobly.

∾ CHAPTER 2 ∾

(1) First, therefore, it is necessary for one who is just beyond boyhood to embark on the practice of hunting with dogs; and then on the other parts of education—after having examined one's substance.[30] If it is sufficient, it should be spent to the extent that it is beneficial to him, and if it is not, then at least let the desire be present, omitting nothing within his power.

(2) As to how much and what sort of preparations are needed for embarking on the practice, I will speak about these things and the knowledge pertaining to each, so that one can undertake the work with foresight. And let no one believe that these things are of no importance; for without them there would be no activity.

(3) It is necessary that the net-keeper be desirous of the work, speak Greek, and be about twenty years old. His form should be nimble and strong, and his soul should be sufficient so that, being superior to the toils in these ways, he may enjoy the work.

(4) The short nets should be made of a chord of fine flax from Phasis or Carthage, as should the road nets and the trap nets.[31] Let the short nets be of nine threads, in three strands, where each strand has three threads; the length should be five spans; the meshes should be two palms wide; let the drawstrings be on the outside, without knots, so that they run easily.[32] (5) The road nets should have twelve threads, the trap nets sixteen threads. The length of the road nets should be two, three, four, or five fathoms long, while the trap nets should be ten, twenty, or thirty fathoms; if they are any larger, they will be difficult to manage. Both of them should have thirty knots, and the interval between the meshes should be equal to that in the short nets. (6) Let the road nets have wool fastened along the edges, but let the trap nets have rings, with drawstrings made of twisted chords.

(7) Let some of the forked props for the short nets be the length of ten palms, but let others be less. Those of unequal length are to be used on ground that slopes to one side, so that the upper part of the net is raised up to an equal height, while those of equal length are to be used on level ground. Since it should be easy to pull the short nets off, their props must be smooth. The props for the road nets are to be twice as long as those for the short nets, and the props for the trap nets are to be five spans long and have small forks, with cuts that are not very deep. All of them are to be firm, and their thickness should not be disproportionate to their length. (8) The number of props used in the short nets can be either many or few: few, if the nets are to be tightly stretched in their position, but more if they are to be left loose.

(9) Let there also be a sack made of dog- or calfskin where the short nets and road nets will be kept, as well as the scythes, in case it is necessary to cut brush and block up places.[33]

∾ Chapter 3 ∾

(1) The dogs are of two species, the Castorian and the fox-like. The Castorian have their name for the reason that Castor, because he

took pleasure in the work, guarded the purity of the breed closely; the fox-like are so called because they were bred from dogs and foxes, and, over a long time, their nature became a blend.

(2) The inferior, and also the more numerous, specimens are of the following sorts: small, hook-nosed, bright-eyed, short-sighted, ugly, stiff, weak, hairless, long-legged, ill-proportioned, without soul, without a sense of smell, and lacking good feet.

(3) Those that are small, on account of their size, often abandon their task. The hook-nosed are unable to bite and thus cannot hold onto the hare. The bright-eyed and short-sighted have inferior eyes. The deformed ones are ugly to behold. The stiff in form end the hunt in a bad condition. The hairless and the weak are incapable of toil. The long-legged and ill-proportioned are uncoordinated and move their bodies slowly. Those without soul leave their tasks, stay out of the sun, and lie down in the shade. Those without a sense of smell rarely and only with difficulty perceive the hare. Those without strong feet, even if they possess good souls, are unable to withstand the toils, but they grow weary on account of the pain in their feet.

(4) The same species of dogs have many ways of tracking. For when some detect the track they pass over it without a sign, so that one does not know that they are on the track; and some only move their ears but keep their tails still; and others hold their ears unmoved but wag the end of their tail. (5) Others draw their ears together, and, looking ferocious along the track, they run about, dropping their tail and letting it fall. Many do none of these things, but running around madly, they bark at the track when they rush upon it and mindlessly trample upon the scent. (6) There are some which, by making many circles and wanderings, get in front of the tracks and thus miss the hare; when they overrun the tracks, they guess at it; but when they finally do see the hare ahead, they tremble and do not approach until they see it move slightly.

(7) Those which, in tracking and pursuing, run ahead, frequently watching the discoveries made by the other dogs, have no trust in themselves. And the rash ones will not allow their wiser coworkers to advance in front, but keep them back by causing a tumult. And some are delighted with falsehoods and get terribly excited if they have a chance of taking the lead, while being conscious that they are being deceptive; others, however, do the same thing, though without

knowing. The ones that do not move away from the beaten roads are worthless; they do not know what is correct.

(8) Those dogs that are ignorant of the tracks to [the hare's] resting places, and run swiftly over its courses, are not well bred. Some chase the hare vehemently at the beginning, but then give up on account of their softness; others, however, cut in hastily and then go wrong; and others go wrong by thoughtlessly running ahead in the roads and by being unwilling to listen. (9) There are many that give up the pursuit and come back because of their hatred for wild animals; others do so because of their love for human beings. Some try to deceive others by yelping away from the tracks, thus making what is false [appear] true.

(10) There are some that will not do this, but, when they hear a cry in the middle of running, get carried away without forethought and abandon their tasks. Some pursue without clarity; others make big assumptions, but then come to believe something else. Some out of pretending, others out of envying, hunt away from the others, alongside the track—then come together at the end.

(11) Those that have these qualities—most of which are possessed by nature, though some are due to being trained ignorantly—will be of no use. Such dogs as these will turn away even those who desire to hunt with dogs.

But what sort the dogs of this kind ought to be, in form and the rest, I will explain.

∼ CHAPTER 4 ∼

(1) First, then, they should be large; next, they should have heads that are light, snub-nosed, well knit, and sinewy below the space between the eyes; the eyes raised up, black, and bright; between the eyes, broad, and deeply divided; the ears small, slender, and bare on the back; the neck long, pliant, and rounded; the breast broad, and not without flesh; the shoulder blades set a little apart from the shoulders; the front legs short, straight, round, and firm; the knees straight; the ribs not down low on the ground but running obliquely; the loins fleshy, of medium size between long and short, neither very

pliant nor stiff; the flanks between large and small; the hips rounded, fleshy on the back, not tied together on the upper parts, but joined on the inside; the part below the flanks and the lower flanks themselves hollow; the tail long, straight, and flexible; the thighs not stiff; the lower thigh large, carried around, and compact; the legs much longer in the back than in the front, and wiry; and the feet rounded. (2) And if the dogs be such as these, their forms will be strong, light, symmetrical, swift-footed, appear bright in the face, and have good mouths.

(3) And when tracking, they should get swiftly away from the beaten paths, slanting their heads to the earth,[34] smiling in the direction of the scent, and letting their ears down; and they should, with eyes swiveling frequently, and wagging their tails, all together advance toward the resting spots, in many circles along the tracks. (4) When they are near the hare itself, they should make this manifest to the hunter by going more quickly, and making it known from their greater spiritedness, from their heads, from their eyes, from the changes in their bearing, from looking upward, from looking straight at the woody undergrowth, from straining on toward the seat of the hare, as well as from throwing themselves back and forth and sideways, and from this making it known that they are now truly elated in their souls and exceedingly delighted that they are near the hare.

(5) They should pursue vigorously and not relent, with much noise and barking, coming together everywhere with the hare. They should run after it swiftly and clearly, frequently changing course and, with justice, crying out again and again; but they should not leave the track to go back to the hunter.

(6) Along with this form, and such work, they should have stout souls and also good noses, good feet, and good hair. They will have stout souls if they do not leave off hunting even in stifling heat. They will have good noses if they smell the hare in places that are bare, dry, and in the sun, during the dog days. Their feet will be good if, in the same season, they are not torn up as they run in the mountains. They will have good hair if it is fine, thick, and soft.

(7) In color, the dogs should not be completely red, black, or white. For this is not a mark of good breeding; the unmixed coloration indicates wildness. (8) So those that are red or black should have white

hair showing about the face, and those that are white should have red hair there. At the top of the thighs the hairs should be straight and thick, and also at the hips and the lower tail—but of moderate thickness higher up.

(9) It is better to lead the dogs out often to the mountains, but less often to the cultivated fields; for in the mountains they are able to track and run freely, while in the fields they can do neither on account of the beaten paths. (10) It is also good to lead the dogs out to the rough ground without discovering the hare; for they will come to have good feet, and toiling in such places benefits their bodies. (11) In the summer they should be led out until midday, but in the winter throughout the day, in late autumn all except midday, and in the spring before evening. For at these times the heat is measured.

～ CHAPTER 5 ～

(1) The scent of the hare lasts long in the winter because of the length of the nights, but for a short time in the summer, for the opposite reason. In the winter, however, there is no smell of it early on, when there is rime or frost; for rime by its strength draws the heat in and holds the scent inside while the ice congeals it. (2) Even the noses of the dogs, becoming numb, are not able to perceive when it is like this, before the sun or the advancing day thaws. Then, the dogs do smell, and the tracks, vaporizing, give off odor. (3) Much dew also makes the scent disappear, suppressing it; and rains, coming after a time, draw odor from the earth, making it bad for scent until it dries out. The southerly winds also make it worse; for their moisture scatters it. But the northerly winds, if the scent has not been lost, concentrate and save it. (4) Heavy rains, and even drizzles, wash away the scent; and the moon dulls the scent through its warmth—most of all when there is a full moon; then the scent is scarcest. For the hares, delighting in the light, leap up high and long as they play with one another. The scent also becomes confused when foxes have passed through earlier. (5) Spring, with its beautifully temperate weather, makes the scent clear unless something flowering on the earth hinders the dogs, mixing in the smell of the blooms. In the summer, the

scent is faint and unclear: being hot, the earth renders the heat that
the scent holds unapparent; for it is but faint; and also the dogs have
less ability to smell on account of the relaxation of their bodies. But
in late autumn the scent is pure; for, of what the earth bears, what is
cultivated has been gathered in and what is wild has withered with
age so that the odors of the fruits do not trouble the dogs in being
brought forth with the scent. (6) In the winter, summer, and late autumn the tracks of scent are mostly straight, but in the spring they
are complicated. For the wild animal, which is indeed always coupling, does so most of all in this season, so that on account of this out
of necessity they wander about with each other and do such things.
(7) The tracks around the resting places of the hare smell for a longer
time than those about the places where it runs: for the hare goes to
the resting places in a halting manner, but goes quickly through the
places where it runs. The earth of the former is thus densely covered
with the scent, but that of the latter is not so full. And it smells more
in the woods than in the bare places, for in running about and sitting
up the hare touches many things.

(8) They lie down in what the earth naturally gives rise to or
has upon it—under all things, on them, in them, beside them, in
between them, or at a distance from them that is much or little.
They sometimes even throw themselves as far as possible into the
sea, and into freshwater, if there be anything growing over it or in
it. (9) In its resting place the hare makes its bed mostly in sheltered
places when it is cold, in densely shaded places when it is hot, but
in the sun in the spring and late autumn, although those that are
on the run do not do this, on account of becoming frightened by the
dogs. (10) It lies down by putting its thighs under its flanks, and for
the most part putting its forelegs together, stretching them out, and
putting its lower jaw down on the ends of its feet and spreading its
ears over its shoulders so that its tender parts are covered; and the
hare also has its fur as a covering, for it is thick and soft. (11) When
it is awake, it blinks its eyelids, but when it lies down to sleep its
eyelids are opened up and motionless and the eyes hold still. When
it is asleep its nose moves frequently but when it is not asleep, less
often.

(12) When the earth abounds with produce, they frequent the cultivated fields more than the hills. If it is being tracked, it stays wher-

ever it is unless it is very frightened with the coming of night—when thus affected, it moves away.

(13) It is so prolific that when it has brought forth young, it is bringing forth again, and is also conceiving more. There is more smell from the small young hares than from the large hares. For, since their limbs are still tender, they drag them all upon the earth. (14) But the lovers of hunting with dogs let the newborns go, for the goddess.[35] Those that are at this time a year old run the first course swiftly, but not the rest, for though they are nimble, they lack power.

(15) To find the tracks of the hare, lead the dogs from the cultivated fields downward. As for those hares that do not come into cultivated fields, go to the meadows, glens, streams, rocks, and woods. And if the hare moves away, do not cry out, lest the dogs go wild and have difficulty recognizing the scent. (16) Once the hares are discovered and pursued by the dogs, they cross streams, and double back, and slip down into gullies and holes. For they are afraid not only of dogs but also of eagles; for when they cross over slopes and barren places they are snatched up, until they are yearlings. (17) But the bigger ones are run down and caught by the dogs.

Hares in the mountains are the swiftest of foot, while those that live on the plains are less so, and the marsh dwellers are the slowest. Those that wander in all these places are difficult to pursue, for they know the shortcuts. They mostly run uphill or on level ground, and not so much on uneven ground, and least on the downhill slopes.

(18) When pursued, they are most conspicuous where the earth has been moved, if they have redness in their coat, and through stubble, because it reflects light.[36] But they are also conspicuous in the beaten paths and roads, if these are level, for the brightness of the hares is lit up in turn. But when they run away through rocks, hills, stony ground, or thickets, they are inconspicuous, on account of similarity in color.

(19) When they are ahead of the dogs they come to a stand, and, sitting up, they raise themselves and listen for barking or noise of the dogs anywhere nearby; and from wherever they hear the sound, they turn away. (20) But sometimes, also, even when they do not hear anything, but believe or have persuaded themselves that they hear them, they run by and through the same things, changing over their leaps, making tracks on top of tracks. (21) Those discovered on barren grounds, because they are clearly seen, run the furthest,

while those discovered in the thickets run the shortest distance, since the darkness is a hindrance to them.

(22) There are two species of hares: those that are big are dark in color and have a lot of white on the face, while those that are smaller are lighter, having less white. (23) In the former, the tail is spotted all around, but in the latter along the side; in the former, the eyes are bright, but in the latter somewhat gray. In the former there is black on much of the tips of the ears, but in the latter it is on a small part. (24) Many of the islands, both the desolate and the inhabited, have the smaller sort of hares, and they are more numerous on the islands than on the mainland, for on most of them there are neither foxes, which approach and carry them and their offspring away, nor eagles, for the big mountains have more eagles than the small ones, and the mountains on islands are for the most part smaller. (25) But hunters with dogs seldom come to the desolate islands, and even on the inhabited ones there are but few men, and most[37] are not lovers of wild game. And it is not possible even to take dogs to the islands that are sacred. So when only a few of the hares and their offspring are hunted out, they are by necessity abundant.

(26) The hare does not see keenly, on account of many things: for it has eyes that stick out and deficient eyelids, providing no screen for the pupils; on account of these things, its vision is dim and dispersed. (27) Along with these things, though the animal is asleep much of the time, this does not benefit its vision. Its swiftness of foot also contributes much toward its being dim-sighted; for it quickly turns its eyes away from each thing before it can grasp what it is. (28) And when being pursued, its fear of the dogs behind it takes away its ability to grasp what is ahead of it so that, on account of these things, it runs into many things without noticing and falls into the nets. (29) If it fled straight ahead it would seldom suffer such a thing, but now, being fond of the places in which it was born and raised, and frequently circling about them, it is caught. Yet, on account of its swiftness of foot, it is not often seized on the run by the dogs; when it is caught, this is contrary to the nature of its body, by chance; for none of the beings of an equal size is similar with respect to structure.[38] For its body is composed from such parts as these: (30) a head that is light, small, carried downward, narrowed in the front; in the neck it is slender, rounded, not stiff, sufficient in length; the shoulder

blades are straight, unconnected on top; the forelegs are attached to the shoulder blades and are nimble, with the limbs close together; the breast is not heavy; the sides are light to bear, symmetrical; the loins are rounded; the thighs are fleshy; the flanks are supple; the hips are sufficient; the haunches are well rounded, full, separated on the top as needed; the hind legs are large, compact, with the muscle stretched on the outside, not swollen on the inside; the upper thighs are large and firm; the front feet are extremely supple, narrow, and straight; the hind feet are solid and flat, thinking nothing of rough ground; the hind legs are much larger than the front and less bent inward on the outside; and the hair is short and light.

(31) Therefore it is not possible that, being composed in such a way, the hare not be strong, supple, and exceedingly nimble. This is a sign of how nimble it is: when it passes through without trembling it hops (no one has ever seen it, or ever will see it, walking) by putting the hind feet beyond and outside the front feet; and it runs in this way, for this is clear in snow.

(32) But it has a tail that is not helpful for running; for because of its shortness it is not sufficient to steer the body. This the hare does with each of its ears. And when it is roused by the dogs, it lowers and turns aslant one of the ears on the side from which it is troubled, and supporting itself in this way, it then quickly turns away, in a moment leaving the attacker much behind. (33) So charming is the wild animal[39] that there is no one who, seeing it being tracked, discovered, pursued, and caught, would not forget if he was passionately in love with someone.[40]

(34) When hunting with dogs on cultivated fields, keep off whatever the season brings forth, and leave alone the springs and streams; for to touch such things is shameful and bad, and also may set onlookers in opposition to the law.[41] And when there is no hunting,[42] everything connected with hunting with dogs should be removed.

∼ CHAPTER 6 ∼

(1) The equipment order for the dogs consists in collars, leashes, and girth-belts. Let the collars be soft and wide, lest they wear off

the hair of the dogs. The leashes should have loops for the hand, but nothing else; for those who fashion the collars and leashes in the same piece do not treat their dogs in a noble manner. The girth-belts should have wide straps, lest they rub on the flanks, and have spikes sewn in, in order to guard the breed.

(2) The dogs must not be led out to the hunting grounds when they do not accept with pleasure the food before them (for this is a sure sign that they are not strong), nor when the wind blows hard, for it scatters the scent and the dogs are not able to smell it, and also because the short nets and the trap nets are not able to remain standing. (3) When neither of these poses a hindrance, lead the dogs out every other day. The dogs should not become accustomed to pursue foxes; for this is the greatest form of corruption, and the dogs will never be present when they are needed. (4) Lead the dogs onto hunting grounds of varying sorts in order that they will have experience of the hunting grounds and oneself of the country. But go out early, lest the dogs be kept from the track, since those who go late deprive the dogs of the discovery of the hare and themselves of the benefit; for the nature of the scent, being faint, does not remain the whole day. (5) Let the net-keeper go out to hunt in apparel that is not heavy. Let him set up the nets in passages that are rough, sloping, hollow, and dark, or in streams, gullies, and ever-flowing watercourses; for the hare mostly flees to such places, but to say how many others there are would be endless. (6) But let the nets be set up on paths that run along or across these, clearly or faintly manifest, and at daybreak, but not earlier, in order that if the net-stand is near the places where the hare is to be sought, and it hears noise at the same place, it is not frightened (although if they be very far from each other, the early time poses less of a hindrance), and make the short nets unencumbered (7) so that nothing clings to them. Fix the forked props leaning forward so as to hold tension when the nets are pulled. On the tops, let the meshes be put on so that they are even, and fix them in the same way, lifting the pouch in the middle. (8) Let the net-keeper tie a stone, long and large, to the cord that runs round the top in order that the net does not pull away when it has the hare in it. Let him set up the nets over a long ways, and high, so that the hare does not leap over them. In

tracking, do not delay, for this surely does not pertain to hunting or the love of toil; what does pertain, however, is to catch the hare by any means quickly.

(9) Let the net-keeper stretch the trap nets in level places, but let him put the road nets in the roads, and from beaten paths to the places where they meet, fastening the cords running around the net to the earth, bringing the lines of the nets together, sticking the props in between the upper edges of the net, putting the upper ropes on the top and pressing together the ropes running alongside each other. (10) Let him then stand guard by going around; if any pole or net is leaning over, let him raise it up.

When the hare is pursued into the nets, let him allow it to run ahead in front and, as he runs after it, let him then shout. When the hare falls into the net, let him stop the frenzy of the dogs, not by touching them, but rather by soothing them; and let him make clear to the hunter by shouting that it is caught or that it has run by on this side or that, or that he has not seen it, or where he saw it.

(11) The one hunting with dogs should go out on the hunt wearing casual, lightweight clothing and footgear, with a club in his hand, and the net-keeper should follow him. He should proceed toward the hunting ground in silence, lest the hare, if it is somewhere nearby, move away upon hearing his voice. (12) Having tied the dogs to trees, each separated so that they will be easy to set loose, set up the short nets and the trap nets in the manner discussed. After this, the net-keeper should be on guard. The one hunting with dogs, taking the dogs, should proceed to lead them on to the hunting ground (13) and, having promised in prayer to give a part of the game to Apollo and Artemis the Huntress, he should loose one of the dogs, whichever one is most wise at tracking—if it is winter, at the same time the sun is rising, but if it is summer, before day, and in the other seasons, between these times.

(14) When the dog finds the right track—of those going now this way, now that—he should loose another dog in addition; and if the track goes on, he should send forth the others, one after another, leaving not much of an interval between them, and follow without pressing upon them, addressing each by name, but not often, lest they be excited too early. (15) The dogs will advance with joy and vigor, disentangling the lines of scent that are brought forth in twos or threes; and they run to and fro beside and across the tracks that intersect, circle

about, are straight or curved, close or separated, recognized or unrecognized; and the dogs run beside each other, rapidly wagging their tails, lowering their ears and flashing their eyes. (16) When they are near the hare, they will make this visible to the hunter by shaking their tails back and forth along with their entire bodies, by warlike charges, by racing past one another in love of rivalry, by running together in a love of toil, by quickly uniting, separating, and then again charging. Finally they will come to the resting place of the hare and overrun it.

(17) The hare will suddenly start up, arousing the baying and barking of the dogs behind it as it flees. Let him shout toward the hare as it is pursued: "Go, dogs, go![43] Wise[44] dogs!" Wrapping his cloak around his hand, and taking up his club, he should run with the dogs after the hare, but should not head the hare off, for that would be perplexing to them. (18) The hare quickly runs off, gets out of sight, and often comes around again to the place where it was discovered. The hunter should then shout out to the slave: "Strike, boy! Strike now, strike now!" And let the slave then make clear whether or not it has been caught.

(19) And if it is caught in the first run, the hunter should call in the dogs and seek another; but if not, he should run along with the dogs as quickly as possible and not give up, but rather go forth with a love of toil. And if the dogs, as they are in pursuit, encounter the hare again, the hunter should shout: "Well done, well done, dogs! Follow it, dogs!" If the dogs are far ahead of him, so that he is able neither to run with nor to follow them, but fails to reach their course and cannot find or see them—although they are casting about somewhere nearby or yelping or staying on the track—he may find out as he runs along at the same time by shouting aloud to anyone: "Hey, have you seen the dogs?" (20) When he has already found out, and if they are on the scent, he should stand by them and urge them on, calling each dog by name, altering the tone of his voice in as many ways as possible, making it sharp, deep, quiet, or loud. In addition to the other ways of calling them, if the pursuit is in mountains, he should call upon them in this way: "Well done, dogs! Well done, o dogs!"[45]

But if they are not near the tracks, but have overrun them, call to them: "No, back! No, back, dogs!"

(21) But when they hold fast to the track, he should lead them around, making many tight circles; and whenever the track is dim

for them he should set a pole as a marker for himself and from this point bring them together, urging them on and patting them until they recognize it clearly. (22) But then when the track is clear they will pursue it swiftly, throwing themselves upon it, leaping over it, acting in concert, conjecturing, making signs, and setting recognizable boundaries for themselves. But whenever the dogs thus rush closely across the track, do not press hard upon them, lest they, through love of honor, overrun it.

(23) But when they are near the hare and display this clearly to the hunter, he should take heed lest it move forward for fear of the dogs. By wagging their tails, leaping over and falling upon each other many times, giving tongue again and again, lifting up their heads and looking at the hunter and making it known that these things are true, the dogs will by themselves make the hare stand up, and, yelping, attack it. (24) And if it falls into the net or gets past, on the inside or outside, in each case let the net-keeper announce it. And if it has been caught, search for another, but if not, pursue it, using the same means of urging the dogs on. (25) And when the dogs are already somewhat tired of pursuing, and it is already late in the day, then the hunter should continue to seek the worn-out hare, neglecting nothing of what the earth sends up or has upon it, making frequent returns so that the hare is not overlooked (for the animal lies down in a small place and from tiredness and fear does not rise); and, leading the dogs on, urging them, encouraging much the one that loves human beings, little the one that is self-satisfied, and a measured amount the one in the middle, until he either kills the hare on the run or drives it into the nets.

(26) After this, having taken up the short nets and the trap nets, he should rub down the dogs and leave the hunting ground, having waited, if it is midday in the summer, so that the feet of the dogs do not get burnt on the paths.

∾ Chapter 7 ∾

(1) For breeding, relieve the bitches of toils in the winter so that, having rest, they may generate a well-born nature toward spring; for this season is the best for the growth of the dogs. There are

fourteen days in which they are held in the grip of necessity. (2) In order that they may become pregnant more quickly, lead them to the good dogs toward the end of this time. But when they are near giving birth do not lead them out on the hunt continuously, but leave intervals, lest they miscarry through love of toil. They are pregnant for sixty days.

(3) When the puppies are born, leave them under the mother and do not put them under another bitch: for they will not grow if they are looked after by others. The milk of the mothers is good, and her breath and embraces are dear [to the puppies]. (4) When the puppies are already wandering about, give them milk for up to a year and whatever they will live on for the whole time, but nothing else; for heavy feeding of the puppies warps their legs, introduces sicknesses into their bodies, and generates injustices[46] within.

(5) They should be given short names, in order that they are easy to call up. The names should be such as these: Psuchē, Thumos, Porpax, Sturax, Lonchē, Lochos, Phroura, Phulax, Taxis, Xiphon, Phonax, Phlegōn, Alcē, Teuchōn, Huleus, Mēdas, Porthōn, Sperchōn, Orgē, Bremōn, Hybris, Thallōn, Rhōmē, Antheus, Hēba, Gētheus, Chara, Leusōn, Augō, Polus, Bia, Stichōn, Spoudē, Bruas, Oinas, Sterrhos, Kraugē, Kainon, Turbas, Sthenōn, Aethēr, Actis, Aechmē, Noēs, Gnōmē, Stibōn, Hormē.[47]

(6) Lead the puppies on the hunt, the females at eight months, the males at ten months. Do not set them loose on the track to the resting place of the hare, but, tying on a long leash, follow the tracking dogs and let them run over the track. (7) And when the hare is discovered, if [the puppies'] form be noble for running, they should not go up to it straightaway. Rather, send forth the puppies when the hare is ahead on the course so that they no longer see it. (8) For if the hunter should set them loose from near at hand, those that have noble form and stout souls will, upon seeing the hare, strain themselves and break down because their bodies are not yet composed. The hunter therefore needs to be on guard against this. (9) If, on the other hand, they are but shamefully suited for coursing, nothing should hinder the hunter [from letting them run], for they have no hope of catching the hare and will not suffer from this. But on the course, the puppies should run along the track until the hare is caught, and, once it is captured, the hunter should give it to them to tear apart.

(10) But when they are no longer willing to remain by the nets and scatter, the hunter should retrieve them until they are accustomed to discover the hare by running toward it, since by seeking it when they are not in order, they eventually become the sort that keep hunting about, which is a terrible thing to learn.

(11) Give them their food beside the net—at least while they are young—and when the nets are being taken up, so that, if they wander on the hunting ground through lack of experience, they will come back to this place and thus be saved. But they will leave off from this when they begin to regard the wild animal with hostility; and they will be attentive about the latter, rather than giving thought to the former. (12) It is also necessary that for the most part the hunter himself give the dogs what is suitable when they are in need; for when they are not in need[48] they do not know the cause of this, but when, desiring something, they take it, they are attached to the giver.

∼ CHAPTER 8 ∼

(1) Track the hare when the god snows and the earth disappears: for if there are dark[49] areas on it, it will be difficult to search for the hare. When it has snowed and there is a north wind, the tracks will be manifest on the surface for much time, for they do not melt quickly. But if there is a south wind and the sun shines they will be manifest for little time, for they quickly dissolve. When it is snowing continuously, one should not go out, for the tracks will be covered up; nor if it is blowing hard, for it heaps the snow up and makes the tracks disappear.

(2) Never go out on the hunt with the dogs in these conditions, for the snow burns the noses and feet of dogs and the smell of the hare disappears on account of the excessive frost; but taking the trap nets and setting out with another, go to the hills, away from the cultivated fields, and whenever one picks up the tracks, follow them.

(3) But if the tracks intersect, come back from the same places to the same place, making circles and seeking the place where they go out. The hare often wanders about, since it is perplexed about where it will lie down and at the same time because, as a consequence of

always being pursued, it is accustomed to employ art in walking. (4) When the track appears, proceed on ahead. It will lead either to a shady place or to one that is steep; for the blowing winds carry the snow over such places. The winds therefore leave behind many places that are good for sleeping, and the hare seeks out one of these. (5) When the tracks bring one to such places do not approach near, lest the hare move away, but go out and around in a circle, for it is to be expected that the hare is there and that it will become visible, for the tracks will nowhere pass out of such places.

(6) But when it is clear that the hare is there, let it be, for it will stay there, and search for another before the tracks become invisible, taking into consideration the time of day so that, if one discovers others, enough time remains to place round the nets. (7) At this point, stretch the trap nets around each of them in the same way as on dark ground, encompassing any hare that may be close within; and, when the nets are standing, approach and set the hare in motion.

(8) If the hare extricates itself from the trap net, pursue it along the tracks; it will come to other such places if it does not press itself down in the snow. Looking into this, then, it is necessary to set up nets around any place that it might be. If it does not stay behind, run after it; for it will be caught even without trap nets, since it will quickly grow weary on account of the depth of the snow and the amount that attaches to the bottom of its feet, which are hairy.

❧ Chapter 9 ❧

(1) For fawns and deer, the dogs should be Indian, since they are strong, large, swift-footed, and not lacking in soul; having these qualities, they are able to toil.

The newborn fawns should be hunted in the spring, for this is the season in which they are born. (2) Look for them by going first into the glades, where there are the most deer. Wherever they may be, the keeper of the hounds should come into this place with dogs and javelins before daybreak, and tie up the dogs far off, out of the woods, so that they do not bark upon seeing the deer; and he himself should then keep watch for them.

(3) At daybreak he will see them leading the fawns to the place where each will put its own to bed. Each one, having lain down and given milk and looked about to ensure that they are not seen by any one, guards its own as it goes off to the other side. (4) On seeing these things, he should loose the dogs, and, taking up the javelins himself, approach the first fawn where he saw it bedded down, taking the places into consideration so that he does not go astray; for when approached up close the places are often altered in appearance from how they seemed from afar. (5) When he has seen the fawn, he should approach up close. For it will keep still, press itself down on the earth, and allow one to take it up, crying loudly, if it has not been rained on—but if this has happened, it will not remain; for the rapid condensation of the moisture that it has within it, being contracted by the cold, makes it withdraw. (6) Then it will be caught by the dogs, pursuing it with toil. Having taken hold of it, he should give it to the net-keeper. The fawn will cry out; and the deer, seeing some things and hearing some things, will run at the one holding it, seeking to take it away. (7) At this moment, he should urge the dogs on and use the javelins. Having prevailed over this one, he should go on to the others and use the same form of hunting against them.

(8) The young fawns are caught in this way. But those that are already big are caught only with difficulty; for they graze with their mothers and other deer, and when they are pursued, they withdraw into the latter's midst—and sometimes at the front, and occasionally at the back. (9) The deer, defending the fawns, trample upon the dogs and are therefore not easily caught, unless someone comes directly in close to them, dispersing them away from each other so that one of them is left alone. (10) When this violence occurs, the dogs are left behind in the first chase, for the absence of the other deer frightens the fawn, and the swiftness of fawns of such age is like nothing else; but on the second or third course they are quickly caught, for their bodies are not able to withstand the toil on account of their youth.

(11) Foot traps are also laid for deer, in the mountains, around the meadows and the streams and the vales, on the pathways and cultivated fields to which they may go. (12) The foot traps should be made by plaiting yew that has been stripped of its bark all round in order that it not rot, and they should have well-rounded crowns and spikes of wood and iron alternately woven into the plait; but the

iron spikes should be larger so that the wooden ones will give way to the foot, while the former will press upon it. (13) The noose of the rope that is to be put on the crown should be of plaited hemp, as also the rope itself; for this is least likely to rot. And let the noose itself, as well as the rope, be strong; and let the wood to which it is fastened be of common oak or evergreen oak, three spans long, with bark all round, and one palm in thickness.

(14) Set up the foot traps by excavating a round hole of earth five palms deep, equal in size to the crowns of the traps above and tapered toward the bottom. Also, excavate enough earth to seat both the rope and the wood. (15) Having done these things, put the trap at a depth below ground level, put the noose of the rope around the crown, and lower the rope and the wood each into place. Put sticks over the crown, but not so many that they extend beyond the outside, and over these put thin leaves, as the season may offer. (16) After this, throw some earth on the leaves, first what was lifted from the surface of the excavation, and then, above this, solid earth from far away in order that the position of the trap may be especially inconspicuous to the deer. Carry the remaining earth far away from the trap, for if the deer smell recently moved earth—and they quickly do this—they will be timid.

(17) Holding the dogs, inspect the traps that are set up in the mountains, in the morning especially, though this is also necessary at other times of the day—and in the cultivated fields early; for in the mountains, the deer is not caught only at night, but also in the day on account of being deserted; in the cultivated fields, however, it is caught at night on account of its fear of human beings during the day. (18) Whenever one discovers that the trap has been turned up, pursue it—setting loose and encouraging the dogs—along the furrow made by the wood, looking to see in what direction it may lead. It will not be unclear, for the most part; for stones will have been moved, and the trail of the dragging wood will be apparent on the cultivated fields; and if it goes over rough places, the rocks will hold the bark of the wood, tearing it off, and by this the pursuit will be easy.

(19) Now if it is caught by the front foot, it will quickly be taken; for on the run, the piece of wood will beat it all over its body and face; and if it is caught by the rear foot, the piece of wood trailing

along behind impedes its body as a whole, and sometimes, as it is carried along, it falls into forked branches of the bushes, and if that does not break the rope it will bring the deer to a halt on the spot.

But you must not—if you take the deer in this way, or if you prevail over it through toil—approach near, if it is male; for it will strike with its antlers and feet; and if female, with its feet. Hurl a javelin from a distance.

(20) They are caught even without traps, through pursuit, when it is summertime; for they grow very weary and when they are brought to a stand they can be speared with a javelin. They even throw themselves into the sea if they are followed close, and into fresh waters if they have no way out; and sometimes they fall down because they have difficulty breathing.

∽ Chapter 10 ∽

(1) For the wild boar one should acquire dogs—Indian, Cretan, Locrian, Laconian—nets, javelins, boar-spears, and snares.

Now in the first place, the dogs that are needed from each breed must not be merely chanced upon if they are to be ready to battle the wild animal.

(2) And the nets should be of the same flax as those for the hares; let them be of forty-five threads in three strands, with each strand of fifteen threads; from the upper edge the length should be ten knots; the depth of the meshes should be a *pygnon*.[50] The cords that run round [the top and bottom] should be one and a half times the thickness of the nets. They should have rings on the end and let the cords be woven in above the meshes and let their ends go out through the rings. Fifteen nets will suffice.

(3) Let the javelins be of all sorts, with blades of good breadth and sharp, and shafts that are strong. The boar-spears should first have heads five palms long and, in the middle of the socket, strong teeth forged, and shafts of dogwood the thickness of a spear. The foot traps are similar to those for deer. But let there be fellow hunters, for the wild animal is difficult to capture even by many. How each of these things should be used in hunting, I will teach.

(4) First then, when they have gone to wherever they suppose the boar to be, it is necessary to loose one of the Laconians, while keeping the others tied up, and to go around with the dog. (5) When it has picked up the scent of the boar, they should follow in a row along the track, which clearly guides those following. And for the hunters there will be many indications: tracks in the soft ground, broken branches in the bushy part of the woods; and where there are trees, scratches from its tusks. (6) The dog, in tracking, will usually arrive at a densely wooded spot, for the animal usually lies down in such places; for they are warm in the winter but cool in the summer. When the dog arrives at the boar's lair, it barks. Most often, however, the boar will not rise.

(7) Then, taking the dog and tying it up with the others far away from the lair, set up the nets in their places of anchorage, throw the meshes upon large forked sticks, and make the hollow part of the net extend a long way, standing branches within on each side as props in whatever way the beams of light may pass through the meshes and into the hollow as much as possible, in order that for the one running toward it, it is as bright here as it is on the outside. Fasten the cord running round the net to a strong tree, and not from a bush. For in the barren places, briars keep together.[51] Beyond each net, stop up even the difficult passages with wood, so that the boar makes its run into the nets and does not change course.

(8) When the nets have been set up, return to the dogs, loose them all together, and, taking the javelins and the boar-spears, advance. The one who is most experienced should urge on the dogs, the others should follow in order, leaving much distance between them, enough for the boar to run through. For if, retreating, it should fall upon them when close together, there is danger of being struck. For it vents its anger on whomever it falls upon.

(9) When the dogs are near its lair, they will press forward; aroused by the tumult, it will rise up, and that dog that is brought before its face will be tossed up; and, running ahead, the boar will fall into the nets; but if not, it is necessary to pursue. And if the ground slopes where the net holds the boar, it will get back up quickly, but if the place be level, the boar will straightaway stand firm, having the net around. (10) And at this moment the dogs will press hard; the hunters, being on guard, should use their javelins, and throw stones,

standing around behind the boar at a considerable distance until, by running forward, it stretches tight the edge of the net. Then, whoever among those present is the most experienced and the strongest should approach from the front and strike the boar with the spear.

(11) But if, despite the javelins and stones, it will not stretch the edge of the net, but rather, drawing back, turns around toward the man before it, it is then necessary, whenever this holds, to advance, taking the boar-spear and holding it with the left hand in front and with the other behind; for the left hand keeps it straight, while the right hand thrusts it in. And let the left foot follow the left hand forward, and the right the other hand. (12) Advancing, one must project the boar-spear, with legs not much further apart than in wrestling, turning the left side toward the left hand, and then watching the wild animal in the eye and taking heed of the motion of its head. He should present the boar-spear while guarding lest the animal, by jerking its head, knock the spear out of his hands; for the boar will follow through on the force of this swing of its head.

(13) But if one does suffer this, he must throw himself flat on his face and hold onto the wood beneath him; for if the wild animal falls upon him in this position, it cannot pick him up because of the upward curve of its tusks; but if he is raised into the air, he is necessarily struck. So it tries to raise him into the air. And if it cannot, it stands over him and tramples him. (14) There is only one deliverance from these things, when one is in this necessity: that is, for one of his fellow hunters to come close, holding a spear, and provoke it by pretending to throw; but he must not throw, lest by chance he hit the one who has fallen. (15) When it sees this, abandoning the one it has beneath it, it will turn out of anger and spiritedness to the one provoking it. The other must leap up quickly, having remembered to hold onto his spear as he stands up. For safety is not noble unless one prevails. (16) He should bring his spear to bear again in the same way and thrust it within the shoulder blade where the throat is, and, holding firmly, push back vigorously. It will advance on account of its rage, and, if the teeth of the spearhead did not prevent it, would shove itself along the shaft until it reached the one holding the spear.

(17) Its power is so great that one would not believe what belongs to it. For, when it has just died, if someone puts hairs on its tusks, they shrivel up; they are that hot. But when it is living they are in-

flamed, when it is provoked. Otherwise, it would not set fire to the tips of the hairs on the dogs when it misses a strike on their bodies.

(18) The male is captured after providing these, and even more, troubles. But if it is a female that falls in, he should run up and strike it, guarding against being pushed down. But if he suffers this, he is necessarily trampled and bitten. So one should not fall down willingly. But if he falls unwillingly, the ways to get up are the same as when one is under the male: when rising it is necessary to strike with the boar-spear until one kills it.

(19) And they are captured also in the following way. Short nets are set up for them in the passages of the groves, in the thickets, the hollows, the rough places, and where there are entrances to meadows, marshes, and waters. The one who has been assigned this guards the short net, holding his boar-spear. The others lead the dogs out, seeking the most beautiful places; and when it is discovered, it is pursued. (20) If it falls into the short net, the net-keeper, taking up his spear, should advance and use it as I described; but if it does not fall into the net, he should run after it. It is also caught, when it is stiflingly hot, by being pursued by the dogs; for even though the wild animal is exceedingly powerful, it gets exhausted when it runs out of breath. (21) But many dogs die in such a hunt, and the ones who hunt with dogs are themselves endangered, especially when, in pursuits, they are compelled, holding their spears, to approach it when it is tired out in water, standing on a steep place, or in a thicket from which it is unwilling to come out. For neither a short net nor anything else will prevent it from bearing down on the one who is drawing near. Nevertheless, they should advance when it is like this, and demonstrate the stoutness of soul on account of which they chose to exercise fully this desire. (22) They must use the boar-spear and forward positions of the body as has been described; for then if one should suffer something, it would not be from failing to do it correctly that he would suffer.

Foot traps are set up for them the same as for the deer, in the same places, and with the same inspections, pursuits, approaches, and uses of the spear.

(23) When their newborns are caught, they suffer this with difficulty; for they are not left alone as long as they are small, and whenever the dogs find them, or they foresee something, they quickly

disappear into the woods, and they are generally followed by both [parents], who are then fierce and fight more when battling on their behalf than on their own.

∾ CHAPTER 11 ∾

(1) Lions and leopards, lynx, panthers, bears, and other wild animals of that sort are caught in foreign lands—around Mount Pangaeus and Cittus beyond Macedonia, others on Mysian Olympus and Pindus, others on Nysa beyond Syria, and on other mountains to the extent they are able to support them. (2) Some of the ones in the mountains are caught, because of the difficulty of the ground, with the drug aconite.[52] The hunters[53] scatter this, mixing it into whatever [food] each likes, around waters and other places where it goes. (3) Others of them are caught going down into the plains at night, being intercepted with horses and weapons, placing their captors in danger. (4) And for some of them they make round, big, deep pits, in the middle of which they leave a pile of earth. Upon this, toward nightfall, they set a goat that has been tied up and they fence in the pit with wood in a circle so that it cannot see over it, leaving no way in. Hearing the [goat's] cry at night, they run around the fence in a circle and, when they do not discover a way in, they leap over it and are caught.

∾ CHAPTER 12 ∾

(1) Concerning the practices involved with hunting with dogs, they have been spoken about. But those who desire this activity will be benefited in many ways: for it provides for the health of their bodies, improves seeing and hearing, and lessens aging; and especially educates in things connected to war. (2) For first, when they march on difficult roads carrying weapons, they will not be at a loss; for they will withstand the toils because they are accustomed to them in taking wild animals. Then they will be able both to go to sleep

on hard ground and to be good guards of what has been assigned to them. (3) And in marches against enemies they will be able both to pursue and to do the things they are ordered because this is the way they catch the prey. Those who are assigned to the front will not depart from their stations because they are able to endure. (4) And when their enemies are in flight they will correctly and safely pursue those in front of them over every sort of ground because of habituation. But if their own army suffers misfortune in a place that is wooded and precipitous or otherwise difficult, they will be able to save themselves in a fashion that is not shameful, and also save others; for habituation of this work gives them an advantage in knowledge. (5) And further, some such men, when a large mass of their allies was turned to flight, have, by their own good order and boldness, renewed the fight and turned the victorious enemy to flight when it erred because of the rough ground. For it always belongs to those whose bodies and souls are in a good condition for good fortune to be near at hand.

(6) And because our ancestors knew that this is why they were fortunate against the enemy, they were attentive to the young; for, though crops were rare at the beginning, they believed nevertheless that they should not at all hinder the hunters with dogs from giving chase over the crops growing on the earth. (7) In addition to this, there was to be no night hunting within many stadia[54] [of the city], in order that those who possess this art not take away the prey; for they saw that for younger men this pleasure alone provides the most goods. For it makes them moderate and just, through being educated in the truth. For they perceived that, both in other matters and in the matters of war, they are fortunate on account of these things. (8) And if they want to practice one of the other noble things, it deprives them of none, as do other bad pleasures, which should not be learned. From ones such as these, therefore, come good soldiers and generals. (9) For those from whose soul and body toils remove the shameful and hubristic things, and increase desire for virtue, those are the best; for they will overlook neither their city being done injustice, nor the land suffering badly.

(10) But some say that they should not fall passionately in love[55] with hunting with dogs, so that they do not neglect their households—not knowing that all those who do well toward their cities

and friends are more attentive to their households. (11) If, therefore, those fond of hunting are preparing themselves to be of use to the fatherland in the greatest things, they will not neglect their own private affairs; for the households of each are saved or destroyed along with the city. The result is that, in addition to their own things, such men also save the things of other private persons. (12) But many of those who say such things are unreasonable because of envy and would rather choose to be destroyed through their own badness than to be saved through the virtue of others. For most pleasures are also bad; by giving in to them men are induced to say and to do worse things. (13) And then, through their vain words they arouse hatreds; and from their bad deeds they bring sicknesses, penalties, and deaths on themselves, their children, and their friends, insensibly holding onto bad things, but more sensitive to pleasures than others. Who would use any of these to keep a city safe?

(14) From these bad things, however, there is no one who is passionately in love with what I recommend who not will abstain; for a noble education teaches one to live under laws and to speak about and listen to the just things. (15) Those, then, who submit themselves always to working hard at something and being taught obtain for themselves lessons and toilsome cares, and safety for their cities. But those who are not willing to be taught through toil, but pass their time in unseasonable pleasures, these are by nature the worst. (16) For they obey neither laws nor good speeches; for, since they do not toil, they do not discover what a good man should be; so they are able to be neither pious nor wise; and, being uneducated, they censure very much those who have been educated. (17) Therefore, through these men nothing would be in a noble condition, but everything that is beneficial to human beings has been discovered through the better sort—and the better are those who are willing to toil.

(18) And this has been demonstrated by a great example; for among the ancients, those who were with Cheiron when they were young, whom I mentioned, started from hunting with dogs and learned many noble things; from which great virtue came into being for them, on account of which they are admired[56] even now. It is quite clear that all men are passionately in love with her,[57] but because it is through toils that one chances upon her, the many stand aside. (19) For while achieving her by labor is unclear, the toils she

entails are manifest. Perhaps then, if her body were manifest, human beings would be less negligent of virtue, knowing that just as she was manifest to them, so too are they seen by her. (20) For whenever someone is seen by his beloved,[58] every man is better than himself, and neither says nor does anything shameful or bad, lest it be seen by the beloved. (21) But men, not supposing that they are watched by virtue, do many bad and shameful things in her presence, because they do not see her. But she is present everywhere on account of being immortal, and she honors those who are good with regard to her and she dishonors the bad. So if they knew this, that she watches them, they would hasten to the toils and the education by which she is with difficulty caught, and they would acquire her.

~ CHAPTER 13 ~

(1) But I wonder at those who are called sophists, because the many say that they lead the youth to virtue, when in fact they lead to its opposite. For we have not seen a man anywhere who has been made good by the present-day sophists, nor do they produce writings by which men are made to become good. (2) But many things have been written by them about frivolous matters, from which there are empty pleasures for the young, but in which there is no virtue: things that otherwise provide a waste of time to those who vainly hope to learn something from them and that hinder them from other useful things and also teach them bad things. (3) I blame them, then, in matters of great importance to a greater extent; but concerning what they write, the meaning of their words has been sought, and they do not have any knowledge at all by which the young are correctly educated in virtue.

(4) I am a private individual, but I know that it is best[59] to be taught the good from nature itself, second from those who truly know something good, rather than by those who possess the art of deception. (5) Perhaps, indeed, I speak using expressions in an unsophisticated manner, for this is not what I seek. But I seek to express correct judgments that those who have been nobly educated in virtue need; for expressions do not educate, but judgments do, if they are noble.

(6) But many others also accuse the present-day sophists (not the philosophers) because they are sophisticated in expressions, but not in thoughts. And it does not escape my notice that someone, perhaps from among this type, will say that things that have been written beautifully and orderly have been written neither beautifully nor orderly; for it will be easy for them to blame quickly and incorrectly. (7) And indeed, things have been written in this way in order to hold correctly, and make men not sophistical but wise and good; for I do not want them to seem, but to be, useful, in order that they be unrefuted forever.

(8) But the sophists speak and write in order to deceive and for their own gain, and they do not benefit anyone in any way; for not one of them ever became wise, nor is wise, but it suffices for each to be called a sophist—which is a term of reproach, at least among those who have good sense. (9) Against the precepts of the sophists, therefore, I advise being on guard, but not to dishonor the thoughts[60] of the philosophers. For while the sophists hunt the wealthy and young, the philosophers are sharers and friends with all; and with respect to the fortunes of men, they neither honor them nor dishonor them.

(10) Nor should one emulate those who seek advantage wherever they can, whether in private or in public affairs—taking to heart that the best of them are recognized as better but are burdened with toil, while the bad ones suffer badly and are recognized as being worse. (11) For by robbing the substance of private men as well as of the city, they are more unbeneficial to the common safety than private men; and their bodies are in the worst and most shameful condition with regard to war, being incapable of toil. But those who hunt with dogs provide both their bodies and their possessions, nobly maintained, to the community of citizens. (12) And whereas these go after wild animals, the others go after their friends. And then those who go after friends have a bad reputation in the eyes of all, but those who hunt with dogs, going after wild animals, have a good reputation. For if they make a capture, they win victory over enemies; but if they do not make a capture, they are still praised, first because they assailed what is hateful to the whole city, and then because they set out with a view neither to injuring a man nor to love of gain. (13) Moreover, through the exercise itself they become better at

many things and wiser, for the reason that we will teach: for if they do not excel greatly by means of toils, contrivances, and many cares, they will not capture their prey. (14) For their opponents, contending for their soul[61] and in their own home, are in great strength; accordingly the toils of the one who hunts with dogs come to be in vain unless he prevails over them by greater love of toil and much intelligence. (15) Therefore, those who want to take advantage in the city take care to gain victory over friends, but one who hunts with dogs over what is commonly hated; and this very care makes the ones better against other enemies, the others much worse. And, for the ones, the prey is taken with moderation, but for the others with shameful boldness. (16) The ones are able to despise bad character and the shameful pursuit of gain, but the others are not able; the voice of the ones gives utterance to what is good, the others to what is shameful; with respect to divine matters, for the ones, nothing impedes their being impious, but the others are the most pious. (17) For, ancient accounts hold that even gods delight in this work, both practicing and watching it; so the young who do as I advise, by taking these things to heart, will be both dear to the gods and pious, thinking that these things are seen by one of the gods. And these will be good to their parents, to their whole city, and to each one of their friends and fellow citizens. (18) And not only did as many men as were passionately in love with hunting with dogs become good, but also the women to whom the goddess, Artemis, gave these things—Atalanta, Procris, and whoever else.

An Introduction to The One Skilled at Hunting with Dogs

Michael Ehrmantraut

Among Xenophon's works, *The One Skilled at Hunting with Dogs* may appear to be the one least in need of an interpretive essay. What is at issue in the work may seem unequivocal: it presents what one needs to know in order to practice the art of hunting with dogs. That this is the subject matter of the work receives additional confirmation through the fact that lovers of hunting down through the ages have found this to be an instructive and enjoyable account of their favorite pursuit.

Yet the author makes a claim on behalf of this work that goes far beyond what one would expect of a work concerned with technical matters. Anticipating criticisms of the work, he maintains that, "indeed, things have been written in this way in order to hold correctly, and make men not sophistical but wise and good; for I do not want them to seem, but to be, useful, in order that they be unrefuted forever" (13.7). *The One Skilled at Hunting with Dogs* is thus intended to educate its readers in the most fundamental sense: to make them "wise and good." But education is not only the intention of the work but also one of its themes. It concerns the knowledge by which the young are educated for virtue (13.3, 5). However, the reader may remain puzzled as to what the education to virtue, wisdom, and goodness has to do with the knowledge possessed by the skilled hunter, the presentation of which constitutes the large part of this work.

The One Skilled at Hunting with Dogs is divided into three distinct parts: the introduction (chapter 1), the central part that concerns the activity of hunting (chapters 2 through 11), and the conclusion (chapters 12 and 13). In what follows we will consider first the work's introduction and conclusion, and then its central part, with the hope of learning something about what constitutes a good education, paying special attention to the role of hunting in this education.

∾ On Chapter 1: Cheiron's Students ∾

The intention of the first chapter is to promote education: it aims to persuade "the youth" that they should not "despise hunting with dogs nor the rest of education" (1.18). Here, as throughout the work, hunting is said to constitute only one part of education (see 1.2, 5: 2.1; 12.18). The other parts remain unspecified, although they appear to include "noble things" (1.2; 12.18). The class of readers to whom this advice is directed is not made up of those who are already practitioners of hunting. Indeed, it is not presumed that they have any interest in hunting, or even have a favorable opinion of hunting and hunters. To the contrary, the aim of Xenophon's rhetoric in chapter 1 is to overcome the prejudices of the young against hunting and the rest of education. One must infer, from what is adduced on behalf of hunting, why it might be held in contempt. Apparently, the youth are disposed to disdain hunting because they do not believe that it has anything to do with their aspirations to be the kind of men they wish to be: those who are highly honored for their virtues, noble deeds, and contributions to Greece or human civilization (1.17; 12.17). For such ambitious, honor-loving young men, hunting must look like pointless toil. As regards "the rest of education," we can surmise that the youth similarly have the opinion that they are not in need of it. It likely seems to them that what they already possess in the way of knowledge, virtue, or wealth suffices for them to be able to procure what they wish (see *Memorabilia* 4.1.3–5).

The education of the youthful reader therefore requires both that his prejudices about hunting and the rest of education be altered and that he comes to need this education, or at least comes to see it as something beneficial for the community and, therefore, as something that should be tolerated (see 12.7). In this context education is not regarded as something desirable for its own sake; it is not seen as the "greatest good for human beings" (see *Apology of Socrates to Jury* 21). It is rather to be esteemed because "it is from these things that one becomes good both at war and at the other things as a result of which one necessarily thinks, speaks, and acts nobly" (1.18). Hunting and the rest of education first come to sight as means to other more obviously noble ends.

In order to arouse a need, perhaps even a passionate love for "hunting and the rest of education," Xenophon must appeal to the desires, wishes, and longings that the youth already possess (1.17). This is accomplished through the presentation of the example of the ancients who were students of Cheiron, attained "great virtue," and are admired "even now." Implied in the admiration of the youth for the heroes and their virtue is a wish to emulate them and a hope to attain at least something like what they are said to have attained. Perhaps the aspirations of these youths have already been formed by poetic legends of such figures. In any case, since it is by starting from hunting that the heroes learned many noble things and attained their great virtue, hunting and education are made to appear attractive to the reader when they come to be seen as the means by which he can become who he wishes to be (12.18).

The depiction of Cheiron's school is a "great example" (12.18) of education in two ways: not only does it provide models for emulation by the "youth" who is the immediate addressee of the work; it is also an example through which another kind of reader can reflect on what belongs to a genuine education and what might facilitate or obstruct it. Accordingly, Xenophon reveals for us, through the depiction of the much-admired students of Cheiron, something about the "students" he is attempting to reach, the promising candidates for a genuine education.

Xenophon's account of Cheiron's students focuses attention on their respective virtues and accomplishments, and the attainments—human or divine—that follow from these. These are clearly related: on the one hand, their peculiar virtues are what enabled them to perform their great deeds, and, on the other hand, what they acquired in the way of prizes was accorded to them by other men and by gods for their virtuous deeds. Accordingly, Xenophon says about the students as a group: "[They] were wondered at for their virtue" (1.5). Attention is also paid throughout the account of the heroes to the fact that their virtue "came to be great" through what was learned in hunting (12.8; 1.5, 12, 13, 14, 16, 17). Thus even if hunting is only one part of Cheiron's educational program, it appears to be the most important part.

In several cases Xenophon mentions the particular virtues by which Cheiron's students distinguished themselves as individuals: love of toil (Meilanion, Menestheus), moderation (Hippolytus), piety (Hippolytus, Aeneas), and wisdom (Palamedes). In keeping with the exhortatory character of this whole chapter, it seems likely that the purpose of highlighting these particular virtues is to direct the interests of the youthful reader toward them. In this light, the attention paid to the "love of toil" (*philoponia*) is especially noteworthy. In the later elaboration of what we might call the problem of acquiring virtue (in chapter 12), Xenophon maintains that although all men love virtue, the many stand aside from it on account of the "toils" involved in its acquisition (12.18). The willingness to "toil" or "labor" (*ponein*) thus seems to constitute a basic condition for the attainment of human virtue as such (12.9). Yet throughout this text the cultivation of this virtue or disposition is also strongly associated with hunting. For example, it is from "attentiveness to hunting" that Menestheus became superior in the love of toil (1.12). One way in which hunting "educates for war" is that through carrying heavy weapons in the pursuit of wild animals one will be accustomed to similar toils on campaign (12.1–2). In the main part of the treatise, Xenophon frequently mentions the toils that the net-keeper, the dogs, and the hunter himself must endure in the course of the activity. Love of toil is a quality possessed by both the better dogs and the hunters. There are occasions, however, when love of toil in the dogs must be restrained out of the master's sense of what is proper to the pursuit, or in order to prevent young dogs with unformed bodies from overexerting themselves (7.8), or for the sake of their offspring. When pregnant, for example, dogs must be kept in at times "lest they miscarry through love of toil" (7.2).[62] The meaning of "love of toil" is perhaps most visible in the description of what is demanded of the hunter himself when the hare that he is seeking eludes his efforts to catch it. Xenophon says that the hunter should "run along with the dogs as quickly as possible and not give up, but rather go forth with a love of toil" (6.19).[63] The hunter must prove himself superior — in both love of toil and intelligence—if he is to prevail over quarries who have "much strength" and are "contending for their soul and in their own home" (13.14). It is thus through love of toil and exercise of the faculties of soul in hunting that one is made "better and wiser" (13.13–14).

Among the virtues of the heroes, wisdom is also highlighted in that it is the superior excellence of Palamedes, the central figure in the registry of Cheiron's students.[64] It should also be recalled here that Xenophon's stated intention in writing is to make men *"wise* and good."[65]

Xenophon also calls attention to what the students of Cheiron gained on account of their superior virtue, including fame, immortality, and desirable marriages. From the outset, Xenophon appeals to and reinforces the opinion that virtue both makes its possessor deserving of such extrinsic rewards and leads to their acquisition. Indeed, hunting and dogs are said to have been gifts from the gods to Cheiron in honor of his justice (1.1). The concern with just desert—one presumably shared by the intended reader—is brought out in this striking and far-reaching statement about the ultimate fate of the heroes: "Let no one wonder that many of them, although pleasing to the gods, nevertheless died—for this is nature; yet their fame came to be great" (1.3). Xenophon must enjoin that the reader not "wonder" at their death because he, the reader, is presumably disposed to find in the fact of the death of the virtuous something that confounds his view of how things ought to be.[66] Within this disposition to wonder there lurks then both a concern for justice and the corresponding belief that men of this sort, on account of their superior virtue and the great things they do for their communities, deserve better than to perish like all other men, good and bad. Within the admiration for the supremely virtuous, and deeply linked with the concern for justice, there lies a wish or hope for immortality. Xenophon thus adds, by way of consolation upon acknowledging the mortality of the heroic, that nevertheless "their fame came to be great" (1.3). Throughout the descriptions of Cheiron's students, Xenophon also highlights their fame, glory, and reputation. The admiration or longing for great fame to which Xenophon here appeals would seem then to grow out of the concern with justice and the awareness of death as "nature" or natural, that is, as a necessity that limits what even the gods can do. In any case, Xenophon's remark has the effect of momentarily illuminating the hope or wish for immortality lurking in the reader's admiration for superior virtue. Xenophon can thus help make his intended reader, the one he is trying to persuade that hunting and education are noble pursuits, more fully aware of what he already yearns for (see *Memorabilia* 3.1.1).

Divine favor, in various forms, is bestowed upon a number of these men. Cephalus and Hippolytus associate with goddesses (1.6, 11). Amphiaraus, and Castor and Polydeuces, are granted "everlasting life" and "immortality," respectively. That these gifts are mentioned immediately after the statement about death as something natural points to the difficulty of attaining and preserving clarity about death. In any case, the strong identification of death and nature seems to preclude the possibility that everlasting life can be in accordance with nature (see also 6.4). If men actually do become immortal, this can only be against nature, by divine dispensation.

Peleus and Telamon are rewarded with marriage to notable women—as is Meilanion (though not expressly by gods). The emphasis on marriage here, along with divine immortality and enduring fame, is suggestive of the erotic character of the longings inherent in admiration for heroic virtue.

While celebrating all these splendid rewards for heroic virtue, Xenophon conspicuously overlooks or downplays the misfortune and suffering to which some of these men were subject (see *Anabasis* 5.8.26). Meilanion, for example, may indeed have won the hand of Atalanta, "in what was the greatest marriage of the time"—but by all other accounts their marriage was not exactly a happy one. Of Hippolytus, Xenophon says that "having been deemed blessed for his moderation and piety, he died" (1.11). Xenophon does not mention that the young man was killed at the behest of his own father, Theseus, in reaction to an accusation against him that proved to be false (and that seems to have arisen *because* his moderation and pious devotion to Artemis brought on the hatred of his stepmother, Phaedra). With Palamedes, again, it is precisely his distinguishing virtue, his superior wisdom, that elicits the envy of the bad men who killed him. Although he is rewarded with "vengeance from the gods such as no other being has," it appears that he, apart from his reputation, was never in a position to enjoy any benefit from this revenge.[67]

While the depiction of these men seems at first to celebrate them as worthy of admiration and emulation, further consideration of the fact that although all of these students of Cheiron were distinguished for their virtue, many of them suffered death and misfortune, and that not one of them is said to be "happy," may undercut that initial impression of the heroes.

⚭ On Chapter 12: Hunting, Education, and Virtue ⚭

The exhortation to take up hunting is resumed at the beginning of chapter 12 with a succinct account of the "many ways" in which those who are enthusiastic about it will be benefited. It is noted, without explanation, that it provides for good health and improvement of sight and hearing. However, the way in which it benefits "most of all"—by educating men for war—must be less obvious, for a detailed explanation is proffered. Hunting can educate for war because there are similarities between the two activities in what is experienced, what must be done, and what must be known. The one activity can thus function as a likeness or image for the other.[68] In both hunting and war, one must endure toils, keep watch, coordinate with others, and obey orders—all in the course of an attack upon and pursuit of the "enemy."[69] Xenophon highlights the advantage in "knowledge" that being accustomed to the works of hunting gives to those whose army has experienced misfortune in difficult country, thus enabling them to save themselves without dishonor "and also save others" (12.4).[70] From this it also becomes clear that the real benefits of hunting are supposed to redound not only to the individual, but also to "others," that is, one's fellow soldiers and citizens. Accordingly, the promotion of hunting in this work seems to make the activity appeal not only to the individual in his concern with his own good, but to the individual whose own good appears to him to be bound up with others (12.11). Accordingly, from here the case for hunting moves beyond the claim that hunting is good for one's health and instills habits and skills that are useful on campaign to suggest that the activity of hunting is conducive to human virtue—especially the particular virtues of justice and moderation—and, thereby, to the formation of the kind of men who will be useful to others (12.8). Hunting contributes to this sort of virtue in part because it, unlike other pleasures (and "most pleasures are bad") does not draw one away from "other noble things" if one wishes to engage in them (12.8, 12).

The question remains, however, as to what makes hunting—the only pleasure of the young favorable to virtue—truly pleasant. Something of the nature of this pleasure may be inferred from the description of the experience of capturing the hare: "So charming is the wild animal that there is no one who, seeing it being tracked, discovered, pursued, and caught, would not forget if he was passionately in love with someone" (5.33). Pleasure is experienced insofar as one has discovered, pursued, and captured the hare. It does not appear to arise from the possession or consumption of the animal itself—something of negligible worth that may be tossed to the dogs for them to tear to apart (7.9; *Memorabilia* 2.1.19; 3.11.7). The charm of the sight then accompanies the hunter's exercise of his own powers of soul and body in the course of the hunt.[71] The corresponding pleasure may then lie in the experience of the confirmation of the sufficiency of those powers—including the hunter's knowledge and skill—through the successful capture of the animal.

In any case, the pleasure of hunting is not impaired by the toils that it involves, although toils, unless they be accompanied by a good hope (such as the hope of making progress), are usually associated with pain that one would prefer to avoid (12.15, 18).[72] Xenophon treats the sorts of toil that hunting involves as labors which will make one "better at many things" (13.13). The willingness to toil in the hunt thus belongs to a broader willingness to undergo hardship for the sake of learning and improvement. Both toil and learning are necessary here because becoming a good man requires that one first "*discover* what a good man should be" (12.16, emphasis added). What constitutes the truly good or "better sort" of men is, at least prior to genuine education, not evident. Xenophon nevertheless maintains that through them "everything that is beneficial to human beings" has been discovered and that they are those who are "willing to toil" (12.17). In this context, Xenophon once again holds up the ancient heroes as examples of men who attained great virtue through their willingness to toil and through their having learned "many noble things," beginning with hunting, under their teacher,

Cheiron. The example of the heroes thereby demonstrates that the willingness to toil is a basic condition of human virtue. "It is quite clear that all men are passionately in love with her, but because it is through toils that one chances upon her, the many stand aside" (12.18). Chapter 1 held out the promise that education in hunting and other things could make one virtuous like the heroes. The argument of the conclusion, without explicitly retracting that promise, hints at potential difficulties in the lover of virtue's attempt to possess his beloved. Great virtue, on this account, requires a willingness to toil, but the presence of this willingness is not to be taken for granted, for even the lover of virtue appears to need to know that he is being "watched" by "her"—the divine object of this love—if he is to work hard enough to possess her.[73] But if Virtue is an incorporeal and invisible goddess, men cannot "know" (*eidotes*: 12.19) if they are in fact watched by her and they therefore appear to lack sufficient incentive to toil for her. In other words, in lacking a body, Virtue herself is insufficiently attractive to bring men to toil and sacrifice themselves for her sake. Perhaps this is why, in chapter 1, the presentation of the heroes' virtues is accompanied by attention to the many great rewards that these men acquired through their great deeds (fame, immortality, and marriage). In the face of these difficulties, however, the lover of virtue may nevertheless find reassurance in Xenophon's insistence that, despite her invisibility and incorporeity, Virtue is in fact "present everywhere," "immortal," and capable of honoring those who are good with respect to her and dishonoring those who are bad (see *Memorabilia* 1.4.18–19; 4.3.14). Nevertheless, the question remains open whether, without "*knowing*" that "she" watches them, this assurance is enough to resolve the problem of how one can engender the willingness to toil necessary for the possession of virtue or genuine education (12.21). Xenophon seems to leave open the question as to whether the willingness to toil requires, on the one hand, the knowledge or, on the other hand, the mere "belief" (*oiomenous*: 13.17), that one's actions are watched by the gods. However, we have also seen that lovers of hunting toil with pleasure in their pursuit of wild animals without either knowing or believing that they are watched by a beloved. Indeed, the sight of a hare as it is pursued and captured makes the hunter "forget" his beloved, if he has one (compare 5.33 and 12.18).

On Chapter 13: Teachers and Sophists

Xenophon's intention in this work is to say what is needed for an education to virtue (13.3). The argument of chapter 12 holds that the student must be willing to toil and "to be taught" so as to learn what it is to be good (12.15–16). The argument of chapter 13 explicitly addresses the need for a teacher who is in possession of the knowledge of what is good. Teaching and teachers have been at issue from the beginning of the work, at least implicitly: for example, in the depiction of Cheiron as educator of the heroes, as well as in the presence of Xenophon himself who addresses the reader directly throughout this work as a new teacher of hunting and as an advocate for "the rest of education" (see 1.18; 12.14; 13.7). Xenophon appears here as the teacher who may surpass even Cheiron, since he can convey his "knowledge" through his writings. Xenophon's teaching is thus not limited by the length of his own life, as was Cheiron's, but may endure "forever" (compare 1.4 and 13.7). As regards Cheiron, Xenophon emphasizes throughout chapter 1 that the heroes "became such as they were" from their attentiveness to hunting and the other things that they learned from him (1.17). Cheiron's activity as an educator thus makes possible the education of the men who "made Greece invincible" (1.17). Education is necessary, in the first place, because men lack knowledge of the good, including knowledge of "what a good man should be" (12.16). For this especially, it seems, a teacher is needed. While Xenophon holds out the possibility that someone can be self-taught—perhaps like his Socrates[74]—he addresses the reader as a potential student who will need to be taught by someone else who "truly *knows*" (in the strictest sense) the good—knowledge that is at once of oneself and of "nature," since it is gained from one's own nature (13.4).

If the young are persuaded that education would be advantageous for them and their cities, they will be led to seek the guidance that they need. But the young may then also be receptive to sophists who claim that they can "lead the youth to virtue" (13.1). Xenophon's intention of directing the youth toward those who are more capable of educating them toward virtue (or of making them "wise and good") is the basis for his criticism of the sophists and their writings. He first disputes the sophists' claim on the grounds of experience: "we" have not seen anyone "made good" by those who are now sophists (13.1, 8). But the most basic criticism of the sophists concerns their lack of knowledge (*gnomai*) of the good, a knowledge that one must have if one is to teach what is truly useful (13.3, 8). It is also suggested that these sophists, in lieu of that knowledge, employ the arts of deception and mislead others into believing that they do possess it and that they are therefore wise and competent teachers (3.9). Further, Xenophon suggests that their motive for doing so is their own gain, understood in terms of wealth.

The critique of the sophists' competence as teachers intends not only to deter the reader from seeking their guidance, but also to cast into relief those who are in fact qualified to educate the young through speech or writing: Xenophon himself and "the philosophers." While Xenophon neither expressly affirms nor denies that he belongs among the philosophers here, the extraordinary claims that he makes on behalf of his own knowledge (13.4) and intentions (13.7) as a writer would seem to place him among them as someone from whom one might learn "something good." In any case, this disclosure of the author's self-understanding—of his intention and his worth as a thinker and educator—at the same time makes evident the extent to which he must then conceal his own wisdom and downplay his own competence as an educator everywhere else in his writings.

∽ On the Hunter's Dogs ∽

Consideration of how the introduction and conclusion of this work aim to persuade the readers to take up hunting reveals how the central part of the work—which treats the breeding, care, training, and guidance of hunting dogs—also concerns education. The training and leading of dogs may in fact be an elaborate likeness for the education of those who, in accordance with Xenophon's advice in chapter 13, become students of the philosophers.[75]

Dogs, in Xenophon's account, clearly also participate in the "work" of hunting—as the very title of our text and the name for the activity indicate. Dogs are so much a part of the activity that in this treatise everything about them—their qualities of body and of soul, as well as their characteristic ways of behaving—is considered solely with a view to the "work" (*ergon*) of the hunt. For the dog, the "work" of hunting is to contribute to the capture of the elusive hare and of other wild animals. However, this involves many subordinate tasks, including detecting the invisible and evanescent scent of the hare; following the line of scent as it winds about and overlaps with the scent of other hares and animals; signaling to the hunter when it has picked up the scent or seen the hare; withstanding fatigue and adverse conditions while tracking and pursuing; swiftly pursuing the hare to its hiding place or into the hunter's nets; not letting up until it is called off by the hunter or the hare is captured; and obeying the commands of the master. In all of this, the dog must also cooperate with the other dogs, neither impeding nor deceiving them even as it vies with them to distinguish itself and attain honor from its master. In the description of the qualities, habits, and tendencies of the dogs—both those that make them good (chapter 4) and those that make them bad (chapter 3) at their work—it first becomes evident that Xenophon's depiction of the dogs is also a likeness for young human beings and that his description of their training and guidance in the activity of hunting the elusive *lagos* (hare) or *therion* (wild animal) is a likeness for their education. Moreover, since, as we have seen, the sort of education promoted in this work ultimately requires study of writings of the philosophers, the hounds depicted here are not simply like students, but also like *readers* of philosophical works. Accordingly, Xenophon's account of the bad and good habits of the dogs as they follow the track of the *lagos* at the same reveals the characteristic traits, both good and bad, of his own readers, that is, of those he intends to make "wise and good" through his writings (3.8–10).

Of special importance here is the treatment of the qualities of soul that make a dog proficient or deficient at its tasks. With dogs—as also with human beings—such qualities ultimately depend on the fitness of the body (12.1–2, 9; 2.3). This obviously holds with respect to the faculties of perception, which require good eyes and organs of smell (3.3). It is also the case with respect to the dog's ability to endure toil. For "those without strong feet, even if they possess good souls, are unable to withstand the toils, but they grow weary on account of the pain in their feet" (3.3). In addition to such characteristics of the bodily "form" (*eidos*) of the dog,[76] Xenophon also addresses what pertains to its "soul," such as its desires, concerns, and passions. For a dog to have a good (or "stout") soul (*eupsuchia*) means, above all, that it is spirited and "able to toil" in pursuit of the animal and not be too "soft" in this respect (7.7; 9.1).[77] The dog's ability to do its work well also depends on the kind and degree of its affection for the object of its pursuit and for its human masters. "Many," Xenophon says, "give up the pursuit and come back because of their hatred for wild animals (*misothēron*)" (3.9). "Love for human beings" (*philanthropia*) also leads some dogs to abandon the chase and return to the company of their human masters, something that a good dog should not do when it is on the scent (4.5). These passions, dislike of the wild animal and love for human beings, appear to be especially problematic because they so closely resemble concerns that dogs should possess in order to be effective hunters. On the one hand, such hatred of the animal is detrimental because it leads the dog to give up the pursuit; on the other hand, the dog must yet be willing to attack, and, in some cases, fight and kill, the animal. Since Xenophon's hunter uses praise and encouragement in guiding and urging the dogs onward, a dog that lacks affection for the human being and any desire to be honored by him would be stubborn and "unwilling to listen" to the master's commands and exhortations (3.8; 6.25).

In the treatment of the dogs, the qualities that render them "useless" are considered first and at greater length than their good qualities. Xenophon directly addresses the question of the sources of these bad qualities. Most of these, he says, "are possessed by nature," though some are due to ignorant (or "unscientific") training (3.11).[78] "Education" or training may thus improve or corrupt a dog's nature depending on whether the teacher "truly" possesses "scientific" knowledge of what is by nature good, as Xenophon indicates in his account of the difference between the good teacher and the sophist (13.4). The absence or presence of the love of toil, for instance, is from nature, yet appears to grow weaker or stronger in accordance with the degree to which it is rewarded. Although the dog's attachment to man (*philanthropia*) does not strictly speaking come from nature, it arises and persists through the natural tendency of the dog to have affection for whoever satisfies its needs. Xenophon accordingly advises that the hunter should himself feed his dogs, but only when they are hungry,[79] on the grounds that "when they are not in need they do not know [who is] the cause of this, but when, desiring something, they take it, they are attached to the giver" (7.12). On the other hand, Xenophon suggests that at a certain point in the dog's life it naturally cares more about pursuing the hare than about its own food—implying, at the same time, that the motivation of the dog is not reducible to the desire for food (7.11).

Throughout the account of hunting, Xenophon calls attention to the differences between dogs. There is much variety in their qualities and habits, both with regard to whether they do or do not possess them, and in the degree to which they are possessed. The hunter must know the characteristic differences between his dogs, as this has bearing upon how the dogs are to be trained and led. Different dogs must be treated differently. For example, in pursuit of the hare, the hunter must encourage "much the one that loves human beings, little the one that is self-satisfied, and a measured amount the one in the middle" (6.25).

Moreover, in Xenophon's account, dogs manifest not only such characteristic differences but, like human beings, even seem to possess individuality (at least when compared to hares, as Xenophon discusses them). Xenophon accordingly stresses the importance of giving each dog its own name and of exhorting each individually by this name as one is urging them on after the hare (7.5; 6.20). The utility of addressing and praising each of the dogs by name stems from the fact that the dogs possess a "love of rivalry" (*philonikōs*) and "love of honor" (*philotimias*) on account of which they compete against one another for distinction and recognition, both from fellow dogs and the human masters (6.16, 22). Because the dogs so desire honor, the master urges them on and calms them, if need be, through praise and exhortation conveyed through speech, and by running along with them as they track and pursue the wild animal (6.9, 17). Xenophon nowhere—even in the chapter on the training of dogs—mentions an occasion where one would punish or discipline a dog.[80] Indeed, while there are many times when approbation of the dogs—both as a group and individually—is called for, there is never occasion for so much as a rebuke—although if they overrun the track one will need to call them back (6.17, 19–20, 25). This silence about punishment or any other means of correcting the behavior of the dogs is striking in light of the extensive attention accorded to all the bad characteristics and habits of the dogs (3.2–11). Although the master relies on speech in guiding the dogs, there is certainly no indication that the defective dogs could be made good through the wise speech of their master alone or that all dogs could be ruled like gentlemen.[81] As "most" of the characteristics of the useless dogs are possessed "by nature," it is perhaps not possible to educate or reform their nature in a way that allows them to become proficient at their work. Any attempt at correction with respect to the kinds of dogs and qualities that the skilled hunter is concerned with may come much too late. Accordingly, Xenophon teaches that in order to bring forth dogs that have a "well-born nature" one must be sure to breed the females with only "good dogs" and limit their hunting during the breeding season (7.1–2). But such precautions, however prudent, clearly will not prevent altogether the birth of defective dogs. As with the treatment of the problem of educating the young, Xenophon's account of hunting dogs—of their nature, their training, and their guidance—directs us to a consideration of limitations in the education of human beings.

～ On the Love of Hunting ～

With the recognition that education is at issue throughout the whole of the work we should not overlook the differences between the introduction and conclusion, on the one hand, and the main part of the treatise (chapters 2 through 11), on the other hand. The most striking difference concerns the presentation of the activity of hunting. In the work's introduction and conclusion, Xenophon is clearly addressing those who are not hunters, who as yet seem to have no interest in hunt,ing and who may even despise or reproach hunters and the activity itself. Xenophon accordingly promotes hunting by appealing to *other* interests of the reader: his longings for the rewards bestowed upon men for their superior virtue—fame, marriage, immortality, and divine favor. Hunting is thus presented as an activity whose worth lies in its conduciveness to such ends. In defending the exercise of hunting against detractors who assert that the love of hunting leads to a neglect of one's household, Xenophon holds that "if" the hunters are preparing themselves to be useful to the city, they will not neglect their own private things, "for the households of each are saved or destroyed along with the city" (12.10–11). Xenophon's defense of hunting here rests upon two assumptions: first, that the activity of hunting is not good or profitable enough for the private individual to justify its pursuit;[82] and second, that hunters are ultimately devoted to the sport because they desire to "be of use to the fatherland," and thus take part in hunting as a military exercise (12.11). These assumptions appear questionable, however, when we consider the main part of the work, where there is no indication that the skilled hunter practices hunting in order to make himself useful to the city or for any other end that is extrinsic to the activity itself. That is not to say that, in the main part of the treatise, the hunter is oblivious to concerns that may seem to point beyond the activity of hunting. For, prior to coming to the practice of hunting, the youth must first undertake an examination of his "substance" in order to determine whether it is sufficient for him to truly benefit from the activity (2.1). Also, Xenophon describes how the hunter, at the outset of the activity, first promises part of the game to Apollo and Artemis (6.13; 5.14). Last, Xenophon enjoins that the hunter observe certain customary constraints on where he should hunt (for example, not in springs or streams) lest the onlookers follow his example and are turned against the law (5.34; cf. 5.25). Yet in each of these cases, the concern with what seems to lie "outside" the practice of hunting (economics, gods, law) can in fact be in support of the practice. For example, hunters should avoid influencing onlookers in a way that makes them disrespectful of law because it might undermine the reputation of hunters for piety and law-abidingness—the very sort of reputation that Xenophon promotes in the conclusion of the work (12.14; 13.17).

That hunting can be practiced for its own sake (or, rather, for the benefit that lies in the activity itself), rather than as a means of making oneself useful to the city, is clear from a passage in the *Education of Cyrus*. Cyrus here teaches one of his captains—described as a "lover of hunting" (*philotheria*)—how he must depart from his usual practice as a hunter of wild animals when he is leading men against the enemy on a "hunt" for allies and "riches in their entirety" (*Education of Cyrus* 2.4.22; 4.2.46):

> Do not do as you sometimes do, Chrysantas, on account of your love of hunting, for you are often busy the whole night without sleep. But you now must allow the men to rest a measured amount so that they might be capable of fighting sleep. Nor, since you have human beings to guide, should you wander up and down the mountains, and run wherever the animals lead you. And do not now go along the paths that are hard to walk, but order your guides to lead along the easiest road, unless it is much long, for the easiest is the quickest for an army. (2.4.26–29)

In sum, hunting itself as practiced by the lover of hunting—without subordination to political or military ends—is a more solitary, self-sufficient, and unconstrained activity than politics or war. Chrysantas, however, is said to "exult" in his charge; this lover of hunting is willing to adapt his ways and consequently becomes Cyrus's most loyal and trusted subordinate. The attractions or satisfactions of hunting for gain with or under Cyrus must outweigh, for this character at least, any good found in the activity of hunting alone.

∾ What the Hunter Needs to Know ∾

Hunting is thus not necessarily in the service of ends extrinsic to the activity itself. But what then is hunting? What makes someone a "skilled hunter"? What is distinctive about hunting and makes it deserving of such high praise? These questions may be addressed through a close consideration of the hunter's relation to his quarry. Generally speaking, "hunting" as it appears throughout Xenophon's works is the activity of attempting to acquire something that one does not possess, something that even eludes attempts to possess it. Not only wild animals, but also friends, riches, "the young," "virtue," "soft breezes," and other things can be "hunted." In the hunting of wild animals, however, the possession of what is hunted is not necessarily the aim of the activity. Aside from the injunction to let newborn hares go free, only once does Xenophon say anything about what one might do with an animal after capturing it: when the dogs catch the hare, "give it to them to tear apart" (7.9). Moreover, concerning the hunting of the hare, Xenophon teaches that "if it has been caught, search for another"—suggesting that the animal, once caught, is of complete indifference to the hunter and that the end of hunting somehow lies in the activity of "searching" (6.24). The wild animal must be "sought out" (*epizetein*) because it is not present in its bodily form, either to the hunter or to his dog. Although the hunter possesses a sense of smell, he himself cannot perceive the scent of the hare. His apprehension of the hare is here indirect, mediated by the work of his dogs. He becomes aware of the presence of the hare only through his own interpretation of the perceptible "signs" (such as barking and tail wagging) that his dogs give when they have picked up the hare's line of scent (6.16). Although the scent itself is thus imperceptible to the hunter, it is yet indirectly accessible through other things that he is in fact able to see, hear, and touch: the dogs or visible tracks in the snow, for instance. For the hunter, the scent is nothing but evidence that the hare is nearby. Although the scent belongs to the animal, it can be detached from its body. The scent is thus a trace of the hare that lingers on the ground and remains available to the dogs even when the hare is not bodily present. Moreover, there are circumstances—in winter, for example—when the hare is out and about but does not leave a scent upon the ground because of snow or frost. The conditions under which the hare itself is manifest are not necessarily the same conditions under which the scent is accessible. Xenophon here dwells on the latter at length because the hare usually becomes present through the line of scent. The description of these conditions demonstrates a knowledge of the different causes of both the appearance and the absence of the scent of the hare as these conditions would be experienced from the perspective of the hunter (see especially 5.1–4).

There are many things that the skilled hunter must understand, as is evident from the teaching of chapters 2–11. Much of the work presents instruction about the means by which the hunter can capture his prey, including such matters as the construction and placement of nets and snares, the equipping, training, and handling of dogs, the tasks of net-keepers, and so forth. But much of chapter 5, not to mention other parts of the work, teaches or conveys knowledge of a somewhat different sort, of such matters as where, when, how, and under what conditions the wild animal or its tracks can be discovered by the hunter, in addition to matters concerning the "nature" of the animals—hare, deer, boar—that are of interest to the hunter. Whereas the former sort of knowledge must originally arise from repeated experience of what works and does not in the field,[83] the latter—the knowledge of the favorable and unfavorable conditions for discovering the hare and other such things—requires extensive experience and observation of the animals and the ever-varying circumstances under which they are or are not present.

As regards the scent of the hare, in particular, such conditions are in the first place understood to bear upon the presence or absence of the animal by first acting upon the scent itself, as when, for example, "rime by its strength draws the heat in and holds the scent inside" (5.1). But the same conditions in their own way also act on the perceiver, in this example, the nose of the dog; for "even the noses of the dogs, becoming numb, are not able to perceive when it is like this, before the sun or the advancing day thaws" (5.2). So whereas rime or ice affects both the dog and the scent so as to prevent the appearance of the scent, the warming sun affects both so as to make the scent manifest. The example suggests that the very appearance and perceptibility of the trace of the hare depend on a chance concatenation of a multiplicity of conditions that affect both the perceiver and what is perceived. The midday sun happens to thaw out the ground where the scent lies and also warm the nose of the dog. This example also highlights how both the conditions of the appearance of the scent and scent itself are changeable and impermanent: "for the nature (*physis*) of the scent, being faint, does not remain the whole day" (6.4).

Similarly, the hare itself does not endure in appearance. Being alive, it actively flees before the approach of the dogs. It eludes detection, pursuit, and capture through both movement and stillness. The hare stays in place if it is being tracked, "unless it is very frightened with the coming of night" and so "moves away" (5.12). As a being with the power of sense perception, a sort of "thinking" (*noesai*: 5.27), and passions like fear, the hare responds to what it perceives. In this way also the presence (or absence) of the hare is in part determined by the presence of the hunter and his dogs with their own (limited) powers of perception. Thus even when it is chased out into the open, the hare may be visible or invisible in accordance with varying conditions such as the light, the color of the terrain, and the coloring of the hare's coat (5.18). Here again, the "causes" of the presence of the hare remain on the level of what is perceptible by the hunter and what is changeable (or perishable). The hunter's grasp does not extend beyond what shows itself to him. For example, he has an understanding of all the weather conditions and seasonal changes that bear on the presence or absence of the hare's scent, but his grasp does not appear to encompass the motions of the heavenly things responsible for those changes, let alone any unchanging necessities that might be responsible for the coming-into-being of those things and their motions.

In chapter 5, Xenophon describes the presence of the hare as it is given first, through its scent (and thus indirectly); he then describes the hare in the manner in which it becomes visible to the hunter when it is on the run, in flight from the dogs; and finally as it is available for close examination after it has been caught. First, with the description of the hare as it appears when it has been flushed out into the open and is on the run, we are given an account of the two kinds (*genē*) of hares, the "big" and the "smaller," which can be distinguished by their visible features: comparative size, color of coat, color of eyes, and the sort of terrain upon which one sees them.

As the hare is being pursued one will also see it "runs into many things without noticing and falls into the nets," a tendency indicative of its poor vision (5.28). Xenophon provides an account of what is responsible for its poor eyesight (weak eyelids, excessive sleep, and the quickness of its movement) that also helps to explain why the hare can be captured at all. For if the hare is in fact driven into the nets, this happens "by chance" (*tuchē*) and "contrary to the nature of its body," a nature that makes it swifter than its pursuers (5.29). As the observations of the skilled hunter seem to be directed by his own concern with discovering and catching the wild animal, the description of the nature of its body is focused upon that aspect of the

hare that is most important from the point of view of the hunter:
its superior speed and ability to elude capture.[84] To come to know
the nature of the hare one thus proceeds from observations on the
animal's characteristic motion, its exceptional swiftness, and then to
the underlying causes of this motion in the nature of its body. Xenophon's description accordingly attends to the features that make
this animal so swift: the structure of its legs and haunches, as well as
the overall "harmony" of its bodily composition. It is also noteworthy that the description begins with the body as a whole and moves
on to address its parts: head, shoulders, chest, loins, haunches, and
feet. In articulating the body of the hare into its parts, its wholeness
or integrity is preserved. Each of these parts is regarded compara-
tively, that is, considered with reference to analogous parts of other
animals (e.g., the head is small) or with other parts of the hare (e.g.,
the back legs are much larger than the forelegs). To speak of the "nature" of the body then is to speak of it in relation to other similar or
dissimilar things appearing to the human observer. Moreover, the
view of the hunter is focused on the *formed* body of the hare. There
is no indication that the form (*eidos*) could be separate from the body
of the animal; for the "form" is always the form *of* the body of something (see 2.3; 3.3; 4.2, 6; 7.7, 8).

In addition to such things, the skilled hunter must also have an
understanding of certain forms of natural "necessity" that can be
experienced and observed in the course of hunting wild animals.[85]
These necessities appear to be of two sorts: first, those that become
manifest in the inclination of animals to mate, generate their kind,
and care for their young; and second, those present in the suscep-
tibility of wild animals, dogs, and even the most skilled of hunters
to bodily harm, death, and the corresponding need to avoid such
danger. One can infer from the work's teaching regarding what
the hunter needs to know in order to find and prevail over his prey
that the skilled hunter requires an understanding of these necessities (10.3–4; 13.13).[86] For example, the necessity that impels hares to
couple and reproduce also induces them to "wander all about" in
the spring, thus complicating the lines of scent left behind for the
dogs and the hunter (5.7). An especially striking example of how the
skilled hunter puts his knowledge of such necessities to use is exhibited in Xenophon's instruction in the hunting of fawns and deer.

Having captured a young fawn (in the manner described in 9.2–6), one can employ it as bait to lure the mother, which can then be speared as she rushes in to save "her own" (9.7). The hunter prevails over the mother deer by taking advantage of her love for her off-spring. Such a strategem may strike one as unseemly and heartless.[87] Evidently, however, the hunter's understanding of erotic necessity is accompanied by a measure of freedom from the power that it might otherwise have over his own heart and mind — a freedom that allows him to make use of his knowledge.

The hunter's activity has even more to do with natural necessity as it is manifest in the mortality of the living being. For, in the first place, the hunter's prey are always "contending for their soul" (13.14), and the successful hunt usually results in the death of the animal. Furthermore, the wild animal's fear — for itself and its off-spring — of pursuers, be they dogs, men, or other predators, like eagles, clearly affects the lives and habits of the wild animals as they show themselves in the course of hunting (5.12, 16–21, 24; 6.23; 8.3; 9.10, 16; 10.18). Aside from such threats, the lives of the wild animals are also clearly constrained by the often harsh extremes of the elements. The hunter must understand these constraints because they are conditions that determine where, when, and how his prey are to be discovered and caught (5.1–6; 7.4; 8.8; 10.6).

But the most striking instance of the skilled hunter's encounter with natural necessity in the form of mortal danger is depicted in the terrifying description of the hunter's own confrontation with the wild boar (10.20). One finds the most references to "necessity" (*anagkē*) in the context of the account of the dangers posed by the boar to the hunter's own life. Here it is not only a matter of what the hunter must do in order to catch the wild animal; it is a question of what must necessarily be done if the hunter is to save his own life (and, if he is to act "nobly," the lives of his fellow hunters) from the raging boar (10.15).

∾ HUNTING AND PHILOSOPHY ∾

In the course of this reading of *The One Skilled at Hunting with Dogs* we have considered passages that suggest that there is a resemblance between hunting and philosophy. Chapter 13 brings hunting and philosophy together as components of the best education. Peculiarities in the treatment of the training of hunting dogs indicate that it may serve as a likeness for the education of the young to the philosophic life. In addition, consideration of the central theme of the work, the skilled hunter's pursuit of wild animals, suggests that this activity may function in the work as an image for the theoretical investigation of nature, a central concern of the philosophic life.

Because it may not be evident that either Xenophon or his Socrates had any serious theoretical interest in coming to know the "natural things," this last suggestion requires explanation. Socrates, according to Xenophon, was "always conversing about human things" (*Memorabilia* 1.1.16). Xenophon presents himself as someone who is engaged in political and military affairs. Indeed, in the *Memorabilia*, Xenophon presents Socrates as a severe critic of those thinkers who hoped or claimed to discover the natural "necessities" or "causes" of "each thing coming to be" (See *Memorabilia* 1.11.15; cf. 4.7.5). Socrates is here said to have "wondered whether it was not visible to them that it is impossible to find these things out" (1.1.13). However, various considerations suggest that, this critique notwithstanding, the Socratic philosopher may still be preoccupied with questions of a theoretical character. In the first place, it seems that the very judgment that the fundamental causes are "impossible" for a human being to discover must arise from a comprehensive reflection upon what is and is not given to us, as well as upon what we can and cannot know of that world, that is, a reflection on the possibility of a science of nature. Moreover, Xenophon's statement that Socrates "did not converse about the nature of all things *in the way* most of the others did" suggests that he might have nevertheless conversed about such things in a way that *differed* from "most of the others" (1.1.11). It also leaves open the possibility that the subject matter of his thinking may not be equated with that of his public "conversation." In any case, Xenophon presents one instance where Socrates does engage in a theoretical examination of the nature of light and fire before breaking it off with the comment that the social setting may not be appropriate for such an inquiry (*Symposium* 7.4). There are then reasons for concluding that, despite appearances to the contrary, Xenophon considered theoretical inquiry in some form to be a worthwhile pursuit, at least for Socrates and those like him.

If, however, theoretical pursuits do indeed belong to the philosophic life as Xenophon understands it, and perhaps lives it, one must conclude that the presence and importance of such concerns have in some way been concealed by the author. The reasons why it might be necessary to exercise reserve in the presentation of the theoretical inquiry into nature are not so difficult to discover. Xenophon's account of Socrates' critique of the "other thinkers" aims to distinguish him from those who sought to find the fundamental causes of the world in "nature," as opposed to the gods, and thus to absolve Socratic philosophy from the reputation for impiety or atheism that is attached to such pursuits (*Memorabilia* 1.1.1). But if theoretical investigation is central to philosophy, and if Xenophon is sincere in his express intent to "make men . . . wise and good" through his writings, it would seem to be an important or necessary concern of the author that this component of the philosophic life not be simply concealed, and thus perhaps forgotten, but that it be preserved and bequeathed to posterity—just as Cheiron receives the gift of hunting and teaches it to his students, and just as Xenophon does something similar for the readers of *The One Skilled at Hunting with Dogs* (1.1). However, an enterprise that might be endangered if promoted openly may yet be advanced covertly with success and safety under the cover of an activity that appears, not merely less threatening, but even beneficial for the individual and the community. So, for example, in the *Education of Cyrus*, the Persians disguise the young peers' instruction in the arts of deception and harming human beings as exercise in the practice of hunting animals that is conducive to the formation of good citizen soldiers; and so Cyrus himself later disguises his advance on the Armenian, his "hunt for friends," as an unthreatening hunting expedition. We are thus led to consider the possibility that the description of hunting in this work may at once serve to depict the otherwise hidden theoretical pursuits of the Socratic philosopher. The figure of hunting, as Xenophon presents it, seems to be well suited for the purposes of both protecting and advancing the philosophic life. In the first place, hunters are evidently not so open to the suspicion and charge that they and their activity are impious. Xenophon insists that the hunters are in fact "the most pious" and argues that "ancient accounts hold that even gods delight in this work, in both practicing and watching it" (1.17). Moreover, with their unpretentious, unprepossessing appearance, Xenophon's hunters are unlikely to incite in other men the sort of envy and hatred that bring about the downfall of those who appear to possess superior wisdom and nobility.[88] Finally, the presentation of hunting in this work seems to be well suited for the purposes of education concerning the theoretical life. For if the activities of hunting and theoretical inquiry do indeed resemble one another, one might come to learn something about the latter through reflection on Xenophon's account of former.[89] We are thus left with the question, does Xenophon's depiction of the outlook and understanding of the hunter reveal something of the philosopher's perspective on the world and what can be known of it?

In the preceding discussion we have for the most part limited our attention to Xenophon's account of the hunting the hare. If the skilled hunter's search for this and other animals is in fact an elaborate likeness for the Socratic philosopher's theoretical pursuits, it seems possible that Xenophon's treatment of the hunt for deer, boar, and other big game may provide the reader further clues as to what constitutes the central concerns of the philosophic life. In any case, a reading of these chapters may lend further support to the main suggestion of this introductory essay: that *The One Skilled at Hunting with Dogs* may be something more than a technical manual on the art of hunting wild animals.

Notes

Editor's Introduction

[1] Many of the major manuscripts are now available online through Princeton University, making possible new discoveries in the study of Xenophon. http://library.princeton.edu/byzantine/search/site/xenophon.

[2] Rev. J. S. Watson, *Xenophon's Minor Works* (London: H. G. Bohn, 1857).

[3] E. C. Marchant, *Xenophon in Seven Volumes* (Cambridge, MA: Harvard University Press, 1923). The original edition did not include the *Regime of the Athenians*; G. W. Bowersock added the work to a later edition (1968) under the authorship of "Pseudo-Xenophon."

[4] H. G. Dakyns, *The Works of Xenophon in Four Volumes* (London: Macmillan, 1890–97).

[5] For a list of every occurrence of every word in Xenophon's shorter writings, see Francisco Martin Garcia and Alfredo Rospide Lopez, *Index Xenophontis Opusculorum* (Hildesheim: Olms-Weidmann, 1994).

[6] Marchant, *Xenophon in Seven Volumes*, 4:xxvi–xxvii.

[7] Marchant and Bowersock, *Xenophon in Seven Volumes*, 7:469–70.

[8] Xenophon, *Hiero the Tyrant and Other Treatises*, trans. Robin Waterfield (London: Penguin, 1997; reissued in 2006 with minor changes).

[9] Robin Waterfield, *Xenophon's Retreat: Greece, Persia, and the End of the Golden Age* (London: Faber and Faber; Cambridge, MA: Belknap Press of Harvard University Press, 2006), xii.

[10] Xenophon, *Hiero the Tyrant*, trans. Waterfield, xvi.

[11] J. M. Moore, *Aristotle and Xenophon on Democracy and Oligarchy* (Berkeley: University of California Press, 1975; reissued 2010).

[12] In fact, the division of Xenophon's works into chapters and paragraphs was not even introduced until the end of the seventeenth century by Edward Wells in his Xenophon, *Opera quae extant omnia* (Oxford, 1691–1703).

[13] *Cyropaedia* 1.3.16–18.

[14] *Cyropaedia* 1.2.10.

[15] See *Cyropaedia* 3.1.14 and context; *Symposium* 4.63; *Memorabilia* 2.1.18, 2.6.28 and ff., 3.11.3–18, and 4.7.4.

[16] *Memorabilia* 4.2.1. See Amy L. Bonnette's essay in this volume, "An Introduction to *On Horsemanship*."

1. HIERO, OR THE SKILLED TYRANT

My grateful thanks to Thomas Pangle for his careful reading and detailed editorial suggestions; he has saved me from many errors and has helped my version conform more closely to the editorial practices of this volume as a whole. The volume editor and an anonymous reviewer have also improved the translation. The Greek manuscript history of the *Hiero* is convoluted, and I have made no attempt to sort it out, but have simply relied on E. C. Marchant's OCT edition (1900), supplemented by the helpful report of the manuscripts in Ralph E. Doty's edition and translation (2003).

[1] "Simonides the poet": A great lyric and elegiac poet, Simonides lived ca. 556–468 BC. Like many of the great poets of his age, he composed victory odes commissioned by winners in the festivals, celebrating their triumphs. He was also famous for his dirges and his hymns celebrating heroic exploits in the Persian War, including an epitaph for those killed at Marathon that was chosen over the effort of Aeschylus, a younger contemporary. Simonides, again like many leading poets and other literary figures of his age, had cordial relations with various tyrants who were his patrons. He was a friend of the family of the Athenian tyrants Hipparchus and Hippias, on which see note 19 on 4.5. He also visited Hiero of Syracuse ca. 476 BC. Simonides was reputed to be rather ugly and fond of money.

"Hiero the tyrant": Hiero ascended to the tyranny of Syracuse in 478 BC, defeating his brother Polyzelus. He was a very successful military leader, winning his greatest victory in 477 BC, over the Etruscans. He was a patron of many literary figures, and often sponsored victorious chariot teams in the common festivals (see 11.5). He died around 466 BC.

[2] "Man": Throughout this translation, "man" is never used in a gender-neutral way. It always translates the Greek *anēr*, which refers emphatically to masculinity, as in the English "He's a real man." Thus one Greek word for "courage" (translated at 5.1 as "manly"), built on this root, is *andreia*. *Anēr* contrasts with the Greek *anthrōpos*, always translated as "human being"; for the contrast, see especially 7.3. When contrasted with each other, *anēr* and the Greek word for "woman," *gunē*, mean "husband and wife," as at 3.3.

[3] "Private person" translates the Greek *idiōtēs*. This word has nothing to do with our ideas of privacy as a legally and morally privileged realm. The *idiōtēs* contrasts with one who is professionally involved or specially trained in some activity. For example, at 4.6 Hiero contrasts trained athletes with "private persons" to illustrate the relation between tyrants and "private persons." In this sense, *idiōtēs* is like "amateur," and can tend toward the sense of "amateurish" or "unskilled"; compare "idiotic." But the other primary sense of *idion*, the root of *idiōtēs*, is seen in the English word "idiosyncratic." The *idion* is what is one's own, in contrast to what is the city's, for example (11.1). It has always been translated as "private," as in "private [affairs]." Thus "the private life" can connote both a life that avoids political involvement, whether by taste or talent, and a life focused on oneself and one's own affairs. The term gets a determinate meaning only in specific contrasts.

⁴ "Sex": An ugly English word for the beautiful Greek *ta aphrodisia* (literally, "the things of Aphrodite"), from Aphrodite, goddess of love. The Greek is also translated as "sexual relations," which is even uglier.

⁵ "Soul": The Greek *psuchē* is always translated as "soul"; but *psuchē* sometimes is closer to "life," as at 4.8 and 7.12.

⁶ "Emulous": Translates the Greek *zēloein*, here and at 6.12. Both words connote an envious admiration that tends to inspire emulation. This relatively benign type of envy contrasts with the hostile type that looks more to the fall of the one envied than to the rise of the envier. The Greek word for this hostile envy is *phthonos*, always translated simply as "envy" (at 7.10, 11.6, and 11.15).

⁷ "Get less": Much of the comparison of the two lives asks whether one "gets more" (*pleonektein*) or "gets less" (*meionektein*) than the other (for an example, see 1.14). Sometimes these could be translated as "get more/less than one's fair share," sometimes as "do better/worse," sometimes as "have an advantage/be at a disadvantage"; but for consistency it seems better to retain the etymological connection to "more" (*pleon*) and "less" (*meion*).

⁸ "Common festivals": "Festival" translates *panēguris*; the word refers primarily to the great Greek gatherings for competitions (in athletics and other cultural events), the most famous of which, of course, are the Olympic Games. But the word can also be used of other festive assemblies, as at 11.10.

⁹ Simonides here uses a plural form of "you" to refer to a characteristic of tyrants in general, not just of Hiero. Both speakers often use the plural forms this way, but English does not distinguish the plural and singular forms of "you," so the reader should be alert to this nuance. In many passages "you" could be translated with phrases such as "you tyrants" or "you private persons." But deciding which general group is implied in any passage is a matter of interpretation.

¹⁰ Despite some awkwardness, "erotic" has always been used to translate Greek words with the root *erōs*. The root refers primarily to erotic love, but as this passage shows, it can be extended to cover anything that might be done or pursued "with passion"; see also 7.3, where erotic interest is extended to honor and praise. It is never translated as "to love" or "to be in love," since "love" is used to translate *philein*; see note 17.

¹¹ "Sophistications": Translates *sophismata*, with its root *sophos*, "wise." The connection between "contrivances" and "sophistications" in 1.22–23 foreshadows the tense relation between tyrants, the wise, and contrivance in 5.1.

¹² "Have intercourse with": In many contexts, the Greek *suneinai* would be more naturally translated "spend time with" or "be with"; see, for example, 6.2, where Hiero uses this verb of being by himself or keeping his own company. But the word was definitely a euphemism for "have sexual intercourse," which of course is itself a euphemism. To preserve the possible sexual and erotic connotations, *suneinai* is always translated as "have intercourse with."

¹³ "Beautiful": *kalliston*. Words with the Greek root *kal-* are notoriously hard to translate consistently. They cover a range of meanings from "physically beautiful" to "noble."

¹⁴ "The proudest": Translates *mega phronein*, which literally means "to think big," and has connotations of haughtiness, classiness, and self-assertion. Note the contrast with slavish behavior.

¹⁵ "Boys": Translates the odd Greek expression *paidika*, a neuter plural whose literal meaning is "things to do with boys." Its usual reference is to male adolescents involved in pederastic relations with older adult men, rather than to peers in a homosexual relationship. This typical age difference helps to explain the worry about old

age at 8.6. The neuter plural was used to refer to even a single erotic favorite, though in this translation it has always been taken as plural in sense.

[16] Hiero probably means to personify "erotic longing" (erōs) in this sentence as the god Eros, since erōs is "not at all willing" and "aims at . . . pleasures."

[17] "Friendship": Nouns with the Greek root phil- have been translated as "friend" and its cognates; but verbs with the root have been translated as "love" (see note 10). The verb philein could sometimes be translated as "like" or "feel affection for," but not as "be in (erotic) love with." To love and to have an erotic interest are two distinct things, even if, as in this passage, they are combined.

[18] Plural "you."

[19] "Cities greatly honor one who kills the tyrant": Hiero may well have in mind the fate of Hipparchus, reputed in popular tradition to have been tyrant of Athens ca. 527–514 BC. (Thucydides reports that Hipparchus's older brother Hippias was in fact the tyrant, and that Athenian bias against tyranny caused the popular account of the story to be inaccurate; see Thucydides 6.54–59, which is worth comparing to Hiero.) In 514 BC, Hipparchus was assassinated at a public festival by Harmodius, an attractive youth Hipparchus had courted, been rejected by, and then insulted, and Aristogeiton, Harmodius's lover. Both tyrannicides were killed, and Hippias kept control. But Harmodius and Aristogeiton were greatly honored as heroes of freedom, and their statues were in fact erected in temples. The example would be especially striking to Simonides, since he had very close ties with the family of Hippias and Hipparchus. Xenophon may also have intended to remind his readers of the assassination of Jason, tyrant of Thessaly. In 370 BC, Jason was poised to take military control of most of the Greek mainland, but he was killed during preparations for a public festival. Most of the conspirators got away, and, says Xenophon, "were honored in most of the Greek cities to which they escaped" (Hellenica 6.4.32). Xenophon's entire presentation of Jason in the Hellenica provides an interesting comparison to the Hiero.

[20] "Life": The Greek (psuchē) can also be translated as "soul."

[21] "Personal guards": It was a common practice of Greek tyrants to hire foreign mercenaries as a personal bodyguard.

[22] "Blessed": This does not mean he is holy or pious. The Greek word makarios carries instead the connotation of great success founded in unchangeably good fortune.

[23] "Gentlemen": Literally, "the people who are beautiful and good." This phrase is a more or less formulaic way to refer to the better people, in status, wealth, and character, in the community. In other works, Xenophon shows a keen interest in analyzing the criteria by which one could truly be said to be "beautiful and good."

[24] For this particular sort of claim about "appropriateness," see 1.32.

[25] The text is corrupt here. The bracketed translation is speculative.

[26] For a far more comprehensive treatment of the Hiero, see Leo Strauss, On Tyranny (Chicago: University of Chicago Press, 2000). My interpretation is thoroughly indebted to that of Strauss: my treatment of the conversation leading up to Simonides' account of how a tyrant should rule attempts to recapitulate the most important points of Strauss's analysis (ibid., 36–64); my subsequent discussion of Hiero's dissatisfactions, Simonides' advice, and the relative ranks of the tyrannical and private lives relies heavily on Strauss's observations (see especially ibid., 66–102).

[27] I rely on David O'Connor's translation in this volume; I make only a few minor changes to the translation in order to highlight important details for my argument.

[28] Throughout, I translate aner as "real man" in order to distinguish this important term from mere human beings. See translator's note 2 on 1.2.

[29] Contrast Vivienne Gray, ed., Xenophon on Government, Greek text with introduction and commentary (Cambridge: Cambridge University Press, 2007), 128–29,

211–13. Gray argues against Strauss's interpretation of Hiero's fear of the wise (*On Tyranny*, 43–44, 111–12n48), and suggests that all three classes mentioned in 5.1, the brave, the wise, and the just, are threats to tyrants because they work for freedom. That is, she overlooks the distinction between the aims of the brave and those of the just, and on this basis concludes that the wise too aim at freedom. Furthermore, Gray does not address the supporting facts, mentioned above, that Simonides encourages the thought that he has tyrannical ambitions, and that Hiero, as 6.12 shows, has been affected by this. Gray agrees with Strauss that Hiero "exaggerates his miseries and then contradicts them," but offers no explanation for this beyond saying that the "exaggeration is the natural product of his emotion" (*Xenophon on Government* 124, 132).

³⁰ Consider the obvious defect of Simonides' claim at 1.14 (cf. 1.15–16).

³¹ In 5.1, Hiero denies that tyrants are really able to admire virtuous men. Perhaps more tellingly, in 6.15–16, Hiero treats virtuous men as desirable because of their utility rather than treating virtue as an end in itself.

³² In this regard, consider especially Simonides' seeming preoccupation with bodily pleasures in light of his statement about real men's preferences (cf. 1.16, 20, 26 with 2.1). Consider also the distinction between "many" and "everyone" in 1.9.

³³ That is, Hiero wishes for love (*philia*), both in response to his sexual love and from others more generally. See translator's note 17 on 1.33.

³⁴ See also Gray, *Xenophon on Government*, 115.

³⁵ As 6.12 indicates, Hiero only responds to Simonides' statement in 2.2 about helping friends in 6.13.

³⁶ Note also that Hiero would prefer the companionship of his countrymen to that of foreigners, if he could trust his countrymen (5.3; 6.5; cf. 1.28).

³⁷ Simonides also suggests that "perhaps it turns out that only the enjoyments of sex produce the desires in you to be a tyrant. For in this respect, you can have intercourse with the fairest you see" (1.26). Simonides does not make entirely clear the basis of his suggestion about the sexual origin of tyrannical desire; he suggests later that Hiero may seek tyranny for the sake of honor (7.2); and it is clear that Hiero finds more about tyranny attractive than its capacity to provide sexual pleasure. Still, Simonides' initial emphasis on the importance of sexual desire is perhaps supported by the following consideration. After Simonides suggests that tyrants seek honor, he observes that people give honors to tyrants and to "anyone else they happen to honor at the moment" (7.2). Thus an explanation of why a person seeks honor as a tyrant is required, and Hiero's subsequent description of the superior honor that would be available to a popular ruler (7.6–10) makes more acute the question of why Hiero would have sought honor in the unpopular way that he did. Simonides' observation that rulers are rendered more attractive to beloveds by ruling then explains how a man could be moved by sexual desire to desire tyranny (8.6), and this explanation, which relies on the potential tyrant's concern for his sexual favorites rather than his fellow citizens in general, is compatible with the tyrant's undertaking generally unpopular actions, as Hiero evidently has done.

³⁸ Contrast Gray's claim that "Hiero seeks friendship rather than power" (*Xenophon on Government*, 213).

³⁹ Consider *Memorabilia* 4.6.12.

⁴⁰ On the distinction between oneself and one's own, consider 11.14.

⁴¹ It is imaginable that a man could desire to be a tyrant for purely utilitarian or cruel reasons, but such a man would find the tyrannical life defective insofar as merely retaining his power requires him to undertake great risks and toils to keep order in his city, and he finds no pleasure in thus benefiting his city (cf. 7.1–2).

[42] Cf. the less ambiguous word choice of Simonides' praises of tyranny in 1.8 and 2.2.

[43] Consider in this regard Simonides' concession that Hiero will need mercenaries; that Hiero will not be equal to his subjects, which implies that the subjects will necessarily bristle under his rule; that precisely the good conditions Simonides' proposals would bring to the city will increase the insolence of some of the citizens (8.10; 10.2, 4). Despite his beneficence, the tyrant's power will be resented, and some will want to rebel against it. It is doubtful that this tyrant could avoid being envied.

[44] On this usage of "happiness," see 2.3–4, as well as Aristotle, *Rhetoric* 1.5, 1360b15–17.

[45] This is not to say that these honors derive solely from the benefits given: in 8.2–5, Simonides shows that the response to gifts from rulers is not based solely on the value of the gifts.

[46] The connection between forgetting and friendship helps explain why Hiero begins his list of pleasures in 6.2 by mentioning the time he spent with friends and concludes his list with social pleasures, but places the "rest" he could find by himself at the center of the list: in an important respect, the time with friends also provides "rest," i.e., rest from his worries. Note also that Hiero's statement in 6.2 concludes with a remark about the "desire for bed," and that his next statement about his current condition culminates in his expression of regret at having now to "guard against strong drink and sleep" (6.3). (On Simonides' view of sleep, see 1.6; 7.1–3.) That Hiero does not regard the forgetting permitted by spending time with friends as altogether satisfying is shown, among other ways, by his insistence in chapter 3 on praising friendship above all for the additional benefits that come from it (see especially 3.5).

[47] Consider also the psychological demand of following the suggestion of 11.14.

2. Agesilaus

I have used the text of E. C. Marchant, Xenophon, *Opuscula*, vol. 5 of *Opera Omnia* (1920; Oxford: Clarendon Press, 1992), although I have also consulted the following editions and commentaries: *Xenophon's Agesilaus*, ed. R. W. Taylor (London: Rivingtons, 1880); *Xenophons Agesilaos*, ed. Otto Guethling (Leipzig: B. G. Teubner, 1888); *Agesilaus of Xenophon*, ed. H. Hailstone (Cambridge: Cambridge University Press, 1891); and *L'Agesilao di Senofonte: Tra Commiato ed Encomio*, ed. Emma Luppino Manes (Milan: Jaca Books, 1992). A valuable contribution is Rosemary Wieczorek's doctoral thesis, "Xenophon's *Agesilaus*: A Collation, Stemma, and Critical Text" (Iowa City: University of Iowa Press, 1975). All modern editors are inclined to emend the text of the *Agesilaus* to make it accord with the related or parallel accounts in the *Hellenica*, using the latter to "correct" the former. But if one does not assume that Xenophon was guided by the same intention in both works, one should be open to the possibility of his having used different formulations to describe even the same events. I have therefore mostly kept to the reading of the MSS of the *Agesilaus* in the cases that seemed to bear on the meaning of a sentence.

[1] Although Xenophon makes no mention of the fact here, the Spartan kingship was in fact a dual kingship, one king being selected from among the Eurypontids (descendants of Eurypon), the other from among the Agiads (descendants of Agis); both lines claimed descent from Heracles and hence ruled by a kind of divine right.

2 Ca. 400–399 BC; see *Hellenica* 3.3.1. All dates in the notes are BC.

3 Agis II, son of Archidamus, ruled as king of Sparta ca. 427–ca. 399; Agesilaus (ruled ca. 399–360) was also a son of Archidamus, by his second wife, and hence half-brother to Agis II.

4 Or "most excellent" (*kratistēi*).

5 It is thought that Agesilaus was in his midforties; perhaps he was, if not "young," then "youthful" (*neos*).

6 The reading of the MSS. In the *Hellenica*, however, Xenophon says two thousand (3.4.2), as does Plutarch, *Agesilaus* 6.2.

7 Tissaphernes was the Persian satrap of the coastal provinces of Anatolia from about 413 until his assassination (see 1.35) in 395. See also *Hellenica* 3.1.3 and 3.4.6.

8 That is, instead of heading south to Caria, Agesilaus headed far north, to the Hellespontine Phrygia.

9 Compare 1.13–16 with *Hellenica* 3.4.11 and following.

10 That is, his love of or fondness for human beings.

11 Pharnabazus was the Persian satrap or governor of Phrygia ca. 413–370.

12 A daughter of Zeus and sister to Apollo, Artemis is known as a huntress and so makes a suitable goddess to be worshipped by soldiers.

13 That is, those who have been in military service for no more than ten years; these would be the youngest of the soldiers.

14 The MSS read "with him." Here I follow the modern editors, who alter the text in accord with *Hellenica* 3.4.2.

15 Compare 1.23–32 with *Hellenica* 3.4.15–24.

16 For this last sentence, see *Hellenica* 4.3.21 end. One hundred talents is a vast sum of money, to say nothing of the original thousand talents this tithe suggests.

17 Artaxerxes II (ca. 436–358), son of Darius II and Parysatis, became King of Persia in 404.

18 For this sentence, see *Hellenica* 3.4.25. Tithraustes thus became the satrap of Sardis.

19 See *Hellenica* 3.4.27.

20 Agesilaus was recalled to Sparta in 395 in order to help fight the Corinthian War.

21 The reference is to Xerxes in 480; see, e.g., Herodotus 7.105–32 and 179–201.

22 Compare *Hellenica* 4.2.8.

23 The reading of the MSS. The modern editors emend the text in accord with that of the *Hellenica* (4.3.4): "He sent along to the rear the cavalry from the van of the army, except those with him himself."

24 The reading (*aphronōs*) of the MSS. The modern editors emend the text in accord with that of the *Hellenica*: "and the others followed them very moderately [sensibly] (*sōphronōs*)." "The others" here are Agesilaus's troops.

25 Compare 2.2–5 with *Hellenica* 4.3.3–9.

26 The modern editors insert here "Argives," which is not present in the MSS but is in the margin of two of them and in the *Hellenica* (4.3.15). The Argives are mentioned at 2.9.

27 That is, the Opuntian Locrians, on the Gulf of Euboea east of Thermopylae, and the Ozalian Locrians, on the Gulf of Corinth between Phocis and Aetolia. Compare *Hellenica* 4.2.17, where the two Locrians are mentioned separately.

28 The precise size of a Spartan *mora* or regiment is unknown. Estimates range from 512 to 1,280 men, and so Agesilaus may have had as few as 768 Spartiates with him or as many as 1,920. For the larger figure, and a helpful discussion of the question, see J. F. Lazenby, *The Spartan Army* (Warminster: Aris & Phillips, 1985), 5–10.

[29] Compare *Hellenica* 4.3.15.

[30] That is, with Cyrus the Younger in his attempt to overthrow his brother, the sitting King of Persia. Xenophon was among these soldiers, as he tells us in his *Anabasis of Cyrus*; consider also *Hellenica* 3.1.2.

[31] Or "and indeed" (*ou mentoi . . . ge*): the sense depends on whether *mentoi* here has its asseverative or adversative meaning.

[32] Compare 2.9–16 with *Hellenica* 4.3.16–21.

[33] Since the Athenians, Boeotians, Argives, and other allies were waging war against the Spartans and using Corinth as a base, the territory of Corinth suffered badly. As a result, a peace party arose in Corinth that was in turn the victim of an impious plot on the part of the Corinthian war party, thus weakening Corinth from within. In due course, Argos came to take over Corinth as its own: see *Hellenica* 4.4.1–6 and 4.5.1. The Argives were not directly involved in the fighting and so suffered less than their neighbors ("taking pleasure in the war").

[34] The port of Corinth.

[35] A large festival celebrated every year at Amyclae by the Amyclaeans and Spartans together. According to R. W. Taylor (ad loc.), the festival "was held in honour of the Amyclaean Apollo and of the hero Hyacinthus, on the longest day of the month Hecatombeus, when the sun was hottest. On the first and third days sacrifices were offered to the dead, accompanied by dirges and funereal laments. On the second day, however, the chief day of the feast, there was nothing but rejoicing and amusements. There was a horse-race, followed by a singing of the paean and of national songs, and by a procession of maidens riding in chariots of wicker-work." For this last, see also 8.7.

[36] A large promontory at the eastern end of the Corinthian Gulf, north of the Isthmus and opposite Corinth.

[37] A Boeotian port on the Gulf of Corinth and Thebes's nearest seaport.

[38] Compare *Hellenica* 4.5.4, where Xenophon gives a more detailed, and very different, account.

[39] Wieczorek suggests a lacuna here after "asking," Marchant in the place indicated. Consider *Hellenica* 4.6.1–9.

[40] Compare *Hellenica* 4.6.4–12: Xenophon there says that Agesilaus had hoplites capture the heights.

[41] See *Hellenica* 4.7.1.

[42] See *Hellenica* 5.1.29.

[43] That is, the Persians, or more precisely Tiribazos the satrap, who had been working closely with the Spartan Antalcidas to effect a peace between the Spartan, Athenian, and Persian sides: see *Hellenica* 4.8.12 and 5.1.25 and following.

[44] The Peace of Antalcidas (*Hellenica* 5.1.36), also known as the King's Peace, in 387. See *Hellenica* 5.1.32–33, for Agesilaus's demand that the Thebans not be permitted to deny autonomy to the other cities of Boeotia; and *Hellenica* 5.1.34, for his demand that the Argive garrison leave Corinth (see also 4.4.6; 4.5.1).

[45] See *Hellenica* 5.2.8–10: in fact the attempted reconciliation of democratic and oligarchic factions goes badly, and Agesilaus is compelled to besiege the city for one year and eight months before it surrenders; see also *Hellenica* 5.3.16.

[46] "The partisans of the Lacedaemonians in Thebes": in 382, a pro-Spartan faction in Thebes, led by Leontiades, persuaded the Spartan commander Phoebidas, without approval from home, to occupy the Cadmea, the acropolis of Thebes, a disastrous move once the hoped-for oligarchic revolution in Thebes failed to materialize. The Spartans were killed when they attempted to leave the acropolis, despite having secured an agreement from the Thebans to do so peaceably. See *Hellenica* 5.2.25–36; 5.4.10–12.

[47] Not the mountain range of the same name ("Dogs-head") in Thessaly, but the one in Boeotia.

[48] Xenophon's account here is highly compressed: compare *Hellenica* 5.4.35–49.

[49] Under the command of the outstanding Theban general Epaminondas in 371, whom Xenophon at this point in the *Hellenica* declines to name, the united Boeotians soundly defeated the Spartan army led by King Cleombrotus—the first significant defeat suffered by Sparta in more than 150 years and one from which the city never quite recovered.

[50] The phrase "with the force of the Lacedaemonians" does not appear in the MSS, although it has been added to one. See *Hellenica* 6.5.10 and context.

[51] Compare *Hellenica* 6.5.1–21.

[52] Compare *Hellenica* 6.5.23–32.

[53] Compare *Hellenica* 6.5.25 and 32 end.

[54] Autophradates was satrap of Lydia, ordered by the Persian King to punish those who had revolted from him, among them Ariobarzanes satrap of Phrygia. The *Hellenica* makes no mention of this episode.

[55] A Persian satrap in Caria.

[56] The reading of the beginning of this sentence is uncertain, and Marchant posits a lacuna.

[57] King of Egypt, mentioned also at 2.28. The MSS. here read the adverb "quickly" (*tacheōs*), but the modern editors make the slight change needed to give the name of the Egyptian king or pharaoh. See also Plutarch, *Agesilaus* 36.

[58] Messene neighbored Sparta and had long been under its thumb: the majority of Sparta's slave population, the Helots, were originally from Messene. Sparta, and Agesilaus, found the demand that it give Messene its freedom particularly galling.

[59] Under the command of Nectanebis according to Diodorus Siculus (15.32) and Plutarch (*Agesilaus* 37).

[60] The other "king," in addition to Nectanebis, hailed from Mendes, Agesilaus siding with the former (see the references in the preceding note).

[61] There is a lacuna in the text, and I supply what I take to be missing.

[62] The modern editors emend the text here to read "one thousand horses and two thousand targeteers," as the text of *Hellenica* 4.1.3 has it. Cotys is sometimes also called Otys.

[63] Compare *Hellenica* 4.1.37 and context.

[64] The only appearance in the text of this abstract noun (*eusebeia*), although the related adjective appears at 11.1 end. The related verb (*sebō*: "revere") appears at 1.27, 3.2, and 11.1. *Theosebēs* appears at 10.2.

[65] There is a difficulty with the text, although the general meaning seems clear.

[66] See *Hellenica* 4.1.6 and 28.

[67] This is the striking reading (*lian manikon*) of the MSS. All modern editors read a suggested emendation: "daimonic" or "more than human" (*daimonion*).

[68] That is, by the twins Castor and Pollux. This is Dindorf's emendation (*ou tō siō*) of the MSS, which contain no oath, but the adverb "Thus" or "So it is" (*houtōsi*).

[69] The verb (*dokimadzō*) means in the first place "to test," then "to approve of after having tested."

[70] There is a lacuna in the text, and I follow Marchant's text.

[71] The verb can also mean "to chasten or punish."

[72] Artaxerxes II.

[73] See, e.g., *Hellenica* 4.1.2.

[74] *Eucharis*: good grace, perhaps "urbanity."

[75] Otherwise unknown. Some editors suggest emending the text to read "Callias," who is mentioned at *Hellenica* 4.1.15.

[76] According to Herodotus (6.52), Aristodemus was the great-grandson of Hyllus, the son of Heracles. The suggestion is that the gates are very old and presumably in poor repair.

[77] The modern editors, following Plutarch, *Agesilaus* 19.5, add the phrase "his daughter," which would thus be subject of the verb: "Let him hear how his daughter . . .": it was evidently young maidens who so participated in the festival (see note 35 above).

[78] Evidently to celebrate the Hyacinthia, an important Spartan religious observance in honor of Apollo and the young man he loved, Hyacinthus. See note 35 above as well as *Hellenica* 4.5.11 and Thucydides 5.23.4 and 5.41.3.

[79] The phrase "nobility and goodness" translates the common Greek formula *kalokagathia*, which might also be rendered as "gentlemanliness."

[80] The word (*deisidaimon*) often has a negative connotation: "superstitious."

[81] The term (*megalophrōn*) can also mean "arrogant." Consider *Hellenica* 4.5.6.

[82] There is a lacuna in the text. As the text stands, "great and noble" modifies no noun, although "reputation" does appear to have been added by Petrus Victorinus on his copy of a fourteenth-century MS (see Wieczorek, "Xenophon's *Agesilaus*," 18 and her apparatus criticus).

[83] On this unusual phrase, consider the suggestions of C. J. Cressey, "Two Notes on Xenophon: *Agesilaus* 6.7 and 11.15," *Liverpool Classical Monthly* 11 (1986): 109.

[84] References in the body of this essay are to chapter and section of *Agesilaus*, unless otherwise identified.

[85] Consider, e.g., Plutarch, *Agesilaus* 10.6; 22.1–2; 26.1–5; 35.3; 36.1.

[86] William Mure, *A Critical History of the Language and Literature of Ancient Greece* (London: Longman, Brown, Green, Longmans, and Roberts, 1857), 5:434.

[87] Leo Strauss, "The Spirit of Sparta or the Taste of Xenophon," *Social Research* 6 (1939): 502–36.

[88] Noreen Humble, "The Author, Date, and Purpose of Chapter 14 of the *Lakedaimoniōn Politeia*," in *Xenophon and His World*, ed. Christopher Tuplin (Munich: Franz Steiner, 2004), 216.

[89] Strauss, "Spirit of Sparta," 521.

[90] Leo Strauss, "Greek Historians," *Review of Metaphysics* 21.4 (1968): 665.

[91] Leo Strauss, *Xenophon's Socratic Discourse* (South Bend, IN: St. Augustine's Press, 1998), 125–26.

[92] In general the textual discrepancies between the "repetitions" in the two works tend to redound to the benefit of Agesilaus in the encomium. Compare, e.g., 2.2 end and *Hellenica* 4.3.4: in the former, Agesilaus sends along the troops with him himself; in the latter, he keeps them with himself. Also 2.20 and *Hellenica* 4.6.4–12: here he has the light infantry capture certain heights; in the *Hellenica*, it is the hoplites, a much more difficult task given the weight of their arms and armor. Consider, finally, 3.4 in the light of *Hellenica* 4.1.3: a certain deal is twice as profitable according to the *Agesilaus* as it is according to the *Hellenica*.

[93] See Leo Strauss, *On Tyranny*, ed. Victor Gourevitch and Michael S. Roth (Chicago: University of Chicago Press, 2013), 31.

[94] Consider the "conjecture" or "guess" at 8.7. See also Plato, *Theaetetus* 175a5–b4.

[95] Consider *Hellenica* 5.4.58 (also 3.3.3) and 5.5: Agesilaus was not exceedingly beautiful or strong or swift.

[96] By juxtaposing the deeds of Dercylides in particular to those of Agesilaus, the *Hellenica* makes plain how little the fuss and bother of Agesilaus really accomplished in Asia Minor: Dercylides captures nine cities in eight days, protects eleven or twelve cities on the Chersonese from Thracian plundering, and takes the city of Atarneus. So skilled a man at "contriving things" was Dercylides that he

earned the nickname "Sisyphus," and he liked to be away from home (*Hellenica* 3.1.8–9 and following).

[97] Compare 8.7 end, where one expects to find mention of a daughter but does not, with Plutarch, *Agesilaus* 19.5–6, where one does.

[98] For a slightly different chronology, see Charles D. Hamilton, *Agesilaus and the Failure of Spartan Hegemony* (Ithaca, NY: Cornell University Press, 1991), 18n46.

[99] W. P. Henry calls this the "most poetic moment of description in the whole of the *Agesilaus*": Henry, *Greek Historical Writing: A Historiographical Essay Based on Xenophon's "Hellenica"* (Chicago: Argonaut, 1967), 152.

[100] See also Strauss, "Spirit of Sparta," 521.

[101] For his earlier refusal to fight against Mantinea, see *Hellenica* 5.2.3.

[102] On Agesilaus's pious acts, consider *Hellenica* 3.3.4; 3.4.3–4, 15; 4.3.10, 20–21; 4.5.2, 10; 4.6.10; 5.1.33; 5.3.14; 5.4.37, 41–49; 6.5.12, 17–18.

[103] The discussion of the virtues of the soul begins with piety or pious reverence (3.2–5) and then turns to justice (4.1–6), just as Xenophon presents, in the summary chapter, pious reverence (11.1) together with justice (11.3) or justice (11.8) together with the fear of the divine (11.8; see also 10.2).

[104] The whole of Xenophon's exposition of the wisdom of Agesilaus (6.4–8) takes the form of a further description of those of his actions or deeds that displayed it: his obedience to the fatherland (compare 1.36), the obedience he instilled in his troops (compare 1.25–28), the good he could do for friends (1.17–19, 34; 2.23) and the harm to enemies (e.g., 1.29–34). Xenophon has taken up each of these elsewhere under a heading different from "wisdom." Hence his usage of the term is exceedingly loose: Agesilaus "practiced wisdom in deed rather than in speeches."

[105] On the meaning of this pseudonym, see Eric Buzzetti, *Xenophon the Socratic Prince: The Argument of the "Anabasis of Cyrus"* (New York: Palgrave Macmillan, 2014), 301–11.

[106] "Xenophon knew that there were duties higher than those imposed by gratitude and loyalty, that the duties imposed by gratitude and loyalty may sometimes have to be superseded by the duty to see things as they are and to communicate one's insights to those who are by nature and training fit for them. The proof of this is the difference between his obtrusive and his unobtrusive judgments on Agesilaus": Strauss, "Greek Historians," 665–66. See also Strauss, "Spirit of Sparta," 536.

3. Regime of the Lacedaemonians

We have used the text of E. C. Marchant, Xenophon, *Opuscula*, vol. 5 of *Opera Omnia* (1920; Oxford: Clarendon Press, 1961). We consulted in addition the editions of Michael Lipka, *Xenophon's Spartan Constitution, with Introduction, Text, and Commentary* (Berlin: Walter de Gruyter, 2002), Vivienne J. Gray, *Xenophon on Government* (Cambridge: Cambridge University Press, 2007), and François Ollier, *Xenophon: La République des Lacédémoniens* (Lyon: A. Rey, 1934). Also helpful was J. S. Watson's translation with notes in *Xenophon's Minor Works* (London: George Bell & Sons, 1891).

[1] The first line of the treatise begins with *alla* ("but" or "rather"), as if Xenophon is picking up a thought midstream or responding to an argument. His only other work to begin in this way is *Symposium*.

[2] Xenophon will use different terms to refer to the people and area of "Lacedaemon." "Lacedaemonian" and "Laconian" (*Laconikos*) typically refer to all free people of Lacedaemon, even those who do not enjoy full political rights. By contrast, "Sparta" (*Spartē* or *Sparta*) refers specifically to the city within Lacedaemon and "Spartan" or "Spartiate" (*Spartiatēs*) only to full Spartan citizens, that is, to the Spartan warriors (cf. Gray, *Xenophon*, 147, with Lipka, *Xenophon's Spartan Constitution*, 99).

[3] *Nomoi* (*nomos*): "Usages," "customs," and in this broad sense, "laws" of the Spartan mode of life, as compared to *rhetra*, the term in Sparta for specific laws.

[4] *Eudaimonein*: Verb related to the Greek word for "happiness" (*eudaimonia*). It has the sense of "to prosper" or "to be well off," and some translators use "flourish." In the Greek, the word is connected most fully with the idea that the life well lived is the best, and so happiest, life. We consistently translate both the noun and the verb with the related English terms, "happiness" and "to be happy" (see 1.2; 9.3), but the reader should keep in view the full sense of the Greek.

[5] *Eis ta eschata*: An adverbial phrase generally translated "extremely," but it can be translated literally as "with respect to the extremes" or "in the extremes." We use a close English equivalent to try to capture the two meanings. See especially Leo Strauss, "The Spirit of Sparta or the Taste of Xenophon," *Social Research* 6 (1939): 512n4. Cf. Lipka *Xenophon's Spartan Constitution*, 101. "To wonder at" here is the same verb as above (*thaumazein*), having the sense of "to admire."

[6] *Nomizein*: Xenophon uses this verb frequently in this work, signaling its importance. It can mean "to enact" or "to legislate," but also more simply "to believe." When its connection to the act of legislating is clear, we will translate it as "legislate," but otherwise as "believe" and, twice, as "deem" (4.4; 10.7). For the importance of the distinction between what Lycurgus "believed" and "enacted" (or "legislated") in contrast to what he "saw" and "observed," see Strauss, "Spirit of Sparta," 518n1.

[7] *Phulon*: The Greek has the primary meaning of "tribe, race, or class," but can also be translated "sex." The important point is the distinction between the female "tribe" and the male "tribe," and Lycurgus's focus on the animal natures of women in particular. On this point, see especially Strauss, "Spirit of Sparta," 505–6.

[8] *Adeomein*: Here translated as "to be immodest," it could also be translated as "to be shameful," but in this work it connotes something closer to the English sense of "modesty" or even "bashfulness" (see Strauss, "Spirit of Sparta," 506–7, 529–30). We translate it in this sense at 2.10 and 3.4, as we do the comparative or substantive adjective *adēmōn* at 2.10 and 3.5. Xenophon refers here to the coming and going of the man to and from his wife's bedroom: he was expected to dine at his *philition* (common mess) before visiting his wife, using the appropriate stealth. See Plutarch, *Lycurgus* 15 for an account of the nuptial arrangments.

[9] With Marchant and Lipka, we follow Haase's emendation *blastoi* or "engendered" (see Lipka *Xenophon's Spartan Constitution*, 108). But three MSS read *blaptoien*, in which case the line could be translated, if awkwardly: "Thus, the couple would necessarily have greater longing for intercourse with one another and would become more robust, if they should thus hinder anything, more than if they should be sated with one another."

[10] Or "each of the two," the plural genitive of *hekasteros*. On the one hand, Xenophon appears to indicate that he is carrying forward the contrast between the Spartans and the other Greeks; on the other hand, he makes statements that would seem to indicate that he is about to deal with the education of both the boys and the girls. Cf. Lipka, *Xenophon's Spartan Constitution*, 114–14, 123; Gray, *Xenophon*, 153; with Strauss, "Spirit of Sparta," 505n3; Watson, *Xenophon's Minor Works*, 206n3; Nigel M. Kennell, *The Gymnasium of Virtue* (Chapel Hill: University of North Carolina Press, 1995), 45–46.

[11] *Paides*: That is, beginning with the youngest, the children. Xenophon will shortly refer to the *hēbontes*, "the young men" (2.2), as well as those who have just come into puberty (*to meirakiousthai*, 3.1). In general, the cohorts were divided into *paides* (from six to seven years old to puberty), *paidiskoi* (from puberty to nineteen to twenty years old), and *hēbontes* (from twenty to thirty years old), who are eligible for military service but not yet in the ranks of the mature men. See Lipka, *Xenophon's Spartan Constitution*, 115–16, 135–36, and 140–41; Gray, *Xenophon*, 152–53; Kennell, *Gymnasium of Virtue*, 29–48; see Kennell, 116–20, for discussions of the age cohorts, about which ancient testimony varies. Cf. *Cyropaedia* 1.2.4; LSJ, s.v. *hēba*, I.1.c.

[12] *Paidōgogoi* (pedagogues) were slaves who attended children on their way to and from school and their *didaskaloi* (teachers), to whom Xenophon next refers.

[13] *Paidonomos*: Literally, "child law." First attested here, the term refers to a particular supervisory office, for which men over thirty were eligible (see also 4.7). According to Plutarch (*Lycurgus* 17.2), there was only one such supervisor at Sparta.

[14] *Aidōs*: A difficult word to translate, *aidōs* connotes shame, reverence, and respect. We translate it here and at 5.5, its other appearance, as "modesty" to indicate the connection with *adeomein* (1.5; 2.10; 3.4) and *adēmōn* (2.10, 14; 3.5) and to distinguish it from *aischunein* (to be shameful, 9.4) and *aischros* (shame, 2.13; 6.2; 9.1), as well as *aischrourgia* (shameful conduct) and *aischrologia* (shameful speech) at 5.5.

[15] *Arrēn*: We follow the reading of the MSS here and at 2.11. In these passages, *eiren* is offered as an emendation by Schneider and Cragius; it refers to a youth who has completed his twentieth year. See Lipka, *Xenophon's Spartan Constitution*, 130–31, for an argument in support of the emendation; and Strauss, "Spirit of Sparta," 505n3, and Kennell, *Gymnasium of Virtue*, 16–17, for a defense of the MSS reading.

[16] The opening phrase could also be translated "it was not out of ignorance . . ." We seek to capture the two possibilities allowed by the Greek: Lycurgus acted neither because he was at a loss for resources nor because he was simply at a loss, that is, ignorant. See Lipka, *Xenophon's Spartan Constitution*, 125.

[17] See *Anabasis* 4.6.14–15 for Xenophon's ironic comment regarding this same practice, and *Cyropaedia* 1.6.31–32 for his account of the Persian view of such practices; see also Strauss's treatment of these passages in "Spirit of Sparta," 507–8.

[18] Orthia is a Laconian name for Artemis, the goddess of the hunt. For details of the rite, about which little is certain, see Lipka, *Xenophon's Spartan Constitution*, 127–28, 255–57; Gray, *Xenophon*, 155–56; Kennell, *Gymnasium of Virtue*, 149–61.

[19] Here, too, we follow the MSS and accept *arrēn* in the plural genitive, rather than the emendation *eiren*. See again Strauss, "Spirit of Sparta," 505n3.

[20] *Ilē*: Generally "band" or "troop"; at Sparta, it was a subdivision of the *agelē*, a term that means generally "herd."

[21] Literally, "the erotic love of boys"; Xenophon refers to the arrangements related to pederasty among the Spartans, which he introduces with some reluctance. See Lipka, *Xenophon's Spartan Constitution*, 132–35; Gray, *Xenophon*, 156–57; Kennell, *Gymnasium of Virtue*, 124–25; Strauss, "Spirit of Sparta," 511.

[22] The Greek text is flawed (see Lipka, *Xenophon's Spartan Constitution*, 133; Gray, *Xenophon*, 157), but the general sense seems to be clear.

[23] *Ta kala*: "The noble things," meaning more specifically in this case "all the privileges of citizenship." See also 4.4, where *ta kala* includes the honor of being chosen for the *hippagretai*.

[24] *Toi kēdomenoi*: Or "the relatives," but literally, "those who care for [or take charge of] each"; the contrast is with those who hold public office. Hence Xenophon seems to be referring also to the *erastai* in addition to relatives. Cf. Gray *Xenophon*, 158, with Lipka, *Xenophon's Spartan Constitution*, 138.

[25] We take *tōn parthenōn* as "maidens" rather than as a synonym for "eyes" and, following the main MS, read *tois thalamois* instead of *tois opthalmois*. See Strauss, "Spirit of Sparta," 511–12, for a defense of the MSS reading (see also Watson, *Xenophon's Minor Works*, 210). Cf. Lipka for the alternative reading and translation: "You would consider them shyer than the very pupils in their own eyes" (Lipka, *Xenophon's Spartan Constitution*, 73, 139–40; see also Gray, *Xenophon*, 158–59).

[26] *To philition*: Or *phidition*, "friends mess," the Spartan word for "common mess."

[27] Reading with the main MS *paidikoi*, instead of *paidiskoi* with Haase. See Strauss, "Spirit of Sparta," 511n4, for a defense of the reading of the MSS. Cf. Lipka, *Xenophon's Spartan Constitution*, 140–41.

[28] *Aretē*: This is the first appearance of the word for "virtue." It appears again at 9.2, 10.1, 10.4, and 10.7.

[29] *Andragathia*: From *anēr* (man) and *agathos* (good), the word connotes especially courage.

[30] See 8.3–4 for Xenophon's discussion of the ephorate, five annually elected "ephors" or "overseers." See also 11.2 and 15.6–7.

[31] *Hippagretai*: Literally, "gatherers of the *hippeis*" (see Gray, *Xenophon*, 160), the term refers to the leaders of the *hippeis*, an elite unit (the famed Three Hundred) that also formed the bodyguard of the kings (see also Lipka, *Xenophon's Spartan Constitution*, 143–44; Kennell, *Gymnasium of Virtue*, 121, 129–30). The leaders are *hēbontes* around the age of thirty (in the "prime of life"), and are therefore the most experienced soldiers of their cohort; as Xenophon next says, each enlists one hundred young men to serve in the elite unit. Although *hippeis* refers more generally to cavalry, the Spartan bodyguard comes from the hoplite soldiers, and the name thus refers to their elite or aristocratic status.

[32] The Greek admits of another translation: "But each group exercises separately as well, in order that they will always be at their strongest, and, if there be any need, will as one give aid to the city, with all their strength" (see, e.g. Gray, *Xenophon*, 160).

[33] *Diaita*: "Way of life" or "mode of living." The term can also denote a particular regimen, especially of diet.

[34] *Antiparaballein*: As Watson (*Xenophon Minor Works*, 213), following Weiske, suggests, both prefixes of the verb contribute to its meaning and indicate that the wealthy contribute (*paraballein*, lay before the others) wheat bread in exchange for (*anti*) extras that have come from the hunt. Also the term *arton* (wheat bread) is supplied by editors in place of *argon* (without work or idle) in the main MSS; Proietti suggests, then, the line may read: "They contribute in behalf of (in place of the contribution of) one who is idle" —he points to *Cyropaedia* 1.2.15 as comparable. Gerald Proietti, *Xenophon's Sparta: An Introduction* (Leiden: E. J. Brill, 1987), 53n15.

[35] There is a lacuna in the text, and we have supplied terms that make sense of the line in its context. See also Lipka, *Xenophon's Spartan Constitution*, 155; Gray, *Xenophon*, 162.

[36] The Greek is ungrammatical, and several emendations have been suggested, though the sense of the sentence is generally clear. We follow Gray (*Xenophon*, 163) in accepting Richards's suggestion. See also Lipka, *Xenophon's Spartan Constitution*, 158–59.

[37] The final phrase may also be translated as "and after making use of it, returns it in fine (*kalōs*) condition."

[38] Following the main MS (*tous pepaumenous*) rather than Zeune's correction (*tous pepamenous*, "those who have them"), which is accepted by most editors. See Lipka, *Xenophon's Spartan Constitution*, 162–63, for an explanation, as well as a description of the practice of leaving sealed provisions in storage places in the countryside for those who were on an extended hunt.

[39] *Euexia*, which is the reading of the MSS, but *eutaxia*, "good arrangement," is a frequently accepted correction by Dindorf. Cf. Proietti, *Xenophon's Sparta*, 56–57, with Lipka, *Xenophon's Spartan Constitution*, 168.

[40] *Kratistoi*: The superlative of *kratos*, meaning also "best" or "most excellent." Here the term carries the sense of both "strongest" and "most excellent," referring to the leading citizens; see also 8.5. The earlier and later uses of the term refer specifically to bodily strength (see 4.5 and 11.8), and there is the sense of such strength in the usage here. But cf. 10.3 in which the comparative, *kreittōn*, is used to designate the superiority of soul to body.

[41] *Aneleutheros*: The privative of *eleutheros*, "free" or "freeborn."

[42] The office of the ephorate was occupied by five annually elected ephors or "overseers." Xenophon enumerates several of their powers. See also Aristotle, *Politics* 1265b31–66a1; 1270b6–35; 1271a6–8; 1272a4–7, 26–34; 1272b33–37; 1275b9–11; 1294b29–31; 1313a23–33; Plato, *Laws* 692a, 712d. As Lipka notes (*Xenophon's Spartan Constitution*, 169–71), there are different accounts even among the ancient authors of the origin of the ephorate: Herodotus, for example, identifies Lycurgus as its source (1.65.5), whereas Aristotle locates its origin in the reforms of Theopompus (*Politics* 1313a25–33).

[43] *Kataplēxein tous politous hupo tou akouein*: We render this phrase with the emphasis the Greek suggests on the fear that the Spartans wished to strike into the hearts of their citizens, and we keep the reading of the MSS, *hupo tou akouein* (into submission), against Schneider's deletion, though the use of the genitive is unusual, as Lipka points out (*Xenophon's Spartan Constitution*, 171). We translate *akouein* here and above (8.2) as "being submissive" and "submission" to distinguish it from the term that Xenophon typically uses for "obedience," which is the middle/passive of *peithō* (see 1.2; 2.2; 4.6; 8.1–3, 5; 14.7). Each of these terms can connote a willing obedience—hearkening to or having been persuaded of—but only in one instance in the text (8.5) does Xenophon clearly speak of "willing" obedience.

[44] In the Greek, the phrase "on trial for their life" (or a capital trial) is literally "the contest that concerns the soul." The Greek expression becomes important in Xenophon's complicated discussion in 10.2 of the "contests" that have to do with the "soul" and those that have to do with "bodies." The same phrase, with the same sense, is repeated there.

[45] Xenophon here offers a particular version of the source of the Lycurgan laws and their relation to the oracle at Delphi. Other versions identify the source of the laws as either Crete or Delphi itself. See, e.g., Tyrtaeus, fr. 4; Herodotus 1.65–66; Plato, *Laws* 624a, 632d; Aristotle, *Politics* 1271b20–32.

[46] *Aretē* and *kakia* are the usual Greek terms for "virtue" and "vice." In this context, *kakia* has the sense of "cowardice," so we translate it in this way, and *kakos* as "coward," though the reader should keep in view the connection of these terms with overall vice or badness. The usual term for "cowardice," *deilia*, is absent from this work by Xenophon, but see 10.6 for "unmanliness (*anandreia*), as well as 3.3 and 10.7 for "cowardly shirking" (*apodeilian*). The opposite of *kakos* in this context, *agathos* (good), thus connotes the virtue of courage.

[47] The three best MSS read *andreias*, "manliness," though, as Strauss notes, the meaning of the term is thus "exceedingly ambiguous"—so much so that most translators accept the reading of a lesser MS, *anandrias*, "unmanliness" (see Strauss, "Spirit of Sparta," 520–21). Gray (*Xenophon*, 169) argues in favor of translating *anandrias* here as "lack of husbands," and hence suggests the translation "The coward must bear the blame for their (the girls') lack of husbands," but cf. Lipka, *Xenophon's Spartan Constitution*, 178; Watson, *Xenophon Minor Works*, 218–19. See also 10.6, where Xenophon speaks of *anandria*.

[48] Sometimes translated as "senate," the *gerousia* (or *gerontia*, the Laconian term) was a council of thirty members, composed of twenty-eight Spartan elders (*gerontes*, men over sixty years of age) and the two Spartan kings (*basileis*). Plutarch (*Lycurgus* 26.1–4) offers one description of the manner of their election, upon a vacancy, which was by acclamation of the assembly (*ekklēsia*). Aristotle calls the office "the prize of virtue" (*Politics* 1270b24–25).

[49] The phrase "nobility and goodness" translates *kalokagathia*. This term is often translated as "gentlemanliness" and has the sense of "complete virtue" (see also 10.4, where it is used again). As Lipka notes (*Xenophon's Spartan Constitution*, 180–81), citing Bourriot, the quality of *kalokagathia* in Sparta is closely associated with military affairs and especially courage in battle. See also Strauss, "Spirit of Sparta," 520–21.

[50] This is the same phrase as in 8.4, the literal translation of which is "the contest that concerns the soul." The literal translation brings out the ambiguity in what follows, in which the contest that concerns the soul then seems to be identified with the "contest involving the *gerousia*." See also Gray, *Xenophon*, 170; Proietti, *Xenophon's Sparta*, 60–62. As Proietti asks, in light of this ambiguity, which one is the contest that "most of all is taken seriously among human beings": the trial for one's life or the contest for the *gerousia*?

[51] *Nomima*: The plural of *nomimos*, translated earlier as "lawful" (1.8) and then as "customary" (4.7).

[52] *Toi homoioi*: A term first attested in Xenophon, which means literally "the same ones" and refers to full citizens (equals in citizenship). Those who lost their citizenship, as a result either of cowardice or of an inability to make the appropriate contribution to the common mess, were known as *hypomeiones*, a term that does not appear in this work.

[53] Spartan kings traced their lineage back to Heracles. As Lipka notes (*Xenophon's Spartan Constitution*, 187), Xenophon knew of the Spartan lists of kings and of the story of the return of the Heraclids to the Peloponnese (*Agesilaus* 1.2 and *Memorabilia* 3.5.10; see also Herodotus 6.52, 1.65–66). Xenophon's suggestion, based on what "is said," that Lycurgus lived at the time of the Heraclids, as well as his overarching attribution of all the Spartan laws to Lycurgus, are both exaggerations and, in this connection, commentators note the ironical character of this concluding passage (cf., e.g., Gray, *Xenophon*, 171; Lipka, *Xenophon's Spartan Constitution*, 35–36 and 187–88; Strauss, "Spirit of Sparta," 527–33).

[54] A *mora* is a division or battalion in the Spartan army. Commentators debate whether Xenophon means to indicate six *morai* altogether, or six *morai* of hoplites and six *morai* of cavalry. See, in particular, Lipka, *Xenophon's Spartan Constitution*, 195. With the exception of *stratēgos*, "general," we simply transliterate the Greek military terms.

[55] This passage presents the chain of command from the largest unit to the smallest. In the military arrangements of which Xenophon speaks, a Spartan *mora* numbered around 576 men, and was divided into four *lochoi* of 144, eight *penteēkostyes* of 72, and sixteen *enōmotiai*, numbering around 32–36 men. See Lipka, *Xenophon's Spartan Constitution*, 194; Ollier, *Xenophon*, 36; Nick Sekunda, *The Spartan Army* (London: Osprey, 1998), 13–15.

[56] Commentators dispute how to read this line, and most assume that there is a lacuna in the text. The main question is how the Spartans deployed their troops, whether on the march or for battle. Lipka suggests that Xenophon describes here not the internal deployment of the *enomotia*, but their deployment as units: the *enomotia* could be deployed into one long file (the main column) or into three (two *morai*) or six (six *morai*) files. See Lipka, *Xenophon's Spartan Constitution*, 195; Gray, *Xenophon*, 174; Watson, *Xenophon's Minor Works*, 222n3; Ollier, *Xenophon*, 14–15, 36–37.

[57] The advantage of this *exeligmos* or countermarch movement is that the order of the lines is preserved. But since the leader ends up on the left, the hoplites must look left (the shield side), which is more difficult, and if they are attacked on the right side (spear side), they cannot fight the attacker and pay attention to the leader on the left at the same time. On the other hand, the leader himself will be better protected on his shield side should an attack come from the left.

[58] In this case, there is some question as to whether Xenophon describes the countermarch of an *enomotia* or of an entire *lochos*—that is, does not the entire *lochos* of sixteen *enomotia* have to move to get the leaders on the right? See Lipka, *Xenophon's Spartan Constitution*, 200–01; J. K. Anderson, *Military Theory and Practice in the Age of Xenophon* (Berkeley: University of California Press, 1970), 106–7.

[59] As Lipka notes, Xenophon omits crucial details in this difficult passage, such as the manner of the attack, and scholars disagree about the precise set of movements being described here. There are also textual differences among the MSS, as well as different solutions suggested by editors; we accept the reading of one MS, *alla protheousin* (dash forward) and Marchant's deletion of *enantious*, but cf., e.g., Lipka *Xenophon's Spartan Constitution*, 201. One point is clear: depending on the side of the attack, the *lochoi* turn to confront it in such a way that the *lochos* in the rear ends up either on the spear side or on the shield side. Cf. Lipka, *Xenophon's Spartan Constitution*, 200–201; Gray, *Xenophon*, 176; Anderson, *Military Theory*, 109–10. In *Hellenica* (7.5.23), Xenophon employs the same image of a trireme to describe the movement of Epaminondas's successful attack on the Spartans in the battle of Mantinea, 371 BC.

[60] The corners of a square or rectangular camp are harder to defend, enemies being able to attack from two sides.

[61] It is not clear whom Xenophon means to signify by "friends": Helots, allies, or even fellow Lacedaemonians? In what follows, 12.4, he speaks of slaves, i.e., Helots, being barred from the weapons, and in this sense, it would seem that "friends" are at the same time "enemies," but in 12.5, "friends" refers most clearly to Spartan allies.

[62] Numbering six hundred men, the Skiritai were light infantry from the mountains of Arcadia, northwest of Sparta. Although they fought on foot, they were trained to work alongside cavalry (see *Hellenica* 5.4.52–53); cf. Thucydides 5.68, where the Skiritai would appear to fight as hoplites at the battle of Mantinea in 418; see also Sekunda, *Spartan Army*, 49; Lipka, *Xenophon's Spartan Constitution*, 203–4; Gray, *Xenophon*, 177. When Xenophon speaks of a "phalanx" here, he refers to the entire encampment. Also, as Gray notes, what is left out in the ellipsis is not clear, but Xenophon is at least signaling a difference between the practice of the past and that of his own time.

[63] Here and in what follows in chapter 13, Xenophon refers to "the king" in the singular; only one of the two Spartan kings would be sent on campaign.

[64] *Agētōr* or "the Leader" is a Spartan epithet for Zeus. The "gods with him," the reading of the main MSS, may refer to the Dioskouroi, the "twin gods."

[65] The sacrifices performed at the border—called *diabateria* in *Hellenica* 3.4.3—are distinctive of Sparta (cf. *Cyropaedia* 3.1.22; 1.6.1, where Xenophon may be transferring the Spartan practice to Persia).

[66] *Autoschediaztēs*: Or "bunglers." See *Memorabilia* 3.5.21 for a similar statement by Socrates regarding most of the Athenian generals.

[67] Again, scholars give somewhat different accounts of this movement, as the king turns to the right to station himself between two *morai* and *polemarchoi*, but cf., e.g., Thucydides 5.72.5, where the king is in the center at the battle of Mantinea; see also Gray, *Xenophon*, 180; Lipka, *Xenophon's Spartan Constitution*, 218. The "troop of the first *mora*" may refer to the king's bodyguard (the Three Hundred) or to the first *enoōmotia*.

[68] Accepting the reading of the MSS against the emendation of Zeune, but cf. Lipka, *Xenophon's Spartan Constitution*, 220–21, for a defense of the latter. The aulos (or flute)

players "lead" the army by setting the pace of the march (see especially Thucydides 5.70).

[69] *Kala* is the reading of the MSS, as opposed to the emendation *mala* by Castalio ("the following very beneficial things"), which is accepted by most editors and translators. The former reading is defended by Ollier, *Xenophon*, 68–69, but cf. Lipka, *Xenophon's Spartan Constitution*, 222, for a defense of the latter.

[70] *Phaidros*: For the term in the context of battle, see *Anabasis* 2.6.11 and *Cyropaedia* 3.3.59; 4.2.11; 6.2.12.

[71] *Parakeleuesthai* also means "to encourage or exhort," so perhaps: "They call out encouragement to the *enoōmotarchēs*" (cf. Gray, *Xenophon*, 181, with Lipka, *Xenophon's Spartan Constitution*, 224).

[72] As Strauss notes, "The Lycurgus with regard to this is the king" is the reading of the best MSS. Although it is an odd phrase designating a function by the use of a proper name, it is not without precedent in Xenophon (see *Cyropaedia* 1.4.6). For the significance of this suggestion, see Strauss, "Spirit of Sparta," 527–28. The alternative reading of one of the lesser MSS (F), and the preference of most editors and translators, is "The king has authority (*kurios*) over this" (see especially Lipka, *Xenophon's Spartan Constitution*, 58 and 225).

[73] Our rendering of this sentence in the affirmative regarding the king's power follows the reading of the MSS, and there are solid philological and textual reasons for doing so. But Weiske suggests an emendation, accepted by most editors and translators, that would indicate a restriction of the king's power regarding the sending of embassies. Lipka lays out the linguistic and historical evidence on the question (Lipka, *Xenophon's Spartan Constitution*, 225–26; see also Proietti, *Xenophon's Sparta*, 70–71 and n. 41; Gray, *Xenophon*, 181; Ollier, *Xenophon*, 70).

[74] *Hellanodikai*: Little is known of this office, which shares the name of the chief judges of the Olympic Games. Lipka conjectures that they dealt with disputes involving non-Spartans (*Xenophon's Spartan Constitution*, 227).

[75] Commentators dispute the position of this chapter, since it seems to interrupt the flow of the argument, but none of the extant MSS order the chapters differently, and the first section of chapter 15 suggests that it follows naturally from the considerations of the previous chapter. As Lipka notes, furthermore, chapter 15 "ends with an hexameter and thus indicates a special caesura very appropriate for the end of the whole treatise" (*Xenophon's Spartan Constitution*, 28). Lipka (27–31) provides a review of some of the scholarly positions. See also Gray, *Xenophon*, 217–22; Ollier, *Xenophon*, ix–xiii; Strauss, "Spirit of Sparta," 521–25.

[76] *Harmostēs* (or *harmozein*, "to act as a harmost," here in the participle): "One who arranges or governs" and hence a Spartan governor of a subject city or area (see 14.4; Lipka, *Xenophon's Spartan Constitution*, 229–30).

[77] *Xenēlasia*: "Expulsion of foreigners" was a Spartan practice, also attested in Thucydides 1.144 and 2.39; Plato, *Protagoras* 342c and *Laws* 950b; Aristotle, *Politics* 1272b17 (see also Aristophanes, *Birds* 1012; Herodotus 3.148; Thucydides 1.77.6).

[78] Here and in 15.5 and 15.8 are the only times that Xenophon speaks of the kings in the plural, thereby noting, but without comment, the dual kingship of the Spartans.

[79] According to Herodotus (6.57.2), the task of the two Pythioi was to act as public liaisons between the king and the oracle at Delphi.

[80] As many commentators have noted, Xenophon concludes his treatise with a "solemn spondaic hexameter": *tous Lacedaimoniōn basileis protetimēkasi* (Proietti, *Xenophon's Sparta*, 86; Lipka, *Xenophon's Spartan Constitution*, 247–48; Gray *Xenophon*, 186; Strauss, "Spirit of Sparta," 523–24).

[81] There is not a good English word for the Greek term *politeia*. I translate *politeia* as "regime," rather than "constitution," to signify the connection of the Greek not simply to an arrangement of political offices, which is the usual sense of the English term "constitution," but more fully to a shared, and legislated, way of life, ordered with a view to a common good.

[82] Cf., respectively, E. N. Tigerstedt, *The Legend of Sparta in Classical Antiquity* (Stockholm: Almqvist & Wiksell, 1965), 159–79, with Strauss, "Spirit of Sparta," 502–3, 528–31. As will become clear, my own treatment of the treatise is indebted to that of Leo Strauss. Renewed appreciation of Xenophon's art of writing among scholars today—an appreciation that was lost for well over a century—owes much to the recovery of Xenophon achieved by Strauss (see especially Strauss, "Spirit of Sparta," 502–3 and 528–36, as well as Strauss's other works on Xenophon, several of which will be cited in what follows). That Xenophon is a careful, and ironical, writer is now not generally in dispute. As Paul Cartledge observes, "The limpidity of [Xenophon's] style masks a sophistication that requires his text to be read between as well as on the lines." Cartledge, in *The Landmark Xenophon's "Hellenika," ed. Robert B. Strassler (New York: Pantheon Books, 2009), 347; and see especially Strauss, "Spirit of Sparta," 507, 519, and 521. See also Christopher Tuplin, *The Failings of Empire* (Stuttgart: Franz Steiner, 1993); Tuplin, *Xenophon and His World* (Stuttgart: Franz Steiner, 2005) (as well as Tuplin's entry on Xenophon in the most recent *Oxford Classical Dictionary*); Proietti, *Xenophon's Sparta*; W. E. Higgins, *Xenophon the Athenian* (Albany: SUNY Press, 1977), especially 29; Robert C. Bartlett, ed. and trans., *Xenophon: The Shorter Socratic Writings* (Ithaca, NY: Cornell University Press, 1996), 1–6; Eric Buzzetti, *Xenophon the Socratic Prince: The Argument of the "Anabasis of Cyrus"* (New York: Palgrave Macmillan, 2014), 7–36.

[83] However much agreement there exists concerning Xenophon's irony, there is naturally much disagreement about his intention in any particular case. Regarding his treatment of Sparta, compare, for example, Strauss, "Spirit of Sparta"; Gray, *Xenophon*; Noreen Humble, "Xenophon's View of Sparta: A Study of the *Anabasis*, *Hellenica*, and *Republica Lacedaemoniorum* (PhD diss., McMaster University, 1997); Humble, "The Author, Date, and Purpose of Chapter 14 of the *Lacedaimoniōn Politeia*," in Tuplin, *Xenophon and His World*, especially 215n3; Lipka, *Xenophon's Spartan Constitution*.

[84] The most prominent among the modern commentators is K. M. T. Chrimes; the one doubter among the ancient commentators is Demetrius of Magnesia. See Humble, "Chapter 14," 217–18; Lipka, *Xenophon's Spartan Constitution*, 5–9.

[85] On the question of the placement of chapter 14, compare Xenophon's *Cyropaedia*, in which the criticism of the Persians appears at the very end of the work. For an argument in favor of placing it at the end of the treatise, see Ollier, *Xenophon*, ix–xiii. But Ollier's argument is tenuous, given the evidence of all the extant MSS. See Strauss, "Spirit of Sparta," 522–25; Higgins, *Xenophon the Athenian*, 66; Proietti, *Xenophon's Sparta*, 45–46.

[86] On this question, cf. in general Strauss, "Spirit of Sparta," with Gray, *Xenophon*.

[87] Xenophon's own *Anabasis* is one of the two major sources of information about his life, the other being Diogenes Laertius's *Lives of the Philosophers* (2.48–59). Recent accounts of what we know are Lipka, *Xenophon's Spartan Constitution*, 3–5; and Humble, "Xenophon's View of Sparta," 3–21.

[88] Xenophon's interest in horses, an indication that he came from wealth, and his cavalry experience have led to speculation that he served in the cavalry under the Thirty Tyrants and that this was at least one reason he left Athens (Humble, "Xenophon's View of Sparta," 7–8). In his *Anabasis*, however, he never tells us precisely *why* he left Athens, though he does acknowledge Socrates' caution that the Athenians will

not look kindly on his actions. By his own account (3.1.4), he does not play a leading role in Cyrus's army; only in the aftermath does he rise to prominence as a general, and, at one point, he is virtually penniless (7.8.6). See also Xenophon's *Hellenica*
(2.3.1–4.43), where he provides a very critical account of the rule of the Thirty, as well
as Buzzetti, *Socratic Prince*, 54–58.

[89] Scholars debate the exact date of this decree, as well as its grounds, and Xenophon's own account does not settle the matter (*Anabasis* 7.7.57). See Humble, "Xenophon's View of Sparta," 11–14; C. J. Tuplin, "Xenophon's Exile Again," in *Homo
Viator: Classical Essays for John Bramble*, ed. Michael Whitby (Bristol: Bristol Classical
Press, 1987). On the question of when the decree was lifted, see Diogenes Laertius
2.59; Humble, ibid., 17.

[90] But see Humble, "Xenophon's View of Sparta," 16.

[91] More precisely, Gryllus died in a cavalry skirmish before the main battle (*Hellenica* 7.5.17). Xenophon mentions his sons in a beautiful passage of the *Anabasis* (5.3.10).
See also Diogenes Laertius 52. There is a suggestion in Diogenes Laertius, generally
accepted by modern scholars with little other evidence, that Xenophon's sons trained
in Sparta. But see Humble, *Xenophon on Sparta*, 19–21 for criticism of this view, which
is frequently used as evidence of Xenophon's pro-Spartan bias. See also Plutarch, *Agesilaus* 20.2.

[92] See Humble, "Xenophon's View of Sparta," 18–19.

[93] See Leo Strauss, *Xenophon's Socrates* (1972; South Bend, IN: St. Augustine's Press,
1998), 3. See also Christopher Bruell, "Introduction: Xenophon and His Socrates," in
Xenophon: Memorabilia, trans. Amy L. Bonnette (Ithaca, NY: Cornell University Press,
1994), vii–xxii.

[94] Cf., e.g, Lipka, *Xenophon's Spartan Constitution*, 17.

[95] Humble, "Xenophon's View of Sparta," 187.

[96] See again Strauss, "Spirit of Sparta," 512n4, for a discussion of the expression *eis
ta eschata*.

[97] See Strauss, "Spirit of Sparta," 526–27: "The ephors, [Xenophon] says, rule like
tyrants. But tyrants do not rule in accordance with laws." See also n. 4: "The fact that
'constitution' is as such irreconcilable with 'tyranny' shows that the very title of the
treatise is ironic; cf. *Hellenica*, VI, 3, 8."

[98] Cf. Strauss, "Spirit of Sparta," 507–11; Lipka, *Xenophon's Spartan Constitution*,
142; Humble, "Xenophon's View of Sparta," 193–202; Gray, *Xenophon*, 143.

[99] Cf. Strauss, "Spirit of Sparta," 508, 511; Lipka, *Xenophon's Spartan Constitution*,
125, 132–35; Humble, "Xenophon's View of Sparta," 199–201, 195–96; Gray, *Xenophon*,
155, 156–57.

[100] See especially Strauss, "Spirit of Sparta," 533–34.

[101] See especially 2.2, 8–9; 3.6; 6.2; 8.3–4; 9.5; 10.2.

[102] It is curious, to be sure, that Xenophon never uses the term *andreia*, except in an
"exceedingly ambiguous" way at 9.5 (as Strauss, following the MSS, observes) or in
the negative at 10.6. Still, he does speak of *andragathia*, "manly goodness" at 4.3, and
in the context of chapter 9, the terms for "virtue" (*aretē*) and "vice" (*kakia*), as well as
those for "good" (*agathos*) and "bad" (*kakos*), are indistinguishable from "courage"
and "cowardice" in war. See also Strauss, "Spirit of Sparta," 520–21.

[103] Messenian Greeks conquered by the Spartans during the Dorian invasions of the
Peloponnese, the Helots were subjected to an annual declaration of war and the terror
of the *krupteia* (literally, "concealment"): another institution about which Xenophon
is notably silent, the *krupteia* required that a young Spartan man spend a year in the
wilds, fending for himself and killing any Helot who was caught after curfew. See
Plutarch (*Lycurgus* 28.5), who remarks that given the cruelty and injustice involved
in the *krupteia*, it could not have been a practice instituted by Lycurgus but only a

consequence of the Helot revolt of 464. See also Kennell, *Gymnasium of Virtue*, 15–16; Aristotle, *Politics* 1269a34–39.

[104] The second reference to leisure associates it with hunting, which Lycurgus sets down as an activity for the older men so that they will remain fit enough to bear the toils of campaigning (cf. 6.3 with 4.7; see also 3.2 for *ascholia*, "lack of leisure"). Cf. Aristotle, *Politics* 1271a41–b6.

[105] See Ollier (*Xenophon*, xxxiii), who points out that during the retreat of the Ten Thousand, Xenophon preferred Athenian rather than Spartan formations. See also Strauss ("Spirit of Sparta," 525), who notes that other shortcomings come to sight when one compares 12.2–4 with *Cyropaedia* 4.2.1–8 and *Agesilaus* 2.24.

[106] Cf. Aristotle, *Politics* 1270b6–17.

[107] See Strauss, "Spirit of Sparta," 522–28.

[108] The last sentence of the treatise concludes with *tous Lacedaimoniōn basileis pro-tetimēkasi*. See Proietti, *Xenophon's Sparta*, 86; Lipka, *Xenophon's Spartan Constitution*, 247–48; Gray, *Xenophon*, 186; Strauss, "Spirit of Sparta," 523.

[109] See especially *Memorabilia* 4.4.17 and *Cyropaedia* 1.2.7.

[110] On this question, see especially Strauss, "Spirit of Sparta," 528–36.

[111] See especially D-K frr. 6 and 7, as well as frr. 32 and 37, for parallels to Xeno-phon's treatise. See also Strauss, "Spirit of Sparta, 528–29; Lipka, *Xenophon's Spartan Constitution*, 14, 19–20.

[112] See especially *Memorabilia* 4.4.14–18. Cf. Strauss, "Spirit of Sparta," 517–20; Strauss, *Xenophon's Socrates*, 179–80.

[113] See also Humble, "Chapter 14," 222n23.

[114] As Humble remarks, "Much of the difficulty in understanding *LP* has arisen because of the general tendency to regard each of Xenophon's works in isolation, instead of taking them together as a coherent and ongoing dissemination of his own political and philosophical views" ("Chapter 14," 226). But see finally Strauss's state-ment in homage to Xenophon's artfulness and to Xenophon himself, "this truly royal soul" ("Spirit of Sparta," 535).

4. Regime of the Athenians

I have used the Greek text edited by Vivienne J. Gray, *Xenophon on Government* (Cambridge: Cambridge University Press, 2007), but I have also consulted E. C. March-ant, Xenophon, *Opuscula*, vol. 5 of *Opera Omnia* (Oxford: Clarendon Press, 1969). J. S. Watson's translation with notes in *Xenophon's Minor Works* (London: George Bell & Sons, 1891) was also helpful. I would like to thank David Bahr, Alex Priou, Robert C. Bartlett, and an anonymous reviewer for Cornell University Press for their helpful feedback on this essay.

[1] This treatise begins abruptly with the words "but concerning" (*peri de*), as if in midargument or as the continuation of another work. Xenophon's *Hellenica* begins similarly with "But after these things" (*meta de tauta*), and the *Oeconomicus* begins, "But I once heard him" (*ēkousa de pote autou*). Xenophon's *Regime of the Lacedaemonians* and *Symposium* both begin with an even more emphatic disjunctive "but" (*alla*).

[2] "Vulgar" and "worthy" (*ponēroi* and *chrēstoi*, respectively): Xenophon uses terms with economic overtones to distinguish the better and worse citizens, rather than a term more typically associated with superior virtue (*agathoi* or *aristoi*, for example).

[3] "The people" (*dēmos*) carries democratic overtones. It does not refer to the entire population; rather, it refers to the many, who would have been poor, and hence only a part of the total population.

[4] *Pentēkontarchos*: A subordinate officer in charge of a tier of roughly fifty oarsmen.

[5] Hoplites were heavily armed foot soldiers, and only members of the upper and upper middle classes could afford their own expensive armor. Additionally, many hoplites appear to have used slaves to carry their shield.

[6] *Dēmotikos*: Literally, "of the people" or "popular."

[7] *Ponēria*: Related to the word that I have translated as "vulgar" (*ponēroi*). See 1.1.

[8] The verb translated as "deliberate" (*boulein*) is related to the word for the Council of Athens (*boulē*). See note 20 on 3.1.

[9] The word (*anēr*) refers to an adult male and connotes the presence of qualities Greek males supposed real men should possess. It is distinguished from "human being" (*anthrōpos*).

[10] "A city with good laws" translates *eunomeisthai*, whose root is the word for "law" (*nomos*). An alternative translation is "well regulated by law." "Good, lawful order" translates *eunomia* in the next section. Similarly, *kakonomia*, which I have translated as "has bad laws" could be "badly regulated by laws." The word *eunomia* carries oligarchic overtones and so may remind of Sparta. See, e.g., Plato, *Hippias Major* 283e; Thucydides 1.18.

[11] "You," here and in the next sentence, is singular. The word "believe" (*nomizein*) is related to the word for "law" (*nomos*).

[12] Here and at the beginning of 1.18, Xenophon uses the word *andrapodon* for "slave," which refers to one taken in war and sold as a slave. In all other instances, he uses the more common word *doulos*.

[13] Literally, the *prytaneia*, which is a sum of money deposited by each party to a lawsuit before the suit began. The losing party's sum was retained, and was used, in part, to pay jurors.

[14] *Andrapodon*. See note 12 on 1.11.

[15] A trierarch was a person responsible for outfitting a trireme and hence was someone wealthy.

[16] The few (*oligoi*) stand in contrast to the people (*dēmos*). The former term carries oligarchic overtones, and the latter democratic ones.

[17] The word translated as substance (*ousia*) can be translated as "beings" in other contexts.

[18] The text appears to be corrupt here; this is my best effort to construe the sentence.

[19] The verb translated as "love" is *philein*.

[20] The Athenian Council (*boulē*) was a deliberative body of five hundred male citizens that prepared decrees and laws for the entire Athenian Assembly (*ekklēsia*) to vote on.

[21] The text appears to be corrupt here. The meaning seems to be that no amount of money would enable the Athenians to conduct all the business that came before them.

[22] The chorus equipper defrayed the cost of producing a chorus and hence was someone wealthy. The five events mentioned are all dramatic festivals.

[23] Cf. Thucydides 2.13.8.

[24] As previously noted, a trierarch was responsible for outfitting a trireme at considerable personal cost. Someone who was appointed trierarch could dispute his appointment. If appointed, he was also responsible for ensuring the ship was in good order after the service ended, except for damages beyond his control. Thus, he could also dispute his responsibility to provide repairs.

[25] Little is known about the details of these three examples of Athens supporting the "best." For possibilities, see Thucydides 1.113 in the case of Boeotia, 1.115 for Miletus, and 1.101–3 for Sparta. All of the events are thought to have occurred in the

middle of the fifth century, between 467 and 443, before Xenophon was born. These are the only historical events to which Xenophon refers in the entire work.

26 Exceptions include Yoshio Nakategawa, "Athenian Democracy and the Concept of Justice in Pseudo-Xenophon's *Athenion Politeia*," Hermes 123.1 (1995): 28–46; Gray, "Introduction to *Respublica Atheniensium*," in *Xenophon on Government*. Each work is marked by the virtue of investigating the content of the *Regime of the Athenians*, but both authors deny that Xenophon wrote it.

27 J. L. Marr and P. J. Rhodes say: "The arguments for this position [that Xenophon is not the author of the *Regime of the Athenians*], however, need to be examined, since they are by no means as self-evident or conclusive as some scholars assume." Marr and Rhodes, eds., *The "Old Oligarch": The Constitution of the Athenians Attributed to Xenophon* (Trowbridge, UK: Cromwell Press, 2008), 2.

28 Compare, for example, J. M. Moore's statements on the authorship of the *Regime of the Athenians* with his statements on the authorship of the *Regime of the Lacedaemonians*. Moore, *Aristotle and Xenophon on Democracy and Oligarchy* (Berkeley: University of California Press, 2010), 19 and 67, respectively. See also Gray, *Xenophon on Government*, 20–21.

29 "The implication of Diogenes' comment is that the *Constitution of the Athenians* was generally regarded in the first century B.C. as being by Xenophon . . . and that, although this was disputed by Demetrius . . . , his challenge was not regarded by [ancient] scholars as decisive." Marr and Rhodes, *"Old Oligarch,"* 7.

30 David Hume, "On the Populousness of Nations," in *Essays: Moral, Political, and Literary*, ed. Eugene F. Miller (Indianapolis: Liberty Fund, 1987), 429; Montesquieu, *The Spirit of the Laws*, ed. Anne Cohler (Cambridge: Cambridge University Press, 1989), 2.2; 21.7; 24.23.

31 Marr and Rhodes, *"Old Oligarch,"* 7.

32 See Gray, *Xenophon on Government*, 57–58; Hartvig Frisch, *The Constitution of the Athenians*, Classica et Mediaevalia: Dissertationes 2 (Copenhagen: Gyldendalske Boghandel, 1942), 47–62; and Marr and Rhodes, *"Old Oligarch,"* 8–12.

33 Marr and Rhodes say the case for the rejection of Xenophontic authorship on the basis of chronology is "stronger [than the case based on style], though not totally conclusive." Marr and Rhodes, *"Old Oligarch,"* 10.

34 Eric Buzzetti, *Xenophon the Socratic Prince: The Argument of the "Anabasis of Cyrus"* (New York: Palgrave Macmillan, 2014), 303–4.

35 Ibid., 85 and Appendix 1.

36 Christopher Nadon, *Xenophon's Prince: Republic and Empire in the "Cyropaedia"* (Berkeley: University of California Press, 2001), 79.

37 See, for example, Vivienne Gray, "Continuous History and Xenophon, *Hellenica* 1–2.3.10," *American Journal of Philology* 112.2 (Summer 1991): 201–28; David Thomas, introduction to *The Landmark Xenophon's "Hellenika,"* ed. Robert B. Strassler (New York: Pantheon Books, 2009), §§8.4–8.8. Chapter 6 of William Higgins, *Xenophon the Athenian* (Albany: SUNY Press, 1977), is helpful for understanding the change in style.

38 "Some put the break at 2.2.23 and others at 2.3.10" (Thomas, *Landmark Xenophon's "Hellenika,"* 417) or at the end of book 2, after he has discussed The Thirty. "The stylistic evidence . . . puts the break before the account of the thirty" (Thomas, 418). Of course, some scholars explain this change in style as evidence that the work was not composed as a unity.

39 Gray, *Xenophon on Government*, 20n35.

40 Ibid., 20.

41 Xenophon's works seem to demand comparison with one another. The titles of *Cyropaedia* and *Cyroanabasis* invite an obvious comparison. Xenophon's Socratic works similarly invite comparison with one another. Moreover, the symposium in *Cyropaedia* 8.4 should be compared with the *Symposium* as a whole, and the various

trials in Xenophon's works could also be compared (*Apology* with *Memorabilia* 4.8; *Cyropaedia* 3.1, 5.5; and *Hellenica* 1.5).

[42] Gray (*Xenophon on Government*, 187) says that the author "takes for granted that the many poor who constitute the *demos* are bad and the few rich are good." See *Oeconomicus* 11.3–7.

[43] *Memorabilia* 1.6.

[44] Three times in 1.1; also in 3.1, 9.

[45] Compare *Agesilaus* 1.37, *Poroi* 1.1, and *Regime of the Lacedaemonians* 15.1 with *Cyropaedia* (*Education of Cyrus*) 1.2.15 and 8.1.45.

[46] This has led other commentators to refer to this comment as paradoxical, since the praise for the stability of the Athenian regime stands in stark contrast to the supposed oligarchic prejudice. Yet no attempt to resolve this paradox has been undertaken.

[47] See the *Cyropaedia* (*Education of Cyrus*) in its entirety, but especially book 8.

[48] See Glenn R. Morrow, *Plato's Cretan City: A Historical Interpretation of the "Laws"* (Princeton, NJ: Princeton University Press, 1993), 43. Morrow points to the vast literature on *eunomia*.

[49] Indeed, Xenophon tells us that no city wanted to imitate Sparta's way of life (*Regime of the Lacedaemonians* 1.2). For Xenophon's considered judgment of Sparta, see Leo Strauss, "The Spirit of Sparta and the Taste of Xenophon," *Social Research* 6 (1939): 502–36. See also Susan Collins's essay in this volume, "An Introduction to the *Regime of the Lacedaemonians*."

[50] *Anabasis* 5.8.26.

[51] As Thomas Pangle says, "We are given a more lively, if less gentlemanly or polite, expression [of the fact that "'the perfect gentleman' is likely to have only an incomplete, uneasy, and insufficiently grounded awareness of his insuperably out-of-step political situation"] in the discourse by the fictitious character whom scholars refer to as "The Old Oligarch"—created by Xenophon as the (in fact not so elderly) narrator of his comic *Constitution of Athens*." Pangle, *Aristotle's Teaching in the "Politics"* (Chicago: University of Chicago Press, 2013), 18.

[52] The Spartans always had to live in fear of their slaves. See *Regime of the Lacedaemonians* 6, but also 12.2, which seems to indicate that the Spartans maintain a large contingent of enemies within their numbers. For evidence of Spartan fear of their slaves, see Plutarch's discussion of the "secret society" (*krupteia*) in *Lycurgus* 28.

[53] See J. S. Watson, *Xenophon's Minor Works* (London: G. Bell, 1857), 234n6. See also Moore, *Aristotle and Xenophon on Democracy and Oligarchy*, 49. He says this claim must be taken in a metaphorical sense.

[54] *Regime of the Lacedaemonians* in its entirety, but especially 2–4.

[55] Demosthenes 18.257.

[56] Of course, Socrates fits the description of a busybody (Plato, *Apology of Socrates* 31c) and was indeed the object of ridicule in Aristophanes' *Clouds*.

[57] And perhaps also Alcibiades. For Xenophon's judgment of Alcibiades, see *Hellenica* 1–2, esp. 2.1.25 and ff.

[58] *Hellenica* 1.7.12.

5. Ways and Means, or On Revenues

Unless otherwise noted, I have translated the text as presented in the Oxford edition, E. C. Marchant, Xenophon, *Opuscula*, vol. 5 of *Opera Omnia* (Oxford: Clarendon Press, 1920).

[1] The Greek title is *Poroi*. It refers in general to paths or ways through the sea and on land, primarily, and then to the ways of accomplishing or achieving something, and is opposed to the privative word *aporia*, "no way or path," which was commonly used to refer to the confused condition to which Socrates often reduced his interlocutors. In a narrower sense, *poroi* refers to ways of providing resources or money, or to the resources themselves. The subtitle is in the MSS but is now commonly bracketed by editors. The word translated as "revenue" here and elsewhere is *prosodos*, and it occurs frequently in this work.

[2] For similar but slightly different thoughts, see *Cyropaedia* 8.8.5 and 8.1.8.

[3] Literally, "human beings or humans" (*anthrōpoi*). See notes 12 and 20. "The people" (*dēmos*) refers to a political group, the poor majority. In the *Poroi* it occurs only in 6.1.

[4] This probably refers especially to cities allied to Athens.

[5] This is the superlative form of an important adjective, *kalos*, whose forms I will always translate with a word related to "beautiful," "noble," or "fine." It may suggest a contrast not only with what is ignoble or base but also with what is good or useful.

[6] The *metoikion* was a tax on resident aliens alone. See Plato, *Laws* 850b. Athenian citizens, by contrast, received a wage for performing such civic duties as serving on juries.

[7] The Greek word is *astos*, not *politēs*, which is the usual word for "citizen" and which is used in the very next section. "City center" is used below to translate *astu*, which is cognate with *astos*.

[8] The word for "arts" or "trades" (*technōn*) is close to that for "children" (*teknōn*), and some editors substitute it. I translate the MSS.

[9] A similar proposal is made in *The Skilled Cavalry Commander* (9.6), though from a different point of view.

[10] *Nomisma* can refer to anything sanctioned by custom or convention, not merely currency.

[11] When modifying a human being, this combination of adjectives, *kalos kai agathos*, has aristocratic overtones and is often translated "gentleman." To suggest a particular policy is noble (or fine) and good may imply that it would not be characteristic of a democracy.

[12] Literally, "friendly toward human beings" or "philanthropic."

[13] Special contributions (*eisphora*) were sometimes demanded of the Athenians during wartime (*Hellenica* 6.2.1; Thucydides 3.19.1), and they fell most heavily upon the wealthy (consider *Oeconomicus* 2.6). To emphasize that they were compulsory, Thucydides sometimes modifies the word "contribution" with the adjective "forced" (1.141.5). Although Xenophon does not, I think he expects his readers to infer it. All forms of "contribute" in this translation are based on words cognate with *eisphora*.

[14] These events are not well known. It is possible that a Lysistratus commanded the four hundred Athenian cavalry mentioned as allied to an Arcadian force at *Hellenica* 7.4.29, and perhaps Hegesilaus commanded the six thousand cavalry sent to help defeat Epaminondas at the battle of Mantinea (*Hellenica* 7.5.15). It is not known how much was raised by contributions to fund these expeditions.

[15] The obol is the smallest unit of Athenian currency: six obols equal one drachma, one hundred drachmae equal one mina, and one hundred minae equal one talent. Thus, ten minae equal six thousand obols. The premises here are that all citizens receive a dole of three obols per day and that the wealthier citizens, who would be subject to new taxes under Xenophon's proposal, would regard the taxes they pay as an investment, on which their three obols is a return. The required "investments" would be in proportion to the individual citizen's wealth, so the "return" is high for the poor and lower for the rich. More precisely, if a wealthy individual is required to pay ten minae, and this brings three obols per day, as all "investments" do, the "return" is

18.3 percent. (This is the "fifth" mentioned in the text. Three obols per day equal 1,095 obols per year.) If one cuts the "investment" to five minae, of course the rate of return doubles to 36.6 percent ("more than a third" in the text). If most Athenians receive more in one year than they contribute, then most Athenians contribute less than 1,095 obols (equal to a bit less than two minae).

[16] Being poor, they will generally contribute less than the three obols per day they receive.

[17] On the word translated as "the human things," see notes 20 and 12.

[18] Besides the honor of being listed as benefactors, Xenophon does not mention any return for the foreign contributors, but perhaps they too would be paid some unspecified return on their investment.

[19] On "noble [or fine] and good," see note 11 above.

[20] Literally, "human beings [*anthrōpoi*]," but I use "people" except as noted. In this chapter Xenophon appears to use *anthrōpoi* to mean "slaves," as is sometimes done also by other authors (and consider *Memorabilia* 2.7.6). Although "slaves" often seems to fit the context here, I will persist with "people." I accept this awkwardness because Xenophon's own usage departs from his usual practice of using either *doulos* or *andropodon* for "slave," and because he also uses *anthrōpoi* in this chapter in its broader sense. The ambiguity of *anthrōpoi* might also help one question the difference between slaves and free workers. The passages where *anthrōpoi* might mean "slaves" are 4.11, 14, 16, 18, 21, 25, and 39. The passage in 4.42 is especially ambiguous and raises the question of whether Xenophon is suggesting that slaves might be used in war not only as rowers but also as infantry troops. When I use "slave," the Greek word is always *andrapodon*.

[21] The Greek word *chrēmata* means "money" as well as "things."

[22] Nicias is the Athenian general who opposed the Sicilian expedition but was also responsible for leading it. He figures prominently in books 6 and 7 of Thucydides' *History*. Hipponicus is possibly the father of Callias, who plays the host in Plato's *Protagoras* and Xenophon's *Symposium*. Sosias and Philemonides are unknown.

[23] Literally, "in proportion to their power."

[24] Consider Socrates' advice to a comrade in *Memorabilia* 2.8.

[25] Six thousand slaves working 360 days, earning one obol per day, would earn the sixty talents mentioned in the text. A talent was worth sixty minae or thirty-six thousand obols.

[26] In the nineteenth year of the Peloponnesian War, Sparta followed the advice of Alcibiades and built a fort at Decelea in Athenian territory. This denied the Athenians the free use of the land outside of their walls and enabled, in Thucydides' estimate, over twenty thousand slaves to desert. He reports the fortification of Decelea as being one of the main reasons Athens lost the war (Thucydides 7.27–28; 6.91). See also *Memorabilia* 3.6.12.

[27] *Apo koinou*: That is, from the common wealth or property of the city.

[28] This is a conjecture. The Greek is incomplete and unclear.

[29] The Social War or War of the Allies was fought from 357 to 355.

[30] Although *pezoi* means "on foot" and often refers to infantry troops, it can also mean "on land" as opposed to "at sea." It could thus be compatible with the earlier suggestion that resident aliens might serve in the cavalry (2.5).

[31] Thoricus and Anaphlystus were well to the south of Athens, almost to Sunium. The fortification of Thoricus is mentioned at *Hellenica* 1.2.1.

[32] There are about 8 stadia to a mile, so the forts are about 7.5 miles apart.

[33] Five hundred and six hundred stadia are about sixty-two and seventy-five miles.

[34] Since it is not clear with whom Xenophon is agreeing, Richards changes the text to read "I now say."

[35] The precise meaning here is unclear, but surely this sentence emphasizes the importance of compensation, in the form of nourishment, for hard work. Apparently, this compensation was not consistently forthcoming for those leading or participating in the festivals mentioned. The word for nourishment, *trophē*, also means "livelihood" and is so translated in the next section.

[36] Literally, "denser" (*puknoteran*); the obscurity of this term has led to various emendations of the text.

[37] The conclusion of the sentence is a surmise based on the context; the text is uncertain.

[38] Several editors delete this curious item from the list.

[39] Literally, "silver."

[40] This appears to refer to those who work with what the poets produce, such as actors and chorus trainers, but it might extend to anyone engaged in the activities of one of the four groups just mentioned.

[41] "Leadership" translates *hēgemonia* here and in its other two appearances. Although it is a gentler term than "empire" (*archē*), which occurs only in the next section, it does not require that all followers be willing subjects. "Leaders," on the other hand, translates *prostatai*, which can also refer to leaders within a city, as in 1.1.

[42] Literally, "the Medean things." Xenophon refers to the growth of the Athenian empire after the Persian War. To accept Xenophon's invitation to consider whether Athens' leadership was rooted more in violence or benefaction, see Thucydides' so-called Pentecontaetia, 1.89–117. Taken by itself, 1.96 offers some support for Xenophon's present claim.

[43] He refers to the so-called Second Athenian Empire or Second Delian League, which was formed in 378 especially to resist Spartan domination. The "islanders" refers to the allied cities, most of which were located on islands in the Aegean.

[44] He perhaps refers to the particular episode described in *Hellenica* 5.4.62.

[45] He perhaps refers to the decisions debated and reached in *Hellenica* 7.1.1–14.

[46] See the very last section of the *Hellenica*.

[47] I translate an emendation. The MSS read "whoever was seeking to take over the temple since the Phocians have abandoned it."

[48] Xenophon offers a brief defense of his use of this phrase in *The Skilled Cavalry Commander* 9.8.

[49] The Greek word here and in the previous sentence is *eikos*, and it may mean either "fitting" or "likely," which is how I have translated it elsewhere.

[50] This essay is a revised version of a paper presented at a panel on Xenophon, at the annual meeting of the American Political Science Association in September 2010, and posted on the Social Science Research Network, http://papers.ssrn.com/sol3/papers.cfm?abstract_id=1641727.

[51] See my chapter, "The 'Infrastructure' of Aristotle's *Politics*: Aristotle on Economics and Politics," in *Essays on the Foundations of Aristotelian Political Science*, ed. Carnes Lord and David K. O'Connor (Berkeley: University of California Press, 1991).

[52] Leo Strauss, *Xenophon's Socratic Discourse: An Interpretation of the "Oeconomicus"* (Ithaca, NY: Cornell University Press, 1970), 199–204.

[53] This short dialogue perhaps justifies Karl Marx's taunt about Xenophon's "characteristic bourgeois instinct." Marx, *Capital* (New York: Modern Library, n.d.), 402, cited in Strauss, *Xenophon's Socratic Discourse*, 203.

[54] The likeliest time frame for the composition of *Poroi* is the closing period of the "Social War" of 357–355 BC, in which Athenian control over its subject cities was gravely weakened. While some in Athens called for an attempt to restore Athenian hegemony, the times were propitious for the consideration of an alternative policy.

Philippe Gauthier, *Commentaire historique des "Poroi" de Xénophon* (Geneva: Librairie Droz, 1976), 1, 6.

[55] References of this type (e.g., 1.1) in the text are to Xenophon, *Poroi*.

[56] Gauthier (*Commentaire historique*, 38) notes the "Socratic" turn of phrase; these leaders do not claim to know what justice is, only to be no more ignorant of it than other men.

[57] *Politics* 6, 1317b34–37.

[58] *Politics* 6, 1317b31–34. Translations from Aristotle's *Politics* are from *Aristotle's "Politics,"* trans. Carnes Lord, 2nd ed. (Chicago: University of Chicago Press, 2013).

[59] *Athenian Constitution*, 24–25.1.

[60] *Politics* 4, 1292b25–93a10.

[61] While this is not the same as the modern notion of "representative democracy," the underlying motivation and reasoning would not be entirely inconsistent with that of the authors of the *Federalist*, who sought in devices such as representation "a republican remedy for the diseases most incident to republican government." *The Federalist*, #10 (ed. Edward Mead Earle [New York: Modern Library, n.d.], 62).

[62] Cf. Thucydides (1.2.5), who says that Athens has "thin soil," and that this explains why Athens' early history was relatively peaceful: compared to other parts of Greece, Attica was not worth fighting over.

[63] See also Aristotle, *Politics* 6, 1318b9–12: "The best people is the farming sort, so that it is possible also to create [the best] democracy wherever the multitude lives from farming or herding."

[64] For Aristotle, mining takes an intermediate position between "natural" and "unnatural" modes of acquisition. It is "natural" in the sense that it takes something useful that nature provides; however, Aristotle appears to regard it as less natural in that the material gained is not the product of a natural process of growth. He defines it as the taking from nature of "unfruitful but useful things that grow from the earth." *Politics* 1, 1258b27–32.

[65] See note 65 above.

[66] Xenophon's explicit reference to the fact that Attica is not an island seems connected to his repudiation of the strategy of naval imperialism. Pericles, a major exponent of that strategy, famously advised the Athenians to think of themselves as an island, by virtue of the walls that protected Athens and the Piraeus from the invading Spartan armies. Thucydides 1.148.5.

[67] *Politics* 7, 1327a11–40.

[68] *Politics* 7, 1327a37–40. Xenophon, by contrast, explicitly says that homes and shops for the resident aliens or metics should be established not only in the port of Piraeus but in the center of Athens (3.13).

[69] *Politics* 7, 1327a29–31. *Pleonexia*, the Greek word here translated as "aggrandizement," is hardly a morally neutral term; perhaps "grasping for more [money]" would better convey the political and moral sense. Nevertheless, Aristotle does not make a blanket condemnation of *pleonexia*: he allows that some cities might have no choice but to make use of otherwise regrettable sources of revenue.

[70] This requirement to enforce the law impartially is captured neatly by Shakespeare in *Merchant of Venice*, when Antonio explains to Solanio why the Duke will not stop Shylock from collecting his pound of flesh:

> The Duke cannot deny the course of law;
> For the commodity that strangers have
> With us in Venice, if it be denied,
> Will much impeach the justice of the state,
> Since that the trade and profit of the city
> Consisteth of all nations.
>
> (3.3.26–31)

[71] In *The Skilled Cavalry Commander*, Xenophon describes the cavalry's participation in various religious processions, something that goes to the symbolic heart of Athenian identity.

[72] At 4.40, Xenophon recognizes that the taxes levied during the years of the "Social War," which was just ending, might cause the Athenians to believe they could not bear the burden of an additional tax.

[73] Thus, Xenophon tries to assuage the likely resistance of the richer citizens (for example, those who would be required to pay ten mina) by noting that, if they received three obols a day for their civic activities, they would be receiving the same "rate of return" as if they had lent the ten mina to a merchant or ship captain to engage in foreign commerce (3.9). Those who are assessed smaller amounts (Xenophon considers the cases of those who would have to pay five or one mina) would do correspondingly better.

[74] It is these latter (houses and shops for retail traders) that Xenophon specifically says should be located not only in the Piraeus but in "town," that is, in the "city center" of Athens (3.13). As noted, this is significant because it highlights Xenophon's disregard for the putatively polluting effects of a foreign presence in the heart of the city.

[75] "Il faut admettre que la cité athénienne est morte avant que les filons soient épuisés." Gauthier, *Commentaire historique*, 119.

[76] *Politics* 1, 1256b30–37.

[77] An invasion of Attica, for example, would require Athens to import more of its food than it usually did.

[78] It is intriguing to find that Keynes repeats Xenophon's arguments (albeit with respect to gold, the monetary commodity of his time) almost exactly: "Increased stock of gold . . . does not, as in other cases, have the effect of diminishing its marginal utility. Since the value of a house depends on its utility, every house which is built serves to diminish the prospective rents obtainable from further house-building and therefore lessens the attraction of further similar investment. . . . But the fruits of gold-mining do not suffer this disadvantage." John Maynard Keynes, *The General Theory of Employment, Interest, and Money* (London: Macmillan, 1936), 130. Keynes's argument, however, depends on the existence of substantial unemployment, in which case putting the additional gold supply in circulation will increase economic activity overall, rather than the price level. He admits that, under conditions of full employment, increases in the supply of gold could lead to inflation, i.e., a reduction in the value of gold.

[79] Here and elsewhere the reference is to adult male citizens (i.e., not including women and children).

[80] It would appear that Xenophon ignores another source of income from the silver mines, i.e., whatever royalty Athens charged the entrepreneurs for the right to remove silver ore from a given territory. Unfortunately, we cannot estimate the magnitude of the revenue that Athens would have received from this source, even in general terms. Gauthier (*Commentaire historique*, 114–15) discusses the various unknowns that preclude us from even the grossest estimate of the magnitude of this revenue.

[81] The Athenian population was divided into ten "tribes."

[82] Xenophon does not provide any information on, for example, the number of slaves working in the mines when they were at their peak. However, he notes that Nicias had one thousand slaves in the mines, a number that was regarded as huge, a sign of his tremendous wealth. Thucydides says (7.27) that, as a result of Spartan depredations in Attica, twenty thousand slaves fled Athenian control. Thus, it seems unlikely that Xenophon's target of sixty–ninety thousand slaves can be regarded as a serious proposition.

[83] For example, at 4.39, he admits that "everyone" will fear overcrowding the mines, and that it would be advisable to limit the number of men working in the mines on a year-by-year basis.

[84] The reasoning appears to be that, during the previous year, Athens' nonwar-related expenditures were roughly equal to its regular revenues (i.e., revenues from ordinary taxes, not including the wartime property tax, or *eisphorai*). Thus, if the regular revenues increase with the return of peace, but expenditures do not, there would be an excess available for investment.

[85] Xenophon oddly refers to this urban agglomeration as itself being a city (*polis*), implying political independence, although the context makes clear that it would remain part of Athens (4.50); see below.

[86] Thucydides (6.91.6–7) reports that this was done at the suggestion of Alcibiades.

[87] Thucydides 7.27.

[88] Thucydides 2.55.1.

[89] This is the only instance in which Xenophon makes reference to the fact that Athens will continue to have a navy; in general, of course, his entire argument is directed against traditional Athenian navalism.

[90] That Xenophon is thinking along these lines is indicated at 5.13, where Xenophon admits that, if wronged, Athens might have to fight back. But Xenophon claims that if Athens had been following a pacific policy, the aggressor would not find any allies for its war with Athens.

[91] Xenophon discusses a possible defensive Athenian military strategy in *The Skilled Cavalry Commander* (7.7–13). He proposes an essentially "Fabian" strategy of harassing an invader rather than confronting him head-on. This implies that Athens is likely to be weaker than the invader with respect to infantry; nevertheless, it differs from the Themistoclean-Periclean strategy of ceding the territory of Attica to the invader outright.

[92] Thucydides 2.35–46.

[93] That military preparedness is part of Xenophon's scheme is indicated at 5.51–52, where he argues that the ability to provide pay for those engaged in military training and guard duty will raise proficiency and make the city more prepared for war.

[94] This (to conservative eyes) pleasing picture masks the fact that Xenophon's proposals are essentially subversive of the "old" Athens. For example, we recall that Xenophon had earlier suggested that metics be allowed to enroll in the cavalry, the aristocratic military unit par excellence (2.5).

[95] He also avoids imitating the apparent mistake he made prior to joining Cyrus's attempt to replace his brother on the Persian throne, as recounted in the *Anabasis*. Having been advised by Socrates to seek the advice of the oracle, he failed to ask whether he should join Cyrus, but limited himself to asking to which gods he should sacrifice to ensure his success. Socrates criticized him for this failure. *Anabasis* 3.1.4–7.

[96] The use of slaves as rowers was not unprecedented in Athens, but presumably involved offering them a reward.

[97] In any case, if Athens is to win the goodwill of the Greeks by means of its "manifest efforts" on behalf of peace, on sea and on land (5.10), then it would presumably need at least enough of a navy to deal with piracy.

[98] *On the Peace* 130.

[99] See Aristotle's discussion of the various forms of democracy, cited above.

[100] At the same time, as noted, Xenophon appears to suggest that the slaves could be sufficiently well treated so as to make them recruitable as soldiers in war, let alone

not a security threat. Even in the light of Xenophon's blurring of the distinction between free and slave (as discussed above), this seems far-fetched. Does Xenophon envision that the slaves could become the equivalent of an industrial proletariat?

[101] In this connection, we recall Xenophon's strange statement (see note 38 above) to the effect that his proposal would give rise in the Laurion area to a densely populated city (*polis*). The problem is that the word *polis* refers not to an urban agglomeration, but to a politically independent (sovereign) "city-state" (to use modern language.) For the silver mines to serve as a source of revenue for Athens, Laurion would have to remain part of the Athenian *polis*, rather than become the nucleus of a new *polis*. But does Xenophon envision an actual new *polis*, that is, an industrial-commercial city with capitalists and workers (and slaves) instead of aristocrats and common people?

6. THE SKILLED CAVALRY COMMANDER

Unless otherwise noted, I have translated the text as presented in the Oxford edition, E. C. Marchant, Xenophon, *Opuscula*, vol. 5 of *Opera Omnia* (Oxford: Clarendon Press, 1920).

[1] The title of the work, *Hipparchikos*, is an adjective related to the Greek words for "horse" (or "horseman") and "ruler" (*hippos* or *hippeus* and *archon*). The suffix of this particular adjective, *-ikos*, refers to a skill or art. *Hipparchikos* does not mean merely "cavalry commander" (*hipparchos*) but "[the man] skilled in ruling cavalry" or "[account of the] skill of ruling cavalry." Xenophon's titles most similar to *Hipparchikos* are *Kunēgetikos, Oikonomikos,* and *Hieron ē Turannikos,* for they too imply skills or arts and could modify an understood "man" or "account." (*On Horsemanship* [*Hippikēs*] refers to the skill required to ride well, not to the person who possesses it.)

[2] This clause could also be translated "if the gods are propitious." It does not promise divine favor.

[3] "Horseman" (*hippeus*) is linked by etymology to the word translated as "cavalry." *Hippeus* could also be translated as "knight," as it commonly is in the title of Aristophanes' play, *Knights*.

[4] Xenophon's essay makes several points that applied directly to Athens in about 365 BC. Although there were supposed to be 1,000 horsemen, the cavalry at this time had dwindled to about 650. At one drachma per day per knight, the cost of a force of this size would be about forty talents, the figure referred to in 1.19.

[5] Xenophon's *On Horsemanship* explains this in some detail.

[6] This is the first use of the important Greek adjective *kalos*. I translate it (and only it) as "noble," "beautiful," or "fine," save in 7.3, where I use "fair," and 9.6, where I use "honors." When translating its related adverb, I also try to use a word sharing the root "beautiful," "noble," or "fine," as in the next sentence.

[7] The Greek word is *eikos*, and it may mean either "likely" or "fitting." It thus allows an important ambiguity between what probably is the case and what would be fitting if it were the case. A beautiful example of this ambiguity occurs in the very last section of the *Hipparchikos*. Except here and at 4.20, I translate it as "likely."

[8] The Greek word is *phylarchos*, and its more literal meaning is "ruler of a tribe (*phylē*)." It thus helps remind the Greek reader that each of the ten Athenian tribes provided eighty to one hundred horsemen and a leader for them. In contrast to "colonel,"

the Greek word calls attention to a political division that underlies the cavalry; this point is made even clearer in 1.21.

[9] I presume he means that fear of Athenian political authorities might help the troops be more willing to exercise regularly and be more courageous in facing the enemy, for example. See 1.13 for a simple example. See also 7.7.

[10] Xenophon refers in this way to his essay or to parts of it also in 3.1 and 9.2.

[11] That is, if you show that you cannot be bought off by the most powerful, you thereby show you cannot be bought off by the less powerful.

[12] Literally, "those who are authoritative over them."

[13] This passage may allude to the case of Pheidippides in Aristophanes' *Clouds* 73–86, where the young man's enthusiasm for horses and racing led his family to the brink of financial ruin. Xenophon presents cavalry service under a good leader as a possible solution to this problem, whereas in Aristophanes' comedy the solution attempted was to send the young man to study with Socrates. Disaster ensued.

[14] Or "more prudently." The root of the Greek word is *sōphrosunē*, which Xenophon's Socrates identifies with wisdom in *Memorabilia* 3.9.4. Its only other appearance in this text is at 4.14.

[15] Literally, "of the weight of a mina," which was a unit of currency.

[16] That is, I think, the hooves will grow large and strong, the best ancient approximation to horseshoes. See also *On Horsemanship* 4.4–5.

[17] If the horsemen were paid a drachma per day, as historical sources suggest the Athenians were (partly to help defray the cost of maintaining their horses), an expenditure of forty talents would support about 650 horsemen. A talent was six thousand drachmae.

[18] I will often use words cognate with "ambition" to translate the cognates of *philotimia*, "love of honor."

[19] Other sources suggest that hoplites received two obols per day and horsemen received a drachma, which was three times as much. They also received an indemnity to maintain their horses. This difficult passage suggests that the colonels could insist that their troops use some of these funds to arm themselves and their horses; thus, the colonels could insist that their troops be well armed without having to contribute to the expense of making them so. See also 9.5.

[20] I translate the Greek word literally. It is clear that this group was under the direct command of the cavalry commander, but it is not clear whether he used them especially for communication, for protection, or for some other purpose.

[21] I imagine that the spectacles referred to are like those described in chapter 3.

[22] On the usefulness of contests and prizes, see also *Hellenica* 4.2.7, *Hiero* 9. 3–11, and *Education of Cyrus* 1.6.18. The question of who awards the prizes is stressed in the *Hiero*, as is the parallel question of the distribution of punishments for those who fall short.

[23] The Dionysia was a major Athenian festival devoted to the god Dionysus; it provided an important occasion for competitive performances of tragedy and comedy. The "Twelve" are the twelve Olympian gods and goddesses.

[24] This temple was apparently at the foot of the Acropolis and was involved in celebrating the famous mysteries dedicated to Demeter and Persephone.

[25] The Athenians had two cavalry commanders, not one. See also 3.11.

[26] Literally, "human being (*anthrōpos*)," not "the people (*dēmos*)" as a political class.

[27] With their columns offset, the two groups race at one another but pass through each other's lines, with the dramatic effect of a bull passing under a matador's cape.

[28] Xenophon perhaps refers to Protagoras's doctrine that "man is the measure of all things," which is examined in Plato's *Theaetetus* (see especially 151d7–152a4 and

183b7–c4). Xenophon's curious passage invites doubt about whether men are good judges of how sore horses' backs might be and even whether a particular man's experience of "hard work" can be generalized to others. (Xenophon's Cambyses expressed the different view that labors are felt to be lighter by those in positions of honor than by ordinary soldiers who do not enjoy this extra reward [*Education of Cyrus* 1.6.25].)

29 Consider the story of Araspas at *Education of Cyrus* 6.1.31–44 and 6.3.11–20.

30 The ruler of five is thus responsible for leading his short file up to the front whenever it is opportune to change the order from one that is long and narrow to a more shallow order with a broader front.

31 Perhaps the stealing is done primarily by stealth, while the seizing is done primarily by the sudden use of force. Xenophon is probably thinking of seizing advantageous positions as well as of property. Consider *Education of Cyrus* 3.2.1–11.

32 I translate the MSS. An emendation reads, "snatches up whatever it has."

33 See *Education of Cyrus* 6.3.29–30, where Cyrus used the women and their carriages to increase the apparent size of his outnumbered army, while also making it more difficult to encircle.

34 Literally, "with the god." Similar phrases occur at 6.1, 6.6 (but in the plural), 7.3 (twice), 7.14, and 9.3 (in the plural). Xenophon defends his use of this phrase in 9.8–9.

35 The Greek of the purpose clause is emended differently by different editors. I translate the Oxford text, which keeps the verb but changes "chance" from the object to the subject; the Bude changes the verb but keeps chance as the direct object. It would read, "in order that we might seize chance." The very last phrase appears also in 1.2, and the note there explains its ambiguity.

36 Hoplites were the heavily armed infantry in a Greek army. The enemy in question is identified as the Boeotians in 7.3. Thebes was the leading city of Boeotia.

37 Or a "complete" or "consummate" man: *apotetelesmenos anēr*.

38 I have translated the MS, but Marchant proposes this emendation: "that he be capable of thinking in advance for himself" (*pronoein* for *ponein*).

39 The end of the sentence appears to be lost. Perhaps "this is a manageable task" was the thought. The task of bringing people and goods to safety in case of attack is also fraught with danger, as the episode described at *Hellenica* 7.5.15–17 makes clear.

40 A few words appear to have dropped out of the Greek text. My conjecture follows that of Marchant's Oxford text.

41 See *Education of Cyrus* 1.5.11 for a similar contrast.

42 I have followed the Oxford text in transposing the negatives here. The MSS read, "have not exercised so much that they get winded in their hard work."

43 So too at *Education of Cyrus* 6.2.32.

44 I here translate the MSS. Editors move "with the help of the gods" to the previous sentence.

45 The word for "foreign," *xenos*, can also mean "hireling" or "mercenary."

46 The text in this clause is variously emended by editors. There is no doubt that some are so averse to cavalry service as to be willing to buy their way out of it.

47 Orphans enjoyed some immunity from service. The text suggests they might still be taxed to fund the cavalry.

48 That is, men with an intense dislike or hatred of the enemy, as might be the case with the Plataeans, for example, who were driven out of Boeotia (*Hellenica* 6.3.1).

49 Closely related passages include *Education of Cyrus* 1.6.3–6 and *Memorabilia* 1.1.9, 19; 1.4.18; and 3.9.14–15.

50 "Prudent" and its cognates are the closest thing to an exception. They appear eleven times, far more than any other virtue. "Wiser" appears once: men should be "wiser" than "prudent" animals, like wolves and kites, which know when to attack

and when to retreat (4.20). Even a virtue we might expect, courage, is mentioned only once (4.13).

⁵¹ Contrast, for example, the open and vigorous critiques of law by the hero of the *Education of Cyrus* (1.3.16–18) and by a notorious student of Socrates in the *Memorabilia* (1.2.39–46).

⁵² Contrast this restraint with the bold opening sections of the *Education of Cyrus*, for example, which promise a solution to the problem of stable rule in general.

⁵³ The first sentence uses a verb in the second person singular; it also uses the pronoun "yourself." It thus appears that the essay is written to a single individual, one who is or is about to become a cavalry commander. The second person singular is used also in 1.2, 8–12, 17, 20–21, 25, and perhaps six other occasions in later chapters. There are, nonetheless, passages that are addressed to a wider audience.

⁵⁴ And yet the first sentence refers to ruling in general, not to commanding a cavalry in particular. So too with chapter 6, 7.1, and several other passages referring to "rulers" rather than "cavalry commanders." And the text frequently discusses subjects like obedience, which are important to rulers of all kinds. It also turns out that the cavalry commander should know how to lead infantry troops and "teach" the city (5.13).

⁵⁵ Prudence is vitally important for the commander. See especially 6.1 and 7.1. The commander's knowledge must also extend to the terrain best suited for cavalry and how to deceive the enemy, for example. Verbs pertaining to knowledge are frequent throughout the essay. But Xenophon's emphasis falls first on the importance of using one's knowledge, not on the intellectual challenge of being a ruler.

⁵⁶ In stressing the insufficiency of knowledge, Xenophon may appear to part company with his teacher (cf. *Memorabilia* 3.1.4; 3.9.10).

⁵⁷ Because Xenophon speaks here of ruling in general, it is easier to see that he departs from one of his teacher's lines of argument (*Memorabilia* 3.4.4–6).

⁵⁸ Even so astute a student as Xenophon's Cyrus was surprised to learn that rulers need to concern themselves with the material conditions of their rule as well as the ruling itself (1.6.9–11), and he too later stressed the importance of such little details as straps (6.2.32). On this point Xenophon follows his teacher (*Memorabilia* 3.3.3).

⁵⁹ This and other translated passages in this essay may differ in minor ways from the preceding full translation of the *Hipparchikos*, for I have adjusted them to suit the immediate context.

⁶⁰ Cambyses' advice to his son also begins and ends with the gods. His theology is often similar to that in the *Commander*, especially in its concluding emphasis on our inability to compel the gods to reveal their secrets. *Education of Cyrus* 1.6.1–5, 44–46.

⁶¹ See especially *Memorabilia* 1.1.9, 19, 1.4.18; 4.3.16–18, 4.7.10; *Oeconomicus* 5.18–20; *Apology of Socrates* 11–13.

⁶² Similar phrases occur at 6.1, 6.6 (but in the plural), 7.3 (twice), and 7.14. His defense is not so much of this exact phrase as of the importance of the gods to the commander.

⁶³ For a similar passage, see *Education of Cyrus* 1.6.3. "More likely" (*eikos de māllon*) might also mean "more fitting," which would dilute even further the faint hope of divine counsel that Xenophon here raises.

⁶⁴ Consider the story of Menelaus and Proteus for the case of a mortal who actually compels a god to help him (*Odyssey* 4.351–592).

⁶⁵ The essay does not indicate that the gods either demand justice of us, for example, or reward it.

⁶⁶ Compare Aristotle's suggestion that it promotes the health of pregnant women to have them walk regularly to appropriate shrines (*Politics* 1335b12–6).

[67] It appears from the present passage and from 9.3–7 that Athens' public spirit has waned. Chapters 7 and 8 indicate that Athens is being threatened by its powerful neighbor Thebes, as other sources report Athens was in and around 357.

[68] See also *Education of Cyrus* 1.6.19. Although elevated in tone, the intriguing first sentence of the *Commander* emphasizes the importance of effective speech; it does not call for honesty.

[69] See especially 6.1; 8.21–22; and, again, 9.3–6. The role of the peers in the successes recorded in the *Education of Cyrus* shows that even a political genius needs good soldiers to start with; his "education" of the commoners shows how (and to what extent) a leader can, under some circumstances, make good troops on his own.

[70] *Education of Cyrus* 2.2.23–28.

[71] The most important passages are 1.7, 24; 2.2–9; 6.1–6; 8.21–22; and 9.3.

[72] Socrates' mostly parallel discussion of obedience with a newly elected cavalry commander points explicitly to the need to teach that it is both more noble and safer for soldiers to be obedient (*Memorabilia* 3.3.8–10). But is it?

[73] Consider *Education of Cyrus* 4.1.8.

[74] 1.11, 22–23, 19; 2.2; 8.7, 22; 9.3, 6.

[75] Shakespeare's Falstaff is the most memorable such doubter: *Henry IV*, Part I, 5.1.127–39.

[76] 2.3; contrast *Education of Cyrus* 3.3.41–42. Consider, however, that the mobility of cavalry troops also makes it difficult to use rearguard troops to force the ones in the front to fight.

[77] See *Education of Cyrus* 1.6.21–22 for a closely related discussion. Among other things, this discussion considers compulsion as an alternate route to obedience.

[78] Xenophon himself had to beat a soldier into obedience. *Anabasis of Cyrus* 5.8.1–26.

[79] In contrast to the *Commander*, this is the main subject of the conversation between Socrates and the newly elected cavalry commander in *Memorabilia* 3.3.

7. On Horsemanship

Édouard Delebecque edited the Greek text used for this translation: Xénophon, *De l'art équestre* (Paris: Les Belles Lettres, 1978). The notes below indicate where he records manuscript variations worth mentioning. I follow his designation of the two best manuscripts as A and B. I have also consulted with profit the translations and notes of J. S. Watson, *Xenophon's Minor Works* (London: George Bell and Sons, 1891), A. Nyland, *The Art of Horsemanship: Xenophon and Other Classical Writers* (Lexington, KY, 2010); J. K. Anderson, *Ancient Greek Horsemanship* (Berkeley: University of California Press, 1961); Morris H. Morgan, *The Art of Horsemanship* (Boston: Little, Brown, 1893); and E. C. Marchant, *On the Art of Horsemanship*, in *Xenophon in Seven Volumes*, vol. 7, *Scripta Minora* (Cambridge, MA: Harvard University Press, 1971).

[1] Xenophon uses the "royal we" here at the beginning, but not consistently throughout this treatise. The verb *hippeuein*, translated as "to be in the cavalry," is also translated below as "to be a horseman," or simply, "to ride horses." One could also translate it as "to be a knight (*hippeus*)." The word *hippos* (horse) is the root of the feminine adjective used as a noun, *hippikē*, "skilled riding," or "horsemanship," in the title of this work, *Peri Hippikēs*. Xenophon was presumably a member of the political class of "knights." We have no knowledge of his serving in the Athenian cavalry or in

the position of cavalry commander in his native city (cf. *Memorabilia* 3.3). He recounts in the *Anabasis* that he embarked on an expedition to Persia with several of his own horses as a personal friend to one of the Greek generals hired by Cyrus the Younger. He hastily formed a successful Greek cavalry after disaster befell that army.

² A omits the name "Simon," about whom little is known outside of this text. The Eleusinion was a temple precinct in Athens devoted to Demeter and Persephone (the goddess of agriculture and consort of Hades, and her daughter, both worshipped in the cult of the Eleusinian mysteries). This temple was perhaps near the Acropolis, and at the starting point of the procession along the "Sacred Way" to the town of Eleusis during the celebration of the mysteries.

³ A has "how someone may deceive least" in horse buying.

⁴ I translate *pōlos* as "colt." However, the Greek word can refer to a young un-trained horse of either sex; cf. Euripides, *Andromache* 621. The English word "colt" usually refers to an uncastrated male under three or four years, but the term can be used more loosely. Anderson (*Ancient Greek Horsemanship*, 39) states that working horses in ancient Greece were generally male and that castration was rarely prac-ticed, although Xenophon does appear to approve of that practice (*Education of Cyrus* 7.5.62). I generally use the pronouns "it" for the horse or colt and "he" for the rider or the groom. *Anabainō*, the verb, translated as "mounted," means more generally "to ascend," as in the title *Anabasis*. The related word, *anabatēs*, is translated as "rider."

⁵ "Beautiful" is *kalos*, also translated below as "noble," "fine," or "kind." The word can refer to both moral beauty and physical beauty. Its first appearance in this treatise in a sentence with *chresthai* and *agathos* is fitting, since the relation between the beauti-ful or noble (*kalos*) and the good (*agathos*), and hence between the noble and the useful (*chrēstos*), is a recurring Socratic theme in Xenophon's writings. "Use" translates *chres-thai*, rendered below also as "manage," "deal with," or "treat," "utilize," "employ." It is a common yet important word for Xenophon, as is indicated by this very passage, which implies that there is both an overlap and a distinction between *kalos* and *agathos* related to benefit or use. Socrates explores this ambiguity in his quest to understand the gentleman (*kalos k'agathos*; *Oeconomicus* 6.11–16).

⁶ "Horn of its hoof" (*onuchai*) is distinct from "hooves" (*hoplai*). *Onychai* can mean "talons," "claws," or "fingernails." "Differ from greatly" is another translation for "far superior to" (*diapherein*).

⁷ Delebecque deletes "or whether they are flat," which is in B but not A.

⁸ "Swallow" (*chelidōn*) is a literal translation. English riders calls this the "frog," the rubbery interior sole of the horse's foot surrounded by the nail of the hoof. "Put the same weight on" (*homoiōs bainō*) is literally "walk evenly." He seems to mean that the soft part of the foot bears too much weight, as he thinks happens in human beings whose knees knock.

⁹ Xenophon does not name here these short bones of the front leg (called pasterns) that angle down toward the hoof from the bone called the "fetlock" (*kunepodon*), which angles backward and in turn attaches to the more upright "cannon" bones (*knemon*; also translated as "shins" below in reference to human beings, 7.2, 6).

¹⁰ "Knotty" is thought to mean "varicose." The "skin will pull away" perhaps means "separate from the leg, causing an abscess." The word translated as "ligament" (*perone*) can mean the "small bone of an arm or leg," the "radius" or "fibula." There is no secondary bone in this part of the horse, but the tendon may have seemed analo-gous to the radius or fibula in humans.

¹¹ "Flexible" (*hugrō*) might also be translated as "supple" or "fluid." In this sentence Xenophon for the first time uses a verb form that refers to the reader as "you" (sing.). In 1.3 Xenophon referred to "one" or "someone" who is making the assessment of the

young horse. It also first becomes clear here that Xenophon is "moving up" from the hooves, pasterns, fetlocks, and cannons of the front legs of the horse, rather than the rear legs, for only the front legs have something resembling "knees" (*gonata*), or a joint bending forward, on the lower leg. The equivalent lower joint bends backward in the horse's hind legs. The word translated as "when it is ridden" (*hippeuein*) is also translated below as "to exercise" (one's horse).

12 In other words, like thick biceps in a man (*anēr*). Xenophon calls this part of the horse's front leg a "thigh." English riders call it a "forearm."

13 "Act up" is literally "act violently" or "use force" (*biazesthai*). It refers to the horse resisting its bridle.

14 "Horses with jaws of uneven [sensitivity]" (*heterognathoi*) have one side of the mouth more hardened than the other. Such a horse tends to pull its head more to the hardened side because of insensitivity to the bridle-bit there, thus leading to difficulties in training, even obstinacy. See 3.5 and 6.9 below.

15 There is comparable language regarding Socrates' eyes and nostrils at *Symposium* 5.5–6.

16 Equestrians call "shoulder points" (*akromia*) the "withers," or "acromion process." What *prosphusis* ("point of attachment") means is unclear, perhaps it should be read as "grip" or "place for the rider to cling to the shoulders and body." It can mean literally "grown to."

17 "As for the back" is an addition to the text, accepted by Delebecque.

18 The "loins" (*osphus*) are the lower back; cf. 11.2–3 below.

19 The flank is the hollow part between the rib cage and stomach.

20 "Hip joints" (*ischia*) or "haunches," the points of the hip.

21 "By a wide gap" is literally in "a broad line" (*grammē*).

22 By "crouching" (*hupobainō*) the horse makes it easier for the rider to mount. But if the "fiercer" applies to the crouching as well as the riding, perhaps *hupobainō* refers here to the horse "squatting" to lift up its front legs for show (see 11.2–3 below).

23 The ankle joint or hock (*astragalon*) is the large joint of the hind leg that bends rearward, as one sees also in a dog.

24 "Good" (*euchrestos*) could also be translated as "useful" or "decent." "Ugly" (*aischros*) can be translated as "shameful."

25 See note 1 above on "horsemen" (*hippeis*), which could also be translated as "cavalrymen" or "knights." It signifies high social rank as well as a military class. "Character" (*hexis*) might also be translated as "condition," as it could refer to either the moral or physical state of a person.

26 Alternatively, "his slave for apprenticeship." The same word (*pais*) could be used for "child," "boy," or "slave." See Delebecque, *De l'art équestre*, 45. The word translated as "put down in writing" (*sungraphein*) is the same as for "writing a treatise" above in 1.1.

27 "Notes" or "reminders" (*hupomnēmata*) is also used below at 3.1 and 12.14 with reference to Xenophon's writing this treatise.

28 Cf. *Oeconomicus* 13.7. "Home" (*oikia*); "horse groom" (*hippokomos*).

29 A has "pebbles" (*psēphois*), B has "sounds" (*psophois*).

30 An alternative translation: "It suffices in my opinion as a private individual (*idiotēs*), to tell (one) to do this much." *Idiotēs* can mean "private individual" or "amateur," as opposed to a professional or a public official, and, in this sentence, it could refer to Xenophon or to his advisee.

31 Xenophon mentions selling here, when the stated purpose here and above (1.1) is buying a warhorse. It is unclear whether he means to imply reselling or horse trading, or simply striking a good bargain with the seller.

[32] See note 14 on 1.9 above and note 58 on 6.9 below. If its jaws are unevenly sensitive, the horse yields more readily in one direction and is more obstinate (literally, "unjust," *adikos*) in the other. "Fettering" (*pede*) is an exercise making the horse ride in figure eights, allowing for equal exercise on both sides of the body.

[33] Cf. *Oeconomicus* 11.17.

[34] B has "self-controlled," instead of "strong."

[35] "From horseback" is literally "from itself" (*apo heauton*).

[36] "Signs of willfulness" is literally "noddings" (*neumata*) in A and B. Delebecque accepts an emendation, "wheeling" (*dineumata*).

[37] "Driving" (*elasis*) is a noun related to the verb translated as "galloping" (*elaunō*).

[38] "Fine" is "beautiful" or "noble" (*kalon*). Words related to *oikos* are translated as both "home" (*oikade*) and "estate" (*oikia*) in this sentence. Since managing the *oikos* is the subject of the *Oeconomicus*, *On Horsemanship* could be understood as a supplement to that work, as well as to Xenophon's *The Skilled Cavalry Commander* and his political works.

[39] Dangers of war, most obviously, although hunting and riding itself are risky.

[40] "Throwing its food out" translates *ekkomizō*. It could also mean "carry out," rendering the possible alternative "when the horse is not furnished with food." The meaning of this passage is unclear, and has been rendered differently by those knowledgeable about horses. See J. K. Anderson, "Notes on Some Points in Xenophon's ΠΕΡΙ ΙΠΠΙΚΗΣ," *Journal of Hellenic Studies* 80 (1960): 1–2.

[41] "Body" is an emendation; the MSS have "mouth." "Weakness" could also be translated as "lack of vigor" (*arrōstia*).

[42] "As large as can be grasped" (*amphidochmōn*) is an emendation. MSS have "cut on both sides" (*amphitomōn*). It is not perfectly clear whether the stones would weigh a mina or the load would cost a mina, for it is a unit of weight as well as currency. Anderson (*Ancient Greek Horsemanship*, 89) translates "rounded oval stones of about a pound's weight."

[43] "Bother by flies" (*muōpizein*) here and at 2.3 is the same verb as "use a spur" (10.1).

[44] See note 8 above on 1.3. The "swallow" is vulnerable to injury or pain if one rides on rough surfaces.

[45] The horse's mouth must be tender so that it remains sensitive to the bridle-bit, by which one signals and controls the horse.

[46] Delebecque, with A, has the verb "to educate" in the perfect tense here. "Man" is *anēr*. *Anthrōpos* is translated as "human being."

[47] The MSS have "move" (*kinōn*), instead of "scrape" (*knōn*).

[48] "At being bridled" is missing in A.

[49] The "seat" (*hedras*) is the back of the horse where the rider sits.

[50] A and B have the singular "god," but the verb "gave" is in the plural form in the next clause. Delebecque has "gods."

[51] A Greek rider (*anabatēs*) typically mounted by grasping the mane and lifting himself up.

[52] "Rule out" (*aphaireō*) is translated as "omit" in 1.1.

[53] "Brush down" (*psēchō*) and words related to it could also be translated as "curry" or "groom"; see 5.1, 3, 10.

[54] "Wrongly" is *adikos*.

[55] "In close order" (*athroi*) for battle, or just "assembled" or "collected in a group."

[56] "Withers," the shoulder blades. See note 80 on 10.6 below on the mouthpiece (*stomion*) and the bridle or bridle-bit (*chalinos*).

[57] "Headstall" (*kekruphalos*) is part of the headpiece (*koruphaion*) of the bridle (*chalinos*).

[58] See note 14 on 1.9 and note 32 on 3.5 above on the importance of mouth sensitivity in the horse.

[59] Cf. *The Skilled Cavalry Commander* 1.17.

[60] Another possible reading noted by Delebeque is "the same horse serves different people at different times."

[61] Using the spear somewhat like a pole for vaulting.

[62] "Ugly" or "shameful" (*aischros*). The word translated here as "shin" (*knēmon*) is the same as that for the cannon bone of the horse; see 1.5.

[63] The MSS have "go up" (*anabainō*), which Delebecque emends to "reaches up" (*anateinō*).

[64] Xenophon switches in the same sentence from one term for "left" (*aristeron*) to another (*euōnuma*). The MSS have begin "on the incline (*epiklēsis*)" or "toward the bend" (or "inclination," *klisis*). Delebecque has the emendation "at first bound (of the gallop)" (*episkelisis*). Xenophon is describing how the rider may direct the horse to lead the gallop with the left leg, which an armed horseman (with weapons in his right hand) may find more convenient, according to Anderson (*Ancient Greek Horsemanship*, 104).

[65] A has "again" (*authis*), while B has "suddenly" (*exaiphnēs*).

[66] "Dismount" (*katabasis*), the opposite of *anabasis*.

[67] "Uphill" (*orthia*) is an emendation. The MSS have *oreia* or *horeia*, which are difficult to construe; the adjective *oreios* means "of the mountains," and *oreion* is "mare's tail." "Thoroughly" or "as a whole" (*katholou*) with Delebecque and the MSS. Some editors delete the word or transpose it to the next sentence to modify "more useful."

[68] "Gathered together" (*hathroō*) could also be translated as "collected" or "in close order." Part of this sentence is difficult to construe and is emended in various ways by editors. Delbecque's reading (*an hen ei pēi*) means "if the hind parts are somehow one." I follow Brodaeus, "if it leaves the hind parts out" (*an ekleipē*).

[69] This is the reading of A and B. An alternate reading: "they should be encouraged by learning."

[70] "Oppressed" could be more literally "weighed down." *Kalon* ("kind" or "fine") is the reading of A and B, while other MSS have "bad" (*kakon*) or "not fine" (*ou kalon*). If the reading adopted is correct, the action is presumably beautiful, fine, or kind on the part of the rider because he is thinking of the comfort of the horse. In the previous sentence the rider was thinking of how to avoid falling off. In the next sentence the comfort of the horse seems less important than the safety of both horse and rider.

[71] "Fine" is *kalos*.

[72] "With the spear" is not in B.

[73] In this section "deal with" is *chrēsthai*. See note 5 on 1.1 above. "Ruin" (*diaphtheirai*) could also be translated as "corrupt," and "prove" (*apodeiknuein*) is translated below as "show." The word for "horseman" here is *hippeus* rather than *hippikos*.

[74] "Brief" is the reading of the manuscript, defended by Delebecque; Brodaeus changes it to "slow."

[75] "Agitation" (*tarachos*) can also mean military or political disturbance, confusion, or tumult.

[76] B has "most competitive" (*philoneikotatos*) instead of "most victory loving" (*philonikotatos*).

[77] That is, holding on with the legs.

[78] The MSS have "posture" (*schēmata*) instead of the emendation "mouths" (*stomata*).

[79] "Making itself fierce" or "behaving hotly or spiritedly" (*gorgoumenos*). Words related to the adjective *gorgos* are translated as "fierce" and its variants, to distinguish it from words related to *thumos* (spiritedness).

[80] The whole bridle (*chalinos*) consists of a headstall, bit, and reins, and the noun form is related to the verb "to bridle" (*chalinoō*). Xenophon sometimes refers to a mouthpiece (*stomion*), but here and elsewhere he uses the word *chalinos* to refer to the bridle-bit, which can be smooth or rough, and have rings hanging down from it. Delebecque offers useful diagrams of the bridle and bit used by Greek horsemen. Anderson (*Ancient Greek Horsemanship*, 40–78) discusses the subject at length.

[81] Or, according to other editors, "by wrapping and tightening." Nyland renders it "by keeping it loose or tight" (*Art of Horsemanship*, 52). Editors disagree on the text here.

[82] A has "to be ridden" (*hippasasthai*). Delebecque follows B, "to stop" (*pausasthai*). Rather than "pat" (*thōpein*), perhaps "wheedle" or "caress." The word can mean to "flatter" or "fawn over." Marchant translates "coax him as when you want to stop."

[83] A has "pressed" (*piestheis*), B has "persuaded" (*peistheis*).

[84] "Display" (*kallōpismos*), "adornment," or "beautification."

[85] "Under" (*hupo*) is the reading of B; Delebecque follows A, "above" (*huper*).

[86] "He has" (*echonta*) is the reading of the MSS; an emendation is "willingly" (*hekonta*).

[87] For "depicted as riding on such horses," Delebecque adopts the reading of B, while A has "depicted as riding horses with such a form."

[88] "Admirable" (*agaston*) is an emendation accepted by Delebecque. The MSS have "good" (*agathon*).

[89] "Phylarch" and "hipparch" are transliterations for "colonel" and "cavalry commander." See *The Skilled Cavalry Commander* 1.22.

[90] Cf. *Memorabilia* 3.10.9–16, where Socrates visits a breastplate maker.

[91] A greave (*knemis*) is a piece of armor or legging covering the leg from the knee to the ankle.

[92] The "frontlet" protects the forehead. Marchant, following Weiske, changes "side protectors" (*parapleuridia*) to "thigh-protectors" (*paramēridia*). Cf. *Education of Cyrus* 6.4.1.

[93] Two different words for "saddlecloth" are used: *ephippion* in the prior sentence, and *epochon* here. "Back of the horse" is literally the "seat" (*hedron*) where the rider sits on the horse.

[94] The curved knife (*kopis*) is Persian; the saber (*machaira*) was used by both Spartans and Persians.

[95] Spears are longer than javelins.

[96] "Notes" (*hupomnemata*); see note 27 on 2.2 above, as well as *The Skilled Cavalry Commander* 1.9; 3.1; 9.2.

[97] For example, see Nyland, *Art of Horsemanship*. References in the body of this essay are to chapter and section of *On Horsemanship* (*Peri Hippikēs*), unless otherwise identified. Abbreviations that refer to the works of Leo Strauss are noted at first citation.

[98] In the *Anabasis*, Xenophon indicates that he brought at least a few horses with him to Persia, and that he was particularly attached to one of them (3.3.19; 7.8.6). He does not mention in *On Horsemanship* the unpleasant topic of when one must kill one's horse (*Hiero* 6.15; cf. *Anabasis* 4.5.13).

[99] Xenophon notes an overlap between friendship and political allegiance (*Memorabilia* 2.6.17). And his *Oeconomicus* as a whole reveals how a regime can influence life within the household.

[100] Xenophon's other equestrian work, *The Skilled Cavalry Commander* (*Hipparchikos*), is more political in tone and includes many references to Athens. *On Horsemanship* only occasionally alludes to Athens or even to Greeks (1.1; 12.3; 6.12; 8.6).

[101] These mentions of horsemanship in the Socratic writings can be in fascinating contexts. For example, Xenophon uses a bridle shop as the setting for his single overview of Socrates' course of education in the *Memorabilia* (4.2.1); Leo Strauss, *Xenophon's Socrates* (Ithaca, NY: Cornell University Press, 1972; South Bend, IN: St. Augustine's Press, 1998), 95 (hereafter cited as *XS*). Also, the setting of Xenophon's *Symposium* is a party after the horse race of the Great Panathenaia (1.1). At the conclusion of that party several of the men mount their horses and ride home. Without mentioning Socrates, *On Horsemanship* has a few slight allusions to Xenophon's Socratic writings. The description of the eyes and nostrils of a good horse at 1.9–10 could remind us of Socrates' physical description of himself in the *Symposium* (5.5–6). We will discuss below Socrates' comparing himself to a horse at *Oeconomicus* 11.5, as well as the parallel between *On Horsemanship* 3.7 and *Oeconomicus* 11.17. Since the horse is one of the most important possessions of a gentleman, and horsemanship is a necessary art for him to learn, this treatise may be a supplement to Xenophon's treatise on good husbandry (*Oeconomicus* 3.8).

[102] *Memorabilia* 1.11–16. See also Cicero, *Tusculan Disputations* 5.10; Leo Strauss, *Xenophon's Socratic Discourse* (Ithaca, NY: Cornell University Press, 1970; South Bend, IN: St. Augustine's Press, 1998), 83 (hereafter cited as *XSD*); Leo Strauss, *Natural Right and History* (Chicago: University of Chicago Press, 1950), 120.

[103] This section is indebted to Leo Strauss's discussion of the titles of Xenophon's works, especially in Strauss, *On Tyranny* (1948; Chicago: University of Chicago Press, 2000), 31–33, 107nn1 and 2 (hereafter cited as *OT*); cf. *XSD* 84; *XS* 3). Strauss published no analysis of *Peri Hippikēs*, and he mentions it only in two early writings on Xenophon: Strauss, "The Spirit of Sparta or the Taste of Xenophon," *Social Research* 6.4 (1939): 502–36, 508n5, 510n1 (hereafter cited as *SSTX*); and *OT* 107n2. Strauss (*XS* 59) may intend to allude to *On Horsemanship* when he refers to *The Skilled Cavalry Commander* in his treatment of *Memorabilia* 3.3.

[104] This explicit link between two of Xenophon's works is unique, although many of his works are related to one another.

[105] In contrast, for example, Xenophon used *Oikonomikos* instead of *Peri Oikonomikēs* (cf. *XSD* 87–89). The feminine form of adjectives such as *hippikē* and *oikonomikē* could signify the feminine practitioner of the art instead of the art itself, but Xenophon clearly writes *On Horsemanship* for gentlemen (2.1). In his argument that the *Oeconomicus* is a response to the *Clouds*, Strauss draws our attention to a connection between *On Horsemanship* and the *Oeconomicus*. (Strauss [*XSD* 111–12, 163–65] identifies a quotation of *Clouds* 32, "give the horse a roll and lead it home," at *Oeconomicus* 11.18; cf. *The Skilled Cavalry Commander* 5.3). If only to direct us to the *Clouds*, Xenophon chooses to connect horsemanship in the *Oeconomicus* to the householder's expertise in farming and the education of his wife (cf. *XSD* 87; *OT* 32–33).

[106] Xenophon served in a mercenary army of Greeks, as he describes in the *Anabasis*, and lived under the protection of Sparta when he was exiled from Athens (*Anabasis* 5.3.7).

[107] Compare *The Skilled Cavalry Commander* 3.2. For the discredit Alcibiades brought upon Socrates, see *Memorabilia* 1.2.12.

[108] Aristophanes (*Knights* 242) mentions a Simon who was a cavalry commander, but we do not know whether it is this Simon. Xenophon dedicated a shrine to Artemis during his exile in Lacedaemonian territory (*Anabasis* 5.3.9–13).

[109] Alcibiades appeared to have learned the military importance of the divine by the time he was later recalled from exile, if he was not sufficiently aware of it before. Upon his return to Athens, he led the religious procession from the Eleusinion temple in Athens to the town of Eleusis, an act of piety that had been suspended because of vulnerability during the war with Sparta.

[110] Horsemanship is a theme of Aristophanes' *Clouds*, which involves a father approaching Socrates for help because of his son's "horse disease" (*hippikē nosos*), by which he means his son's expensive addiction to horsemanship. The word *hippikē* here is a feminine adjective modifying the noun "disease."

[111] Here we see *On Horsemanship* as a supplement to the broader discussion of the gentleman's education of servants in the *Oeconomicus*. Servants need to know something more specific than "be diligent," but the only substantive art that we hear Ischomachus explain there (to Socrates) is farming (*Oeconomicus* 16.2).

[112] At a minimum, writing enables one to give instructions to those who are absent or unavailable. Xenophon writes notes (*hupomnemata*) in this treatise for his "young friends," but he is also writing for older gentlemen he may never know, and even notes to pass on as written instructions to hired trainers of horses ("just as one would if sending one's child out for an art"), so even such inaccessible people as other men's colt trainers may receive Xenophon's writings.

[113] The perfect gentleman tells Socrates that he is careful not to lame his horse when he takes it out for a ride. The gentleman's cautious prudence as an owner makes him avoid certain maneuvers that a shrewd horse purchaser may legitimately try (compare *The Skilled Cavalry Commander* 3.7, 8.11, with *Oeconomicus* 11.17).

[114] Socrates, too, makes clear that the cavalry commander must be concerned with hoof care (*Memorabilia* 3.3.3–4). Xenophon tells the commander to instruct the gentlemen in other behavior at home as well—for example, training rides to practice for war (*The Skilled Cavalry Commander* 1.18).

[115] Ancient Greek equestrians did not use horseshoes.

[116] "Beautiful" here is *kalon*.

[117] *On Horsemanship* delays the mention of kicking until grooming is discussed (6.1). Kicking is a real danger for the groom as well as others on the ground, including horses. On the other hand, being thrown is potentially more fatal to the rider, especially in battle ("Nobody has ever been kicked or bitten to death in battle," *Anabasis* 3.2.18). Xenophon uses two different words when referring to the hooves. Once he uses "nail" (*onuchos*), a word also for the talons of birds or the fingernails of human beings, but elsewhere he uses a word related to "weapons" or "armor" (*hoplē*). A contrasting use of human art is ointments that keep the horse's mouth soft rather than allowing it to become callous, so that it obeys more readily under the pressure of the bit (4.5).

[118] Xenophon offers comical and scarcely credible evidence for this assertion, claiming that female horses, if allowed to grow their manes long, will not allow donkeys to mate with them (5.8). Mules are more utilitarian animals than horses. They are strong and useful for farmwork and for baggage, but they are not used in battle and apparently not considered beautiful.

[119] Compare *Symposium* 2.9–10, where Socrates asserts that spirited horses are good for practice in dealing with all sorts of horses.

[120] Through horsemanship, according to Socrates, a man may be reduced to want or become quite well-off and even glory in profit (*Oeconomicus* 3.8). Critoboulus should not neglect the art, since he must use it (*Oeconomicus* 3.9; cf. 1.8). A gentleman must also contribute to the rearing of horses for the city, one of several taxes that might lead to household ruin (*Oeconomicus* 2.6). Critoboulus thinks he has some experience in the art, although not enough to know why some people profit and others are ruined by horsemanship.

[121] A few days before that conversation, Socrates claims he came to an important decision as to how to live. This is where he compares himself to a horse (11.3–7). However, *Symposium* 2.9–10 might imply that Socrates has some knowledge of what horsemanship entails. Moreover, Socrates does not ask Ischomachus to teach him

horsemanship as he asks him to teach him the art of farming. It could be that he did not see its utility for his peculiar form of home economics. But compare Socrates' statement at *Oeconomicus* 11.10 with Ischomachus's at 11.8. The gentleman's prayer is for noble preservation and noble increase of wealth "in war" (*en polemoi*). Socrates expresses curiosity about noble safety "from war" and wants to discuss moneymaking only after exploring that (*Oeconomicus* 11.8).

¹²² Socrates' joke should be compared to his exhorting Critoboulus in the *Oeconomicus* to educate his wife. That exhortation is in close proximity to his recommendation that Critoboulus learn the art of horsemanship, following a reference to Critoboulus's love of comedy, which happens to be connected to his neglect of farming (*Oeconomicus* 3.8–16). Strauss explains that the themes of horsemanship, wives, comedy, and farming were suggested to Xenophon by the prominence of these same themes in Aristophanes' *Clouds* (*XSD* 112). The *Oeconomicus* alludes to the dream of a young man in the *Clouds* under the influence of the "horse disease." That young man, like Critoboulus, is entrusted by his father to Socrates for an education.

¹²³ As it turns out, this discussion is the central chapter of the *Memorabilia*. Strauss merely points out that Xenophon, who vouches for the authenticity of this conversation, wrote a treatise on cavalry command (*XS* 59). Strauss does not remind the reader there about Xenophon's treatise on horsemanship.

¹²⁴ *Education of Cyrus* 1.1.1–3. The difficulty of ruling over human beings is contrasted to ruling over animals, including horses.

¹²⁵ Persian hilly terrain played a role (1.3.3), but so also must have the structure of the Persian regime, which was a broad-based oligarchy of "peers" disguised as a democratic meritocracy. Accordingly, military training of the ruling class in Persia was a version of the heavily armed, close-quarter fighting of Spartan hoplites.

¹²⁶ To the degree that Cyrus is a model for Xenophon, horsemanship may also be important for his own enterprise (4.3.15–22; 8.4.11).

8. The One Skilled at Hunting with Dogs

We have used the texts of Édouard Delebecque, *L'art de la chasse* (Paris: Les Belles Lettres, 1970) and of E. C. Marchant, Xenophon, *Opuscula*, vol. 5 of *Opera Omnia* (1920; Oxford: Clarendon Press, 1963). The first chapter of the work has come down to us in two substantially different versions, and we have chosen to follow MS Sigma.

¹ The title of this work, *Kunegetikos*, has as its root the Greek word for "dog," *kuōn*. The kind of hunting that is primarily at issue in this work involves the use of dogs to track and pursue wild animals.

² According to myth, Apollo and Artemis were twin siblings of Zeus and Leto. Artemis, among other things, was the goddess of the hunt and was worshipped at Athens as "The Huntress" (*Agra*; see below, 6.13). One of Apollo's epithets was "God of the Hunt" (*Agraios*).

³ Cheiron, a son of Kronos, was the most famous and wisest of all the centaurs and educated many Greek heroes. He was born immortal but suffered an incurable wound from Heracles and was helped to die by Prometheus.

⁴ Cephalus, son of Hermes and Hersē, was captured, while he was hunting, by the goddess Eōs (Dawn). He accidentally killed his wife while hunting.

[5] Asclepius, the Greek god of medicine, is said to have been taught that art also by Cheiron.

[6] Meilanion (also called Hippomenes) is famous for winning the hand of Atalanta, a huntress in her own right, by defeating her in a footrace by cunning, rather than speed.

[7] Nestor was a leader of the Pylians who fought with the Achaeans in the Trojan War, and he was reputed for his wisdom (see *Odyssey* 3.20).

[8] Amphiaraus was the mythical king of Argos, a great seer, and a warrior. Foreseeing that the Argives would fail in their battle against Thebes, he joined only with great reluctance but played a leading role in the fight.

[9] Peleus, king of Phthia in Thessaly, was the son of Aecus and the father of Achilles. Peleus and his brother Telamon killed their half-brother Phocos in a hunting accident. Afterward, both were purified by Peleus's father-in-law, Eurytion. Peleus subsequently accidentally killed Eurytion on the hunt for the Calydonian Boar.

[10] Telamon was the father of the hero Aias (Ajax) and a close friend of Heracles on the expedition of the Argonauts.

[11] Meleager was prince of Calydon. Meleager's father neglected to sacrifice to the goddess Artemis (1.10), and so she sent a wild boar to ravage his land. Meleager then organized the so-called Calydonian Boar Hunt, in which the following people from Xenophon's list took part: Nestor, Amphiaraus, Peleus, Telamon, Theseus, Castor, and Polydeuces. According to Apollodorus (3.9.2), Atalanta, whom Meilanion won in marriage, joined the men on the aforementioned boar hunt.

[12] Theseus was the mythical king of Athens who undertook many famous hunts.

[13] Hippolytus, the son of Theseus, is said to have preferred a life of chastity and hunting to the things of Aphrodite. He is the eponymous hero of a play by Euripides.

[14] Palamedes was another hero of the Trojan War who was responsible for enlisting Odysseus by trickery. He is said to have invented the alphabet, numbers, and other useful things.

[15] Odysseus was the king of Ithaca, influential general during the Trojan War, and hero of the *Odyssey*. Odysseus was scarred by a boar on a hunt when he was a child (*Odyssey* 19.455–527).

[16] Menestheus was leader of Athens during the Trojan War.

[17] Diomedes was a great leader in the Trojan War who became king of Argos.

[18] Castor and his twin brother, Polydeuces, were often referred to as the Dioscuri, or the twin sons of Zeus.

[19] Machaon and his brother Podaleirius, sons of Asclepius, were leaders of the Thessalians as well as physicians in the Trojan War.

[20] Antilochus was the son of Nestor and a friend of Achilles. He died defending his father.

[21] Aeneas was a Trojan hero, son of Anchises and Aphrodite. He saved his aged father and the statues of his household gods when he fled the sack of Troy.

[22] Achilles was the son of Peleus and Thetis, and the hero of the Trojan War. He is the central character in Homer's *Iliad*.

[23] Xenophon refers to the goddess Eōs (Dawn).

[24] "Rivals in love" translates *anterastēs*, a word derived from *eraō*, which we translate as "love passionately." See note 29 on 1.17.

[25] Reading *aiezōs zōn*, with the MSS, rather than Delebecque's emendation, *aei zōntōn*.

[26] Xenophon refers to Artemis.

[27] The identities of "the one" and "the other" in this sentence are unclear. In one traditional account, Palamedes was killed by Odysseus and Diomedes. See Xenophon, *Apology of Socrates to the Jury* 26; *Memorabilia* 4.2.33.

28 "Philopator" is an appellation meaning "devoted to his father."

29 The verb translated "to love passionately" is *eraō*. Unless otherwise noted, "to love" translates *philein* and cognates.

30 "Substance" here translates *ousia*, a participle form of the word for "being"; it may also be rendered as "possessions," "estate," "thing."

31 Xenophon mentions three kinds of nets: short nets (*arkus*), road nets (*enoidios*), and trap nets (*diktuon*). The short net was a net that could be drawn into the shape of a bag. Road nets were intended to block the animal's pathway. Trap nets were larger and meant to enclose animals after they were driven into the net by the dogs.

32 The Greek measurements used by Xenophon in this chapter are the span, (*spithamē*), the distance between thumb and little finger on an outstretched hand; the palm (*palaistē*), i.e., the breadth of four fingers; and the fathom (*orguia*), the distance between outstretched arms (about six English feet).

33 Following the reading of the MSS and omitting Delebecque's emendation of the text (*heneka thēras*), which would read "Let there be a sack made of dog- or calfskin for the game."

34 Considering the importance that *hē gē* (the earth) evidently has in Xenophon's writings (see, for example, *Oeconomicus* 5.12; 16.2), we have chosen to translate this as "the earth" throughout, even though "ground" may in some contexts seem fitting and less awkward.

35 Xenophon refers to Artemis.

36 By blocking or shading the reflected light, the hares would become more easily detectable.

37 Or "the many" (*hoi polloi*).

38 Here we follow Marchant over Delebecque's emendation.

39 Here we follow Delebecque over Marchant.

40 Or "loved something" (*ei tou erōi*).

41 The law being referred to here is presumably the law allowing hunting on cultivated land.

42 That is, during festival days.

43 MSS B and M here include *kakos* (bad). We have here followed MS A in omitting it. Falbe plausibly emends *kakos* to *kalōs* (nobly). In accordance with this suggestion, the phrase could be translated "Go, dogs, go! Noble, wise dogs!"

44 The MSS has *saphōs* (clearly). We here adopt Falbe's emendation, *sophōs* (wise or clever).

45 Here we have chosen to follow the MS and Delebecque over an emendation accepted by Marchant.

46 Or "wrongs," *adika*. It might seem strange that Xenophon would refer to injustices within dogs. But see *Memorabilia* 4.4.5, where Socrates speaks of the justice of a horse or a cow.

47 Xenophon's list of names with approximate English equivalent:

Psuchē	Soul	Hēba	Youth
Thumos	Spirit	Gētheus	Delight
Porpax	Shield handle	Chara	Joy
Sturax	Spear spike	Leusōn	Looker
Lonchē	Lance	Augō	Sunlight
Lochos	Ambush	Polus	Much

Phroura	Lookout	Bia	Force
Phulax	Guard	Stichōn	Walker
Taxis	Order	Spoudē	Serious
Xiphon	Sword	Bruas	Swollen
Phonax	Eager-for-blood	Oinas	Winey
Phlegōn	Fiery	Sterrhos	Stubborn
Alcē	Prowess	Kraugē	Crier
Teuchōn	Doer	Kainōn	Killer
Huleus	Woody	Turbas	Trouble
Mēdas	Plotter	Sthenōn	Vigor
Porthōn	Destroyer	Aethēr	Sky
Sperchōn	Hasty	Actis	Beam
Orgē	Frenzy	Aechmē	Spear point
Bremōn	Roarer	Noēs	Thinker
Hubris	Hybris	Gnōmē	Knowledge
Thallōn	Bloomer	Stibōn	Tracker
Rhōmē	Strength	Hormē	Impulse
Antheus	Blossom		

[48] Reading, with Gesner, the emendation *mē endeeis* (not in need) in place of *endeeis* (in need).

[49] That is, spots not covered by snow.

[50] A *pugōn* is the distance from the elbow to the first joint of the fingers.

[51] The sense of the MS is not clear here. Editors and other translators read *sunechontai* (to hold or keep together) to mean "give way" or "are pulled down" (or propose emendations of the MS that mean "draw together" or "contract").

[52] A powerful poison made from aconitum plants that causes diarrhea and thus weakens the animals.

[53] Xenophon introduces a new word for hunters here, which makes no reference to dogs (*hoi thērōmenoi*).

[54] A stadion was about one-eighth of a mile.

[55] Here and in what follows, the verb translated as "to love" is *eraō*.

[56] The verb translated as "to admire" (*thaumazein*) is translated as "to wonder" in chapter 1.

[57] In this passage (12.18–21), *arete*, "virtue," appears to be spoken of as a goddess or personified, as in her great speech in *Memorabilia* 2.1. We have accordingly used the personal form of the pronouns ("she," "her") to translate the references to "Virtue."

[58] The word is *erōmenoi*, from *eraō*.

[59] Or, more literally, "the strongest" (*to kratiston*).

[60] Literally, "enthymemes" (*enthumēmata*). The related verb is translated in the following sections as "taking to heart."

[61] Or "life" (*psuchē*).

62 See *Memorabilia* 4.1.3–4, where Xenophon relates Socrates' teaching concerning the qualities possessed by those of the young with "the best natures" and the importance of receiving a good education if they are "to become best and most beneficial." In discussing these promising natures, Socrates employs the image of hunting dogs in a way that sheds light not only on the quality of "love of toil" but on the central portions of the work that concern the qualities of good (and bad) hunting dogs and the manner in which they should be reared and trained. Socrates taught that "in the case of the dogs with the best natures, who love labor and are ready to attack their prey, those that have been nobly reared become best for the hunts and most useful, while without rearing they become useless and mad and most intractable" (*Memorabilia*, trans. Amy L. Bonnette [Ithaca, NY: Cornell University Press, 1994]). Here, the love of toil appears to be a natural disposition of sorts (that has "robustness of soul" as a correlate in human beings).

63 What "love of toil" consists in can be grasped through contrast with its opposite quality, "softness." For example, it is "softness" that leads some dogs to "chase the hare vehemently at the beginning, but then give up" (3.8). Socrates at one point names softness as the opposite of love of toil: "Speak if you know someone who, under my influence has gone from . . . love of toil to softness" (*Apology of Socrates to the Jury* 6, trans. Andrew Patch [in *The Shorter Socratic Writings* (Ithaca, NY: Cornell University Press, 1996)]). Socrates elsewhere says that softness and laziness are "deceiving mistresses," pretending to be pleasures, which keep men from beneficial works (*Oeconomicus* 2.19, trans. Carnes Lord [in *The Shorter Socratic Writings*]).

64 Palamedes occupies the central position in both the list of students at 1.1 and the descriptions given in 1.6–16, even though the order of the descriptions departs from that of the list.

65 However, this brief account of Palamedes contains noteworthy, but puzzling details. When Xenophon maintains that Palamedes was unjustly killed, but "not at the hands of *those* supposed by some," he is most likely exonerating two other men who are said (if by Xenophon alone) to be students of Cheiron—Odysseus and Diomedes (1.13). But, if so, the "some" with whom Xenophon here disagrees includes his own Socrates in the *Memorabilia*, when the latter affirms what he presents as the prevailing traditional view that Xenophon here disputes. In the course of an examination of Euthydemus's opinion that wisdom is indisputably good, Socrates asks, "And have you not heard of the sufferings of Palamedes? For according to what *all* sing of him in hymns, he was destroyed by Odysseus, who envied him because of his wisdom" (*Memorabilia* 4.2.33, emphasis added). Xenophon states, as a reason for rejecting the traditional account, that otherwise Odysseus and Diomedes could not be counted among the best of men. This suggests that the general presentation of the heroes is governed by the intent to uphold the excellent reputation of Cheiron's education and its beneficial influence on those who received it.

66 On death as something that is by nature and necessary but yet ordinarily experienced in terms of the concern with what is just and unjust, consider Socrates' remarks to his distraught, indignant companions as they anticipate his impending unjust death (*Apology of Socrates to the Jury* 27–28).

67 In the prevailing account of his death, Palamedes is killed by the Greek army after being falsely accused of treason by Odysseus (whose envy and hatred of Palamedes is aroused when Palamedes succeeds in a venture where Odysseus failed). Palamedes is then said to be avenged through the actions of his father (who slanders the Greek leaders, including Agamemnon, so that their wives turn against them). Since, however, Xenophon rejects this version of Palamedes' death, the account of his vengeance that accompanies it would also seem to be in doubt, and it remains unclear just how he obtains vengeance. Perhaps, however, the "vengeance from the gods" at

issue here refers to what Socrates says about Palamedes: "And Palamedes, who died in a similar way, also comforts me, for even now he still occasions much nobler songs than Odysseus, who unjustly killed him" (*Apology of Socrates to the Jury* 26). On this account, Xenophon's Palamedes (in *The One Skilled at Hunting with Dogs*) appears to be a stand-in for Socrates, and this Palamedes-Socrates obtains "vengeance" against those who killed him (i.e., the Athenians) not through Olympian gods but through those who "sing" "much nobler songs" about him than about his killers.

[68] On how teaching can proceed through likenesses, see *Oeconomicus* 19.15; 17.15. In the *Education of Cyrus*, Xenophon notes that "it is not easy to find anything missing from hunting that is present in war" (1.2.10, trans. Wayne Ambler [Ithaca, NY: Cornell University Press, 2001]).

[69] Xenophon is here silent about how hunting can also make one experienced in the arts of deception and stratagem, and of how these are useful in war. Just as the Persian youth (including Cyrus, at least up until he assumes leadership of the army and is enlightened by his father) are kept in the dark regarding the way in which their own hunting educates for war, i.e., by covertly instructing them in the arts of deceiving and "taking advantage" of other human beings, so too is the reader of *The One Skilled at Hunting* left ignorant that an education in hunting will teach him how to be "a plotter, a dissembler, wily, a cheat, a thief, rapacious, and the sort who takes advantage of his enemies in everything" (*Education of Cyrus* 1.6.27). Nevertheless, all the modes of hunting described in chapters 2 through 11 require knowledge of how to deceive wild animals. Nets, for example, are constructed and employed so as to produce the false appearance to the animal that there is a clear path of escape from its pursuers where there in fact is not. This type of deception relies on the animal's fears of its pursuers. Traps and snares can be baited with food or even the animal's own offspring (9.6–7), so as to draw it in and deceive it by appealing to its strongest desires. Consideration of nets as modes of deception employed to capture one's prey may thus help to explain the paramount "importance" Xenophon puts on the fabrication and preparation of the nets in chapter 2 (2.2). For Socrates' advice regarding the use of nets in the hunt for friends, see *Memorabilia* 3.11.9–11.

[70] Compare this description of a situation where "one's own" army experiences misfortune in a place that is "precipitous or otherwise difficult" with Xenophon's account of himself and the Ten Thousand in the *Anabasis* (books 3 through 7). Was it "hunting" that educated Xenophon to be able to "save himself, as well as others, without disgrace" from the misfortunes of the Persian expedition?

[71] On the delight and pleasure that attends the "belief that one is becoming better," see *Memorabilia* 1.6.8–9. In the *Apology of Socrates before the Jury*, the pleasure of genuine improvement is attended by the pleasure of "self-admiration" (5).

[72] On the coincidence of both toil and pleasure in the activities of "thinking," on the one hand, and hunting, on the other, see *Memorabilia* 2.1.18. Socrates says, "The one who suffers hardship willingly delights in thinking with a view to a good hope, like those who hunt beasts toil with pleasure in hope of a catch."

[73] For an exploration of the similar difficulty of acquiring or teaching the "diligence" (*epimelia*) necessary for successful household management or virtue, see *Oeconomicus* 12.10; 7.7.

[74] As we learn in Xenophon's *Symposium*, Socrates is self-taught in both philosophy and dancing (though he nevertheless expresses interest in learning new dance routines from the Syracusan) (*Symposium* 1.5; 2.16–20).

[75] The care, training, and leading of dogs are employed as a likeness for the education and leadership of human beings in other writings. See, for example, *Education of Cyrus* 1.6.19, 8.2.4; *Oeconomicus* 13.6–10; 5.5–6; and *Memorabilia* 4.1.3–4; 2.7.13–14, 2.9.2.

[76] The word "form" (*eidos*) refers to the characteristic, outward, bodily appearance or "look" of the dog (or hare) and is distinguished from both its "work" and characteristics of soul (for the distinction between "form" and "soul," see especially 3.3; 7.7–8; and *Education of Cyrus* 1.2.10).

[77] "Goodness" or "stoutness" of soul (*eupsuchia*) is a quality also attributed to the (human) hunter of the boar and demonstrated by him when, despite the danger of being gored, he advances upon his cornered prey (10.22).

[78] In the *Memorabilia*, Socrates describes the qualities of the most promising youths as natural, such that their souls are "naturally formed for virtue" and they are the "best natures." The effects of both education and lack of education on young men are, notably, here likened to the effects of "noble" rearing and lack of such rearing on hunting dogs (*Memorabilia* 4.1.3).

[79] Here see *Memorabilia* 3.12.13: Xenophon's advice that one feed the dogs only when they are hungry agrees with Socrates' advice for Theodote that in trying to attract a "friend" one should gratify him only when he is in need (and, in this case, must induce the need if it is not already present).

[80] Ischomachus, the perfect gentleman of the *Oeconomicus*, expresses a different opinion about what is necessary in "teaching" young dogs to obey: "Puppies, though they are far inferior to human beings both in mind and tongue, nevertheless learn in some way to run in a circle and do somersaults and many other things, and when they are negligent, *they are punished*" (13.8, emphasis added).

[81] See *Anabasis* 2.6.20.

[82] Leo Strauss comments that Xenophon "does not dare to assert that hunting is very lucrative" (*Xenophon's Socratic Discourse: An Interpretation of the "Oeconomicus"* [Ithaca, NY: Cornell University Press, 1970], 202).

[83] Such lessons from experience of what does not work are most visible where Xenophon advises how "not" to do something; for example, that one fasten the cord of a net for a boar to a firm tree and "not" to a clump of briars (10.7).

[84] The swiftness of the hare also has bearing upon the qualities that the hunter will require in his dogs (see 3.3, 8; 4.2, 5).

[85] "Necessity," *anagkē*, occurs nine times in this work: three times in reference to the mating habits of hares (5.6, 25) and dogs (7.1), five times in reference to the experience of mortal danger in the pursuit of the boar (10.9, 13, 14, 18, 19) and once to describe the advantages to be expected from hunter education (1.18).

[86] The knowledge of such necessities not only guides the breeding of the dogs, but even informs the fabrication of their equipment. The dog's belt should "have spikes sown in, in order to guard the breed" (6.1).

[87] See Arrian, *Kunegetikos* 24.4.

[88] Recall that Xenophon must implore the young "not to despise hunting" (1.18). On the danger of exciting envy, see 1.11; 12.12, 15; *Education of Cyrus* 3.1.39; *Symposium* 6.6; *Apology of Socrates to the Jury* 32.

[89] Although in the *Oeconomicus* Socrates suggests that "likenesses" may also be deceptive: the similarity of what one knows to what one does not know may lead one to suppose one "knows" what one in truth does not (19.15).

Index

CPSIA information can be obtained
at www.ICGtesting.com
Printed in the USA
LVOW03*2129080218
565674LV00013BA/20/P